EARLY REVIEWS OF

With Justice For Some

by Lise Pearlman

Armed with a razor-sharp legal mind and imbued with a sense of fairness for all, retired Judge Lise Pearlman examines a dozen landmark trials in U.S. history in With Justice for Some. *At the same time, the author paints a searing portrait of a society divided by class, caste, race and creed. Many, but not all, of the leading historical figures in this book, including Sacco and Vanzetti and "the Scottsboro Boys," are members of minority groups or people of color. With a keen sense of balance, the author also exhumes the trials, and explores the tribulations of millionaire Harry K. Thaw, pro-Nazi celebrity Charles Lindberg and the legendary gamblers who fixed the 1919 World Series.* With Justice for Some *ought to be read, enjoyed, studied and heralded by lawyers, judges, defendants and fans of legendary lawyers such as Clarence Darrow . . .*

Jonah Raskin, author of *A Terrible Beauty:*
The Wilderness of American Literature

Anyone interested in history, courtroom drama or criminal justice should read this!

Barry Scheck, Co-Director of
The Innocence Project

With Justice for Some *is an expertly curated tour through some of our nation's greatest legal scandals, offering dramatic accounts, vivid sketches of scoundrels and heroes, and keen insights not only into our history but contemporary events. By turns shocking and reassuring – a pleasure to read.*

Seth Rosenfeld, investigative journalist
and author of *Subversives: The FBI's War on*
Student Radicals, and Reagan's Rise to Power

D1600569

WITH JUSTICE
FOR SOME

Lise Pearlman is also the acclaimed author of

The Sky's the Limit:
People v. Newton, the REAL Trial of the 20th Century?
[Regent Press 2012]
A history of the American 20th century that compares the
Newton trial to other headline trials from 1901 to 2000.

American Justice on Trial:
People v. Newton
[Regent Press 2016]

The Sky's the Limit was awarded:

U.S. BOOK NEWS 2013 / First Place: Law

IBPA AWARD BENJAMIN FRANKLIN 2013 /
Silver Award: Multiculturalism

INTERNATIONAL BOOK AWARDS 2013 / Finalist: U.S. History

American Justice on Trial was awarded:

INTERNATIONAL BOOK AWARDS 2017 / Finalist: U.S. History

WITH JUSTICE FOR SOME

*Politically Charged Criminal Trials
in The Early 20th Century
That Helped Shape Today's America*

LISE PEARLMAN

REGENT PRESS
BERKELEY, CALIFORNIA

Copyright © 2017 by Lise Pearlman

PAPERBACK:
ISBN 13: 978-1-58790-410-3
ISBN 10: 1-58790-410-1

E-BOOK
ISBN 13: 978-1-58790-412-7
ISBN 10: 1-58790-412-8

Library of Congress Catalog Number: 2017946334

All rights reserved under International and Pan-American Copyright Conventions. No part of this book may be used or reproduced in any manner whatsoever without the written permission of the Publisher, except in the case of brief quotations embodied in critical articles and reviews.

Much of the material in this book first appeared in
The Sky's the Limit: People v. Newton
The REAL Trial of the 20th Century?
Originally copyrighted © 2012 by Lise Pearlman

Printed in the U.S.A.
REGENT PRESS
Berkeley, California

DEDICATION

With Justice for Some is dedicated to victims of hate crimes throughout America's history, the Good Samaritans who came to their defense, and those among us who have overcome mutual distrust to embrace each other – "We the People of the United States" seeking to form "a more perfect Union, establish Justice, insure domestic Tranquility, provide for the common defence, promote the general Welfare, and secure the Blessings of Liberty to ourselves and our Posterity."

This book is also dedicated to all those who risked their lives and who continue to put their lives on the line to preserve our American experiment in democracy from all enemies foreign and domestic. Pakistani-American lawyer Khzir Khan challenged all of us native-born Americans on our knowledge of the U.S. Constitution at the Democratic Presidential Convention in Philadelphia in July 2016. He spoke with passion about his adopted country after a short film honored the life of his heroic son Army Captain Humayun Khan, who posthumously received a Purple Heart and Bronze Star for making the ultimate sacrifice in Iraq in 2004. How many of us could assure Humayun Khan's grieving Gold Star parents today that we have even read the Preamble to our Constitution, to say nothing of its entire contents, including the Bill of Rights?

CONTENTS

In February 2015 FBI Chief James Comey acknowledged past discrimination and abusive treatment of minorities by both federal and state law enforcement and invited us all to reexamine our cultural inheritance with fresh eyes. Hate crimes still occur, though with less frequency and with more condemnation; progress is being made. This book illustrates what Washington super lawyer Edward Bennett Williams asserted over 50 years ago in *One Man's Freedom,* that the individual civil liberties we cherish in the United States evolved in our criminal courtrooms, all too often with minority defendants on trial for their lives.

The Assassination of President McKinley

Buffalo, New York – September, 1901

Anarchist Leon Czolgosz shoots the newly reelected Republican Commander-in-Chief whom Hearst papers had vilified as the "tool of the money-hungry trusts." As the police hold off would-be lynchers, nationally acclaimed *Up From Slavery* author Booker T. Washington sees this as a teaching moment and urges Americans to give Czolgosz a fair trial. Czolgosz gets at least the form of a trial; lynching elsewhere continues unabated.

A Dramatic Murder Brings the Curtain Crashing Down on the Gilded Age

New York City, New York – 1906

Drug-addicted millionaire Harry Thaw is at first lauded by defenders of traditional womanhood for the revenge killing of Gilded Age premiere architect Stanford White for having deflowered Thaw's wife, Evelyn Nesbit, when she was a teenage Broadway chorus girl – the "It" girl of her era before that term was coined. Thaw's lawyer uses the defense of Dementia Americana – temporary insanity compelling a man to defend the honor of his wife or daughter. Soon, revelations of Thaw's own debauchery fuel working class anger at the extraordinary privileges and hypocrisy of the ruling elite.

A hired assassin blows up retired Democratic Governor Frank Steunenberg. Clarence Darrow gains national prominence defending militant
mineworkers' union leader Big Bill Haywood, the champion of the
8-hour day. President Roosevelt uses his bully pulpit to weigh in against
"undesirable citizens" as immigrants across the country rally to Haywood's
defense. Four years later, the bombing of the *Los Angeles Times* building
again pits owners against labor unions as Darrow returns to defend the
McNamara brothers from execution, in a case that both severely dam-
aged the labor movement and lost Darrow his California license.

A sheriff up for reelection frames African-American Ed Johnson for the
brutal rape of a blonde 21-year-old. The record leads the U.S. Supreme
Court to issue its first grant of review of a state criminal trial for fairness
only to have its review thwarted when the sheriff allows Johnson to be
lynched. The high court then oversees its one and only contempt trial.
Its opinions in this case gave rise to 100 years of federalism. Today, the
Supreme Court has been accused of turning back the clock to render
review of the fairness of state court trials once again "toothless."

The murder of thirteen-year-old factory worker Mary Phagan is exploited
by the Hearst papers trying to gain a foothold in the Atlanta news market.
Hearst belatedly tries to dampen anti-Semitic rage against the accused
Jewish factory manager Leo Frank. After Governor Slaton commutes
his sentence, Frank is lynched by white supremacists roused by political
kingmaker Thomas Watson to avenge Phagan's death as a symbol of the
antebellum South. The Knights of Mary Phagan launch the modern KKK
and Frank's supporters create the Anti-Defamation League.

INTRODUCTION

This book looks back at riveting early 20th century criminal "trials of the century" as a cultural backdrop for divisive issues we face as a nation today. What can we learn from these trials? Plenty. We start with a remarkable speech two years ago by a public servant then basking in bipartisan praise. In February 2015, former FBI Director James Comey was not the center of controversy that he became just a year and a half later. That month, it was racial prejudice, not his conclusions about the use of Hillary Clinton's email server or the tumult surrounding his dismissal by President Donald Trump that loomed large in Comey's mind. Then only in his second year as head of our nation's chief law enforcement agency, the former Deputy Attorney General eagerly accepted an invitation from Georgetown University to speak on Lincoln's birthday about the highly-charged topic of race bias.

Georgetown's early history included profiting from the slave trade (for which it has recently issued a formal apology). Yet less than a decade after the Civil War, Georgetown embraced emancipation by appointing the nation's first African-American university president, the son of a former slave. When Comey took the podium on Lincoln's birthday in February 2015, the new FBI head took the opportunity to confess his own agency's past sins. He candidly admitted what no one in his position had ever owned up to – an ugly truth about the office long identified with J. Edgar Hoover. Comey conceded the historic bias of both his agency and state and local police: "All of us in law enforcement must be honest enough to acknowledge that much of our history is not pretty. At many points in American history, law enforcement enforced the status quo . . . that was often brutally unfair to disfavored groups." The FBI director's remarks were particularly forceful because Comey had served as U.S. Attorney and later Deputy Attorney General under President George W. Bush, years before Bush's Democratic successor, Barack Obama, named

1

him to head the FBI. So it was a transcendent moment when Comey chose this special platform during Black History month to invite all Americans to reexamine our "cultural inheritance" with fresh eyes.[1]

The next day a federal judge in Mississippi provided a stunning example of the changing times when he sentenced three young white men for a spate of hate crimes committed in 2011. Just the year before those crimes, Judge Carlton Reeves was sworn in as only the second African-American federal trial judge ever appointed in a state with a population historically more than one-third black. Explaining the lengthy sentences he imposed, Judge Reeves detailed in graphic terms how the white defendants appearing before him gleefully recruited others to join them in "a 2011 version of the nigger hunts" that, in the decades from the 1880s to the 1960s, resulted in the deaths of over 4700 blacks – a figure that includes "legal lynchings" (patently unfair speedy trials followed by too hasty executions) as well as torture killings and hangings at the hands of mobs.

Judge Reeves observed that in Mississippi's past, even if a grand jury were convened to investigate a lynching by white supremacists, and even in cases where they openly carried out the murders, the official inquiry would likely be dropped with the notation "died at the hands of persons unknown." He concluded: "The legal and criminal justice system operated with ruthless efficiency in upholding what these defendants would call White Power . . . Today . . . black and white, male and female . . . work together to advance the rule of law [for a] criminal justice system [which] must operate without regard to race, creed or color."[2]

Before deciding on the appropriate prison sentences for the young men in his courtroom, Justice Reeves considered letters submitted by family and friends to show the youths' general good character apart from the horrific crime they had committed. He then posed this question: "How could hate, fear or whatever it was transform genteel, God-fearing, God-loving Mississippians into mindless murderers and sadistic torturers?"[3] But it was not just God-fearing White Southerners who tried to justify their inhumane conduct towards their fellow man, nor solely African-Americans who were victims of domestic terrorists. As FBI Director Comey pointed out in his 2015 speech, his own

Irish-American ancestors also faced mistreatment at the hands of the criminal justice system. Native Americans, Mexican-Americans, Italian and German immigrants, Chinese and Japanese immigrants, and islanders in American territories often endured appalling abuse.

Historically, Catholics and Jews were also among those often shunned, stigmatized and oppressed. Sometimes the stigma stemmed from political activity such as that of militant union organizers and strikers, anarchists and other radicals. Both sides might engage in lawless behavior only to wind up in court where company owners, captains of industry and government officials could usually count on the prosecutors and judges they put in office to ignore their own misconduct while meting out harsh sentences to opponents labeled subversive.

In many instances, publishing giant William Randolph Hearst played a pivotal role – creating or feeding a public appetite for scandalous headlines with little or no regard for the truth or for the lives at stake. One telling example was how Hearst helped ruin the career of silent movie megastar Roscoe "Fatty" Arbuckle, of "Keystone Kops" fame. By the 1920s, the Hearst newspapers boasted a circulation of twenty million people in eighteen cities – almost a fifth of the country's total population. In the first year of Prohibition the obese comedian signed an unprecedented million-dollar contract which he celebrated over Labor Day 1921 with friends at a three-day drinking party in his suite at the St. Francis Hotel in San Francisco. A young actress named Virginia Rappe attended the party, fell violently ill and died a few days later. An ambitious prosecutor pursued false but headline-grabbing charges that Arbuckle had raped Virginia Rappe and ruptured her bladder.

Hearst papers made Arbuckle the face of Hollywood's loose morals that appalled so many conservative church-goers. (At the time, rumors were rampant that Hearst himself, a married father of five, was keeping Hollywood leading lady Marion Davies as his own mistress.) Arbuckle endured three sensationalized trials before being acquitted. The truth was that Virginia Rappe was already feeling poorly when she arrived at the party and never accused Arbuckle of any untoward conduct, and the doctors who examined her concluded she died of natural causes.[4] The third jury met just long enough to pen a rare written apology for the

Starkly different headlines before the first criminal trial of Hollywood megastar Fatty Arbuckle in September 1921 and after the third trial in March 1922. Arbuckle never actually faced the death penalty. The charge was manslaughter, for which he was ultimately exonerated.

Source: File: Roscoe Arbuckle Trial - 1921.jpg from Wikimedia Commons

Source: http://www.chcemywiedziec.pl/wp-content/uploads/2015/02/Roscoe-Arbuckle-Exonerated-Creative-Commons-CC-SA1.jpg

Above: *On Sept. 17, 1921, Hearst-owned papers trumpeted the Hollywood star's likely execution.*

Left: *April 18, 1922, news bulletin after a third trial ended in acquittal and an apology from the jury. Six days later, new movie czar Will Hays banned Arbuckle from appearing in any films. Publisher William Randolph Hearst boasted that he sold more papers by his lurid coverage of the Arbuckle trials than the sinking of the ocean liner Lusitania in 1915 that helped prompt the United States to join World War I.*

Source: Wikipedia Keystone Kops file

Source: Wikipedia Brewster's Millions file

The Keystone Kops

Source: Wikipedia Roscoe Arbuckle file

Top left: *Roscoe "Fatty" Arbuckle stands furthest right as a star member of the Keystone Kops – a silent slapstick comedy series popular in movie theaters from 1912 into the 1920s. Arbuckle joined the cast in 1913.* ***Top right:*** *Arbuckle starred in "Brewster's Millions" in 1921, a year after he signed his record-setting million-dollar contract with Paramount Pictures (roughly $17 million today).* ***Above:*** *what Arbuckle's San Francisco hotel suite looked like after a 3-day binge over Labor Day weekend 1921 (shortly after Prohibition took effect). Among the party's attendees was an out-of-work actress in poor health named Virginia Rappe, who died just days later, triggering the headline trial that ruined Arbuckle's career.*

great injustice done in besmirching Arbuckle's name without "the slight-
est proof . . . to connect him in any way with the commission of a crime."[5]

While the trials against Arbuckle remained pending, Hearst's sensationalized coverage of the rape and manslaughter prosecutions fanned
the church-going public's animosity toward Hollywood's corrupt morals. Local boards of censors across the country had already created
headaches for Hollywood moguls; their distributors sometimes had to
edit films heavily for showing in culturally conservative venues or see
them banned outright. The studio heads responded to the mounting
pressure by opting for self-censorship. They formed the Motion Picture
Producers and Distributors of America and paid President Harding's
former campaign manager, Postmaster General Will Hays, a hefty salary
to leave the administration to head the new organization.

Within a week of Arbuckle's acquittal, Hays barred the Hollywood
star permanently from the movies. The dramatic action mirrored that
of baseball's new czar the summer before – banning eight White Sox
players for life for fixing the 1919 World Series (see Chapter 6). Just
as Shoeless Joe Jackson became the scapegoat for vice-ridden professional baseball, Arbuckle stood in for the sins of Hollywood. Perhaps
not coincidentally Hays took that bold action just days after *The Wall
Street Journal* broke the Teapot Dome bribery scandal in which Hays
later turned out to be a key figure, secretly taking oil company contributions to pay off campaign debts when chair of the Republican Party.

After making an example of the industry's biggest star, Hays later
blacklisted nearly two hundred other actors and imposed a new morality code by which Hollywood endeavored to censor its public image
for decades. Among the "Working Principles" of The Motion Picture
Production Code of 1930, it specified that "no picture should lower the
moral standards of those who see it."[6] The voluntary code expressly prohibited a film from ridiculing or belittling natural or divine law in any
way or creating sympathy for violators. Instead, filmmakers were urged
to "stress proper behavior, respect for government and 'Christian values'."[7] (Today, its successor organization is in charge of film ratings).

Unrepentant at his role in ruining Arbuckle's livelihood, Hearst
boasted that his coverage of the three unwarranted trials "sold more

newspapers than any event since the sinking of the Lusitania"[8] – the British ocean liner torpedoed by Germans off the Irish coast in May 1915. (The nearly 1200 casualties of that act of war included 198 Americans. The sinking of the Lusitania helped convince the United States to join World War I on the side of the British and French.)

Once in a while, over-reaching tactics backfired by prompting heroic responses that helped precipitate major reforms. As explored in the chapters that follow, a few courageous policemen, prosecutors, judges and other elected officials in these early decades of the 20th century stood out for their adherence to constitutional ideals despite strong pressure to do otherwise. Some paid a high price. Alabama Sheriff Matt Wann was murdered in May 1932, reportedly while attempting to make a late-night house arrest of a husband for failure to pay support. The sheriff had been accompanied by three deputies, but, somehow, the shooter fled and was never prosecuted. Rumors began spreading shortly after the sheriff's death that it was a KKK hit job in collusion with his deputies in retaliation for Wann's successful efforts the preceding year to prevent a lynch mob from stringing up prisoners in his custody – the Scottsboro Boys. At the time of Sheriff Wann's death, eight of the defendants remained on death row awaiting Supreme Court review of their group trial. Back when the nine had originally been arrested on rape charges, Sheriff Wann had provoked the Klan's ire by threatening to kill anyone who interfered with his prisoners and calling in the National Guard to protect them. Had the Scottsboro Boys never stood trial – like so many victims of vigilante "justice" before them – there would have been no record for the Supreme Court to review to issue two landmark rulings establishing basic, now widely accepted, procedural rights for criminal defendants.

In light of recently revived interest in the Scottsboro Boys case, a blogger detailed the suspicious circumstances surrounding the murder of Sheriff Wann and concluded that county records did not support the official story. He pressed for the murder to be reinvestigated, urging that "the truth must be revealed for justice to occur."[9] That assumption reflects the premise of this book as well. Getting at the truth in all the cases in this book includes evaluation of key details sometimes revealed long after the trials ended. We also benefit from the passage of time allowing us to assess the societal factors at play more clearly. Many cases where the system fell woefully short of justice have belatedly been reinvestigated. One such case involved a handyman named Ed Johnson, the victim of a kangaroo trial for rape, who was lynched while seeking to establish the right to federal review of state criminal trials for fairness (see Chapter 4). Ten years of research at the end of the 20th century by lawyer Leroy Phillips, Jr., and investigative reporter Mark Curriden convinced a Tennessee judge to conduct a posthumous retrial and clear Johnson's name. Their efforts spawned, just last year, an eponymous memorial project in Chattanooga aimed at promoting racial harmony.

Reviewing other early 20th century cases, we also see examples of men whose principled insistence on affording disadvantaged defendants their rights ultimately helped them achieve high office. Two such heroes profiled in this book – Judge Frank Murphy of Detroit (see Chapter 10 on the 1925–26 Sweet trials) and police officer John Burns of Oahu (see Chapter 12 on the 1932–33 Massie trials) – deserve enormous credit for helping institute major policy changes toward a more inclusive and just society.

By revisiting several high-stakes criminal trials of the early 20th century we can gain a better understanding of the extent to which cultural bias has permeated the fabric of our culture – and a better premise from which to move forward as a nation than the whitewashed history so many of us were taught in school. In *One Man's Freedom*, Washington super lawyer Edward Bennett Williams described how the individual civil liberties we so cherish in the United States evolved in our criminal courtrooms, where the government often prosecutes "the weak and friendless, the scorned and degraded, or the nonconformist and the unorthodox."[10] Cases guaranteeing civil liberties emerged because so many innocents were wrongly convicted without such protections and too often paid with their lives. Mark Curriden, who co-authored an acclaimed book on the Ed Johnson case and its impact on state criminal defendants' constitutional rights, restates Williams' observation more graphically: "the liberties and prerogatives we so frequently take for granted were written in blood."[11]

The lack of concern for minority defendants' rights that characterized the swift rush to judgment in so many early century trials contrasted dramatically with the handling of the most widely watched trial of the late 20th century – that of African-American football legend O. J. Simpson. When the professional athlete turned actor was charged with the stabbing deaths of Simpson's blonde ex-wife and her Caucasian friend Ronald Goldman, Simpson had the luxury to afford a Dream Team of lawyers to defend him.

An estimated 100 million people followed some part of the marathon reality soap opera that prompted nightly analysis on the television news by legal experts hired to explain the intricacies of constitutional law and criminal procedure. Before a riveted audience of viewers around the world, Simpson's lawyers claimed that their client was framed by the Los Angeles Police Department with evidence that clearly would have condemned to death a defendant lacking Simpson's celebrity status and resources. When the long-awaited verdict was announced, Simpson was acquitted by the jury of ten women and two men, nine of whom were black. All viewers had the opportunity to be exposed to the same testimony, evidence and legal arguments. Yet post-trial polls revealed that more whites disagreed with the verdict exonerating Simpson than accepted it, while the vast majority of African-Americans interviewed shortly after the verdict issued endorsed his acquittal.[12] Today, looking back, more than half of the nation's African-Americans believe Simpson was in fact guilty of murder.[13]

In *Lessons From the Trial: The People v. O.J. Simpson*, Dream Team member Prof. Gerald Uelmen noted that "The most remarkable aspect of every 'trial of the century' . . . has been the insight it provides into the tenor of the times in which it occurred. It is as though each of these trials was responding to some public appetite or civic need of the era in which it took place."[14] Decades, sometimes even a century, later investigative journalists and historians have unearthed far more evidence of what really happened in the events that made banner headlines in the early 20th century.

Back then, segregation of African-Americans was reinforced by rule of law. Other disfavored minorities often received similar treatment

to the descendants of slaves. Police, prosecutors and judges were
almost all white men, who also largely monopolized panels of a "jury
of one's peers." Poor men of color accused of rape and murder were
often executed with little regard for fair process – with or without a
trial. Yet rapists and murderers with money might walk free, never so
much as arrested. Even if prosecuted, the wealthy and privileged sometimes obtained startlingly lenient punishment – as Clarence Darrow
engineered for four clients in Honolulu in 1933, three of whom were
caught about to dump the body of their victim in the ocean, the fourth
arrested while cleaning up the site of the killing.

Politics and power routinely trumped the requirements of due
process. Details that were overlooked, underreported or purposely distorted in times past can now be placed in the more balanced perspective that FBI Director James Comey suggested. Just after the November
2016 election, documentary filmmaker Stanley Nelson made an observation similar to Comey's. As the acclaimed African-American director
received a lifetime achievement award, he observed that the biggest
reason for the bitter divide we see today is because "we have failed to
tell the whole American story . . . creat[ing] a fear and a longing for a
past that never existed."[15] So here, in this book, is a baker's dozen of the
most famous headliners of the early 20th century for us to reexamine in
the rearview mirror – trials involving charges of murder, rape, kidnapping, class warfare, fraud on the public, evolution versus Creationism,
and abuse of power.

At the same time as prosecutors in these famous trials claimed to
take the moral high ground, lynching remained tacitly condoned by
the federal government. State legislatures monopolized by white men
authorized involuntary sterilization of thousands of the poor, minorities and other groups presumed to have inferior genes. Politicians
also incited their constituents to scorn "hyphenated-Americans."
Today, despite our nation of immigrants' history as a melting pot,
some politicians still gain traction fanning contempt for "the other."
Hate crimes are again on the rise. In 2009, then FBI Director Robert
Mueller and former Homeland Security Secretary Janet Napolitano
informed a Senate committee that they remained as concerned about

"homegrown" terrorists as those from overseas.[16]

In 2015, the Southern Poverty Law Center reported that a "dramatic resurgence" of hate groups dated from President Obama's 2008 election.[17] In its spring 2017 report it sounded even greater alarm at a "wave of hate crimes and other bias-related incidents that swept the country" following the 2016 election. The SPLC report attributed the dramatic increase in hate crimes to inclusion of white nationalists in setting the White House agenda by advisors apparently "set on rolling back decades of progress." That objective was no secret. Former Ku Klux Klan leader David Duke boasted in writing that "our people played a HUGE role in electing Trump!" [emphasis in original].[18]

Millions of Trump voters disagree with the objectives of the KKK and disavow racism. Many who voted for Hillary Clinton or other candidates harbor their own prejudices, whether conscious of them or not. There are also underlying truths to the dissatisfaction felt by large numbers of Trump supporters that Democrats failed to address sufficiently: American labor has been displaced (though more often by technological advances than by foreign workers) and white Americans are often worse off than their parents, including noticeably shorter life spans than in the past (due in part to record levels of addiction to pain killers). What has gone largely unremarked upon by the mainstream media until recently is an observation made by financial analyst Jeff Guo in the *Washington Post* in early April 2017: "Black Americans have long been dying faster than white Americans. They've long been less happy than white Americans. Now, though, the two groups are starting to look more and more alike. Particularly among those on the bottom rungs of the socioeconomic ladder, class has become equally – if not more important – than race as a predictor of people's health and emotional well-being." [19]

Why is that so many people emphasize their differences rather than their shared experiences? Americans as a whole have absorbed a skewed cultural legacy. This book is meant to promote dialogue between those with nostalgia for the good old days of white Protestant supremacy and those who view those days less fondly or have only hazy ideas about what America was like in past generations.

Many who pine for the time when they believed America was greater than now apparently mean the 1950s and early 1960s – when white men still held near monopoly power in government and industry. Those who view that era with fondness recall it as a time when the middle class was developing with greater opportunities than their parents – the product of heavy federal investment improving the lives of average Americans with historic educational opportunities through the G.I. Bill, suburban housing developments and massive investment in interstate highways. For others, the 1950s were a time of suppression and fear, including political witch hunts, persecution of gays, back alley abortions, impenetrable glass ceilings, and brazen lynching in the South. As the new TV sitcom "Leave It to Beaver" enchanted viewers across the country with the wholesome values of white suburbia, widespread publication of gruesome photos of the mutilated corpse of fourteen-year-old Chicago teenager Emmett Till in Money, Mississippi, had already launched the Civil Rights Era.

The socioeconomic gains for the average American in the 1950s were only made possible by dramatic gains in two prior eras of the 20th century. That earlier history is particularly relevant now. Nobel prize-winning economist Joseph Stiglitz, in his 2013 book, *The Price of Inequality: How Today's Divide Endangers Our Future,* compared the record-setting disparity between the richest one percent and the overwhelming majority of Americans in the first years of the 21st century to both the Gilded Age of the late 19th century and the Roaring Twenties. "In both of these instances, the country pulled back from the brink. Our democratic processes worked. The Gilded Age was followed by the Progressive Era, which curbed monopoly power. The Roaring Twenties was followed by the important social and economic legislation of the New Deal, which strengthened the rights of workers, provided greater social protection for all Americans, and introduced Social Security, which almost completely eliminated poverty among the elderly."[20]

Both eras of reform were triggered by widespread revulsion at the misery endured by so many have-nots as the wealthy few wielded increased power and privilege. Yet throughout these early eras, those with inordinate clout masked their almost insatiable greed and undue influence with misdirected blame against racial and religious minorities, workers striking for decent pay and living conditions, the influx of immigrant labor, and Americans with unorthodox political views. While often living dissolute, amoral lives themselves, key players wrapped themselves in piety and patriotism, making scapegoats to draw the ire of those in the white majority who felt threatened by changing times and expanded rights for women and minorities.

Professor Stiglitz sees the nation today at a perilous crossroads with a crying need for bipartisan action. "Traditionally, persons in both parties have understood that a nation divided cannot stand – and the divisions today are greater than they have been in generations, threatening basic values, including our conception of ourselves as a land of opportunity. Will we once again pull back from the brink?"[21]

It might help all of us who wish to address that question to look back at America as the Gilded Age grudgingly gave way to the Progressive Era and, two decades later, as the Roaring Twenties laid the groundwork for the New Deal: when the Ku Klux Klan reemerged in the 20th century, unions gained clout, women got the vote and major reforms were enacted. And what better window into society at those pivotal times than to have ringside seats at headline trials that riveted Americans and shaped their reactions? Before television and the Internet, folks got their news from traveling lecturers, newspapers and radio programs wielding similar power to influence and manipulate public opinion. Taking this journey back in time with fresh eyes, perhaps we can achieve far greater insight into the tenor of American society in those earlier decades, how far we have come in this democratic republic founded by immigrants, and how far we still have to go to achieve "one nation, indivisible with liberty and justice for all." Progress has never been linear.

1. A BITTER TEACHING MOMENT

The Assassination of President McKinley

That's all a man can hope for during his lifetime – to set an example – and when he is dead, to be an inspiration for history.

– WILLIAM McKINLEY[1]

Like Rupert Murdoch today, publishing giant William Randolph Hearst wielded enormous power shaping public perception of newsworthy events in the first several decades of the 20th century. One tactic that backfired was his editorial attacks on President McKinley early in the formation of Hearst's publishing empire.

Before moving to Manhattan in 1896 to pursue his political ambitions, Hearst had developed a winning formula transforming his father's *San Francisco Examiner* into the top-selling local newspaper. Hearst filled its pages with wildly entertaining stories, comics, and pictures – the print world equivalent of a P. T. Barnum circus. On political issues, Hearst courted the working class: he railed against vested interests like the powerful railroads and utilities, and championed the eight-hour day and the income tax. Hearst could count on the popularity of taking such stances. Over 30,000 strikes had taken place in the past three decades throughout the nation, with the eight-hour day as the primary objective.

Flushed with success in the Bay Area, in 1895 Hearst bought the *New York Journal* to start a cut-throat readership battle with his role model and mentor, Joseph Pulitzer of the *New York World*. Neither publisher viewed truth as an essential ingredient so long as attention-grabbing stories sped from the hands of corner newsies. Staid competing papers invented the

15

put-down "yellow journalism" to describe how the two-penny tabloids hawked colored cartoon supplements and ran oversized banner head-lines to vie for the loyalty of the city's teeming numbers of immigrant workers, many of whom learned English reading the tabloids.

In the hotly-contested 1896 presidential election Hearst was the only publisher in the financial heart of the nation to support populist William Jennings Bryan against Republican William McKinley. This was the campaign in which Bryan made his famous "cross of gold" speech. The debate centered on how best to recover from the nation's then worst-ever depression, which had hit three years before. Like the sub-prime mortgage bubble that burst into an economic crisis in 2008, overbuilding of railroads on shaky financing precipitated large-scale bankruptcies and job loss in the panic of 1893.

The question in 1896 was whether the United States would remain on the gold standard – as favored by banks, investors and industrialists – or whether the nation would return to coining silver as well. Farmers, workers and small business owners favored the silver standard, which would lower the value of the dollar, but pump far more money into the economy. Bryan's "cross of gold" speech fired his audiences up to a fever pitch: "If they dare to . . . defend the gold standard as a good thing, we shall fight them to the uttermost, having behind us the pro-ducing masses of the nation and the world. Having behind us the com-mercial interests and the laboring interests and all the toiling masses, we shall answer their demands for a gold standard by saying to them, you shall not press down upon the brow of labor this crown of thorns. You shall not crucify mankind upon a cross of gold."[2]

Hearst's papers focused on the role of huge campaign donations in this pivotal election. Political boss Mark Hanna raised an unparalleled $3.5 million (about $93 million today) to elect the Republican Civil War veteran – five times the amount raised by his Democratic oppo-nent. McKinley won by more than half a million votes. (For good or ill, Hanna has been credited with launching the modern role of money in politics.) Though Bryan lost, Hearst's formula proved hugely successful in his new headquarters in the nation's largest metropolis, ten times the population of his San Francisco home base.

Source: Wikipedia article on yellow journalism, reproducing cartoon in the collection of the Independence Seaport Museum

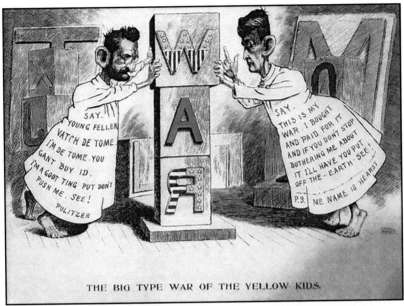

THE BIG TYPE WAR OF THE YELLOW KIDS.

Source of both pictures : "The American Notion of Privacy, The First Wave of Assault on American Privacy: Joseph Pulitzer and William Randolph Hearst."

Top: contemporary political cartoon lampooning publishers **Joseph Pulitzer** (pictured lower left) and **William Randolph Hearst** (pictured lower right) for the "yellow" of their papers filled with sensational headlines and colorful cartoons. The pair were credited with creating public fervor to push President McKinley to wage the 1898 Spanish-American War. Hearst had his own presidential ambitions. Hearst political cartoons caricatured President McKinley as a tool of the money-hungry trusts. One editor called the president "the most hated creature on the American continent" and another Hearst columnist suggested that the president deserved killing.

Source: https://en.wikipedia.org/wiki/Cross_of_Gold_speech

Left: William Jennings Bryan first ran for president in 1896 as a populist advocating the silver standard instead of gold so that money would become more widely available. He became famous for his fiery "cross of gold" speech given at the 1896 Democratic Convention, arguing the nation would be "crucified" on the gold standard. Political boss Mark Hanna raised an unparalleled $3.5 million in 1896 (about $93 million today) to elect Bryan's opponent, Republican Civil War veteran William McKinley — five times the amount raised by Bryan — launching the modern role of money in politics.

Below: Campaign poster for McKinley's reelection in 1900, running with Spanish-American War hero Teddy Roosevelt. McKinley handily defeated Bryan for a second time. Note the disavowal of foreign aggression in that war, which ended with the United States annexing the Philippines, Guam and Puerto Rico, and denial of empire-building in annexing Hawaii as a territory – "The AMERICAN FLAG has not been planted in foreign soil to acquire more territory but for HUMANITY'S SAKE."

Source: https://commons.wikimedia.org_Administration%27s_Promises_Have_Be/wiki/
File:Theen_Kept.jpg

In the second year of McKinley's presidency, rivalry with Pulitzer motivated Hearst to exploit the sinking of the battleship U.S.S. Maine in Havana Harbor on February 15, 1898, as a secret enemy attack. No proof of the charge would ever surface. With his repeated war-mongering headlines, Hearst induced Pulitzer's paper to do the same, urging readers to "Remember the Maine!" Together they created such public clamor they helped pressure President McKinley into precipitating the Spanish-American War. What Hearst cared most about was that circulation for the *Journal* rose fifty percent.

By the war's end, the United States had emerged as a world power acquiring the Philippines, Guam and Puerto Rico from the Spanish Empire as well as control of Cuba. At home, rapid industrialization and consolidation of power in trusts fueled the economy; new waves of Eastern and Southern European immigrants provided a cheap, renewable source of labor. American workers felt increasingly exploited. In editorial cartoons, Hearst's *New York Journal* characterized McKinley as a tool of the money-hungry trusts. One of his editors called the president "the most hated creature on the American continent" and another Hearst journalist suggested that the president deserved killing.[3]

On September 5, 1901, few people were genuinely surprised to learn of an attempt on the president's life by an unemployed worker among the crowd greeting McKinley at an international exposition in Buffalo, New York. Two political assassinations had made headlines the year before. In February of 1900, the new governor of Kentucky had been killed; five months later, on July 29, 1900, King Umberto of Italy was shot in retaliation for brutally suppressing a workers strike. Indeed, in the United States, many older citizens had searing memories of two presidents who had been assassinated – Lincoln in 1865 and Garfield in 1881. Since President Garfield's death, political assassins overseas had also felled Russian Czar Alexander II, French President Sadi Carnot, Spanish Premier Antonio Canovas del Castillo and Empress Elizabeth of Austria.

The disaffected Polish-American who fired his mail-order Sears Roebuck hand gun at President McKinley had been inspired by the recent assassination of King Umberto in Italy. Leon Czolgosz grew

San Francisco Chronicle.

VOL. LXXIV.   SAN FRANCISCO, CAL., SATURDAY, SEPTEMBER 7, 190-—SIXTEEN PAGES.   NO. 34.

PRESIDENT M'KINLEY SHOT BY AN ANARCHIST AT BUFFALO FAIR.

Two Bullets Fired by the Assassin, but Only One Penetrates the Body— Surgeons Hopeful of Recovery—An Attempt Made to Lynch the Cowardly Murderer.

WOUNDED AT A PUBLIC RECEPTION.

Stricken by a Man Who Grasped His Hand—Crowd Sought to Mete Out Swift Punishment.

A RECENT PORTRAIT OF PRESIDENT M'KINLEY

DOCTORS DECLARE INJURIES SEVERE.

The Chances of Recovery Said to Be Against President—Cheering Reports Untrue.

FAVORABLE REPORT ON PRESIDENT'S CONDITION

BUFFALO, N. Y., September 7.—At 3 A. M. the following bulletin was issued:

"The President continues to rest well. Temperature 10½, pulse 118, respiration 24.

"P. M. RIXEY."

Source: Oakland Public Library

The nation reacted in shock to the attempted assassination of the president.

up in the Midwest and once worked in the steel industry. His politics were strongly influenced by the revolutionary speeches of Russian emigrant Emma Goldman. Historian Eric Rauchway suggests that Czolgosz also believed he was dying of untreatable syphilis when he decided to exchange his life for President McKinley's.[4] At first, President McKinley appeared to be recovering from his two wounds. But he took a sudden turn for the worse a week later and died of gangrene resulting from botched emergency medical care. Much ridiculed during his tenure, McKinley instantly became a martyr about whom few were willing to speak ill. Prohibition crusader Carrie Nation was an exception, claiming "he got what he deserved."[5] Goldman also voiced her dissent. She publicly praised Czolgosz as a modern-day Brutus for killing a 20th century Caesar, the "president of the money kings and trust magnates."[6] But these two outspoken women proved rare exceptions.

Pioneering social worker Jane Addams captured the mood of most Americans: "It is impossible to overstate the public excitement of the moment and the unfathomable sense of horror with which the community regarded an attack upon the chief executive of the nation, as a crime against government itself which compels an instinctive recoil from all law-abiding citizens."[7] Many shocked readers blamed newspaper publisher William Randolph Hearst for the attack on President McKinley. Effigies of Hearst were set afire. The *New York Journal* was boycotted for months.

* * * * *

President McKinley had arrived at The Pan-American Exposition in the thriving city of Buffalo to celebrate the nation's emergence as a world power at the dawn of the new century. The huge fair showcased innovations like electricity and the x-ray machine and featured exotic exhibits from around the globe. The president's visit had been postponed from the opening of the festival in May 1901 to the week of Labor Day – a national holiday established just seven years before to honor the working class.

The Secret Service agents guarding the president had scarcely noticed the innocuous-looking Czolgosz in the long queue of well-wishers on September 5 until after Czolgosz fired a gun camouflaged under his handkerchief. At the time, the agents had their eyes on a suspicious-looking six-foot-six "colored man" with a black moustache who was next in line.[8] James Benjamin "Big Ben" Parker reacted quickly. The 41-year-old former slave knocked the weapon from Czolgosz's hand before he could fire again and tackled him as others joined in the fracas. Parker enjoyed national publicity for a short while as a quick-thinking hero credited with saving the president's life. But soon the government supplanted stories of Parker's heroism with a new version of the shooting incident giving an Irish Secret Service agent complete credit for capturing Czolgosz.

While Czolgosz remained in pretrial custody, locals from the Buffalo area stormed the jail twice looking to lynch him for his attempt on the president's life. Whites were not alone in thirsting for immediate vengeance. Big Ben Parker had already bragged to the newspapers that, when he tackled Czolgosz, he was bent on cutting the assailant's throat on the spot like the vigilante justice Parker had witnessed when he was growing up in Georgia. Just the week before, an angry lynch mob of African-Americans in a Kentucky town had made headlines. White jailers stepped aside to let the mob rush the jail and hang several black men arrested for the murder of one of their community's respected elders. In Parker's view, Czolgosz deserved no better.

Educator and orator Booker T. Washington read with great alarm the accounts of mobs storming Buffalo's police headquarters bent on lynching the anarchist. In early 1901, Washington had published his best-selling autobiography *Up From Slavery*. A pragmatist, Washington drew support from both African-Americans and Progressive whites by accepting segregation as the best path forward to economic prosperity for his race. For the last twenty years, Washington had headed the Tuskegee Normal School for Colored Teachers, attracting generous support from philanthropists to turn the Tennessee campus into a prestigious industrial college. By the turn of the century, Washington was recognized as the most influential African-American in the country.

Washington seized upon the frenzied response to the attack on the

Source: https://en.wikipedia.org/wiki/Leon_Czolgosz

Leon Czolgoz

Source: https://en.wikipedia.org/wiki/James_Benjamin_Parker

James Benjamin Parker

Source of photo: http://www.loc.gov/pictures/item/96521677/

Top left: *Leon Czolgosz, the unemployed anarchist who shot President McKinley.* **Top right**: *"Big Ben" Parker, the former slave who wrestled Czolgosz to the ground as depicted* (**above**) *in this 1905 drawing by T. Dart Walker reconstructing the scene of the shooting at the Pan-American Exposition on Sept. 6, 1901. Parker's heroism was soon obscured by the government crediting a Secret Service agent with tackling Czolgosz instead.*

president as a teaching moment. In a widely-published opinion letter to a Montgomery newspaper, he compared self-proclaimed anarchists like Czolgosz to the ubiquity of lynch mobs in America. Washington asked his readers to consider: "Is Czolgosz alone guilty? Has not the entire nation had a part in this greatest crime of the century?"[9] At the time, a black man was lynched somewhere in the South every few days. Washington made a point of tracking grim statistics gathered by the *Chicago Tribune* recording more than 2500 lynchings in the past sixteen years. He estimated that on average fifty people participated in each lynching during that period totaling "nearly 125,000 persons." Washington concluded: "We cannot sow disorder and reap order . . . One criminal put to death through the majesty of the law does more . . . to prevent crime than ten put to death by lynching anarchists."[10]

Editorials in other African-American newspapers echoed Washington's plea. But it was more likely the eyes of the world on Buffalo that ensured a jury trial for Czolgosz. Desire for quick revenge remained intense. The district attorney put the despised social outcast on trial for his life just nine days after President McKinley died. The judge rejected Czolgosz's attempt to plead guilty. Czolgosz refused to cooperate with the lawyers appointed to represent him. The prosecution presented all of its testimony in two days, and Czolgosz's defense lawyers called no witnesses to back up a defense of not guilty by reason of insanity. One of Czolgosz's court-appointed lawyers told the jury that even though anarchists did "not believe in any law" they still merited "the form of a trial."[11] Half an hour later, the jury came back with the expected verdict of first degree murder.

Within a month after the jury voted for the death penalty Czolgosz was electrocuted. Cameras focused on the outside of the prison as background for a ghoulish filmed reenactment of his death distributed widely a few weeks later. Czolgosz had not made any statement at his trial, but he had told the arresting officer, "I done my duty," and admitted he was an anarchist.[12] As he was about to be placed in the chair he elaborated: "I killed the President because he was the enemy of the good people – the good working people. I am not sorry for my crime."[13]

His only regret was not being able to say good-bye to his father.

After his electrocution, his body was dissolved in acid to prevent medical experts from seeking to reexamine his brain and to dissuade souvenir hunters from digging up his remains.

A doctor who analyzed the case in 1902 had serious doubts about Czolgosz's sanity. In a later era, a jury determined that John Hinckley, Jr., was insane when he attempted to assassinate President Reagan. In the first decade of the century, national outrage against Czolgosz would permit no such dispassionate analysis even had evidence been offered to support the insanity plea his court-appointed lawyers had raised at trial. Defendants without status or resources commonly received short shrift in the courts. In this instance, the lawyers were prominent members of the bar, but given no time to prepare. Czolgosz got as little due process as the system could then pass off for justice — a rush to the electric chair Booker T. Washington recognized as an instance of "legal lynching." He was familiar with many municipalities that used the trappings of the law to make preordained hangings less seemingly barbaric.[14]

* * * * *

Less than three weeks after Czolgosz was sentenced, but before his execution, President Theodore Roosevelt invited Booker T. Washington to dine with the first family at the White House. Washington had been a trusted advisor of Roosevelt back when T. R. had been Governor of New York. The President now welcomed Washington's advice on prospective appointees in the South. When news of the private dinner leaked out, blacks and Progressives applauded Roosevelt's egalitarian gesture. Southern Democrats exploded in rage.

On occasion, Presidents had welcomed black leaders to the White House before. Lincoln had opened that door by warmly greeting abolitionist Frederick Douglass at a reception late in the Civil War. But no president had ever sat down at the first family's dinner table with a black man. Roosevelt's violation of strict segregation spawned angry opinion letters and vulgar political cartoons. A Memphis paper called it "the most damnable outrage ever perpetrated by any citizen of the United States."[15] As far as most Southern whites were concerned, President

Source of photo: http://www.philosophersguild.com/blog/?p=2003 Library of Congress /
Contributor Editorial # 640486723 Collection: Corbis Historical

*Artist portrayal of Booker T. Washington dining with new President Theodore
Roosevelt in October 1901 – first African-American ever invited to join the First
Family for dinner in the White House. The backlash was so powerful that no
president invited another black person to dine at the White House for another
three decades.*

Source: Library of Congress's Prints and Photographs division digital ID cph.3c04434

Benjamin Tillman 1845–1918

*South Carolina Sen. "Pitchfork Ben" Till-
man boasted of terrorizing freedmen as a
member of the "Red Shirts" in the late 19th
century, whose exploits included a violent
racial confrontation in 1876 known as the
Hamburg Massacre. An unabashed white
supremacist, he won election as governor
in 1890 and engineered the adoption of
the state's 1895 constitution that stripped
the right to vote from most blacks and poor
whites for more than two-thirds of a century.
Enraged by Booker T. Washington's dinner
with President Roosevelt, Sen. Tillman rallied his followers with calls for a thousand
retaliatory lynchings. Southern politicians
continued to encourage lynching as a power
ploy for decades. A statue in Tillman's hon-
or remains at the South Carolina Capitol in
Charleston to this day.*

Source: This reprint is from the *Kentucky New Era*, March 13, 1903. https://en.wikipedia.org/wiki/Niggers_in_the_White_House

NIGGERS IN THE WHITE HOUSE.

Six Months Hence.

Things at the White House,
Looking mighty curious;
Niggers running everything,
White people furious.

Niggers on the front porch,
Niggers on the gable,
Niggers in the dinning room,
Niggers at the table.

Niggers in the sitting room,
Making all the talk;
Niggers in the ballroom
Doing cakewalk.

Niggers in the East room
Make a mighty throng,
Niggers in the music room
Singing coon songs.

Niggers in the hallway
Taking off their wraps,
Niggers in the billiard room
Shooting game of craps.

Niggers in the storeroom
Packing way their plunder;
Niggers in the bedroom
Snoring like thunder.

Not a room in the White House
Without a nigger many;
Baby in nursery
A nigger pickaninny.

Niggers on the stairway
With very much satiety.

Niggers in the Blue room
Assembled for society.

Niggers in the front yard,
Niggers in the back;
Niggers in the omnibus,
And niggers come in hack.

On they go to Washington
With a mighty rush;
Forty thousand niggers
Getting in the push.

There is trouble in the White
House,
More than you can tell,
Yelling like wild men,
Niggers raising hell.

I see a way to settle it,
Just as clear as water—
Let Mr. Booker Washington
Marry Teddy's daughter.

Or, if this does not overflow,
Teddy's cup of joy,
Then let Miss Dinah Washington
Marry Teddy's boy.

But everything is settled:
Roosevelt is dead.
Niggers in the White House
Cut off Teddy's head.

—Unchained poet in Democratic
Leader, Missouri.

How much have times changed? Written in 1901, this inflammatory poem was published following news that President Roosevelt had invited Booker T. Washington to join the First Family for dinner at the White House earlier that fall. The poem recirculated in a number of Southern newspapers in 1903 and again in the 1920s. A copy has been preserved in the Library of Congress. Those who today disparage the Obamas as having "embarrassed" the country by their tenure in the White House have recently been called out for harboring the exact same racist sentiment. See John Pavlovitz, "No, White Friend – You Weren't 'Embarrassed' by Barack Obama," May 26, 2017, http://johnpavlovitz.com/2017/05/26/no-white-friend-you-werent-embarrassed-by-barack-Obama/.

Roosevelt might just as well have signaled his approval of intermarriage of the races, which some states had prohibited since colonial days and still prosecuted as a felony.

Mississippi Senator James Vardaman complained that "the odor of the nigger" at the White House forced the rats to take "refuge in the stable." In a speech to Congress, South Carolina Senator "Pitchfork Ben" Tillman, another leading white supremacist, characterized the invitation as a grave insult to 7,000,000 Southerners and two-thirds of Northerners. Back home addressing his constituents, Tillman explicitly called for renewed terrorism like that he had engaged in as a youth during the Reconstruction Era: "The action of President Roosevelt in entertaining that nigger will necessitate our killing a thousand niggers in the South before they will learn their place again."[16] Credible death threats were made against Booker T. Washington. The backlash felt by the White House was so powerful that no president invited another black person to dine at the White House for another three decades. All the while, Southern politicians encouraged lynching as a power ploy for more than half a century after Senator Tillman's blood-thirsty appeal.

* * * * *

When anger at Hearst had subsided following McKinley's assassination, the ambitious publisher again tapped into labor's ongoing resentment of corporate power. Denouncing members of his own class, Hearst won a seat in Congress as a populist Democrat. Yet the maverick millionaire's personal life differed little from the decadent circle of wealthy degenerates his readers loved to hate. In New York, the handsome transplanted Californian cultivated the backing of Tammany Hall's new top man, political fixer "Big Tim" Sullivan of the Lower East Side.

Hearst had helped himself get elected to Congress in 1902 by offering free trips to Coney Island Amusement Park to every resident, recognizing that workers did not resent the wealthy when they shared their bounty with the public. He then celebrated with an extravaganza at Madison Square Garden, including fireworks that exploded prematurely and killed eighteen supporters. In 1903, the playboy forty-year-old bachelor married a twenty-one-year-old chorus girl, whose mother ran a brothel protected by Big Tim Sullivan. In 1905, Hearst took on Tammany Hall incumbent Mayor George McClellan (the Civil War General's son) and almost beat him.

Hearst now had his eye on becoming Governor of New York and ultimately President of the United States. The setback over the McKinley assassination had not dampened Hearst's enthusiasm for using his newspapers to expose the excesses of his own privileged class. So it was not surprising in 1906 when newsies hawked the very first "trial of the century" – a spectacular shooting death that featured wealthy degenerates, drugs, sex with Broadway chorus girls and defense of traditional moral values by an outraged husband. Hearst instantly realized that a murder trial focused on the dark secrets of New York's elite social circle was a gold mine. Other papers followed suit. No matter their class or occupation eager readers of daily papers focused on the same question: Would murder charges stick when one tuxedoed vulture killed another in full view of a large crowd?

2. DEMENTIA AMERICANA

A Dramatic Murder Brings the Curtain Crashing Down on the Gilded Age

He had it coming to him!
— HARRY THAW[1]

Harry Thaw must have played the scene out in his head many times before. He could not have picked a more theatrical moment to kill the fifty-two-year-old premiere architect of the Gilded Age. The setting was a crowded performance of an open-air musical atop the city's tallest building – a landmark Stanford White himself had designed. The delusional Thaw saw himself as God's emissary to avenge the many teenage girls White had abused and to save countless others. At first, Thaw appeared to the public as a hero upholding old-fashioned values against the decadent new era. Yet Thaw was a Dr. Jekyll and Mr. Hyde whose history of sadistic outbursts made White's predatory behavior pale in comparison. By the time the saga played out, the tarnished Gilded Age was history, as was public respect for the superiority of the sophisticated high society that bred such evildoers.

The object of both men's desire was Evelyn Nesbit. The wide-eyed Gibson Girl with lush chestnut curls and an enigmatic Mona Lisa smile was instantly recognizable everywhere. Her face sold products from soup to sewing machines, toothpaste to playing cards. The former model and Broadway chorine personified the "It" girl before America ever thought to apply the term to a sex symbol.[2] Like the dream of many showgirls, at twenty, Nesbit traded her career for a handsome millionaire. She married Thaw in April of 1905, disappearing from

31

Sources: Postcard of Madison Square Garden, https://commons.wikimedia.org/wiki/File:Madison-square2.jpg; close up of Diana statue, now in the Philadelphia Museum of Art, https://en.wikipedia.org/wiki/File:Diana_MSG. jpg; Stanford White photo circa 1900, https://en.wikipedia.org/wiki/Stanford_White

Left: Madison Square Garden in 1890 as designed by Stanford White (**lower right**) at 26th and Madison to replace the original building of the same name at that location. Its rooftop theater was the site chosen by Harry Thaw for avenging his wife's earlier seduction by White. When fatally shot, the architect was listening to a performer sing, "I Could Love a Million Girls." **Top right**: The scandalous nude statue of the Goddess Diana by sculptor Augustus Saint-Gaudens that adorned Madison Square Garden's tower made it the highest point in New York City – taller than the Statue of Liberty. Even in daylight, "Diana of the Tower" could be seen from New Jersey. At night, it had the distinction of being the first statue ever lit up by electricity. The statue appalled ministers in their pulpits and other defenders of traditional morality – a tension that underscored life in the newly emerged metropolis, rapidly on its way to becoming a center of world trade.

the limelight to the Thaw family mansion in Pittsburgh, ruled with an iron hand by Thaw's deeply religious and disapproving mother, Mary Copley Thaw.

As the public would soon learn, thirty-five-year-old Harry Thaw and his celebrity wife had only returned to Manhattan for a few days' stay before heading on a luxury cruise to England for a vacation with Thaw's family – a vacation they never got to take. On the evening of June 25, 1906, Evelyn looked as spectacular as ever as her maid fastened the pearl buttons on her white satin, black-trimmed gown. Evelyn completed her fashion statement with matching black accessories, long gloves and an oversized hat with a bow. As usual, Harry had done all the planning.

Later that night Evelyn's heart sank when she realized her husband had arranged for dinner and a show at two of Stanford White's known haunts. Evelyn knew how obsessed Thaw was with "the beast" as he insisted they both call White. Ever since Thaw learned that White had deflowered Evelyn at sixteen, Thaw became preoccupied with the subject, making Evelyn repeat the details ad nauseam. He started having White followed by private detectives and made Evelyn report to him whenever she saw "the beast" passing on the street. Though she still had a soft spot in her heart for White, Evelyn always complied, realizing Thaw had spies tracking her, too.

Florence Evelyn Nesbit was the most celebrated beauty of her day. Hers was a Cinderella story with a twist. In Evelyn's case, she exchanged a life of poverty for one with a dangerous loon in a gilded cage. She started out a small-town Pennsylvania girl, the daughter of a doting lawyer. Winfield Nesbit paid for music and dance lessons and encouraged Evelyn's interest in literature. Then in 1895, shortly after the family moved to Pittsburgh, Winfield Nesbit died suddenly, leaving his wife and two children nearly destitute. When the sheriff put them out on the street, Mrs. Nesbit sent her children to stay with relatives and friends, but eventually scraped by with money she borrowed to run a boarding house. Evelyn, her mother, and her younger brother Howard shared one bedroom while the rest were rented out.

A professional photographer first spotted the twelve-year-old naïf sweating in the August sun on the boarding house stoop, wearing a fetching homemade blue dress. Not long afterward the family was again evicted from their home. Evelyn and Howard stayed once more with relatives while Mrs. Nesbit found work in Philadelphia as a seamstress. After the family reunited, Evelyn obtained steady work as an artist and photographers' model. In the summer of 1900, Mrs. Nesbit again sent her children to live with friends and relatives while she spent months looking for work as a dress designer in New York. In December of 1900, both teenagers rejoined their still unemployed mother in Manhattan. Letters of introduction from Philadelphia artists led to Evelyn being hired to pose for a prominent portrait painter. Word spread to others of the "perfectly formed nymph." The sixteen-year-old's modeling work quickly became the small family's principal source of income.[3] The days of making do with sometimes only bread to eat were now behind them.

Several months later, a newspaper interview with alluring photographs of "The Little Sphinx" prompted a theatrical agent to contact Mrs. Nesbit. He arranged for Evelyn to join Broadway's most popular show, "Florodora." The new five-foot-tall, childlike beauty in the chorus quickly caught the eye of one of its regular patrons, Stanford White. White had become the most sought-after architect of an era when America's superrich favored ostentatious displays of their wealth. White asked an older chorine to introduce him to Evelyn, whose first impression was of an ugly old man. The architect was a contemporary of her deceased father. But unlike the quiet and unassuming Win Nesbit, White was large and gregarious with close-cropped red hair, an untamed moustache, and a huge appetite for delicacies from gourmet food to new sexual conquests. White was willing to bide his time. He ingratiated himself with Mrs. Nesbit and became Evelyn's benefactor. He sent her flowers, paid for an upscale apartment with the luxury of its own private bathroom, and sent her to the dentist at his expense. He suggested books for Evelyn to read to expand her cultural awareness as her father had done. White also indulged Evelyn's sweet tooth, and invited her to taste exotic foods at private lunch and dinner parties with other guests.

During the first several weeks of their acquaintance, White never let Evelyn drink more than one glass of champagne or stay up too late. After

Source of both photos: Wikipedia. https://en.Wikipedia.org/wiki/Evelyn_Nesbit.

Source:https://en.wikipedia.org/wiki/Rudolf_Eickemeyer_Jr.#/media/File:IN_MY_STUDIO_EVELYN_NESBIT_TIRED_BUTTERFLY,_1909.jpg

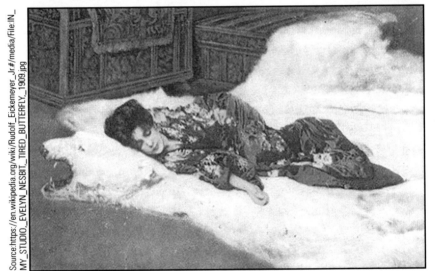

Top left: *America's first sex symbol, Evelyn Nesbit. (Photographer: Otto Sarony, 1901.)* **Top right:** *Gertrude Käsebier's famous 1903 photo of "Miss N."* **Bottom:** *Rudolf Eickemeyer's prize-winning 1909 photo of Evelyn Nesbit in his studio asleep on a bearskin rug, dressed in a loose kimono, and captioned the "Tired Butterfly."*

two months, White had completely won their trust and convinced Mrs. Nesbit that it was safe for her to take a trip back to Pittsburgh and leave Evelyn in his charge. In November of 1901, White lured Evelyn to his love nest on 24th Street on the pretense of another dinner party, plied her with champagne and led her to his bedroom. Over the next several months the two became lovers, which they kept secret from her mother.

Though White considered his adorable "Kittens" quite extraordinary, she was only one of many under-aged chorines the married lecher turned into temporary concubines. Rumors of his debauchery thoroughly scandalized old-fashioned guardians of female purity. The President of the Society for the Suppression of Vice fumed even more when White placed a large, spot-lit statue of a nude Goddess Diana atop Madison Square Garden, higher than any other feature of the cityscape. It was a slap in the face of traditional morality, a tension that underscored life in the newly emerged metropolis, rapidly on its way to becoming a center of world trade.

Harry Thaw's enmity toward White had a different source, dating back at least a year before Evelyn Nesbit first arrived in New York. Thaw envied White as a charter member of the elite New York social circle to which Thaw had been denied entry. White hobnobbed with the Vanderbilts and the Astors, whose Fifth Avenue mansions he designed, and socialized with other millionaires in exclusive clubs which White also designed. Thaw was convinced White had badmouthed him to prevent Thaw's acceptance by the New York "Four Hundred." What fueled Thaw's fury even more was White's interference when Thaw tried to pick up chorus girls at Broadway shows. For their own protection, White persuaded a number of dancers to steer clear of the baby-faced younger Lothario with the glazed expression and weird giggle. Thaw had developed a reputation as a dope fiend with a violent temper.

Thaw's mother had used hush money to quash stories about his prior bouts of scandal, but some negative publicity had still emerged. One college peccadillo that hit the newspapers was a striking example of Thaw's often erratic behavior. It occurred during the brief time the family's influence got the below-average prep school student enrolled at Harvard. At a bar, Thaw might ostentatiously leave a hundred-dollar bill for a three-dollar tab. Yet he had run after a Cambridge cab driver, waving an empty shotgun because he thought the man had stiffed him out of ten cents' change. Soon afterward, Thaw got expelled for unspecified "immoral practices" and threats to fellow students and staff.[4] Thaw later bragged that, while at Harvard, he had spent more time playing poker than attending class; he divided his remaining time among women, cockfights and benders.

Since his expulsion, Thaw had been publicly charged with whipping a woman he dated in New York. Thaw made frequent use of laudanum and carried a special silver case filled with syringes for injecting his own drug cocktails, which reportedly included the original "speedball" mixing cocaine, morphine and heroin. In courting Nesbit, Thaw kept his inner demons well hidden. He even disguised his identity at first, sending her flowers and other gifts under an assumed name.

In 1902, Stanford White still took a strong paternalistic interest in seventeen-year-old Evelyn. White maintained close ties with her mother and paid for her brother's schooling, while he added other young chorines to his list of conquests. At Mrs. Nesbit's urging, White broke up a budding romance between Evelyn and twenty-one-year-old (future matinee idol) John Barrymore by getting Evelyn admitted to a New Jersey boarding school. White also warned Evelyn against Thaw. Evelyn remained at the school through the spring of 1903, visited occasionally by White, but also receiving presents and correspondence from Thaw, who kept proposing. In April, when Evelyn fell ill with appendicitis, it was Harry Thaw who rushed to her side oozing solicitude for the girl he nicknamed his "Boofuls."

When doctors suggested that Evelyn convalesce following surgery, Thaw offered to pay for Evelyn and her mother to take a cruise to Europe. Thaw did not tell them before they embarked that he planned to join the pair in England. Once in Europe, the three traveled together to Paris in June. Thaw again proposed and Evelyn emphatically turned him down, convinced that he would not want her. At Thaw's insistence, she tearfully confessed her reasons. Stanford White had taken her virginity when she was sixteen and kept her as his mistress. Soon after, Thaw succeeded in alienating Mrs. Nesbit and sending her home on his promise to hire a chaperone to take her place. Instead, Thaw isolated Evelyn in a rented Austrian castle where he barged into her bedroom naked in a wild-eyed, drug-induced frenzy. He then beat her legs bloody with a whip, tore off her nightgown, and raped the terrified teenager, saying it was retribution for her past sins.

After they returned to America, Evelyn's mother and Stanford White persuaded Evelyn to avoid all contact with Thaw as she resumed her career in New York. White also had Evelyn sign an affidavit accusing Thaw of abducting and attacking her. White's lawyer kept it safe. Thaw's detectives then gathered dirt on White, and White hired his own men to trace Thaw's gum shoes to their source. Evelyn stayed under White's strong influence for a time, but ultimately chafed at neither being the sole love of White's life, nor in a position to marry anyone else. Thaw resumed the role of solicitous lover. He apologized for his attack on Evelyn and focused his anger instead solely on White.

After being showered with gifts and love letters, Evelyn succumbed to Thaw's incessant pressure and married him in April of 1905. The news horrified Stanford White and greatly dismayed Mother Thaw, a woman devoted to religious salvation who forbade any mention of Evelyn's shameless past. Evelyn soon lamented her decision, trapped in a household of Presbyterian piety that treated her with disdain. Harry Thaw's obsessive jealousy continued unabated. He sent Evelyn to his own dentist to have every bit of dental work White had paid for removed and replaced. She was now his trophy, not White's.

Back in Manhattan at a mid-town luxury hotel on the evening of June 25, 1906, Thaw dressed in his tuxedo and asked Evelyn to meet him at a nearby high-end restaurant for drinks and dinner. Thaw wore a long coat which easily concealed the hand gun he packed. They would be joined by two dinner companions: Tommy McCaleb, an old friend who accompanied them to New York from Pittsburgh; and Thaw's new friend, Truxton Beale. Evelyn mistrusted Thaw's fascination with Beale, who was rumored to have committed an honor killing in California. It fit in too much with Thaw's morbid preoccupation with Stanford White. Yet Evelyn did not attach significance to Thaw's first choice of Sherry's for drinks and dinner, a showplace designed by White's architectural firm. The evening took a different turn when Beale came dressed too casually for Sherry's. Thaw then suggested the foursome go instead to another popular eatery, the Café Martin. By the time they left Sherry's, Thaw had already consumed several drinks.

Evelyn spotted Stanford White entering Café Martin and tried not to react visibly. It now occurred to her that her husband was deliberately trying to force a confrontation. White headed to the restaurant's porch with his son and a friend who were down visiting from Harvard. It would turn out to be the architect's very last meal. Soon, Evelyn realized she could not disguise her angst. Evelyn borrowed a pencil from one of their dinner companions and wrote a brief note to her husband that "the B" had come and gone. Thaw was livid that he had not seen his quarry.

After dinner, the Thaws and their two friends headed for the new musical "Mamzelle Champagne" at the open-air theater atop Madison Square Garden. Thaw had purchased the tickets that same afternoon. He knew White had a regular table five rows from the stage and may have heard from his detectives that White was expected there that evening. The foursome was seated at a table further back in the crowd. They drank more champagne. Evelyn's anxiety lessened when she saw that White's table remained empty. But many people noticed how agitated Thaw appeared as he repeatedly got up during the show, paced, and looked around before sitting back down.

Just before 11 p.m., Thaw was once again out of his chair when Evelyn noticed that White had just arrived. White spoke briefly with the manager to remind him he wanted an introduction to the latest seventeen-year-old ingénue. The architect then headed for his table to catch the last few minutes of the show. When her husband came back to his seat, Evelyn nervously suggested they leave. Thaw and their two guests agreed. The show was painfully amateurish. Evelyn was relieved that Thaw apparently had not seen White enter. The couple headed out to the elevators with their two companions. Then Evelyn noticed her husband was gone; he had darted back into the theater.

By the time Thaw spotted him, White had been served a glass of wine and had his elbow on the table and his chin cupped in his right hand, apparently deep in thought. A male vocalist was just starting to sing "I Could Love a Million Girls." Thaw looked pale as a ghost as he approached White, who likely did not see him coming. Thaw pulled the pistol from under his coat and came within two feet of White's face. Thaw fired three quick shots. One entered through White's left eye; one broke his jaw; and a third penetrated his arm. White's elbow slipped and the table overturned, breaking his glass as the architect thudded to the floor. The singer stopped. Thaw raised his gun high in the air and attempted to reassure everyone he posed no further danger, exclaiming, "He had it coming to him."[5] Then Thaw left for the exit, holding the barrel of the gun, looking for someone to whom he could hand it over.

It took a couple of minutes for the audience to realize this was not part of the show. As blood pooled around White's body, a woman leapt up and became hysterical. Others rose in panic as well. The manager jumped on a table, urging the performers to resume the musical, but the chorines were far too horrified. Then the manager announced that a terrible accident had occurred and asked people to try to leave in an orderly fashion. As patrons rushed for the exits, Evelyn Thaw hurried to White's body and then ran back to her husband by the elevators, crying, "My God, Harry, you've killed him." He asked her for a kiss, and they embraced.

A policeman responding to the sound of gunfire arrived to see White's body on the floor and a woman who had fainted nearby. The officer asked Thaw if he had shot the man lying on the theater floor and Thaw said, "Yes, he ruined my wife." Thaw then asked, "Is he dead?" The policeman told him that he was. Thaw responded: "Well, I made a good job of it, and I'm glad."

Evelyn gave him another hug and kiss, whispering, "I didn't think you would do it in this way."[6]

Having killed the "Beast" who had deflowered his wife, Thaw seemed inordinately calm, some thought dazed. He gave his name to police as Mr. John Smith, though he carried calling cards which revealed his true identity. At the police station, he asked to have his lawyer notified and lit up a cigarette. A doorman familiar with White's many young conquests told a *New York Times* reporter that the shooting

Source: https://en.wikipedia.org/wiki/File:Stanford_White_33_crop.jpg

Front page of the New York American *newspaper June 26, 1906.*

Source: https://en.wikipedia.org/wiki/Harry_Kendall_Thaw

Harry Thaw around 1905 – the year before he murdered Stanford White.

Though a serial sexual predator himself, Stanford White had warned a number of Broadway chorus girls to steer clear of Thaw, a baby-faced younger Lothario with a glazed expression and weird giggle. Thaw developed a reputation as a dope fiend with a violent temper. He made frequent use of laudanum and carried a special silver case filled with syringes for injecting his own drug cocktails, which reportedly included the original "speedball" mixing cocaine, morphine and heroin.

came as no shock. He later testified at trial that the only surprise was that White was killed by a husband: "Everyone always figured it would be a father."[7]

Like the lawyers for Czolgosz, Thaw's lawyers pleaded insanity as a defense to gunning down his victim in front of hundreds of witnesses. Yet the public reaction to Thaw's crime, the nature of the trial, and its outcome were vastly different – a reflection obviously of the magnitude of Czolgosz's crime, but also of the difference in the two men's class, their wealth and their rationale. With Mother Thaw footing the bill, Thaw had the best defense they could buy. In an era when so many Americans openly supported vigilante justice, Thaw invoked an age-old chauvinistic code of ethics that reinforced traditional community values vilifying debauchers of young virgins. His crime was not perceived to threaten society; it provided an entertaining lesson in morals.

Within a week of White's shooting, inventor Thomas Edison's New York movie studio churned out a short, dramatic reenactment, *Rooftop Murder*, which instantly attracted the most nickels in thousands of arcades across the country. By then, the new art of silent picture shows was well on its way to drawing 30 million fascinated people a week. Postcards of Evelyn Nesbit sold out so quickly that printers kept their presses going around the clock, generating millions more. As voyeurs flocked to nickelodeons and souvenir vendors, moralists on and off the pulpit, appalled by the city's sexual permissiveness, applauded Thaw's defense of his wife's honor. Monsters like White who ruined young girls deserved to be shot.

When even Adolph Ochs' dignified *New York Times* played up the murder of Stanford White in effusive detail, a consensus was reached. The prosecution of millionaire Harry Thaw for killing high-society architect Stanford White would be the "trial of the century."[8] *The New York World*'s editor Frank Cobb drooled over the irresistible cast of characters: "rich old wasters, delectable young chorus girls and adolescent artists' models . . . artists and jaded debauchees . . . Bowery toughs, Harlem gangsters, Tenderloin panderers, Broadway leading men, Fifth Avenue clubmen, Wall Street manipulators, uptown voluptuaries and downtown thugs."[9]

The seamy side of the city's elite captivated everyone from

housewives to professionals, society matrons and political reformers. Most members of the public responded with gratitude to Thaw for the public service he performed. Exposure of the dirty linen of society leaders like White who did not follow rules of behavior expected of everyone else had great appeal to the disgruntled laboring class: Jews in the lower East Side, the denizens of Little Italy and Harlem, the Irish, and other European immigrants riding on the new subway system to and from their back-breaking, underpaid jobs and overcrowded slums.

In 1906 the desperate poverty and exhausting work schedules of millions of new immigrants caused simmering resentment of the upper class, but little concerted action. In exploiting the trial of Harry Thaw for the murder of Stanford White, Hearst delighted in creating a wide audience for salacious details about White's immoral social circle of plutocrats and the sordid side of New York's theater life. Soon everyone who read the tabloids learned of the "girl on the red velvet swing" that White had hung from the ceiling of one of his Manhattan love nests. They read every horrifying detail of how the debaucher asked each of his young conquests to swing back and forth both in childlike innocence and in various stages of undress while he looked on in lecherous anticipation of bedding his prey.

By the time of trial in January of 1907, publicity about the case had become so pervasive that the lawyers had to question six hundred men before they could agree on an unbiased jury. Women were not eligible for jury service at the time. The judge decided to sequester the jury to keep them from being tainted – reportedly a first. Journalists swarmed all over, including newly hired female reporters mockingly dubbed "The Pity Patrol" for their maudlin descriptions of Evelyn Nesbit's plight. Soon newswomen who appealed to their readers' sympathy would become known as sob sisters.[10]

The prosecutor was a Republican, former judge William Travers Jerome, a talented district attorney with his eye – like Hearst – both on the governor's office and the White House. Why not? President Teddy Roosevelt was himself former Governor of New York. Though Jerome had earned his reputation by routing out vice and corruption, he did not let marriage impede him from dallying with a woman twenty years his junior. In fact, Jerome traveled in the same social circles as White and should not have accepted the lead role in a trial involving so many friends as potential witnesses.

Thaw's original trial counsel was veteran New York attorney Lewis Delafield. Delafield came highly recommended by the family's corporate lawyers, but soon lost Thaw's trust. Jerome had originally approached Delafield with a practical solution: to have Thaw sent to an asylum instead of an expensive trial where he might risk execution. The very idea of pleading insanity met with strong resistance from both Thaw and his mother. Thaw fired the man he called "the traitor." The family only agreed to try the case on a plea of temporary insanity based on provocation by White's conduct. Mrs. Thaw had no intention of airing family secrets, including her son's history of bizarre behavior.

The trial opened with Delafield's partner Gleason presenting a confused array of defenses. Contrary to the Thaws' instructions, the defenses included inherited tendencies toward mental instability. After a heated conference, Gleason volunteered his resignation. His replacement was renowned San Francisco criminal defense lawyer Delphin Delmas. "The legal Napoleon of San Francisco"[11] had never lost a case. His celebrated victories included a murder trial of a Californian who had similarly avenged the honor of a close female relative by killing her debaucher.

Delmas had a term for the defense he would present for Thaw: "Dementia Americana." The concept first surfaced in a United States courtroom shortly before the Civil War. Lawyers for New York Congressman (and future Union general) Daniel Sickles had used it successfully to exonerate Sickles for killing his wife's lover, the son of famed lawyer and poet Francis Scott Key. Unlike the Sickles case, by the time this trial ended, Mrs. Thaw would pour more than a million dollars into her son's defense, including $500,000 for Delmas and an equal amount on a dozen medical experts. The doctors would offer testimony on a new concept they called a "brain storm," by which they meant temporary interference with rational functions. Mrs. Thaw embraced the opportunity to avoid reference to her son's past behavior patterns as well as his feeble-minded uncles.

Delmas focused on transforming Stanford White from victim to villain, the man whose lechery caused Thaw's brain storm. To accomplish his aim, Delmas turned to Evelyn Thaw as his star witness. He would leave his unpredictable client off the stand. With limited questions on direct examination, they could avoid having Evelyn mention Harry's attack on her in Austria, his attempted suicide with laudanum, and other bizarre behavior. The risk was on cross-examination, but Evelyn gladly undertook to paint her husband in the best light possible. She did not want to see Harry executed; her own future support depended on doing her mother-in-law's bidding and saving Harry's life.

The day Evelyn Nesbit Thaw was called to the stand, thousands of would-be spectators tried to get in. But police and temporary barricades kept most of them out in the street. Dressed demurely in a long, navy blue suit and prim white blouse, Evelyn spoke in a soft, childish voice. The whole courtroom strained to hear her much-anticipated account. The basis for allowing Evelyn to tell her life story was that it had all been told to Harry Thaw and had motivated him to kill Stanford White. So Delmas started by having Evelyn explain how Thaw had proposed to her in Paris and how she had tearfully told Thaw that she could not marry him. Evelyn then revealed that she spent one long night explaining to Thaw why she would not make him a good wife. "He wanted every detail and I told him everything. He would sit and sob or walk up and down the room as I told him."

At the defense table, Thaw became upset all over again. He sank down into his chair and shuddered. Evelyn described the poverty of her childhood after her father's death; her life as a model in Philadelphia and New York and the publicity that led to her getting selected as a chorine, giving all the money she earned to "momma." She had turned down the first invitation to a party at White's apartment as not proper, but was reassured by another chorus girl that the architect came from one of New York's best families.

The incredulous prosecutor periodically interrupted Evelyn's answers to defense counsel Delphin Delmas: "You told all this to Harry K. Thaw that night in Paris?" Evelyn affirmed she had. White and another man took her and a girl friend to see his three-story apartment on West Twenty-Fourth Street. The two girls took turns being pushed on a red velvet swing. A Japanese paper parasol hung from the ceiling that the two girls each punctured with their feet when they swung forward. White let her sip champagne. He offered to have a dentist fix her teeth. Finally, Evelyn reached the crux of the story – the night in November of 1901 when White invited her to a party at his apartment on West Twenty-Fourth Street. She said that she almost left when she saw no one else present, but White convinced her to stay for dinner, telling her perhaps the others had forgotten. He gave Evelyn a glass of champagne and after dinner took her up a back staircase to a sitting room filled with fine art and a piano. She played the piano briefly, and then he suggested she join him in the next room, a small bedroom all decorated in chintz.

Another split of champagne sat on a bedside table from which White poured her a glass. Evelyn put it down after a sip, not liking the taste, but at White's urging she downed it all. Thaw hid his face behind his handkerchief. Evelyn said that her head began to buzz and she passed out. Thaw wept, his body heaving with emotion. The whole courtroom was otherwise still. Delmas paused for effect and then asked, "And, will you please, Madam, tell what happened when you regained consciousness?"

"I found myself in bed," Evelyn replied. White was naked beside her. The walls were covered with mirrors. Blood now stained her leg. She told the courtroom that she started screaming. White took her home and she cried through the night.

"And you told all of this to Harry Thaw that night in Paris after he had asked you to marry him?" Delmas finished with a flourish.

"Yes," Evelyn responded simply.[12]

Evelyn was forced to go through the whole story again under harsh cross-examination by Jerome. Jerome's strategy was to demolish both Evelyn Thaw's and Harry Thaw's character. His witness list included handsome young John Barrymore. But Barrymore had left the state after being interviewed and declined to return, claiming he was ill with pneumonia. Jerome made do with a prize-winning 1901 photo of Evelyn sleeping on a bearskin rug, provocatively dressed in White's borrowed kimono, as the "Little Butterfly." As a surprise blow against both

Evelyn and Harry, Jerome produced the affidavit Evelyn had signed and given White's attorney, accusing Thaw of attacking her in Europe and of being a drug addict. The newspapers found that evidence sensational. Yet Jerome took the risk that he painted Harry Thaw as even crazier than the defense did.

In his argument to the jury after three months of trial, Jerome characterized Thaw as paranoid and dangerous, but technically sane. He knew right from wrong when he killed Stanford White. Delmas closed with his plea of insanity based on Dementia Americana:

> The species of insanity which makes every American man believe his home to be sacred; that is the species of insanity which makes him believe the honor of his daughter is sacred; that is the species of insanity which makes him believe the honor of his wife is sacred; that is the species of insanity which makes him believe that whosoever invades his home, that whosoever stains the virtue of this threshold, has violated the highest of human laws and must appeal to the mercy of God, if mercy there be for him anywhere in the universe.[13]

The jury took two full days before they returned deadlocked, with seven jurors convinced of Thaw's guilt and five convinced he was not guilty by reason of insanity. The standing-room-only courtroom erupted in a roar. Reporters rushed for the exits to write the result up for their papers. Thaw was deeply disappointed. He was headed back to jail pending a retrial when he had hoped to go free as the acclaimed defender of innocent girlhood.

The following January, in a less sensational retrial Thaw had a new chief defense counsel, Martin Littleton. Mrs. Thaw had finally realized that she could best save her son from conviction by giving far more ammunition to the temporary insanity defense. She offered up details of trauma experienced by Thaw in utero, serious illnesses he suffered as a child, and many instances of weird behavior. The tales his mother had done her best to keep private over the years included Thaw's history of writhing uncontrollably with a movement disorder (either from rheumatic fever or epilepsy), wild temper tantrums in which he threw china and heavy objects at servants, an attention-grabbing suicide attempt as a teenager, and his propensity for babbling like a baby even as a young man.

During the first trial, the names of White's friends and associates as well as chorus girls other than Evelyn were deliberately kept from public airing to protect their reputations. By the time of the second trial in 1908 no one involved came out unscathed. The public did not feel sorry for the victim, nor did they empathize much with his crazed, self-indulgent attacker. Evelyn Nesbit also was impugned as a gold digger with the spread of false rumors that she was paid a million dollars for her teary-eyed testimony. No faith remained in innocence as the 20th century emerged with a full-blown exposé of the immoral excesses of New York's moneyed class.

Thaw's tendency to lash out violently when angry and Evelyn's new testimony about his suicide attempt with laudanum made it far easier for the second jury to decide that Thaw was not guilty of murdering White by reason of insanity. The judge announced that Thaw was a danger to public safety and would be committed to an asylum. Thaw flew into a rage. He had expected to be set free. Seven years later, in 1915, Thaw was declared sane and released. He and Evelyn divorced soon afterward. By 1917, Thaw was rearrested for whipping a teenage boy and was sent back to an asylum for another seven years. Even after his final release, Thaw faced periodic civil claims from showgirls he dated, who claimed he whipped them. None of these claims ever went to trial as his enormous inheritance came in handy yet again.

Evelyn Nesbit later penned two memoirs, one in 1934, *Prodigal Days: The Untold Story of Evelyn Nesbit*, and one twenty years earlier that would not be edited and published for ninety years – *Tragic Beauty: The Lost 1914 Memoirs of Evelyn Nesbit*. Harry Thaw wrote his own memoir, *The Traitor*. Stanford White's murder inspired several other books and movies. Among them, E. L. Doctorow's 1975 fictionalized *Ragtime* became the best known and was later adapted as a musical. In 2008, historian Paula Uruburu entranced audiences with her dramatic retelling of the tale in her book *American Eve: Evelyn Nesbit, Stanford White, The Birth of the "It" Girl and the Crime of the Century*.

* * * * *

The first "trial of the century" was practically a scripted melodrama. Audiences found compelling the rags-to-riches story that Evelyn Nesbit Thaw told, raged against the power imbalance that led to her deflowering, and applauded Thaw's revenge against the man who had "ruined" his wife. It gave new fodder to those who still viewed females as protected possessions of fathers and husbands. They condemned the decadence of big city life and agreed the lecherous victim had it coming to him. Yet what gave ubiquitous coverage of Stanford White's murder its special oomph was how Thaw triggered new insights into the Gilded Age and permanently tarnished its most vaunted members.

As riveting as Thaw's first trial had been, it was eclipsed within a month by a political murder trial that had labor directly pitted against capital. The charges that radical labor leader Big Bill Haywood ordered the assassination of Idaho's ex-governor had obvious national implications. Though far to the left of most Americans, Haywood had developed a large following in the previous decade as an outspoken champion of the eight-hour day. In June of 1905 he helped convene representatives of militant unions, Socialists and anarchists at a "Continental Congress of the working class." At that meeting, the revolutionaries co-founded the Industrial Workers of the World (IWW), also known as the "Wobblies."

The IWW was dedicated, like anarchist Emma Goldman and her followers, to the overthrow of the capitalist structure. The potential for the IWW's radical message to rally millions of underpaid recent immigrants unnerved industrialists and Progressive reformers alike. President Roosevelt made it his personal mission to see Haywood executed and thereby decapitate his radical union. Socialist Party leader Eugene Debs called the upcoming confrontation the "greatest legal battle in American history."[14]

3. UNDESIRABLE CITIZENS

Two Lethal Bombings Focus Americans on Labor Wars

The solid column swept past – painters, carpenters, hod-carriers, masons, iron workers – every sort of trade-union, each with its own banners – and an extraordinary number of bands all playing the Marseillaise . . . an indescribable color of martial zest . . . Here were 40,000 men marching in New York City . . . because three labor leaders are on trial for murder in a state two thousand miles away. [E]ven a conservative like myself could see . . . how effective it was . . . a sort of contagious fervor.

– NORMAN HAPGOOD, EDITOR OF COLLIER'S WEEKLY, DESCRIBING THE MAY 4, 1907, SOCIALIST PARADE DOWN FIFTH AVENUE[1]

Big Bill Haywood had the intimidating look of a real-life Cyclops. He was built like an ox and had lost an eye in a childhood whittling accident. Haywood never bothered to obtain a glass eye. He wore a tall cowboy hat to tower over companions. On the rare occasions he took off his Stetson, the two-hundred-pound spokesman for the Western Federation of Miners stood just under six feet tall. He was clean-shaven with neatly parted short brown hair, oversized features and prominent jowls. When photographed, he presented a half-profile with only his good left eye facing the camera.

The "Lincoln of Labor" was born in 1869 in the Utah territory where his father was a Pony Express rider. He was three when his father died and nine when he lost his right eye, the same year he first started working in the mines. Violent confrontations over union demands for

51

worker safety, a $3 minimum daily wage and an eight-hour day were
then common throughout the nation. Federal or state troops had to be
called in to restore peace some five hundred times, almost always at the
instigation of politically powerful industrialists.

Haywood was an impressionable seventeen when Chicago's infamous Haymarket Square riot broke out in May of 1886. He devoured
newspaper accounts of how the mayhem started. First, police and private detectives killed six strikers. The following day an unknown pro-
testor threw a bomb at the police, who responded by shooting into the
crowd, some of whom returned gunfire. After the dust settled, seven
policemen and three protesters were dead. About a hundred others
were injured, most of them police officers. Eight leading anarchists and
militant socialists who had addressed the May Day rally were tried for
murder. All were convicted based solely on charges that the deaths were
"the bloody fruit" of their "villainous teachings."[2] Four were hanged
in 1887. The hysteria-driven executions turned the four Haymarket
Square rally organizers into instant martyrs for their cause.

Local unions in frontier states were mired in similar bloody confrontations with owners of gold, silver, copper, lead and coal mines.
The horrendous working conditions of rough-hewn, poorly educated
men, who drank too hard and seldom enjoyed civilizing female com-
panionship, created an extremely volatile situation. Miners typically
worked ten hours a day, six days a week down dangerous shafts. One
third of all men who worked a decade in gold and silver mines wound
up seriously injured from falling rocks or from inhaling clouds of silica
dust sent up by new "widow-maker" compressed air drills; one out of
eight died in the mines.[3]

It was easy to hate the big businessmen back East who exploited the
mine workers. Only able-bodied men were paid. There was no workers'
compensation, no health benefits. Disabled workers simply lost their
jobs and were replaced with others equally desperate for employment.
The mining industry in the late 19th century made extensive use of
dynamite as a new commercial blasting technique. By the mid-1880s,
American anarchists and militant labor leaders had found other uses
for Alfred Nobel's invention.

Banding together in unions that could cripple the mines with strikes was the mineworkers' only hope to improve their lot. But management of the mines infiltrated unions with spies and resorted to private armies. The hired guns used brute force to break strikes and policed the mining facilities with rifles, killing strikers with impunity. Union members fought back with sabotage and violence against scabs. In 1892, alarmed by the increasing class violence in Idaho, President Benjamin Harrison sent out federal troops to conduct mass arrests of union members. Then came the devastating financial collapse of 1893. It caused a ripple effect of bankruptcies and a surplus of out-of-work laborers competing for jobs in the mines.

Facing wage cuts, strikebreakers, armed company guards, and mass arrests, union members in Colorado, Montana, Idaho, Utah and South Dakota merged to form the Western Federation of Miners (WFM). The WFM almost instantaneously developed a reputation as the most militant union in the country. By the turn of the century, pitched battles between the WFM and state-supported owners would become known as the Colorado Labor Wars. It was the closest the United States "has ever approached outright class warfare."[4]

Haywood was twenty-seven when he joined the WFM in 1896. An impassioned speaker, he rose quickly to national prominence as a champion of labor's goals, shouting to enthusiastic crowds, "Eight hours of work, eight hours of play, eight hours of sleep."[5] By May of 1907, the burly activist had served on the Executive Board of the WFM for seven years. President Theodore Roosevelt immediately took keen interest when Haywood was accused with two other WFM leaders of ordering the assassination of Idaho's former Governor Frank Steunenberg. The bombing death looked all too much like WFM payback for the governor having called in federal troops to impose martial law to end Idaho's labor wars. Executing the leadership of the WFM for that crime could throttle the revolutionary Industrial Workers of the World in its infancy.

In 1896, Steunenberg had been nominated as both the Democratic and Populist candidate for Idaho's governor. Both groups enthusiastically endorsed thirty-six-year-old Nebraskan firebrand William Jennings Bryan for President that year in hopes of revitalizing the nation's economy with

silver-backed currency. Though McKinley defeated Bryan, Steunenberg
had won the Idaho election, with labor union backers and the vote of
"Silver" Republicans, by a comfortable margin. Steunenberg became the
first non-Republican to hold that office since the rough and tumble rem-
nant of Eastern "Oregon country" was admitted to the union in 1890, a
year after its neighboring states of Montana and Washington.

Steunenberg was reelected in 1898 with a smaller majority, which
still included the support of union men. During his second term, antag-
onism reached the boiling point between the WFM and the owners of
the Bunker Hill concentrator. A $250,000 smelting plant in Wardner,
Idaho, the Bunker Hill concentrator had been recognized when built as
the largest such facility on the planet. (It would be a multi-million-dol-
lar investment in today's dollars.) Unlike most other mine owners, the
San Francisco owners of Bunker Hill still adamantly refused to recognize unions. The facility's president had recently gone a step further
and begun purging Irish miners from his work force as un-American
agitators. On April 29, 1899, local union members in Burke, Idaho,
retaliated with a breathtakingly bold act of sabotage.

Scores of armed union men kept the employees of the Bunker Hill
concentrator at bay while another couple of hundred masked associates – armed with rifles, bats and shotguns – commandeered a train.
They brought the train to Wardner and unloaded sixty dynamite car-
tons, which a few volunteers then placed at strategic points under the
concentrator. Then all of the men high-tailed it out of Wardner just
before the explosives blew the concentrator and nearby buildings to
smithereens. The union's extraordinary violence shocked Governor
Steunenberg. At the demands of the irate railroad and Coeur D'Alene
mine owners, the governor surprised the union by re-imposing martial law to restore order. With his own National Guard off serving in
the Spanish-American War, Steunenberg asked President McKinley to
deploy federal troops. Within days, the President purposely chose to
send veteran black soldiers in the 24th Infantry Regiment to quell the
uprising, knowing how insulted the miners would be.

The segregated soldiers of the 24th Infantry had been the
most heroic American combatants at San Juan Hill, in the recent

Spanish-American War, though Assistant Secretary of War Teddy Roosevelt's Rough Riders had received most of the credit. But the regiment of black soldiers was bitter at the prejudice the men suffered upon their return and increasingly fractious. Now they had an outlet for their frustration – strict orders from their white officers to indiscriminately round up union members and sympathizing townsmen in the Coeur d'Alene region and lock them up without mercy. As expected, the French-Canadian, Irish, Welsh and Cornish locals then arrested without charges especially resented being herded into filthy bullpens by "niggers" called in by the government at the behest of the hated mine owners. Meanwhile, Idaho's Attorney General Samuel Hays boasted to the press: "We have taken [the union] monster by the throat and we are going to choke the life out of it."[6]

Hays was obviously speaking not just for himself but for the Populist governor the Democratic union had helped elect. Republican governors had previously authorized mass arrests, but this time the illegal round-up was followed by federal troops enforcing a new county permit requiring all mine workers to deny or renounce membership in any militant union. The illegal ordinance was squarely directed at the local branch of the WFM – all done with the approval of Steunenberg. Union men turned on him, calling Steunenberg a "Benedict Arnold" to their cause.

Though the WFM had recently broken with Samuel Gompers' more collaborative American Federation of Labor in the East, the WFM and its supporters retained substantial national clout. Steunenberg was summoned to Washington to answer charges of misconduct. A specially convened congressional committee hearing addressed his wholesale suspension of the constitutional rights of so many Idaho citizens in the Coeur D'Alene region. Though Democrats were livid, the Republican majority stood firmly behind Steunenberg's imposition of martial law. To the WFM, this was the final indignity. Steunenberg was condemned by its leaders, including Haywood, as an enemy of the working class. Death threats against Steunenberg followed.

As the labor strife escalated, opposition to Steunenberg prevented his renomination. He retreated to private life as a farmer, banker and real estate developer. Steunenberg may have thought he was safe on the sidelines, but in the escalating labor wars, it was getting harder to find any haven. In 1904, in just one incident, thirteen strikebreakers died in a bombing at a Colorado train station. Rumor had it that WFM's Big Bill Haywood ordered that hit, though the union claimed the bomb had actually been set off at the behest of local mine owners. By then, use of agents provocateurs was well-documented, but so was murder and mayhem by mine workers, who again faced brutal retaliation.

Reformers in several states had succeeded in getting some protective laws passed, only to see victory snatched away by the United States Supreme Court in April of 1905. In a hotly contested case with national repercussions, a bare majority of justices in *Lochner v. New York* threw out protective legislation limiting bakers to sixty-hour weeks as an interference with freedom of contract. Over a vigorous dissent, the court interpreted the Fourteenth Amendment to protect the right of business owners and workers to negotiate *any* hours of employment they agreed upon, explaining that the employee might want the extra money from longer hours. State laws to protect workers from exploitation violated both the purchaser's and seller's "liberty of contract."[7] In reality, there were always workers desperate enough to take practically any job offered. The landmark ruling protected owners' property interests in imposing working conditions that Progressive legislatures deemed inhumane.

The *Lochner* case foreshadowed the invalidation of a host of other new laws for worker protection, but its most immediate impact was to galvanize the founding of the revolutionary IWW in June 1905. Just six months later, former Governor Steunenberg lost his life when he opened the booby-trapped side gate to his Caldwell, Idaho, farmhouse. The mine owners then secretly gave Idaho's current governor the funds to hire Pinkerton's chief of its Denver office, James McParland, to investigate the explosion. The assassination had all the earmarks of yet another violent episode in the ongoing class strife.

McParland was the most famous private eye in America. He already had substantial experience with the Colorado Labor Wars, where mine owners kept him on retainer. The ace detective, now in his sixties, had catapulted to national fame almost thirty years before for his role in destroying another militant mineworkers' organization in Pennsylvania. The Molly Maguires had originated as a secret society in Ireland that retaliated against oppressive British landlords. In the 1870s they were rumored to have reemerged in the Scranton anthracite minefields, where some Irish emigrants had settled following the devastating mid-century potato famine in their homeland. Yet it was never clear how active the Molly Maguires were in the deadly guerrilla warfare between union organizers on one side and, on the other, a coalition of mine owners, local police, and judiciary whom the mine owners controlled. It benefited management to tag any ardent union man with that label, realizing that "The name of Molly Maguire being attached to a man's name is sufficient to hang him."[8]

The situation in Pennsylvania back in the 1870s differed little from that in the West at the turn of the century: "labor was at war with capital, Democrat with Republican, Protestant with Catholic, and immigrant with native."[9] By early 1875, a newly formed Irish union called a strike to challenge grueling working conditions. The strike ended when starving workers capitulated in June. Later that summer, the Molly Maguires reportedly started regaining strength. The Pinkerton Agency had already sent James McParland to Pennsylvania as an undercover agent using the pseudonym Jamie McKenna. He started out as a drinking buddy of Irish unionizers and eventually became secretary of the Molly Maguires.

McParland succeeded in his charade for more than two years, all the while passing on information to Pinkerton. The Maguires suspected a spy in their midst when vigilantes organized by a mine owner raided a duplex where three members of the secret society resided, killing one of them and his pregnant sister. It did not take long for them to accuse the man they knew as McKenna, who, fleeing from a lynch mob, barely escaped with his life.

McKenna later emerged as Pinkerton Agent James McParland, the state's star witness against the gang. McParland's testimony helped clinch twenty hangings on "Black Thursday" – June 21, 1877 – for the commission of revenge killings, many of which McParland likely knew

about in advance and did nothing to prevent. Some of those who were
hanged may have only been found guilty by association. Labor historian Joseph G. Rayback credits that trial with "temporarily destroy[ing]
the last vestiges of labor unionism in the anthracite area. More important, it gave the public the impression . . . that miners were by nature
criminal in character."[10] McParland's nickname in the agency became
"Pontius Pilate." Three decades later, Irish Catholics in his own community still scorned McParland as a traitor to his people.

By the time McParland arrived in Caldwell, Idaho, in January of
1906 an itinerant sheep dealer going by the name of Thomas Hogan
had already been arrested for Steunenberg's murder. Hogan was found
with incriminating evidence in his hotel room. When questioned by the
sheriff, Hogan admitted his name was Harry Orchard, that he had once
lived in the Coeur D'Alene mining region and knew the WFM leadership. McParland befriended the prisoner and obtained a confession
by assuring Orchard the state was really after the WFM inner circle.
Orchard then implicated WFM Secretary-Treasurer Big Bill Haywood;
its president Charles Moyer; and former WFM executive board member
George Pettibone. Orchard claimed the three men gave him instructions
in Denver to go to Idaho to kill Steunenberg as an example to other
political enemies that they could never escape revenge. Orchard said it
was only the latest of many terrorist acts he performed for the WFM.

The Constitution did not permit extradition of the WFM leaders
in Denver for ordering a murder in Idaho. Undaunted, McParland
colluded with the governors of Idaho and Colorado, other state officials and the Union Pacific Railroad to kidnap the three WFM leaders.
To make the kidnapping look legal, they prepared traditional extradition warrants falsely claiming the three WFM leaders were in Idaho
on the night of the murder and were fugitives from justice. On a cue
from McParland, the three suspects – who were already under surveillance – were then arrested on unspecified charges without being
given an opportunity to alert family or their lawyers. The trio were then
handcuffed and placed in leg irons and spirited across state lines on
a train later dubbed "the Pirate Special." The train arrived in Boise in
record time and the three men were placed in cells on death row while

Source: http://idahoptv.org/productions/specials/capitoloflight/tour grounds.cfm.

Idaho Gov. Frank Steunenberg

After union men blew up a huge, non-union smelting plant in Wardner, Idaho, in April 1899, Steunenberg called in federal troops to enforce a new (unconstitutional) county ordinance requiring all mine workers to renounce membership in any militant union – squarely targeting the Western Federation of Miners that had supported his election. Union men denounced Steunenberg as a Benedict Arnold and forced his retirement from public life after one term.

Source: "Idaho Meanderings" by Gov Steunenberg's great grandson, http://steunenberg.blogspot.com/2011/12/12301905-today-in-history.html

The newspaper caption reads: "Former Governor Frank Steunenberg killed by an explosion at his home in Coldwell, Idaho."

Source: http://idahoptv.org/trial/images/steunenberghouse.jpg.

Retired Gov. Frank Steunenberg was killed by a bomb as he entered the gate at his Idaho home in December of 1905. Photo from "A Good Hanging Spoiled – The Verdict, July 28th, 1907" by John T. Richards, Jr.

Source: http://pynchonclass.blogspot.com /2012/09/western
-federation-of-miners.html

Defendants: three leaders of Western Federation of Miners. Big Bill Haywood (center) goes to trial first. 1907 photo. (WFM button reproduced above.)

Left: *Labor activist Mary Harris Jones (Mother Jones) campaigned for funds to support the WFM leaders' defense.* **Right:** *Socialist Party presidential candidate Eugene Debs sent his attorney Clarence Darrow to represent Haywood.*

awaiting trial for Steunenberg's murder. Meanwhile, the Governor of Idaho publicly asserted his belief in their guilt, and McParland boasted in a press release, "They will never leave Idaho alive."[11]

Socialist Party of America leader Eugene Debs shot back, "If they don't, the governors of Idaho and Colorado and their masters from Wall Street, New York, to the Rocky Mountains had better prepare to follow them."[12]

Irate WFM lawyers challenged the unorthodox arrests and extradition all the way to the United States Supreme Court. But the political pressure was so intense, they stood no chance. At the justices' annual White House visit on the Monday when the high court began its 1906 fall term, Roosevelt weighed in by asserting his opinion that Moyer and Haywood were undesirable citizens – just three days before oral argument on the propriety of the labor leaders' forcible abduction from Colorado. Roosevelt most likely assumed that the justices were already prepared to give short shrift to the radicals' appeal, but could not resist a heavy-handed hint as to how he hoped they would rule. Two months later, the high court issued its opinion. With only one dissenter, the Supreme Court ruled that any challenge to the illegality of the kidnapping had to be lodged in Colorado. Once the men were transported to Idaho, Idaho had authority to try them for conspiracy to assassinate its ex-governor. It is often said that possession is nine-tenths of the law. In this case, possession was ten-tenths of the law. The men had been spirited out of state without having an opportunity to challenge their kidnapping in Colorado. WFM supporters considered the bootstrap Supreme Court ruling to be as odious and unsupportable as the infamous 1857 *Dred Scott* decision that helped precipitate the Civil War.

Eugene Debs wasted no time excoriating McParland and the two governors, linking them with "the capitalist tyrants" who martyred the Haymarket speakers two decades before. Debs threatened all-out war by Socialists: "If they attempt to murder Moyer, Haywood and Pettibone and their brothers, a million revolutionists will meet them with guns."[13] At the same time, Debs called for a broader national labor strike than the crippling railroad strike he had orchestrated in 1894. Colorado's Socialist Party named Haywood its candidate for governor while he sat in his Idaho jail cell facing murder charges. Though he was not expected to win, Haywood amazed observers by quadrupling the party's last gubernatorial vote count.[11] In the meantime, radical union members and Socialists across the country angrily took to the streets with banners, torches and flags, proclaiming Haywood's innocence. They were particularly incensed about the Pinkerton agency's underhanded role in the matter.

Labor had long considered Pinkerton men lowly spies for management and blamed the infamous May 4, 1886, Haymarket Square riots partly on the agency. The bloody riots had caused a severe setback to the growing eight-hour-day movement. The day before the bloodshed in Haymarket Square, Pinkerton detectives helped Chicago police end a violent confrontation between scabs and strikers locked out of the Cyrus McCormick Harvester Works by killing six strikers and wounding many more. The bombing of the local police that started the Haymarket riot appeared to be in retaliation.

Though four of the speakers at the Haymarket rally had been hanged shortly afterward, three of the eight were still languishing in prison in 1898 when a new Democratic governor of Illinois pardoned them for lack of proof of their involvement in the bombing. The chief advocate of that pardon was Chicago labor lawyer Clarence Darrow, who had become Eugene Debs' lawyer four years before when Debs faced criminal conspiracy charges for leading the 1894 railroad strike. Darrow had first made his mark as a corporate attorney for the city of Chicago and then as a railroad lawyer before he defected to the other side to defend Debs.

By 1907, when Debs asked Darrow to join the team representing the three accused WFM leaders, the accomplished fifty-year-old defense lawyer was not yet a household name. He had, however, already earned a formidable reputation as a passionate opponent of the death penalty and champion of labor and underdog causes. Darrow liked to claim that he never lost a client to the death penalty, but that was only true if one didn't count the time he argued a post-trial sanity motion in 1893 for the convicted assassin of Chicago's mayor. It was impressive enough that Darrow could boast that he had never lost a capital case to a jury.

Born in 1857 in rural northeastern Ohio, Clarence Seward Darrow was destined from the cradle for a life of passionate advocacy. The fifth of eight children of Amirus and Emily Eddy Darrow, Clarence inherited an insatiable appetite for knowledge from both parents. Their families had each migrated to Ohio from New England, where their ancestors had fought in the Revolution. Amirus Darrow first trained for the Unitarian ministry, then quit because he questioned his faith in God. Despite becoming an agnostic, Amirus retained firm convictions about right and wrong and a hide impervious to ridicule – traits he also passed on to his famous son. Clarence recalled his father fondly as the "village infidel."[15]

Amirus barely eked out a living as the town undertaker for the hamlet of Kinsman, Ohio, near the western border of Pennsylvania, just south of Lake Erie. He likely played a key role when Kinsman became a stop on the Underground Railroad. His wife Emily was more practical than Amirus, but shared her husband's idealism and fondness for books. She was a passionate suffragette and advocate of other liberal causes, which her son Clarence would likewise embrace with fervor.

Clarence grew up internalizing his parents' abhorrence of slavery and admiration for the fiery John Brown. Brown had been hanged when Darrow was two for a failed raid on a federal arsenal at Harper's Ferry, Maryland, to arm slaves so they could rebel against their Southern owners. Clarence was not quite four when the Civil War began, but old enough to have indelible memories of that war, the abolition of slavery and the assassination of President Lincoln.

Growing up, Darrow remained close to his mother Emily, who died when he was just fifteen. When he reached manhood, he was taller than average and heavy set. He looked like someone used to manual labor. Actually, Clarence loved to dance, but like his father, he was happiest with his nose in a challenging book. It took a number of tries before Darrow was admitted to the Ohio bar in 1878. Two years later, he married the daughter of a local mill owner and settled down to law practice not far from his home town. By age thirty, he had found that life in Ohio lacked worldly stimulation and moved with his wife Jessie and young son Paul to the vibrant, sinful city of Chicago.

Darrow found the company of avant-garde writers and painters irresistible. He admired free thinkers who disdained bourgeois relationships. By 1897, his magnetic personality had attracted a serious new lover. He divorced his wife and spent much of his spare time entertaining his new bohemian friends, reading, writing, and arguing philosophy. Darrow had a handsome, rectangular face with straight brown hair that flopped to one side of his high forehead. Despite his affinity for the cosmopolitan life of Chicago, he never shed the down-home mannerisms of the small town where he was raised. He mesmerized women with his piercing gray-green eyes, soft voice and animated style. Over time, in court, he grew more careless of his appearance, wearing wrinkled, outdated suits and not bothering to keep his hair combed. By 1903, his dissolute life had sapped much of his vigor. Thankful for someone to look after his daily needs, he married Ruby Hamerstrom, a journalist a dozen years younger than himself.

When Darrow accepted his friend Eugene Debs' invitation to help defend the three most militant union leaders in the country, he counted on Ruby to accompany him to Idaho's capital, where he had never been. Darrow expected to face open hostility from Boise's citizens still grieving for their assassinated governor and outraged at the radical WFM, which they blamed for Steunenberg's death. Ironically, Darrow had just published a booklet on the virtues of turning the other cheek. Biographer Irving Stone notes that when Darrow agreed to join the defense team for this sensationalized murder, the veteran Chicago lawyer "knew that it would be the toughest case of his career, a knock-'em-down, and drag-'em-out brawl with no holds barred."[16]

In the spring of 1907, memory of the despised Pinkerton agency's role in precipitating the Haymarket Square massacre still loomed large. The widow of one of the martyrs was featured in a Chicago parade on behalf of the three WFM leaders. Some more conservative labor unions distanced themselves from the WFM for fear that its militant leaders were guilty as charged. But the issues championed by the WFM – grueling work shifts, safety, and living wages – remained top national concerns of conservative and radical unions alike. Close to a hundred thousand men and women gathered on Boston Common to protest the railroading of the champion of the eight-hour day. One reporter called it "the greatest demonstration the Hub has ever witnessed."[17] In Manhattan, an estimated forty thousand polyglot immigrant workers paraded down Fifth Avenue singing "The Marseillaise" and wore red arm bands or kerchiefs in support of the arrested WFM leaders.

Marchers nationwide were particularly angry at President Roosevelt's prejudicial use of his own bully pulpit to condemn the three arrested union officials as "undesirable citizens."[18] Tens of thousands of workers bought buttons proudly identifying themselves as "undesirable citizens," too, with the nickel cost of each button going to the defense fund. Other sympathizers hid their support for fear of being fired. Roosevelt ignored criticism from the press. The feisty president repeatedly characterized the WFM leaders as "thugs and murderers" whom he equated with the notorious Molly Maguires of Pennsylvania.[19]

The upcoming Idaho trial became the focal point of potential class warfare. One of the most prominent champions of the defendants was another co-founder of the IWW, labor organizer Mary Harris "Mother" Jones (*Mother Jones* magazine is named for her). By her late sixties, the Irish widow had already been branded "the most dangerous woman in America" – a proud Socialist most famous for leading a Children's Crusade in 1903 from Philadelphia, Pennsylvania, to President Roosevelt's estate in Long Island to protest the exploitation of child labor.[20] Mother Jones had campaigned hard since the 1870s for the rights of mineworkers from Pennsylvania to Colorado. In 1906, she traveled across the country fund-raising for her colleagues Haywood, Pettibone and Moyer, spreading word of their kidnapping by government agents hell-bent on destroying the Western Federation of Miners.[21]

In May of 1907, mainstream and Leftist media swarmed to cover what the *Boston Globe* called a "determined struggle between labor unions and capital" and Socialists deemed "the greatest trial of modern times."[22] Debs was eager to cover the trial himself for the *Appeal to Reason*. Darrow emphatically told Debs to stay away – it would be hard enough to defend the three WFM leaders without turning the trial into a referendum on Socialism. As the trial began, a reporter for the Boise *Statesman* claimed that "the eyes of the civilized world are on these great proceedings."[23]

Two of Idaho's ablest lawyers headed a team of four prosecutors: six-foot-four unsophisticated "I-dy-ho" bar leader James Hawley, and "Silver" Republican and newly-elected Senator William Borah. Borah was a renowned ladies' man a generation younger than his rough-hewn colleague and had been a close friend of Steunenberg. Borah and Hawley had teamed up successfully before in prosecuting leaders of the mineworkers for the 1899 bombing in Coeur D'Alene. Both felt they now had an iron-clad case for hanging the WFM's national leaders, aided by McParland's detective work.

Neither side had any objections to the appointment of former U.S. Attorney Fremont Wood as the trial judge. The Republican jurist was an imposing Yankee from Maine, known for his even-handed rulings. Judge Wood first pleased the defense by granting their motion for change of venue to Boise from Steunenberg's inflamed hometown of Caldwell. The defense team then added to their table a prominent member of the Boise Bar who had once been Judge Wood's partner. Trying not to miss a trick, they also seated Haywood's crippled wife and freckle-faced nine-year-old daughter in the front row of spectators, along with his mother and older daughter. To the disappointment of the prosecution team, also looking for sympathy from the jury, Steunenberg's widow refused to attend the trial. McParland fumed at how Haywood was being portrayed as such a model husband and father: when arrested in Denver, Haywood had been found "stripped naked in a room in an assignation house" with his young sister-in-law.[24]

For protection against assassination, Idaho's Governor Gooding had law enforcement question all suspicious strangers and usher them out of town. He moved his own family to the same hotel as Pinkerton's McParland, both under armed guard. Gooding also succeeded in getting federal reinforcements stationed at Boise's edge and secretly encouraged armed vigilantes among local businessmen. For extra insurance, the prosecutor placed a sniper in the attic of a grocery store where he had a clear view of the courthouse. President Roosevelt was kept apprised of the situation, but the Secret Service doubted the WFM would be foolish enough to pull anything.

It took a month and a half just to select the twelve jurors – all white males, of course. Under British common law, women had been categorically excluded from jury service in all but a few specialized types of cases due to a "defect of their sex." This practice continued in the colonies and the United States, with each state mostly free to decide for itself what restrictions it imposed on jury qualifications. The high court also gave its approval to keeping women off juries altogether – which almost all states still did at the time of the Haywood trial, with varying justifications.

Darrow had limited choices in the relatively homogenous community that prohibited him from following his usual formula for success in Chicago trials: "Never take a German; they are bullheaded. Rarely take a Swede; they are stubborn. Always take an Irishman or a Jew; they are the easiest to move to emotional sympathy."[25] Among other subjects, Darrow inquired if they would vote to hang an anarchist. One candidate responded, "Yes, if I understand what an anarchist is, I would hang him on sight."[26]

The sheriff's handpicked jury pool was heavily skewed against wage earners, but the two sides ultimately agreed on twelve men. All of the jurors had started out as farmers or ranchers. One had since become a real estate agent, another a construction foreman and one a building contractor. Eleven of the bewhiskered men were over fifty. (Darrow's other rule of thumb was: "Old men are generally more charitable and kindly disposed than young men; they have seen more of the world and understand it.")[27] Eight were Republicans, three Democrats and one a Prohibitionist. Like the Thaw jury in New York earlier that year, the men were sequestered for the duration of the trial. They were permitted to read newspapers only after deputies cut out any coverage of the case. Of course, some of them had read slanted local articles against the WFM leadership before they were picked for the jury panel.

Both teams had secretly conducted extensive investigation of eligible jurors in advance. The defense team eventually discovered that their chief intelligence gatherer was a Pinkerton spy, who skewed his reports and copied them to the other side. The defense may have planted its own mole on the prosecution side. It was an era known for corrupt tactics, and this was an extraordinarily high stakes case. By the time the ten peremptory challenges for each side were used up, the prosecution was satisfied, but the defense hoped only for a hung jury. Darrow and his co-counsel were painfully aware that most of the men had voted for, done business with or otherwise had been familiar with Governor Steunenberg, including one juror who boarded the governor in his Boise home for two years. Only one juror had ever been a member of a trade union. Socialist papers were even more pessimistic. They assumed the panel had already made up their minds to do the prosecution's bidding.

Prosecutor William Borah deliberately sought to inflame the jury with his claim that the trial was for a crime "a thousand times worse than murder." It was "anarchy displaying its first bloody triumph in Idaho."[28] A parade of prosecution witnesses took the stand to describe Steunenberg's violent, agonizing death and the poorly groomed stranger spotted casing the farmhouse beforehand. The spectators in the packed courtroom were mesmerized when the confessed bomber finally took the stand. McParland had worked hard maintaining the good will of the assassin now known as Harry Orchard and in keeping him well-guarded from retaliation. Over the sixteen months since Orchard's arrest, McParland had also "transformed [him] from [an] unshaven, ill-kempt, shifty-eyed felon" to a "carefully attired" and "manicured" man who "might be a Sunday School superintendent."[29]

Orchard, a forty-year-old Canadian whose real name was Albert Horsley, had been accompanied into the courtroom by armed guards. The doors were then locked to keep out the overflow crowd of hundreds of men and women anxious to get a glimpse of the governor's assassin. Inside the courtroom, deputies and plainclothes detectives provided additional security. The remarkably composed star witness then testified in a low, credible monotone for several days, detailing his career as a union terrorist. He claimed that he had participated in the 1899 bombing of the compression mill in Wardner and that he set the bomb in 1904 at a Colorado train depot, killing thirteen scabs. He claimed to have targeted several other political enemies of the WFM, detailing an aborted attempt on the life of Colorado's ex-governor and two members of its Supreme Court. Then came the damning testimony that was intended to seal the prosecutors' case: that Haywood, Moyer and Pettibone promised Orchard several hundred dollars and a ranch if he assassinated Steunenberg to intimidate other WFM adversaries.

The newly beefed up Western Union office worked at a record pace to transmit the news to the nation from the hordes of mainstream and Socialist reporters who had descended on Boise to cover the story first-hand. *Collier's Weekly* magazine described Orchard as "the most remarkable witness that ever appeared in an American court of justice."[30] *New York Times* correspondent O. K. Davis proclaimed that the witness "upon whose testimony the whole case against Haywood, Moyer, and the other leaders of the Western Federation of Miners is based" told "a horrible, revolting, sickening story . . . as simply as the plainest . . . most ordinary incident . . . and as it went on, hour after hour, with multitudinous detail, clear and vivid here, half-forgotten and obscure there, gradually it forced home to the listener the conviction that it was the unmixed truth."[31]

Though Judge Wood was incensed at the prosecution for permitting jailhouse interviews of Orchard to influence public opinion during the trial, Wood privately agreed with Davis's assessment of Orchard's credibility. Unbeknownst to the parties, the judge and the *New York Times* correspondent took several weekend fly fishing trips together during the pendency of the trial.

Meanwhile, observers could not help but notice that WFM's pompous Colorado counsel, Edmund Richardson, had difficulty sharing the leadership of the defense team with the equally egotistical Darrow. The two often disagreed vociferously on strategy, but Darrow reluctantly deferred to Richardson when he insisted on cross-examining Orchard. Though the veteran WFM lawyer brought considerable skills to his grilling of the state's star witness, most observers believed Orchard easily won that courtroom match-up. (In the next trial of WFM's George Pettibone, when Orchard was again the chief witness, Darrow conducted the cross-examination himself. He was credited with doing a masterful job of discrediting Orchard as a convicted felon, bigamist, company spy and tool of Pinkerton's agency. The jury reportedly responded by recoiling from Orchard as if he were "the carcass of a dead animal.")[32]

Yet, in Haywood's trial, Richardson scored some points. Even after

Source: https://en.wikipedia.org/wiki/File:James_mcparland_pinkerton_agency.jpg

*Pinkerton agent James McParland (**left**), then the most famous detective in America, arrested Albert Horsley (a.k.a. Harry Orchard) (**pictured below**) for Steunenberg's assassination. McParland then groomed Horsley as the star witness for the prosecution against the leaders of the Western Federation of Miners, whom McParland kidnapped from Colorado to face the death penalty for allegedly conspiring to hire Horsley to kill Steunenberg. McParland cleaned Horsley up to look far more presentable at trial. One reporter described the transformation as turning an "unshaven, ill-kempt, shifty-eyed felon" into a "carefully attired" and "manicured" man who "might be a Sunday School superintendent"* (John E. Nevins, Milwaukee Journal, *June 6, 1907, 1*)

Source: http://www.3rd1000.com/history3/events/cdamines/1892-1899.htmp

Source: https://en.wikipedia.org/w/index.php?curid=27122232

Harry Orchard (left) when arrested in 1906 and (right) in 1907 as star witness for the prosecution of Big Bill Haywood

In the follow-up trial of WFM leader George Pettibone, Darrow destroyed Orchard's credibility – revealing him as a convicted felon, bigamist, company spy and tool of Pinkerton's agency. The jury recoiled from Orchard as if he were "the carcass of a dead animal" (Irving Stone, Clarence Darrow for the Defense, *New York: Signet Books, 1941, 1969), 280.

months of preparation, Orchard's story was confusing. He claimed to be a paid assassin of the union, but acknowledged that some of the misdeeds he committed were on his own initiative or that of the mine owners. None of the state's witnesses was able to corroborate the complicity of the WFM leader in Orchard's dastardly act in Caldwell. Before trial, one of Orchard's alleged collaborators had disappeared without a trace, and another, Steve Adams, retracted his own confession at the urging of Clarence Darrow. Detective McParland suspected that Darrow bribed Adams, but had no proof. The prosecution was forced to rely only on circumstantial evidence to support Orchard's conspiracy claim. The defense in the Haywood trial put on a hundred of its own witnesses, including Haywood, who denied all of Orchard's charges.

It was customary at the time for closing arguments to last up to a day and a half apiece. Judge Wood allowed all four veteran attorneys that privilege. The courtroom was filled to capacity with Governor Gooding and James McParland showing up for the first time to lend their weight to the proceedings. Hawley went first, attributing Orchard's confession to "the saving power of divine grace."[33] He disavowed any effort by the state to make war on the WFM or that the mine owners had a role in financing the prosecution – statements that Hawley knew to be false, having taken a very active role himself in fund-raising to "rid the West entirely" of the WFM.[34]

Edmund Richardson went first for the defense. The meticulous, balding Denver lawyer in his three-piece suit stood and lectured the jury from a distance. Richardson suggested that Orchard might have acted out a personal grudge against the governor who had authorized the outrages committed by the "colored troops" against Orchard's fellow miners in Coeur D'Alene. "If you had been there, covered with vermin, . . . gentlemen of the jury, . . . you would have attained in your breast a righteous hatred for every person who had anything to do with causing your humiliation and suffering."[35] Alternatively, Richardson suggested that Pinkerton's agency used that lingering wrath as a cover for hiring Orchard to kill Steunenberg and for misdirecting blame on the WFM leadership.

Darrow sensed the jury had already made up its mind to convict

Haywood and invested himself in an extraordinarily moving, closing argument attacking the prosecution as a conspiracy to behead
the WFM. In stark contrast to Richardson, the unconventional, shaggy-haired Chicagoan doffed his jacket and thumbed his suspenders
in animated conversational style within arm's length of the jury. For
eleven hours, Darrow alternately dared them to hang his client if he
was guilty of such a heinous crime and pleaded with them to believe in
Haywood's innocence as he did. He ended with a sterling defense of
self-sacrifice in class struggle:

> [O]ther men have died in the same cause in which Bill Haywood
> has risked his life, men strong with devotion, men who love liberty,
> men who love their fellow men have raised their voices in defense
> of the poor, in defense of justice, have made their good fight and
> have met death on the scaffold, on the rack, in the flame and they
> will meet it again until the world grows old and gray. Bill Haywood
> is no better than the rest. He can die if die he needs, he can die if
> this jury decrees it; but, oh, gentlemen, don't think for a moment
> that if you hang him you will crucify the labor movement of the
> world . . . Think you there are no brave hearts, no other strong
> arms, no other devoted souls who will risk all in that great cause
> which has demanded martyrs in every land and age?[36]

Darrow's aim was to obtain a hung jury by convincing any doubter
among them to hold out for acquittal. By the time he finished, he was
drenched with perspiration and sobbing. At the very least, he had
greatly impressed the motley WFM supporters gathered outside the
courthouse. Yet Senator Borah drew the biggest crowd for his final
argument. Boise's most prominent citizens turned out in full force.
Widow Belle Steunenberg finally made an appearance, arriving from
Caldwell with one of her sons. A thousand people remained outside,
unable to get into the courtroom.

It seemed that all of Boise could smell an historic hanging in the
air. Prominent citizens had already begun planning a huge, multi-day
picnic celebration. Still, Judge Wood reminded the jury that Orchard's
testimony required corroborating evidence of Haywood's complicity in

that specific crime. He instructed them that they should view Orchard's testimony with skepticism if they believed it resulted from promises of leniency by the prosecutor. When the jury left the courtroom, Darrow wearily confided to a newsman, "It only takes one," spawning rumors that Darrow, too, expected a conviction.[37]

After only four hours, the jury sent a note to the judge. A quick agreement on a verdict sounded like bad news for Haywood, but that turned out to be a false alarm. The panel only wanted to review some exhibits. As jury deliberations proceeded through the night, Darrow paced and listened to disheartening talk that the jury had gone from seven-to-five for acquittal to ten-to-two for conviction. Then shortly before dawn someone standing outside the jury's window overheard an eleven-to-one vote and ran to a newspaper office, which issued an exclusive within the hour.

Darrow heard the raucous celebrants in the street and purchased his own copy hot off the press. When he read that only one juror still held out for acquittal his heart sank. At 6:30 a.m. the attorneys were summoned to court to hear the verdict read. Darrow passed women and men in the streets decked out in their Sunday best, giddy with excitement over the upcoming festivities. In stark contrast, both Darrow and Richardson appeared lead-footed and downcast. When Haywood arrived from his cell, Darrow told his client to prepare for the worst.

To Haywood and his counsel's surprise and relief, the eavesdroppers got it backward. The jury had leaned all night toward a defense verdict. Early that morning, the last holdout for conviction changed his mind to make it unanimous. Hawley registered shock as Haywood won acquittal for lack of proof beyond a reasonable doubt. It was the miners who then declared a holiday, hoisting Darrow on their shoulders as they paraded around amid outraged locals who spread rumors the jury must have been bought off. Others, like President Roosevelt, speculated that the jurors feared reprisal if they convicted the hero of the violent labor union. Elated Socialists across the nation quickly proposed Haywood as their presidential candidate. Anarchist Emma Goldman sent President Roosevelt a telegram: "Undesirable citizens victorious. Rejoice!"[38]

Hawley and Borah blamed the result on the judge's careful jury instructions. Jurors themselves indicated that they focused on the need for corroboration of Orchard's testimony. The prosecutors figured Haywood only escaped the noose because Darrow somehow engineered Steve Adams' retraction of his confession that he acted as Orchard's accomplice. Hawley and Borah badly wanted to turn things around when they tried Pettibone. The prosecutors decided to go after Adams again to get him to turn state's evidence against Pettibone.

Darrow had barely gotten back to Chicago to resume his practice when he was summoned back to defend both Adams and Pettibone. Doped up nightly fighting the flu and severe mastoiditis, Darrow won a hung jury in the Adams case. Then, appearing near death, he commenced a brilliant defense of Pettibone. When Darrow reached the point he could only make it to court in a wheel chair, his doctors ordered him off the case to recuperate in California. Co-counsel then completed the case and won Pettibone's acquittal. In jail, Pettibone had been stricken with cancer. He went back to Denver and died that summer following an unsuccessful operation.

By the time of Pettibone's acquittal, Steunenberg's reputation had suffered a severe setback. Borah himself faced federal charges that, when Steunenberg was governor, the two had conspired to perpetrate a series of fraudulent land deals. At this point, Idaho officials cut short their losses in attempting to destroy the WFM leadership. Charges against Moyer were dropped. Moyer had never favored violent tactics. Soon after his trial, he ousted the more aggressive Haywood from the WFM. Haywood went on to head major strikes over the next decade as a leader of the IWW. Yet some Socialists would have much preferred the boost they believed their movement would have gotten had Haywood, Pettibone and Moyer instead been martyred. They assumed Roosevelt would have faced far greater threats of mass strikes had the three labor leaders been hanged.

Roosevelt saw no benefit from Haywood's acquittal, which he called a "gross miscarriage of justice," from a jury he assumed had been terrorized.[39] Yet had the Supreme Court not given its blessing to the illegal extradition from Colorado, no Idaho murder trial could have taken place. Given the blatant due process violation that brought the three labor leaders to Idaho and the extremely prejudicial pretrial publicity, workers throughout the country would never have believed in the legitimacy of a guilty verdict.

Judge Wood's conscientious instructions, the jury's cautious deliberations and the resulting acquittals showed workers everywhere that the fix was not in for conviction. The underdog prevailed, giving them hope their own situations would improve within the current political structure. One wonders how close the nation came to widespread violence, how much anger would have erupted in the streets and exacerbated pre-existing class, ethnic and religious divisions had Boise's citizenry gotten their coveted hangings.

* * * * *

When Darrow's doctors wheeled him out of the Pettibone murder trial before it ended in January of 1908, neither the ailing champion of labor nor his wife Ruby counted on his surviving the agonizing train trip to Los Angeles. A few weeks later a surgeon performed a life-saving operation, draining a swollen mastoid behind his ear, after which Darrow still faced a long, uphill recovery. For months, Darrow did not speak and barely ate. Ruby kept all visitors at bay and shielded her husband from any business decisions, including frantic letters urging him to sell his investments. Darrow's convalescence in Los Angeles coincided with an economic depression that wound up bankrupting the successful lawyer from prolonged inattention to his affairs.

When Ruby finally told her husband all his savings were gone, he threatened never to forgive her for forcing him to go back into law practice and start all over building up a retirement fund. They barely scraped the train fare together to return to Chicago. Darrow rejoined his old law firm, vowing to concentrate on high-paying cases to quickly put together enough money to retire again. He had never even received all the fees promised him for disrupting his practice and jeopardizing his health to defend Haywood and Pettibone in Idaho. But Darrow did receive a solemn vow from grateful labor leaders after the unexpected victories in Boise – they would never ask him to defend a political murder trial again.

Samuel Gompers remembered that promise well when he showed up on Darrow's door step to beg Darrow to come West again in 1911 for an even bigger class confrontation than the Haywood murder trial. Darrow told the head of the American Federation of Labor ("AFL") an emphatic no. The circumstances were dreadful. The bombing of the *Los Angeles Times* building at one o'clock on Saturday morning, October 1, 1910, had shocked the nation. The building collapsed in flames. Twenty-one non-union employees died trying to escape. Somehow, on borrowed presses, key employees of the *Times* published the news in a one-page special edition the same day, placing the blame squarely on union men.

The attack on the newspaper and an undetonated bomb found outside the owner's home had followed four months of escalating labor-capital confrontations. Harry Otis, owner of the *Los Angeles Times*, was the self-proclaimed general of the movement to break the back of the unions, not only in Los Angeles but across the nation, through the militant Merchants and Manufacturers Association (M & M). Otis was also on a mission to destroy businesses that dared to support unions. Labor retaliated with equal fervor against non-unionized businesses. In June of 1910, union members, strikebreakers and police had come to blows. Local judges sided with management, issuing multiple restraining orders and jailing hundreds of strikers. To many labor supporters, the accusation that militant men were behind a retaliatory terrorist attack on the *Times* seemed too pat. The mass murder drew so much outrage that it dwarfed concerns over abusive labor practices and anti-union businesses. Why would union men be that short-sighted?

Coincidentally on the day of the bombing, William Burns, the celebrated sleuth who had already eclipsed Pinkerton as this generation's "Great Detective," arrived in Los Angeles to make a speech. Burns had rocketed to fame when President Theodore Roosevelt sent him to expose rampant political corruption in San Francisco after the city received unprecedented funds for rebuilding following the Great Earthquake and fire of April 1906. That investigation had prompted stunning indictments for graft and bribery against the mayor and entire board of supervisors, as well as political boss Abraham Ruef, the chief of police, and officers of major utilities and of a local railroad. Mayor

Source: http://en.wikipedia.org/wiki/File:Photo-los-angeles-times-building-post-bombing.jpg

Photo of bombed out headquarters of the Los Angeles Times *October 1, 1910*

Source of newspaper image: *L. A. Times*, Oct. 1, 1910, SPECIAL COLLECTIONS, HONNOLDMUDD LIBRARY OF THE CLAREMONT COLLEGES CONSORTIUM

Newspaper headline story put out by the staff on borrowed presses the same day of the explosion. Los Angeles had already developed a reputation as "the bloodiest arena in the Western World for Capital and Labor." Just four months before the bombing, a major confrontation between union members and strikebreakers prompted local judges to issue multiple restraining orders and jail hundreds of strikers. Labor supporters were suspicious that the terrorist attack on the Times *was actually meant to hurt the labor movement. The mass murder dwarfed concerns over abusive labor practices and anti-union businesses. Why would union men be that short-sighted?*

Schmidt was forced to resign; Ruef alone went to prison.

Harry Otis immediately asked Burns to head the investigation into the bombing of the *Times*. Burns soon realized that it bore similarities to suspicious bombings of non-union work sites his agency had investigated across the country. After six months of intensive national effort, detectives zeroed in on two brothers, James and John McNamara, as the key suspects. John McNamara was the national secretary of the AFL-affiliated Bridge and Structural Iron Workers Union. Like the Pinkerton men who illegally kidnapped the WFM leaders in Colorado in 1906 and whisked them to Idaho for trial, Burns' agents kidnapped the McNamara brothers in the Midwest and transported them to Los Angeles before anyone could challenge their extradition.

Labor leaders smelled a frame-up and wanted to provide the McNamara brothers with their biggest legal guns. (It was, in any event, still more than two years before the city would be the first in the nation to employ a public defender.) AFL President Gompers joined Bill Haywood and Eugene Debs in rallying millions of union supporters nationwide – far broader support than for the Haywood trial – with charges that the McNamara brothers were being railroaded for murder.

Gompers tried to convince Darrow that he was the only lawyer in the country with the skills to save the lives of the McNamara brothers and prevent labor from losing its war against closed shops. Darrow still declined. Back when Darrow had been recuperating in Los Angeles, he and Ruby had seen the polarized city first hand. Customers at local stores had to choose between union and "open" shops and expect to suffer retaliation for their partisanship. In its relatively short history, Los Angeles had developed a reputation as "the bloodiest arena in the Western World for Capital and Labor."[40]

Business leaders in Los Angeles attributed the city's rapid rise to the much lower pay scale compared to the unionized city of San Francisco. In the Southern California city, there seemed to be an unending supply of new job-seekers willing to work when management fired employees lobbying for higher pay and better working conditions. Even in San Francisco organized labor faced stiff opposition from owners bringing in replacement workers. A failed San Francisco Streetcar strike in 1907 for an eight-hour day had made national news when it left 31 people dead and 1100 injured, mostly passengers.

L.A. employers took note of other major strikes across the country, particularly the 1909 "Uprising of 20,000" in Manhattan's garment district. Harry Otis figured that by executing the McNamara brothers he might deter similar uprisings across the country. Darrow dreaded being thrust back into the center of the labor wars, but he did not want the McNamara brothers' deaths on his conscience. Against his better judgment, Darrow ultimately yielded to Gompers' entreaties. He would live to regret that decision.

To counter the extraordinarily negative publicity, the union arranged for a movie biography to be filmed of John McNamara, proclaiming his innocence. The popular nickelodeon galvanized workers nationwide. Meanwhile, in March of 1911 at the very same factory where the 1909 garment district uprising had occurred, a great fire broke out. Nearly 150 garment workers lost their lives as panicked young seamstresses vainly tried to escape the flames only to find the exit doors locked. The Triangle Shirtwaist Factory fire was the worst disaster in New York City before September 11, 2001.

While headlines generated sympathy for exploited factory girls in the East, "Great Detective" William Burns was systematically building a strong case to execute the McNamara brothers and break the back of organized labor. Burns' agency uncovered irrefutable evidence from secret files in the Iron Workers' Union that the bombing was the end result of a five-year sabotage campaign carried out at the direction of union leaders on non-union sites. John McNamara even bragged of the Los Angeles bombing in the presence of an undercover agent.

In an early use of bugging devices, Darrow's visits to his clients in jail were recorded without their knowledge. With the array of witnesses and physical evidence against them, Darrow was astounded at the McNamaras' recklessness. Both were extremely remorseful. They said they had intended the bomb to go off at 4 a.m. when the building was empty. Yet as the two were privately confessing their guilt, the Socialist press kept promoting the McNamara brothers' innocence. Big Bill Haywood called for a general national strike to coincide with the first day of the McNamaras' trial.

This time, Darrow expected his string of victories in keeping clients from execution to end in ignominious defeat. Darrow became so depressed that he also began acting recklessly. He renewed an affair with a woman reporter from New York who came out to cover the trial. If their trysts became public knowledge, it would have ruined his own reputation. Meanwhile, the police caught an investigator on Darrow's staff approaching two different jurors with bribe offers. Darrow could see no way that he could pull off an acquittal or a hung jury.

When muckraker Lincoln Steffens interviewed the McNamara brothers, their guilt was so manifest that Steffens strongly urged Darrow to have the brothers change their pleas. Darrow knew that labor leaders would vigorously oppose any such move. They would much rather claim the two men as martyrs. Yet Darrow told Steffens, "I can't stand it to have a man I am defending hang."[11] Darrow convinced the two brothers to save their lives by pleading guilty and publicly repenting the innocent deaths they caused. Darrow saved them from execution – and avoided a crushing defeat – but at the price of having organized labor turn on him. Union members had contributed hard-earned money to raise Darrow's legal fees only to watch the celebrated lawyer pocket the payment and eventually plead the brothers guilty.

As a consequence of the plea bargain that dramatically ended the McNamaras' trial, the labor movement suffered a huge blow to its credibility. The Los Angeles District Attorney then compounded Darrow's personal woes by prosecuting the famed lawyer on bribery charges – by far the worst legal fiasco of his career. Darrow contemplated suicide, but hired another giant in criminal defense, Los Angeles attorney Earl Rogers, to defend him. When Rogers kept showing up to court drunk, Darrow took over his own defense. For the first and only time, Darrow's emotional pleas asked jurors to salvage his own career. In one of the two attempted bribery trials, jury empathy won Darrow an acquittal; the other ended in a hung jury. To avoid a retrial, Darrow had to agree to forfeit his license to practice in California. Fed up with labor, he headed back to Chicago.

So it was not Clarence Darrow that Bill Haywood asked to defend

Source: http://murderpedia.org/male.M/m/mcnamara-brothers.htm

*Labor activists James and John McNamara (**above, left and right**) were arrested for the murder of 21 people in the October 1, 1910, bombing of the* Los Angeles Times. *John McNamara was the national secretary of the AFL-affiliated Bridge and Structural Iron Workers Union. While in jail, the McNamara brothers confessed to a reporter friend of Darrow's that they had intended the bomb to go off when the building was empty. Darrow feared losing his first clients to the death penalty. Police caught one of Darrow's investigators attempting to bribe two jurors. Darrow then saved the brothers' lives by pleading them guilty, alienating the union paying for their defense. Darrow then himself faced prosecution for bribery – by far the worst fiasco of his career. He forfeited his law license in California, and returned to Chicago broke and dispirited.*

Source: https://commons.wikimedia.org/wiki/File:Clarence_Darrow_cph.3b31130.jpg

Clarence Darrow circa 1913

Source: https://en.wikipedia.org/wiki/Harrison_Gray_Otis_(publisher)

Harry Otis, publisher of the Los Angeles Times *and self-proclaimed general of the movement to break the back of unions across the nation through the militant Merchants and Manufacturers Association. Otis was also on a mission to destroy businesses that dared to support unions.*

him in his next political trial in the spring of 1918, the longest criminal trial the United States had ever prosecuted. By then the coalition that had backed the WFM's defense in the 1907 murder trial had long since collapsed. Haywood and the IWW split from WFM leadership shortly after the Boise cases ended. In 1911, the IWW parted ways from Eugene Debs and the Socialists. Yet Haywood remained a formidable labor leader, viewed by the business establishment as the "most hated and feared figure in America."[42] The "Wobblies" whom Haywood championed, ultimately attracted three million factory, mill and mine workers to their ranks, a coalition including non–English-speaking European immigrants, women, and African-Americans in an era when some unions expressly excluded blacks, while others took aggressive steps to block both African- and Asian-Americans from their own labor pools.

The IWW bore many similarities to the radical coalition that supported Black Panther leader Huey Newton half a century later in his own highly politicized murder trial. Like the Black Panthers' strident opposition to the Vietnam War, the IWW strongly opposed America's entry into World War I as a rich man's war fought with the blood of the poor. Urging tactics that the Weathermen would later emulate, the IWW advocated industrial sabotage to undermine American war efforts. Unlike the bitter national divide generated by the Vietnam War, however, when the country joined World War I patriotic fervor spread across America.

The IWW immediately began to feel the backlash as the federal government drafted harsh new laws blocking entry to revolutionaries and deporting radical immigrants. The war-time Espionage Act of 1917 included lengthy prison sentences for anyone whose speech or political activity encouraged draft resistance. In September of 1917, the Department of Justice raided four dozen IWW meeting halls and arrested 165 Wobblies for "conspiring to hinder the draft, encourage desertion, and intimidate others in connection with labor disputes."[43]

The raids resulted in a mass trial with more than a hundred defendants. The only evidence needed to convict them was proof they disseminated inflammatory IWW literature. All were found guilty and each sentenced to varying prison sentences, with Haywood receiving the twenty-year maximum. The following year, Debs was convicted for making an anti-war speech the Wilson administration deemed treason-ous for use of "disloyal, profane, scurrilous, or abusive language" in violation of the 1918 Sedition Act. Debs was sentenced to ten years in prison; the perennial Socialist candidate for President was also disen-franchised. The United States Supreme Court later upheld Deb's con-viction as a war-time necessity, through a narrow interpretation of First Amendment guarantees that has since been discredited.

Despite the Wilson administration's success in jailing radical labor leaders, strikes for increased wages and better working conditions esca-lated dramatically in 1919. Putting Haywood and Debs in prison made them into martyrs for a noble cause. Poet Carl Sandburg was then working as a journalist for a Socialist paper. He compared Haywood's vision for a worldwide labor uprising to that of John Brown's efforts to encourage slave rebellion before the Civil War. Sandburg wondered, "Will there be marching songs written to Bill Haywood someday as the same kind of a 'traitor' as the John Brown who was legally indicted, legally tried, legally shot?"[44]

Government persecution only increased Haywood's stature among laborers. By 1920, Haywood made bail pending appeal and was out fund-raising for fellow IWW inmates when America experienced the worst bomb attack so far in its history. The Wall Street bombing in front of J. P. Morgan's bank at noon on September 16, 1920, killed nearly forty people and injured ten times that number. The date coincided with a special election to fill the seats of five New York City Socialists ousted from the state legislature on the ground that Socialism itself was a treasonous cause. Was this payback from militant radicals?

The horrific bombing on Wall Street added fuel to "a nationwide antiradical hysteria provoked by a mounting fear and anxiety that a Bolshevik revolution in America was imminent – a revolution that would destroy property, church, home, marriage, civility, and the American way of life."[45] Haywood immediately became a prime suspect. Though he had long since publicly renounced violence as a useless tactic, he realized his appeal was doomed. Soon afterward, Haywood made plans to jump bail and escape with a fake passport to Russia to join Lenin's new government as a labor advisor.

Haywood remained in exile for the last seven years of his life. Once settled in Russia, his naïve vision of a workers' utopia gave way as he observed the stark reality of the new Soviet dictatorship. He died utterly disillusioned, but the Soviets gave him a hero's funeral, keeping half of his ashes in the Kremlin. They honored his request to have the remainder sent back to Chicago to be buried near the Haymarket Square martyrs who had inspired his lifelong battle for worker rights.

Pulitzer Prize winner J. Anthony Lukas's epic history, *Big Trouble*, retells Haywood's story and its context. Lukas notes the ironic difference in outcome of Haywood's trial on charges he conspired to assassinate Governor Steunenberg from that of the accidental deaths caused by the McNamara brothers' sabotage. Several Socialist journalists close to both the WFM leadership and the militant Ironworkers Union privately shared the view in the fall of 1911 that the main difference between the two political crimes was that the two brothers got caught red-handed.

A reporter who covered the McNamara trial for *Appeal to Reason* wrote his publisher that "The McNamara brothers are not one bit more guilty of the crime charged against them than were Myer, Haywood and Pettibone . . . Trickery and audacity liberated the miners' officials." But the *Appeal to Reason* refrained from publishing that story because of what it might do to the Socialist cause: to reveal the truth "would disgust hundreds of thousands of people" with their movement.[46] The rallying cry of innocence in each instance was a propaganda war fought against ruthless political adversaries. Neither the prosecutors nor the defense respected the law. These two high-stakes trials were merely cynical games in a deadly class struggle for power in which media on both sides were often complicit.

* * * * *

Ironically, at the same time Roosevelt had been applying heavy pressure in 1906 on the Supreme Court to let the constitutionally questionable Idaho trials go forward against three "undesirable citizens," the president was waging an unprecedented battle in the South for respect for the Supreme Court's authority. Just a month after the WFM leaders were kidnapped by Pinkerton agents, a lynch mob broke a black federal prisoner out of jail and hanged him to prevent Supreme Court review of his rape conviction. With President Roosevelt's full support, what followed was the one and only contempt trial the United States Supreme Court ever conducted – one which would have lasting consequences for the criminal justice system of every state in the union.

4. SHOWDOWN WITH THE SUPREME COURT

The Lynching That Gave Teeth to the Fourteenth Amendment Right to a Fair Trial

"To Justice Harlan. Come get your nigger now."

– NOTE PINNED TO ED JOHNSON'S CORPSE[1]

During Teddy Roosevelt's presidency, novelist and playwright Thomas Dixon was the nation's most popular lecturer. In the age before radio, Dixon spoke to sold-out audiences across the country, waxing poetic on racial purity, the evils of Socialism and the proper role of women – at home raising children. Belittling bi-racial intellectuals like Booker T. Washington and W. E. B. DuBois, Dixon repeatedly warned his audiences that Negroes were a race of savages: "[No] amount of education of any kind, industrial, classical or religious, can make a Negro a white man or bridge the chasm of centuries which separate him from the white man in the evolution of human nature."[2] (Dixon's anger may have been fueled by abhorrence of his own half-brother, the son of Dixon's father and the family cook.)[3]

The national fad since the late 19th century was to gather round the piano and sing "coon" songs. The public could not get enough of comic sheet music that portrayed Negro men as loose-living, watermelon-eating, ignorant buffoons; ridiculed them as lazy, shiftless gamblers and hustlers or drunks, or demonized them as razor-wielding street bullies. White women singers in black face gained followings as "coon shouters." Hundreds more coon songs fed an insatiable public appetite that lasted through the turn of the century. Historian Eric Foner

Source: https://en.wikipedia.org/wiki/Thomas_Dixon_Jr.

During Teddy Roosevelt's presidency, novelist and playwright Thomas Dixon was the nation's most popular lecturer. In the age before radio, Dixon spoke to sold-out audiences across the country, waxing poetic on racial purity, the evils of Socialism, and the proper role of women – at home raising children. Dixon repeatedly warned his audiences that Negroes were a race of savages: "[No] amount of education of any kind, industrial, classical or religious, can make a Negro a white man or bridge the chasm of centuries which separate him from the white man in the evolution of human nature." Dixon's anger may have been fueled by abhorrence of his own half-brother, the son of Dixon's father and the family cook.

Source of book cover and movie poster:https://en.wikipedia.org/wiki/The_Clansman:
A_Historical_Romance_of_the_Ku_Klux_Klan

Dixon published The Clansman in 1906 in homage to the Ku Klux Clan; it became the basis for the nation's first blockbuster movie in 1915, The Birth of a Nation.

notes, "By the early 20th century [racism] had become more deeply embedded in the nation's culture and politics than at any time since the beginning of the antislavery crusade and perhaps in our nation's entire history."[4]

In 1905, one out of six American households bought the sheet music for "If the Man in the Moon Were a Coon."[5] That same year Dixon published the best seller *The Clansman.* A decade later it would be turned into the blockbuster film *The Birth of a Nation.* In a key scene, Dixon reenacted the most frightening moment of his childhood. A Confederate widow got his father and his uncle, who headed the local Klan, to don their white robes and hoods and join other Klansmen in stringing up a former slave accused of attacking the woman's daughter. The Ku Klux Klan hanged the man in the center of town and shot him repeatedly for good measure. Dixon's mother reassured her young son, "They're our people – they're guarding us from harm."[6]

Among those who enjoyed putting on black face to ridicule former slaves were members of the white supremacist Pickwick Club, who paraded annually at Mardi Gras in New Orleans. Since 1874, many of their members also belonged to the Louisiana White League, formed by Confederate Army veterans to oppose Reconstruction by acts of violence and intimidation. The White League was similar to the secretive KKK, but had enough local support to operate openly without hoods. Members of the Pickwick Club and White League joined with other Democrats in passing Louisiana's 1890 Separate Train Act, which required railroad companies to isolate African-American travelers. Eighteen local black activists reacted by forming a Citizens' Committee to Test the Constitutionality of the Separate Car Law. The test case they set in motion would have enormous repercussions for more than half a century.

The New Orleans citizens' committee asked a volunteer named Homer Plessy, who was one-eighth black, to buy a first-class ticket to ride in a car designated "whites only." The committee prearranged with the railroad's management to have Plessy arrested for civil disobedience when he declined to move out of that car. The citizens' committee then paid for Plessy's legal challenge of the $25 fine, expecting vindication in the Supreme Court. After all, the Fourteenth Amendment to

Source of sheet music photos: https://en.wikipedia.org/wiki/Coon_song

Source: https://commons.wikimedia.org/w/index.php?curid=18826048

Sales of sheet music for "Coon Songs" soared nationwide in the late 19th and early 20th centuries. "Coon, Coon, Coon" was advertised as the most successful song of 1901. (A "honey gal" lived with her man in unmarried sin.) **Lower right:** *Irving Berlin as a young immigrant composer – the man who became one of America's greatest songwriters was among many who wrote popular "Coon Songs" for public consumption.*

the Constitution plainly declared that "no state shall make or enforce any law which shall abridge the privileges or immunities of citizens of the United States . . . nor deny to any person within its jurisdiction the equal protection of the laws."

To the civil rights committee's shock, the high court decided *Plessy v. Ferguson* seven-to-one against them. The panel of jurists that rejected the claim that the Separate Car Act violated the Fourteenth Amendment included a proud member of the Pickwick Club Mardi Gras Krewe and of the militant White League who had been raised on a slave-owning plantation. Louisiana Justice Edward D. White joined six other justices who put the blessing of the highest court in the land behind enforced segregation of mixed-blood or Negro citizens so long as the accommodations were called "equal." Covered by that fig leaf, discriminatory Jim Crow laws proliferated in the South and emboldened physical abuse of blacks throughout the land.

* * * * *

In 1905, Chattanooga, Tennessee, maintained a significantly better civil rights record than most other Southern cities. The industrial city of 60,000 included many transplanted Northerners as well as a substantial middle class among its 20,000 black residents. The city had not held a lynching since 1896 – the same year the Supreme Court of the United States decided the landmark case of *Plessy v. Ferguson.* Back in 1887, Chattanooga had elected a black lawyer, Styles Hutchins, to represent the district for one term in the state legislature. Progressive religious leaders fought bigotry and lobbied for peaceful resolution of all conflicts.

As of 1905, publisher Adolph Ochs still owned the *Chattanooga Times,* though the Jewish philanthropist had already moved to Manhattan to oversee his more recent acquisition, the *New York Times.* Despite the city's progress, fifteen percent of Chattanooga's adults couldn't read. A large number of whites held dead-end, menial jobs and increasingly resented the growing prosperity of the city's black professionals. In Tennessee, new Jim Crow laws made race hatred far more contagious. It went viral in Chattanooga that winter.

Since early December of 1905, the papers had been reporting a wave of burglaries, rapes and robberies by Negro men, including a girl attacked in her own bed in an orphanage and another on a downtown street. On Christmas Eve tension rose dramatically when a notorious black gambler, Floyd Westfield, barricaded himself in his house with a gun when a white constable headed a posse sent to arrest Westfield for disturbing the peace in his neighborhood by shooting off fireworks. When the constable and his men broke the door down, Westfield fired, killing the constable. The day after Christmas, Ochs' often Progressive *Chattanooga Times* captured the widespread fear: "Desperadoes Run Rampant in Chattanooga; Negro Thugs Reach Climax of Boldness." The paper blamed the climate of fear partly on the sheriff for not being tough enough. A month later, vigilantes impatiently waited for Westfield's murder trial to reach its foregone conclusion. Given their druthers, they would have already strung the gambler up to send the Negro community a strong message about respect for law and order.

When locals heard what happened after dark on Tuesday evening, January 23, 1906, to twenty-one-year-old Nevada Taylor, all many could think about was vengeance. Someone jumped the popular office worker from behind and brutally raped her as she approached the cemetery gate near her home in the city's St. Elmo District. The pretty blonde still lived with her widowed father, a groundskeeper at the Forest Hills Cemetery, and commuted daily by trolley to her job downtown. Whoever had assaulted her shortly after 6:30 p.m. had almost choked her with a leather strap around her throat and left her unconscious.

Hamilton County Sheriff Joseph Shipp jumped on the case Tuesday evening as soon as Nevada's father contacted him. The sixty-one-year-old diehard Rebel was tall and thin with receding white hair, moustache and goatee. Though he only had a seventh grade education, since his arrival in Chattanooga from his home state of Georgia, the Civil War veteran had done quite well for himself in a furniture business and through real estate investments. After he and his wife raised their seven children, Shipp decided to run for sheriff. The Confederate veteran had all the qualities of a lawman the county's white male voters could trust – a hard-drinking, cigar-chomping, poker-playing champion of

Southern womanhood.

Shipp's bloodhounds sniffed the scent from Nevada's torn dress and quickly found the abandoned black leather strap. City newspapers featured the shocking details on Wednesday together with a $50 reward, almost two months' wages for many workers. By day's end, the reward would grow to $375, a sum larger than many residents earned annually. Nevada had told the sheriff that she did not get a good look at the man who grabbed her from behind and threw her over the fence as she cried out for help. But she heard his oddly gentle voice. At first, she could not specify his race, but said he was dressed in black, wore a hat, was athletic and shorter than average. He might have been five-foot six.

After talking with the sheriff, Nevada became convinced her attacker was Negro. Under the law, that made the rape a capital crime, which it was not if committed by a white man. Sheriff Shipp was up for reelection to a second two-year term at the end of March. He realized that if he identified the rapist quickly, he could get the suspect tried, convicted and executed well before the election. In a newspaper interview on Wednesday, the sheriff made a solemn promise to his constituents: "I know the people thirst for judgment of the Negro who did this. I can assure the people that all at the courthouse agree and will be satisfied with nothing less. I am confident we will find this beast and he will feel the vengeance of our community upon him."[7]

What underlay that desire for vengeance was white Chattanoogans' underlying terror once again being exploited by newspapers and political candidates – as it had been cultivated among white Americans generally from colonial days by preachers, civic leaders and journalists.[8] Despite his boast, Shipp knew he could be thrown out of office if he did not quickly solve the sensational crime that had the city of Chattanooga in an uproar. That same day, the sheriff and his deputies arrested a twenty-five-year-old grocery deliveryman, James Broaden, who worked in the area and fit the general description of Nevada's assailant. Sheriff Shipp subjected Broaden to tough questioning, but kept the investigation open. The next morning, the sheriff was home eating breakfast when he received a call from a man named Will Hixson who worked near the cemetery. Hixson's first question was whether the reward was still available. When told it was, Hixson met with the sheriff and described a black man he claimed to have seen at the St. Elmo trolley stop ten minutes to six on Tuesday evening "twirling a leather strap around his finger."[9]

Tuesday evening had been particularly dark and gloomy, but Hixson said he had offered the same man a light on Monday and believed he could identify the stranger if he saw him again. Late Thursday morning, Hixson called the sheriff to say he spotted the man and learned his name, Ed Johnson. Shipp rushed over to the run-down colored neighborhood on Chattanooga's south side to the shack on Higley Row occupied by Skinbone Johnson and his wife. Their twenty-four-year-old son Ed was not there. The sheriff ransacked his parents' home and that of Johnson's sister who lived nearby, but found no evidence relating to the crime. Shipp had no warrant. Under state law, he didn't need one.

On a hunch, the sheriff hid around the corner and followed Johnson's sister a few minutes later. She flagged down her brother as he rode on the back of an ice wagon. Sheriff Shipp pounced. He had his deputies handcuff Johnson and take him to the county jail for questioning. Johnson asked the sheriff, "Why are you doing this?" but got no response.[10] At the jailhouse, the sheriff followed his usual methods. He tried to beat a confession out of Johnson.

Like many other colored kids, Ed Johnson had left school in the fourth grade. The police never read him his rights and he was not yet offered an attorney – suspects would receive neither immediate protection for decades. Yet Johnson steadfastly maintained his innocence and gave the sheriff a sizeable list of alibi witnesses who had seen him working at the Last Chance Saloon – miles away from the crime – from late Tuesday afternoon through ten o'clock that night. The sheriff did not believe him. Shipp called the District Attorney. The two interrupted a trial then being conducted by criminal court Judge Samuel McReynolds to alert him that they had the rapist in custody. Word quickly spread.

Fearing that a lynch mob might assemble, the sheriff and judge decided to transfer Johnson to Knoxville temporarily. The jail had already been besieged twice before. Sure enough, that night, 1,500 men – many wielding guns and ropes, bricks and rocks – descended on the

Chattanooga jailhouse demanding "the Negro." They cut the telephone wires to prevent calls for reinforcements and shut off power. Refusing to believe Johnson had been transferred elsewhere, they stormed the building, smashed all the windows and used a battering ram to try to break down the front door. Though police responded, they could not disperse the huge, angry crowd. Then Judge McReynolds showed up and called the governor to ask for National Guard reinforcements. The angry crowd stayed put. One man asked the judge, "Going to help us hang that Negro?" Another said, "The jury is in and we find him guilty and sentence him to hang by the neck until dead."[11]

McReynolds told them to go home, but did nothing to try to blunt their anger against a man who had not even been formally accused, let alone had his day in court. Instead, the former prosecutor explained, "We have laws we must follow." He then pledged that he would give the case the highest priority and told them, "I hope that before week's end, the rapist will be convicted, under sentence of death and executed according to law before the setting of Saturday's sun."[12] Such betrayal of bias should have forced McReynolds off the upcoming trial. Just over a decade earlier, the United States Supreme Court had traced back through Ancient Rome and Athenian Greece to the Old Testament the basic guarantee a free society promises all criminal defendants: the presumption of innocence.[13]

Not until Saturday did Sheriff Shipp bring Nevada Taylor to Nashville to view the two suspects then in custody: Broaden and Johnson. Shipp instructed them to speak so she could try to identify her assailant. Sheriff Shipp needed Nevada Taylor to pick the same man as Hixson. He was worried about more than the upcoming election; he was also concerned about his own safety and that of his staff, other prisoners and the jailhouse itself. When Johnson's voice sounded to Nevada different from that of the rapist, Shipp assumed that the prisoner was just trying to disguise it. Soon Nevada told the sheriff what he wanted to hear – that Johnson was "like the man as I remember him." He "has the same soft, kind voice."[14] The sheriff immediately dispatched a wire to the prosecutor in Chattanooga. An all-white male grand jury indicted Johnson that afternoon, after which Judge McReynolds met with the sheriff and prosecutor to plan their joint trial strategy, which nowadays would be unethical but was then routine.

Tennessee was more advanced than many states in requiring trial judges to appoint a defense lawyer in all death penalty cases. But that was often an illusory right since the judge had discretion to choose any lawyer in his jurisdiction, even if the lawyer was clearly not up to the task. The trio thought about appointing a black defense lawyer, but decided that if Johnson somehow won acquittal, the mob would likely take revenge on the judge as well as defense counsel. McReynolds instead selected Robert Cameron, a known lightweight in the local bar who mostly earned his money finding cases for other lawyers. Cameron had no criminal law experience and no contested civil trials under his belt.

On Saturday evening, January 27, former Circuit Judge Lewis Shepherd stopped by Judge McReynolds' home to offer his suggestions for the high-profile case. Thirty-four-year-old McReynolds had only been on the bench three years, but was highly ambitious and pragmatic. He was open to ideas from the balding liberal, who at fifty was one of the leading lawyers in the state and a seasoned state politician as well. Shepherd was then defending gambler Floyd Westfield on the charge of murdering the constable. McReynolds surprised Shepherd by asking him to partner with Cameron as Johnson's lead counsel. Shepherd accepted on the condition that McReynolds would also name a prominent civil trial lawyer to serve as well.

The next morning before church, McReynolds summoned both Cameron and civil lawyer W. G. Thomas to his chambers. Thomas begged to be passed over, but McReynolds would not take no for an answer. McReynolds dumbfounded the pair by telling them he would not give them time to learn the facts and applicable law. The trial would start as soon as the Westfield trial ended, perhaps by the end of the week, when Judge Shepherd could join their team. As they left, Judge McReynolds reminded them they would not get paid, hinting broadly he expected little effort. Neighbors and clients immediately shunned both Thomas and Cameron and subjected them to ridicule. Thomas's secretary quit. Then rock-throwing hooligans attacked the home Thomas shared with his mother. Though Thomas moved her to a relative's for safety, she and

Cameron's wife begged the two men to get off the case.

Johnson meanwhile stayed in the Nashville prison where he had been transferred for safe-keeping. On February 2, he gave a jailhouse interview to the *Nashville Banner* in which he protested his innocence and repeated the alibi he had told the sheriff. Johnson did not meet his lawyers until the following day when Shepherd and Thomas got him to review with them in detail his movements on January 23. Shepherd told Johnson how grim the situation looked because "the people of Chattanooga are very mad and they want someone to die for this crime."[15]

Johnson must have melted their hearts with his reply: "But I don't understand. I never done what they say. I swear to God I didn't. I've never seen the woman they brought up here before. I didn't even know where she lived. I just want to go home."[16] Shepherd embraced his client.

All three lawyers quickly scrambled to gather alibi evidence. Judge McReynolds had already held an improper private meeting with two of the three defense lawyers, the sheriff, the mayor of Chattanooga and District Attorney Matt Whittaker. Like the sheriff, Whittaker was on the upcoming ballot for reelection and under similar pressure to convict Johnson and make him hang for the rape of Nevada Taylor. McReynolds warned the defense team against making a motion for change of venue or asking for a postponement of the trial to allow the community to calm down. Contrary to his duty to decide how Johnson's case would proceed based on the arguments about to be presented in court, McReynolds had made up his mind in advance not to grant either form of relief for fear that it would only infuriate the mob and precipitate a lynching. McReynolds had already indicated to the sheriff and prosecutor that Johnson's acquittal would present the same serious political problem. The judge felt Johnson's life well worth sacrificing to preserve the façade of a law-abiding society. Let the defense lawyers try their best in an impossible time frame, the script was already written – Johnson had to die to satisfy the mob.

Shepherd was determined to succeed against all odds. For assistance, he had already approached the most gifted local African-American attorney for help, Noah Parden, the younger partner of black politician Styles Hutchins. Unlike Hutchins, forty-one-year-old

Parden was scholarly and athletic. He had light skin, tight curly hair, a long straight nose and a bushy mustache. Parden had been raised in an orphanage since the age of six when his mother, a housecleaner, died of illness. He never knew his father, who likely was white.

Among the few possessions Parden's mother had left him was a Bible, perhaps explaining why he embraced his legal career like a religious calling. Like Hutchins, Parden was an impassioned champion of individual rights, but unlike his mentor, he was far more pragmatic. He did not dare offer help to Johnson publicly for fear of retribution from both the white and black communities, both of which wanted the alleged rapist quickly brought to justice and the whole ugly matter put behind them. Yet Parden helped Johnson's lawyers track down alibi witnesses and gave valuable behind-the-scenes advice. Thomas and Cameron worked day and night establishing that Johnson was at the saloon when he said he was from 4 p.m. until 10 p.m. the night of the rape. Yet they recognized that the bar's regulars were considered low-life with little credibility.

The lawyers could do nothing with Parden's other lead. Two black residents in the neighborhood of the assault had told Parden that they had seen a white man washing off blackface on the street about 7 p.m. that fateful night. Burnt cork and greasepaint were then commonly used by whites in minstrel shows, and it would have been a smart move for a white rapist on a dark night to wear such makeup to reduce the chances of being caught. But the two potential defense witnesses realized the sheriff would never believe them; they refused to come forward.

The tabloids meanwhile kept the ire of impatient community avengers at fever pitch awaiting the trial's start. As a precaution, heavily armed guards brought Johnson back from Nashville in secrecy to the Chattanooga jail. When proceedings began on Tuesday morning, February 6, Judge McReynolds filled the courtroom with lawyers and newsmen strongly favoring the prosecutor; he refused admittance to Ed Johnson's parents and his pastor. McReynolds designated an all-white list of names for the jury panel, though such skewed practice was illegal. Two men who had qualms about the death penalty were dismissed. The defense excused others who admitted that they already believed

Johnson guilty. When addressing the jury panel, Shepherd stood next to his slump-shouldered client and told them, "I ask but one thing of you. I ask that you treat this man throughout this trial and during your deliberations as you would a white man. He deserves no less. The law requires no less."[17]

During the three-day trial, the whole gallery openly cheered District Attorney Matt Whittaker and razzed the defense team at will without any reprimand from the judge. Johnson remained listless as both Hixson and Taylor identified him. Sheriff Shipp and his deputies testified that Johnson had told three inconsistent versions of his alibi when they were grilling him at the jail. It was almost dark when Johnson took the stand on his own behalf, but he suddenly perked up and explained to the jury his whole day Tuesday, January 23, in animated detail. Johnson reeled off the names of nine witnesses who saw him at the saloon. The judge kept the trial going late that night and reconvened early the next morning for another full day.

Aside from the alibi witnesses, the most compelling defense witness was an elderly black building supervisor of a nearby white church. His name was Harvey McConnell. McConnell accused Hixson of framing Johnson for the reward money. He testified that on Wednesday, January 24 – the day after the rape – Hixson approached him to ask for a physical description of the roofer Hixson had seen recently working at the church and for the roofer's name.

The defense argued that it was not based on Hixson's own observations Tuesday night but McConnell's description of Johnson that Hixson then went to the sheriff to collect his reward. Other defense witnesses testified that it was so dark Tuesday night before six p.m. that a pedestrian could not identify the race of a passerby at five feet, let alone the features of the stranger Hixson had claimed to have seen twirling a leather strap Tuesday night. Hixson took the stand and denied ever speaking to McConnell and reaffirmed his identification of Johnson.

On Thursday, Nevada Taylor retook the stand but was less sure now then she had been before: "I will not swear that he is the man, but I believe he is the Negro who assaulted me."[18] A juror then yelled, "If I could get at him, I'd tear his heart out right now."[19] Shepherd demanded a mistrial, which should have been declared, but Judge McReynolds had no such intention. After three hours of impassioned oral argument on both sides, it was after 5 p.m. when Judge McReynolds instructed the jury and nearly six when he ordered them to begin immediate deliberations.

It was almost midnight when the exhausted jury came back to the courtroom. Much to the judge and sheriff's shock, the jury announced a deadlock. Even under intense pressure from the prosecutor to "send that black brute to the gallows," four jurors held out for acquittal. McReynolds ordered them to get some rest and return Friday morning. What happened next would only come out in a later federal investigation. "Long after everyone else had left the courthouse, McReynolds, prosecutor Whittaker, and Sheriff Shipp shared a bottle of whiskey in the judge's chambers. They all agreed that a 'not guilty' verdict could not be tolerated, nor could a mistrial – the city could not afford, financially or socially, a second trial."[20] How they followed up on that conspiratorial session never came to light.

Within an hour of when the jurors arrived Friday morning, they surprisingly announced they had reached agreement. Guards brought Ed Johnson into court handcuffed and in leg irons as a crowd quickly gathered to hear the jury verdict of guilty. Death was mandatory since the jury included no recommendation of leniency. Shepherd announced he would seek a new trial the next day, but his co-counsel Thomas disagreed and asked McReynolds to appoint three more attorneys to help resolve the defense team's impasse on what to do next.

McReynolds then met again with District Attorney Whittaker – yet another breach of the judge's required neutrality – and let the prosecutor name two of the three defense consultants. Not surprisingly, the new lawyers joined forces with Thomas to try to pressure Shepherd and Cameron to forego requesting a new trial or appeal even though both men were convinced that the four jurors who changed their minds so quickly had been tampered with. The advisors told the defense team they had now completed all of their ethical responsibilities to Johnson and any further legal action would simply cause a few months' delay of the inevitable hanging. Thomas feared worse: that any further defense of Johnson's innocence might just incite the lynch mob to kill all of them and the sheriff would no longer get in the mob's way.

By the time the attorneys conferred with Ed Johnson in the jail Friday afternoon, they convinced the poor man he had only two choices, both ugly: to forego any further proceedings and die with relative dignity at the hands of the county hangman or to assert his rights and be lynched and mutilated by a rabid mob. With Shepherd now grudgingly silenced, Thomas talked Johnson into waiving his rights and throwing himself on the court's mercy. McReynolds showed none. He praised the jury as among the finest he had ever observed and announced his personal endorsement of their verdict that the defendant was the guilty party. McReynolds sentenced Johnson to be hanged on March 13 – fulfilling his pretrial promise.

On Saturday, February 10, Skinbone Johnson arrived at Hutchins' and Parden's law firm desperate for help. He told Parden that his son did not want to die for a crime he had not committed and had only waived his appeal under duress. Styles Hutchins overheard their conversation and convinced Parden this was an historic occasion that cried out for their help. Money was not an issue; the two were used to poor black clients not being able to repay them with anything but gratitude and a home-cooked meal. Parden already believed Johnson was innocent and the trial a mockery of justice. He came to Shepherd's home on Sunday and enlisted the remorseful older lawyer's aid.

Ed Johnson's chances of regaining his freedom were slim to none in the Tennessee Supreme Court and not much better under federal law. The Bill of Rights guaranteed the right to trial by jury and the right not to be deprived of life, liberty or property without due process of law, but those constitutional rights had been interpreted to apply only in federal courts. After the Civil War, the country enacted the Fourteenth Amendment declaring that "no state" shall "deprive any person of life, liberty, or property, without due process of law." But the Supreme Court had not yet determined whether that controversial Amendment was intended to enforce the Bill of Rights in state criminal trials.

The next five weeks would involve a race against the hangman's noose through four courts, including the highest in the land. On Monday morning, Parden and Hutchins surprised Judge McReynolds with a hastily prepared motion for a new trial. The judge told them to come back on Tuesday when the prosecutor would be available. The next morning Judge McReynolds denied the motion for a new trial as untimely, telling Parden that the three-day deadline had actually run on Monday. When Parden then requested a certified record to permit review by the Tennessee Supreme Court, McReynolds sneaked off on a week's unplanned vacation to stymie that process. Parden persisted anyway.

On March 3, the Tennessee Supreme Court unanimously rejected the plea to delay Ed Johnson's execution. Four days later, Parden raced to the federal district court in Knoxville to challenge the trial. He cited a United States Supreme Court case on Sixth Amendment guarantees for a fair trial and pointed out the skewed handling of seventeen rape cases in the county over the past six years. Most of the victims were black, but only two of those cases resulted in convictions and the rapists got short jail terms. Three victims were white women who accused black men. All three of those cases resulted in convictions, with two of the three men sentenced to death.

By coincidence, Sheriff Shipp was on the same three-hour train to Knoxville as Parden, but traveling in first class the sheriff never saw the Chattanooga lawyer in the "coloreds" car. Shipp was planning to transfer Johnson back to Chattanooga, where he would likely be at the mercy of another lynch mob. Not in any particular hurry, Shipp ran other errands and spent time with old friends before he reached the prison. By the time he arrived, Shipp was shocked to find a marshal with an order signed by Judge Clark keeping Johnson in Knoxville pending a hearing on March 10.

Shipp brought the judge and prosecutor to the unprecedented hearing, which lasted into the night. At lunch-time on March 11, Judge Clark issued his ruling on the merits of Parden's petition. The judge did not grant the requested relief, but issued a ten-day stay of Johnson's execution to allow for United States Supreme Court review. The Chattanooga officials immediately questioned Judge Clark's authority to change the execution date. Judge McReynolds suggested they might disregard the federal judge's ruling and go ahead with the execution on its prior schedule. Instead, the group asked Tennessee's Governor

William Cox to intercede. He postponed Johnson's execution just one week, to March 20.

Ed Johnson resigned himself to death. He had experienced an epiphany and wanted to be baptized. Johnson no longer hated the white people persecuting him for a crime he hadn't committed. His last wish was granted in the Knox County jail. Instead of taking him to the church, officials allowed the black pastor into the prison. Over three hundred congregants crowded into the jail's cafeteria where Johnson joined in a full-throated rendition of "There's Power in the Blood" and "Amazing Grace." Johnson displayed such ecstasy that it enraptured the choir members, who ended with a wildly exuberant "In the Sweet By and By."[21] Parden barely got any sleep as he prepared an emergency writ to file with the United States Supreme Court and booked a train to the nation's capital for the afternoon of March 15. That morning an arsonist set fire to his office building, but it was put out quickly. Parden found a seat in another "coloreds" car and had plenty of time to wonder if he was on a fool's errand as the train stopped at station after station with their segregated toilets and water fountains. Everywhere he looked were reminders of the Supreme Court's stamp of approval on these demeaning daily indignities in its 1896 decision in *Plessy v. Ferguson*. In Washington, D.C., Hutchins had arranged for Parden to meet first with Emanuel Hewlett, one of the few African-American lawyers already admitted to practice before the United States Supreme Court. Parden needed Hewlett to sponsor him to be sworn in, too.

Two days after Parden's arrival, the two men presented Parden's papers to Justice Harlan in the majestic Supreme Court conference room. Parden was hopeful. Harlan had been the lone dissenter in the *Plessy* case, arguing that the Constitution was color blind. It was their good fortune that the civil rights champion was assigned to review emergency requests from the Sixth Circuit, which encompassed Tennessee. The Kentucky-born jurist had himself been raised on a slaveholding plantation. Though Harlan had fought for the Union in the Civil War, he was then pro-slavery, like his father. In forty years, the six-foot-two-inch jurist had evolved from a svelte, brown-bearded Whig into a hefty, balding and clean-shaven Republican. The Presbyterian's conversion to abolition had much to do with seeing his older half-brother Robert face so many painful experiences because Robert was one-eighth black.

Parden's urgency impressed Justice Harlan: Ed Johnson would hang in three days without Supreme Court intervention. The meeting lasted no more than ten minutes. Parden hoped he might hear something the next morning, but there was no news before he had to catch his train. On the long ride home, he anxiously replayed in his mind the extraordinary session on March 17 with the justice, trying to decide if he had been convincing. Meanwhile, Harlan reviewed the papers and conferred with his brethren at the Chief Justice's home on the morning of March 18. At Harlan's urging, the high court – for the first time in its history – agreed to review a state court conviction on constitutional grounds and gave Harlan authority to stay Johnson's execution pending a hearing. He immediately sent notice of the order by telegram.

Hutchins elatedly greeted Parden's return with the telegram in hand. The following day, March 19, the extraordinary relief ordered for the convicted rapist was all over the front pages of local newspapers. Ed Johnson had trouble realizing that a white-haired son of the South on the Supreme Court in Washington, D.C. gave a tinker's damn about a colored handyman in Chattanooga, Tennessee. Shepherd invited Parden and Hutchins to celebrate their historic victory at a dinner in his home. While they toasted their success, a lynch mob was already gathering to descend once more on the Chattanooga jail. This time, the sheriff was forewarned of the mob's plans and removed all but one other prisoner, a white woman moonshiner, from the third floor where Shipp had brought Johnson back for execution. Shipp then gave most of his deputies an unaccustomed night off.

Shipp's chances of reelection had taken a nosedive for not allowing the lynching in the first place. He was determined not to stand in the mob's way again. Instead, he went home to await the outcome, just a few blocks from the jail. Judge McReynolds still smarted from Shepherd's blistering attack on his judicial integrity and the deep personal affront the shocking federal intervention represented. He gave Adolph Ochs' brother at the *Chattanooga Times* a heads-up, but this time refrained from asking the governor to deploy the National Guard. The attack on the jail began around 8 p.m. McReynolds and Whittaker settled by a window overlooking the jail to watch the show.

As Johnson heard the ugly mob invading the Chattanooga jailhouse, he kept repeating to himself the 23d Psalm. During the three-hour siege, Judge McReynolds and District Attorney Whittaker never alerted the police nor interceded with the crowd. Apparently, they also failed to take any notes of people they observed breaking into the jailhouse. When someone contacted Sheriff Shipp at home, he, too, neglected to ask for police support and failed to ask the governor to deploy the National Guard stationed nearby. Shipp arrived at the jailhouse well before the vigilantes found Johnson, but simply let the mob put him in an unlocked side room to stay out of their way.

It was close to eleven-thirty when the poorly executed siege of the almost undefended building finally succeeded. As the mob's leaders emerged triumphant pushing Johnson ahead of them with a rope around his neck, the crowd gained energy with shouts of "Kill him now!" and "Cut his heart out right here!" The men force-marched Johnson at the head of their ugly parade six blocks to the Walnut Street Bridge where the last lynching had occurred a decade before. Johnson shouted, "God bless you all. I am innocent" before they hanged him over the Tennessee River. Even after they had to know he was dead, mob members repeatedly shot at his swinging body. Though no one tried to stop the hanging, there were policemen around. One was spotted bending over Johnson's bullet-ridden corpse to cut off a finger for a souvenir. Someone else pinned a note on what remained of Johnson's torso, "To Justice Harlan: Come get your nigger now."[22]

It was a classic reaffirmation of lynching as spectacular ritual – complete with contemptuous acts of overkill. Demonstration of such extreme disrespect helped maintain white power over blacks who often outnumbered whites in Southern communities. MSNBC newscaster Chris Hayes in his new book, *A Colony in a Nation*, captures the brutal message succinctly: "To desecrate the dead is to humiliate the living, and humiliation may be the most powerful and underappreciated force in human affairs."[23] The gruesome displays of chopped-off heads followed slave uprisings dating back to colonial days. The joyous

Source: wikimedia.org/wikipedia/commons/thumb/0/0f/
Judge.JMHarlan.jpg/

Source: http://www.abajournal.com/gallery/supremecontempt/200

The historic stay order

Justice John Marshall Harlan (left) issued the historic stay order that delayed the execution of Ed Johnson so the Supreme Court could review the fairness of Johnson's rape trial. It was the first time the Supreme Court took up the issue whether Sixth Amendment rights of defendants applied in state court, where most criminal trials have always taken place. The former attorney general of Kentucky had a half-brother who was biracial which was likely a factor not only in this landmark action, but in his lone dissent in the 1896 decision in Plessy v. Ferguson. *Justice Harlan believed the Constitution was color blind. His view would be vindicated more than half a century later when a unanimous high court decided* Brown v. Board of Education, *rejecting segregation of public places as unconstitutional.*

The impact of Harlan's order and of Sheriff Shipp's letting Johnson be killed by a mob is detailed in the prize-winning 1999 book Contempt of Court: The Turn-of-the-Century Lynching That Launched a Hundred Years of Federalism. *Authors Leroy Phillips, Jr., and Mark Curriden graphically illustrated how rights we take for granted today sometimes had to be "written in blood." The authors spearheaded successful efforts in 2000 to have a judge retry the charges and find Johnson innocent – 94 years after he was murdered.*

Source: *ABA Journal*, "A Supreme Case of Contempt," June 2, 2009, http://www.abajournal.com/magazine/article/a_supreme_case_of_contempt

District Attorney Matt Whittaker was up for reelection when Ed Johnson was arrested. He had a cheering squad in the courtroom counting on him to deliver a hanging.

Source: http://bioguide.congress.gov/scripts/biodisplay.pl?index=M000598

Judge Sam McReynolds feared for his own safety from the lynch mob that tried to take Ed Johnson before trial. He placated them only by saying he hoped "before week's end, the rapist will be convicted, under sentence of death and executed." He then delivered a mockery of a trial and later watched from the sidelines as a mob took "justice" into its own hands away from the U.S. Supreme Court to lynch a federal prisoner. McReynolds soon launched a long Congressional career. This painting was done over 30 years later when he was Chair of the House Foreign Relations Committee.

Source: Chattanooga Public Library. https://www.neh.gov/humanities/2014/novemberdecember/feature/chattanooga-versus-the-supreme-court

Sheriff Joseph Shipp was also up for reelection when he let his prisoner be dragged from his jail cell and lynched. For his willingness to let the mob have its way, he won reelection handily. After he served two months in jail for contempt of the Supreme Court, Shipp received a hero's welcome back in Chattanooga as the band played "Dixie."

celebration of mob law and white supremacy gained in popularity in the South in the mid-19th century as a way to intimidate the growing anti-slavery movement. To the rowdy crowds that gleefully participated in such ghastly revenge for the real or imagined crimes of their hapless captives, each macabre gathering constituted the fit "barbarous" end to a "barbarous criminal."[24]

When the excuse was an accusation of rape, the grotesque lynching ceremony also publicly avenged the indignity endured by a defiled white virgin or faithful wife who would otherwise be forced to testify in open court and undergo the humiliation of having to relive the brutal crime. Most of all, devoted sons of the Confederacy wanted to send a strong message to the federal government. Regardless of what the detested Reconstruction Amendments purportedly dictated, the progeny of former slaves were not citizens entitled to trial by a jury of their peers, equal protection or due process rights afforded to the master race – period.

Having just celebrated Johnson's extraordinary reprieve, Chattanooga's black community reacted in shocked disbelief at the free hand the city's sheriff had given a vengeful mob. It was one outrageous humiliation too many, especially following the Supreme Court's unprecedented show of interest in the argument that black men were constitutionally entitled to fair trials in state courts just as white defendants were. The day after Johnson met his horrible fate, Chattanooga's black community boycotted work, shutting down most factories and textile mills. Hardware stores were emptied of guns, knives and ammunition as blacks and whites throughout the city geared up for race riots. Major stores closed early. Fearing an uprising, the sheriff imposed a curfew on blacks. The mayor closed bars that catered to blacks, while leaving open the ones white men frequented. Shipp deputized two hundred men to assist his regular staff; the mayor appointed some additional city policemen. The governor assigned fifty National Guardsmen as backup. Devastated as he was, Parden joined public efforts to maintain calm and focused instead on bringing the lynchers to justice.

President Roosevelt publicly condemned the open defiance of the Supreme Court as the Chief Justice convened the high court to determine what it should do. In an interview with reporters, Justice Oliver

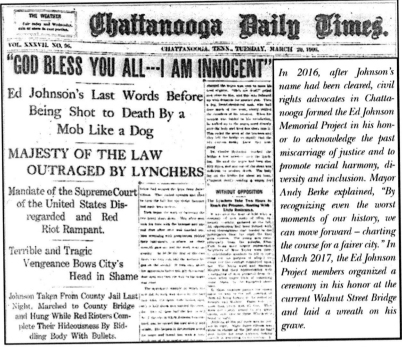

Chattanooga Daily Times.

VOL. XXXVII. NO. 96.   CHATTANOOGA, TENN., TUESDAY, MARCH 20, 1906.

"GOD BLESS YOU ALL---I AM INNOCENT"

Ed Johnson's Last Words Before Being Shot to Death By a Mob Like a Dog

MAJESTY OF THE LAW OUTRAGED BY LYNCHERS

Mandate of the Supreme Court of the United States Disregarded and Red Riot Rampant.

Terrible and Tragic Vengeance Bows City's Head in Shame

Johnson Taken From County Jail Last Night, Marched to County Bridge and Hung While Red Rioters Complete Their Hideousness By Riddling Body With Bullets.

In 2016, after Johnson's name had been cleared, civil rights advocates in Chattanooga formed the Ed Johnson Memorial Project in his honor to acknowledge the past miscarriage of justice and to promote racial harmony, diversity and inclusion. Mayor Andy Berke explained, "By recognizing even the worst moments of our history, we can move forward – charting the course for a fairer city." In March 2017, the Ed Johnson Project members organized a ceremony in his honor at the current Walnut Street Bridge and laid a wreath on his grave.

The lynching of Ed Johnson just after he won a historic Supreme Court order to examine the fairness of his criminal trial almost prompted a race war in Chattanooga.

Source of both images: Mark Curriden, "Supreme Contempt" http://www.abajournal.com/gallery/supremecontempt

Double lynching at the same bridge where Ed Johnson was lynched.

Wendell Holmes echoed Justice Harlan's outrage. The following day Ed Johnson received a martyr's funeral attended by his family, two thousand community members and his three appellate lawyers. Undeterred by the fact that Sheriff Shipp and Judge McReynolds were big political supporters, President Roosevelt immediately met with Attorney General Moody to order an investigation of the lynching. Nor did the Commander-in-Chief back off when warned by leading Chattanooga citizens that "federal intervention in the matter would only incite a race war."[25] Their promises to deal severely with the lynchers themselves rang hollow.

Newspapers quoted the unrepentant sheriff, Judge McReynolds, District Attorney Whittaker and Governor Cox. All of them blamed Johnson's lynching on the United States Supreme Court for butting into purely state business by granting review of Johnson's conviction. Otherwise, they could have just gone ahead with the legal hanging on schedule. The city's leading white Baptist preacher lit into the lynch mob and its lawless supporters in his next sermon. They turned a deaf ear.

Most local white citizens listened instead to the editor of the influential *Chattanooga News*. He urged voters to reelect Sheriff Shipp by a wide margin to send a strong message to the "defenders of such fiends as Johnson." Appealing directly to "Anglo Saxon manhood," the newspaper had nothing but praise for the lawman who had just facilitated the lynching of his prisoner. Only a landslide would "show the whole country that this county proposes to stand by a sheriff who believes in protecting the womanhood of the South."[26] On March 27, an overwhelming majority reelected Sheriff Shipp. (Two years later black voter outrage helped galvanize his crushing defeat for a third term.)

Within days of the lynching, two Secret Service agents had quietly headed to Chattanooga to gather evidence. On the first day, no one would speak to them, but their purpose was whispered about, and three toughs attacked them on the street with pipes. Yet the two investigators refused to leave town. On April 5, local newspapers reported that Baptist minister Rev. Howard Jones had cooperated with the Secret Service men by revealing he had unsuccessfully urged the police to stop the lynch mob on March 19. That night, in retaliation, someone tried to burn down Rev. Jones's home.

The Secret Service agents completed their investigation on April 20, 1906, naming twenty-one co-conspirators in the lynching, including the sheriff and his deputies. Outraged at the murder, the local U.S. Attorney considered prosecution under federal law, but Attorney General William Moody rejected the idea. Moody concluded that white Tennessee jurors would never convict anyone of conspiring to deprive Ed Johnson of his constitutional rights. Filing such proceedings would only exacerbate an already simmering situation. Not surprisingly, when District Attorney Whittaker convened his own state grand jury, it produced no indictments. Neither he nor Judge McReynolds, nor any of thirty-five witnesses Whittaker called, seemed to remember recognizing anyone who broke into the jail that night, even though many participants did not bother to wear masks.

As a protective shield enveloped the lynchers, Parden and Hutchins lost all their paying clients and faced ongoing death threats. Parden and his wife and Hutchins packed up and left the state, not knowing it was for good. Parden was already a much-coveted speaker in the North and hero to blacks elsewhere in the nation for his historic achievement in this case. He offered to assist in the federal prosecution of the sheriff and lynch mob.

By the end of May 1906, the United States Attorney General filed contempt charges against Sheriff Shipp and his co-defendants, the first and only such Supreme Court trial proceeding ever brought. Shipp was defiant. He publicly blamed the Supreme Court for Johnson's lynching and called the grant of review "the most unfortunate thing in the history of Tennessee."[27] By mid-October, the defendants would enter their not guilty pleas. Shepherd had now switched sides and vigorously represented several of the accused. The surprising move alienated Parden. With all of their bravado in Tennessee, before the Supreme Court the sheriff and his deputies defended themselves with lame alibis. None of them had any scruples about concocting a cover-up. Sheriff Shipp and Judge McReynolds also took time for an unannounced visit to the White House, where Roosevelt merely shook hands and exchanged awkward pleasantries.

The first round of arguments addressed the Southerners' claim that the lynching was none of the Supreme Court's business. There was plenty of precedent for its self-restraint. In the fall of 1875, the high court had reviewed the convictions of eight Confederate veterans involved in gunning down most members of a militia of 150 freedmen. The former slaves were protecting the Colfax, Louisiana, courthouse from a white supremacist revolt. It was the worst massacre in the Reconstruction Era. The Supreme Court reversed the convictions and held the federal law unconstitutional, declaring that the Fourteenth Amendment only protected citizens from official state action, not from lawless mobs.[28] (By the time the Supreme Court acted, the blood-thirsty perpetrators of the Colfax massacre had formally established themselves as the first members of the White League.)

In 1883, the United States Supreme Court had played another key role in reducing all blacks nationwide to second class citizenship. The high court had on its docket several cases brought under the Civil Rights Act of 1875 banning discrimination both by government officials and by private citizens who ran public facilities. The Supreme Court issued a blanket ruling in five cases from coast to coast – New York, Tennessee, Missouri, Kansas and California – that Congress exceeded its authority in passing the 1875 Civil Rights Act.[29] With a lone dissent by Justice Harlan, the high court said the Thirteenth Amendment meant only that Negroes were freed from literal bondage, not from blatant disregard of their civil rights.

The Supreme Court's message reinforced its earlier rejection of federal protection of freedmen from mob violence. The *Wall Street Journal*'s Atlanta Bureau Chief Doug Blackmon sums up the result in his 2008 Pulitzer-Prize winning history, *Slavery by Another Name: The Re-Enslavement of Black Americans from the Civil War to World War II*: "In the wake of the [1883] Supreme Court ruling, the federal government adopted as policy that allegations of continuing slavery were matters whose prosecution should be left to local authorities only – a de facto acceptance that white southerners could do as they wished with the black people in their midst."[30]

Still, on December 4, 1906, the Supreme Court began two days of hearings on whether it had the right to entertain contempt charges against state lawmen for failure to protect a convicted black rapist who had been granted its review. Everyone knew that the Sixth Amendment right to a fair trial had never before been applied directly to state proceedings. Defense lawyers argued that the high court could not even consider the question whether the Fourteenth Amendment allowed such review. Otherwise, they would open the door to an enormous array of state criminal cases for potential federal oversight.

Underlying this argument was the firm belief by adherents of Southern states' rights that the Reconstruction Amendments were illegally ratified by pro-Union "rump" legislatures. In their view these constitutional changes abolishing slavery and granting all citizens equal rights enforceable by the federal government ought to be considered null and void – a belief still held by many states' rights advocates to this day.[31] Notwithstanding this entrenched opposition, on Christmas Eve, the court unanimously declared that it did consider itself entitled to address whether Sixth Amendment guarantees applied in state courts via the Fourteenth Amendment.

The Supreme Court's historic ruling cleared the way for the contempt hearing. The high court then appointed a special magistrate to hear evidence. On Parden's advice, the Attorney General strongly urged that the hearing take place in Washington, D.C., to avoid witness intimidation. Defense counsel vigorously objected, claiming undue expense and no reason to worry about the safety of witnesses in Chattanooga. The Supreme Court compromised, letting the hearings proceed in Chattanooga with the proviso they could be moved if need be. Parden quit the team soon afterward. One of the very first white witnesses against the lynchers received a threat that his home would be dynamited if he did not flee the state. The federal agents took it seriously and relocated the man and his family to Georgia. Several other witnesses suddenly disappeared. After a continuance, testimony in Chattanooga concluded in June.

In both sessions, many witnesses braved community wrath by honoring the president's special subpoenas, others never surfaced. Sheriff Shipp's former cook, Julia Wofford, came forward with key testimony that she heard Shipp tell his family he expected a mob if the Supreme

Sources: photo of Noah Parden, http:heblackhistorychannel.
com/wp-content/uploads/2013/07/NoahParden-200x160.jpg;
photo of Styles Hutchins, African American legislators in 19th
Century Tennessee, http://tennsos.org/TSLA/aale/hutchins.htm

Noah Parden

Styles Hutchins

*Two heroic black lawyers who worked to save Ed Johnson in 1906 and later,
at further risk of their careers and their lives, helped prosecute Sheriff Shipp for
abandoning Johnson to a lynch mob. Noah Parden and Styles Hutchins were
pioneering black lawyers, practicing in partnership when asked to help with Ed
Johnson's defense in 1906. Hutchins had earlier served a term in the state legislature. Parden's father was likely white. His mother died when he was a child
and he was raised as an orphan. Parden took a segregated train to Washington,
D.C., to obtain the historic stay order from Supreme Court Justice John Harlan,
but the celebration was short-lived. Shockingly, Sheriff Shipp allowed Ed Johnson
to be lynched that same night. The next day, Chattanooga's black community
boycotted work, shutting down most factories and textile mills. Hardware stores
were emptied of guns, knives and ammunition as blacks and whites throughout
the city geared up for race riots. Devastated as he was, Parden joined efforts to
maintain calm in the city and focused his own efforts on bringing the lynchers
to justice.*

Court delayed Johnson's execution. The African-American woman told the special master she also overheard Shipp on the afternoon before the lynching unhappily exclaiming that the Supreme Court had just granted Johnson a hearing. She quit the next day after news of the lynching, disgusted with her employer. Shipp swore she was mistaken – he had no advance knowledge the mob was coming that night or that Johnson had just won Supreme Court review, making him a federal instead of a state prisoner. The special magistrate ultimately recommended dismissal of seventeen defendants for lack of evidence, but implicated nine of the men, including Sheriff Shipp, crediting Wofford's testimony over the lawman's.

In recognition of the extraordinary precedent being set, the Chief Justice authored the majority opinion himself. He ridiculed Sheriff Shipp's defense that he had no idea the lynching was planned for the night of March 19 and that he did nothing to assist in that lawless act. (Three justices would have found no fault with Shipp's conduct, including, not surprisingly, Louisiana Pickwick Club member and White League veteran Justice Edward White.) The majority dismissed four defendants, but found Sheriff Shipp and four others acted in "utter disregard for this court's mandate" and were guilty of contempt of court by aiding and abetting the murder of a federal prisoner. Barkeeper Nick Nolan had been seen putting the noose around Johnson's neck; defendant Luther Williams had shot Johnson's swinging body five times.[32] An order was issued for the arrest of the five defendants. Shipp's political friends importuned President Roosevelt for a pardon, to no avail.

The remaining question was the penalty to apply. The high court was again divided. Prosecution for conspiring to deprive a citizen of his federal rights permitted a sentence of up to ten years in prison. To discourage another such outrage, Justice Holmes suggested a year in jail and a $25,000 fine as the minimum sentence. The same three justices who believed Shipp had done no wrong would have dismissed the contempt with a simple public reprimand. Instead, on November 15, 1909, the high court ordered the defiant sheriff, Luther Williams and Nick Nolan to serve ninety days in jail; the other two defendants got sixty days.

It was a sad commentary on the high court's perception of its own clout in avenging a major affront to its power and prestige – a lot of sound and fury signifying not so much in the short run. Even so, the ruling met with derision and anger among state officials in many parts of the country, particularly the Cotton Belt. The opposite result should have been unthinkable: that the United States Supreme Court might fail to hold state officials accountable for facilitating the murder of a prisoner to whom the high court had granted a hearing to address claimed violations of his constitutional rights.

Roosevelt's influence seemed quite evident in the manner in which Sheriff Shipp and the other defendants served out their brief sentence. They were held in comfortable quarters designed for women prisoners, where Shipp even got to bring his smoking jacket. Shipp was so impressed with the laxity of his punishment that he decided against asking to be transferred closer to home where his family could visit him. As it was, the men were released early – with time off for good behavior. On January 30, 1910, ten thousand celebrants welcomed Sheriff Shipp's arrival. As he stepped off the train, the band played "Dixie," and the patriotic Confederate crowd burst into song.

The Supreme Court's one major regret was that the Justice Department found no way to charge Judge McReynolds with contempt since he was not responsible for Johnson's safety pending federal review. They considered McReynolds' open disdain for the Supreme Court outrageous. Yet McReynolds' handling of the Johnson case played exceedingly well politically. The primary lesson he took from the landmark case was that criminal defendants had too much opportunity for appeal. He and Shipp lobbied to change Tennessee law to limit "criminal brutes" to just 30 days to seek to overturn any death sentence before the Tennessee Supreme Court.[33] Though that Draconian effort failed, McReynolds later parlayed his tough-on-crime and states' rights platform into nine terms in Congress, from 1922 through 1939. When he died, he was chair of the powerful House Committee on Foreign Affairs.

It took more than another half-century from its historic grant of a hearing to Ed Johnson for the United States Supreme Court to decide exactly which parts of the Bill of Rights were included in "due process of law" enforceable in every jurisdiction and exactly whose conduct besides state officials Congress could regulate under any theory. Diehard states' rightists have never acquiesced in controlling federal law. A movement is currently afoot to repeal that part of the Fourteenth Amendment which guarantees citizenship to all persons born in the United States.

Six decades after Johnson's conviction, the Supreme Court would bar as inherently unreliable jailhouse identifications conducted without a lineup that could be observed for fairness by the suspect's defense lawyer. Its rationale applied equally in 1906: "The influence of improper suggestion upon identifying witnesses probably accounts for more miscarriages of justice than any other single factor – perhaps it is responsible for more such errors than all other factors combined."[34] Witness identifications remain problematic to this day; the national Innocence Project reports that approximately three-quarters of wrongly imprisoned defendants later exonerated through DNA tests were convicted by mistaken eyewitness identification.[35]

Johnson was, unfortunately, like many hapless minorities denied their basic rights when hauled before a criminal justice system hellbent on closing the books on high profile crimes. Johnson was different in that so many courageous people – black and white – made history in attempting to save the itinerant worker from the gallows, risking their own lives and careers in the process. In 2000, a judge in Hamilton County allowed the filing of a posthumous petition to clear Ed Johnson's name. The evidence was painstakingly dug up over ten years by Tennessee lawyer Leroy Phillips, Jr., and journalist Mark Curriden of the *Dallas Morning News*. The year before, the two had just published their acclaimed history, *Contempt of Court: The Turn-of-the-Century Lynching that Launched a Hundred Years of Federalism*. Ed Johnson finally got his fair trial and rightful dismissal of the unproven charges.

In 2016, after Johnson's name had been cleared, some civil rights advocates in Chattanooga formed the Ed Johnson Memorial Project in his honor. Their aim is to acknowledge that ignominious history and to promote racial harmony, diversity and inclusion. As Mayor Andy Berke explained, "By recognizing even the worst moments of our history, we can move forward – charting the course for a fairer city."[36] In March

2017, the Ed Johnson Project members organized a ceremony in the innocent man's honor at the current Walnut Street Bridge and laid a wreath on his grave.[37]

Since *Contempt of Court* was published, federalism has taken a sharp turn in the other direction – toward greater deference to the prior state criminal proceedings, much as Sheriff Shipp's lawyers argued the Supreme Court should have done back in 1906. Some scholars argue that as a practical matter federal review of the fairness of state criminal cases has mostly proved a failure and "squanders resources" in noncapital cases that could be better spent reforming state criminal justice systems.[38]

A 2015 law review article by Ninth Circuit Court of Appeal Justice Steven Reinhardt took the opposite view: that the current Supreme Court has taken a giant step back to making the Sixth Amendment once again "toothless."[39] He cited recent high court decisions rejecting claim after claim that inmates were denied a fair trial in state court without even considering the merits of the inmates' constitutional arguments. He suggested that even inmates on death row now often lack meaningful recourse to the federal courts.[40] He also cited studies showing that restrictive access to federal review of state criminal convictions has had "disproportionate effects on the rights of minorities to obtain equal treatment and equal justice under the law."[41]

Justice Reinhardt's conclusion? "[T]he Court, as currently composed, has little desire to enforce the constitutional rights of individuals who have been subjected to unconstitutional convictions or sentences in state courts, and even less to preserve the Writ [of Habeas Corpus] itself."[42] He found the cutback on federal review of charges that defendants were denied a fair trial particularly disturbing in light of the widespread perception among minorities that our justice system is fundamentally unfair, a perception which "Recent events in Ferguson, Missouri . . . and other communities [across the country], along with the reaction to them, have underscored."[43]

Conservative commentators dismiss Justice Reinhardt and many of his colleagues on the Ninth Circuit as liberals unwilling to follow the Supreme Court's mandate. Yet it is readily apparent that in the last four decades since states began executing prisoners again after a four-year national moratorium, over two-fifths of those executed have been either African-American or Hispanic – almost double the percentage of these two minorities in the population at large. Are minorities more likely to be wrongfully convicted of capital offenses? Charles Ogletree and Austin Jarat's 2006 book, *From Lynch Mobs to the Killing State: Race and the Death Penalty in America,* points out that, of all the death-row inmates exonerated in recent years through DNA testing, most were minorities[11] – not unlike Ed Johnson.

* * * * *

The racial hatred exhibited by white workers in Chattanooga in 1906 was mirrored at the same time elsewhere in the South, including the city of Atlanta. After the voting rights of blacks were suppressed, smoldering resentment of Northern industrialists provided fodder for demagogues and publishers to turn the murder of a teenaged factory worker into a powerful political tool against Atlanta's long-established Jewish middle class. With phenomenal success, yellow journalists – led by William Randolph Hearst – focused local anger on an accused Jewish factory manager. The shocking case unleashed a torrent of anti-Semitism that both helped re-launch Georgia's Ku Klux Klan and prompted the formation of the Anti-Defamation League.

5. MURDER BEGETS MURDER

Two Tragic Deaths in Atlanta Launch the Modern KKK and the Anti-Defamation League

Two thousand years ago another Governor washed his hands
of a case and turned a Jew over to a mob. . . .
If today another Jew were lying in his grave because I had failed
to do my duty I would all through life find his blood
on my hands and would consider myself
an assassin through cowardice.

– GEORGIA GOVERNOR JOHN SLATON[1]

Four years after the historic *Shipp* contempt ruling, Leo Frank's murder trial once again focused national attention on Confederate hardliners rebelling against Northern interlopers. It would end the same tragic way – with local politicians and journalists brazenly inciting a lynch mob to bypass the rule of law. Yet in this case, Georgia's own governor was on the receiving end of widespread defiance orchestrated by a vengeful political rival. Muckraker William Randolph Hearst played a key role in both turning the original quest for justice into a firestorm and in vain efforts to break its destructive path before it became too late.

Still eyeing the White House in 1912, Hearst celebrated his fiftieth birthday and tenth wedding anniversary by purchasing a small Atlanta newspaper, the *Georgian*. He planned to transform the sleepy daily into yet another goldmine for his publishing empire, which was then at the pinnacle of its national influence. Hearst also relished creating a toehold for himself in the Deep South. He transferred to Atlanta a

Source: Mary Phagan Atlanta Journal.jpg archive.org/stream/AtlantaGeorgianNewspaperAprilToAugust1913/atlanta-gogulegorgian-042813#

William Randolph Hearst reveled in the gruesome discovery of teenager Mary Phagan's body in an Atlanta factory basement early on April 27, 1913. The publishing mogul had just bought a newspaper in Atlanta the year before as part of a plan to gain a political foothold for his expanding media empire in the South and promote his chances to run for president. From day one, the Atlanta Georgian's *inflammatory coverage of Mary Phagan's murder hit a nerve among local working class white Christians, galvanizing strong resentment against child labor exploitation by Northern industrialists in general and Jewish factory owners in particular. Georgia politicians and publishers also used the tragedy to whip up anger still harbored over the loss of the antebellum South, a romanticized past which Mary Phagan came to symbolize.*

Kentucky-born managing editor with insights into what would play well with the locals. They made sure to fill the paper with lots of pictures, anticipating a lower literacy level than in his other markets.

As the *Georgian* began competing with the more widely read *Atlanta Constitution* and *Atlanta Journal,* one issue stood out as an easy target. Back in 1909, what had prompted the "Uprising of 20,000" at the Triangle Shirtwaist Factory in Manhattan's garment district had been sixty to seventy-two hour work weeks for immigrant teenage girls earning just $7 per week. After the devastating fire at the factory in March of 1911, hearings on the seamstresses' working conditions revealed routine fourteen-hour days. Both of the company's owners were later charged with first and second degree murders, but had excellent defense counsel and wound up acquitted. (A later civil trial resulted in the owners having to pay $75 for each victim, while they pocketed a recovery worth more than five times as much per victim from their insurer.) The tragedy and its unjust outcome in the courts galvanized support for reforms. Hearst wanted to provoke similar concern for working conditions of youngsters in Atlanta.

Many children of poor whites in Atlanta were like Mary Phagan. Mary had left school at ten to work in a mill and, at thirteen, averaged five dollars and fifty cents per week, working eleven-hour days in a monotonous dead-end job plugging erasers into pencils. Actually, Phagan clocked in less than the average work week in other factories, which included a full day on Saturday, too. Half of Atlanta's kids were malnourished or chronically ill, living in noisome slums that lacked plumbing and other basics taken for granted by the well-to-do. That long-established underclass called themselves "crackers," which was also the name of their local baseball team.

With only scant education, those who joined the work force at age ten had no realistic prospects of ever improving their situation. Social workers wrung their hands at this "awful curse."[2] The President of Coca Cola voiced a contrary view presumably shared by other wealthy industrialists in Atlanta: "The most beautiful sight that we see is the child at labor; as early as he may get at labor the more beautiful, the more useful does his life get to be."[3]

The city's movers and shakers realized how new business complexes and escalating property values owed their very existence to this replenishing resource. Factory workers up North could not be found for anything close to ten cents per hour. Ever the opportunist, Hearst set his transplanted staff full throttle covering Atlanta's exploitation of child labor, joining reformers to point out that Georgia was "the only state that allows children ten years old to labor eleven hours a day in the mills and factories."[4] The maverick multi-millionaire was characteristically uninhibited by his own past as a target of worse claims. For two weeks in July of 1899, thousands of homeless newsboys and girls as young as six went on strike against Hearst and his rival Pulitzer. Their cut-throat circulation wars depended primarily on independent street urchins hawking tabloids from dawn to long past dark to enrich the publishers' coffers. The newsies averaged thirty cents each per day, about two cents an hour.[5]

Hearst hired strikebreakers to break up the rallies. Even after he and Pulitzer settled the strike, the exploited truants' situation remained dismal. Living in the biggest luxury apartment in all of New York City, Hearst had never developed much empathy for the orphans and beggars' children who made his empire possible. But he always knew a hot issue when he saw one, and "the Chief," as his staff referred to him, never let fear of being called out for hypocrisy get in the way of self-promotion. Crime journalist Herbert Asbury, who got his start working for Hearst, claimed that "Had not Hearst owned the *Georgian*, the story [of the Phagan murder] probably would have died a natural death."[6]

Hearst did not create this poisonous stew, he only stirred the pot. The ingredients already existed to explode the local white working class population into uncontrollable rage. Atlanta's business community promoted the city's exponential growth. They aimed to nearly triple the city's current size by the end of the decade despite an already woeful lack of sanitation in the city's growing slums, poor public education, high crime and disease. Turning the city into a modern metropolis meant luring ever more Northern capital investments.

Unlike Atlanta's working class whites, the city's elite had officially decided bygones were bygones: moneymaking was a common bond that, for dedicated capitalists, trumped their anger at cash-rich Yankees over the Civil War. A key selling point to investors was the opportunity to pay wages less than two-thirds of those paid in New England mills. By 1913, Jews owned many local factories. Atlanta's top echelon profited handsomely from their relationship with the Jewish middle class, but excluded them from the city's elite clubs and social circles. The Jews were otherwise largely assimilated in the business community and did not foresee their transformation into scapegoats.

The man who orchestrated the powerful backlash that followed was Georgia's kingmaker, 1904 Populist Party presidential candidate Thomas E. Watson. The lanky, red-headed lawyer born four years before the Civil War had actually co-founded Georgia's Populist Party in 1892 with black voter support. But after a disillusioning election loss, Watson did an about-face and became a rabid white supremacist. By the second decade of the 20th century, Watson was at his feistiest, with a ready platform to spew venom against blacks, Catholics and Jews – his own widely distributed *Jeffersonian Magazine*. Watson knew all along that for the multitude of Georgians the Civil War had never really ended, and he knew exactly how to galvanize that angry base.

* * * * *

With her sparkling blue eyes and auburn hair, Mary Phagan realized she was prettier than most girls her age. A big fan of the movies, Mary dreamed of escaping the tenements of "the bloody fifth" district where she lived with her mother and stepfather, who worked for the city's sanitation department. Her mother worried whenever Mary went about unchaperoned. The buxom thirteen-year-old had turned into quite a tease. On Saturday April 26, 1913, Mary put on an especially fetching outfit to attend the Confederate Memorial Day parade. She never arrived.

The prosecution of factory superintendent Leo Frank for the death of Mary Phagan became the perfect vehicle to focus the wrath of Atlanta's working class whites for their miserable working conditions. Displaced farmers still blamed carpetbaggers for the loss of their ante-bellum society. Significantly, local politicians did not start attacking the Jewish middle class until after they had succeeded in marginalizing black voters. Elder citizens in Georgia could vividly recall their sense of fear and anger when the state fell under martial law because its 1866 state legislature refused to ratify the Fourteenth Amendment.

In Georgia, as elsewhere in the South, the vanquished Rebels abhorred universal male suffrage more than any other consequence of the Civil War. Georgia's 1868 constitution awarded blacks the vote only under duress. But intimidation kept many freedmen from exercising that right, while poll taxes adopted in the 1870s prevented poor people from voting, cutting black turnout in half.[7] Poor whites might expect a local politician to pick up the cost of their poll tax in exchange for their votes. Still concerned that blacks retained a voice in the electoral process, at the turn of the century white supremacists like Tom Watson successfully campaigned for new restrictions throughout the former Confederacy, including whites-only primaries.

To revitalize Atlanta, its civic leaders had already begun to coalesce around a "New South" philosophy predicated on renewed ties with the North, improved technology and education, and a broader based economy. In the first decade of the 20th century, Atlanta's population nearly doubled as impoverished tenant farmers relocated to the city in search of factory jobs. By then, blacks made up forty percent of the city's population and had developed a promising middle class, spurred on by industrialist John D. Rockefeller's founding of three Negro colleges on the city's west side: Spelman (the maiden name of Rockefeller's wife), Clark and Morehouse.

Class rivalry was easy to ignite. A racist gubernatorial campaign helped set off riots in 1906 by playing on fear that the rising black middle class would regain political clout. Journalists egged on local white readers with unverified newspaper accounts about drunken Negro workers emerging from downtown salons and molesting white women. Frenzied mobs then went on a rampage destroying black businesses. They injured hundreds of people and randomly killed over twenty black men. Georgia was reportedly second only to Mississippi in lynchings.

Former Secretary of the Interior Hoke Smith, who made his

fortune as publisher of the *Atlanta Journal,* won the 1906 governor's election. Smith obtained Watson's effusive endorsement on one principal condition: that, if elected, Smith would disenfranchise blacks to ensure they were kept "in their place."[8] As governor, Smith then forged a coalition that in 1908 adopted a state constitutional amendment to add a literacy test for voting with discretionary exceptions for those of "good character," i.e., illiterate whites.[9] By then, nine other Southern States had done the same. Through skewed literacy tests and poll taxes, they succeeded in preventing almost all blacks from voting for more than a half century.[10]

Watson thought Smith owed him personal favors as well. Watson had a long-time friend and supporter, a private detective named Arthur Glover, who shared Watson's devotion to the Confederacy. Glover's twenty-seven-year-old former lover, Maud Williamson, worked at an Augusta cotton mill. Glover showed up at the mill on October 19, 1906, bent on revenge for Williamson's infidelity. He shot Williamson four times in broad daylight in front of witnesses, not stopping even after she fell to the floor. Glover believed he had an absolute right to defend his honor, but the authorities saw it differently and convicted him of murder.

Glover obtained no relief from appeals but must have counted on Watson's clout with Governor Smith when Glover cockily told the press he was certain he would not be hanged.[11] Despite Watson's personal plea, Smith did not commute the sentence. When Smith failed to deliver, Watson switched his allegiance to railroad commissioner "Little Joe" Brown, the son of Georgia's governor during the Civil War, and got Brown elected instead. Watson still did not consider that he had evened the score against Smith. Watson would find that opportunity in the endgame of Leo Frank's tragedy.

In 1913, when the Mary Phagan murder story broke, Watson was otherwise occupied. He was busy fighting obscenity charges instigated by the Catholic Church for repeated scurrilous charges against the Pope. Watson was particularly perturbed about "the sinister portent of Negro priests."[12] The Catholic Church also imposed no ban on inter-racial marriage, a subject that greatly incensed the white supremacist. Watson absolutely abhorred the idea of black men having sex with white women.

It was Watson's book on the white slave trade that prompted passage of the federal Mann Act criminalizing the transportation of females across state lines for immoral purposes. Not surprisingly, the act was selectively enforced from day one. The first time it was ever invoked was against Jack Johnson, the reigning black heavyweight boxing champion. The handsome muscle man contributed enormously to the "Bad Nigger" image that drove this effort. In the 2005 PBS video, "Unforgivable Blackness: The Rise and Fall of Jack Johnson," filmmaker Ken Burns describes how, in the early years of the 20th century, the bald, six-foot-five-inch Texan became "the most famous and the most notorious African-American on Earth."[13] The legendary boxer had a penchant for breaking social taboos, including flaunting his frequent sexual exploits with white women.[14]

Johnson was constantly in the sports news. In 1908 he shocked white boxing fans around the globe by beating the current World Heavy Weight Champion, Canadian-born Tommy Burns, in a historic inter-racial match in Sydney, Australia. On Independence Day 1910, the world-renowned son of slaves – whom Muhammad Ali would later cite as his own role model – challenged retired American heavy-weight champion James Jeffries in "The Fight of the Century." The Johnson – Jeffries match-up marked the first inter-racial heavyweight title fight in the United States. Prominent sports writers like Jack London assumed that Jeffries, though long past his prime, would wipe the "smile from Johnson's face."[15]

The controversial contest was filmed in Reno, Nevada, before an all-white audience, whom security guards first checked for weapons. Energized by spectators' shouts urging Jeffries to "kill the nigger," Johnson won handily. Jubilant blacks took to the streets. Race riots followed in more than half the states across the country. Twenty-three people died, most of whom were black. Hundreds were injured. A feature-length movie of the historic fight was soon distributed across the country and internationally, though many cities prohibited its showing.[16] (Church groups outraged at the moral depravity of the sport soon prompted Congress to ban interstate distribution of any boxing movies, a law that remained on the books for nearly three decades.)

In January 1911, the hard-drinking Galveston Giant shocked America by marrying Etta Duryea, a white socialite divorcee from Long Island. It was when Johnson openly cheated on his wife with a white prostitute that the boxer was targeted for the first Mann Act prosecution. Alienated from her family and depressed by Johnson's highly publicized sexual infidelities, his wife put a gun to her head and killed herself. Johnson then married the prostitute and the Mann Act charge had to be dropped. (Another one would later stick.) Inter-racial marriage had been banned in the state of Georgia since 1788, as it had been in the majority of the former British colonies. Yet many other states had no laws against intermarriage. Public outrage prompted Georgia Representative Seaborn Roddenberry to introduce a federal constitutional amendment in January of 1913 to ban inter-racial marriage in all states as it was already prohibited in Georgia.[17]

When Roddenberry launched this unsuccessful national campaign, the capital of his own state remained mired in poverty. Continued railing against uppity blacks by white supremacist politicians like Roddenberry and Tom Watson played to popular prejudice, but did nothing to address Atlanta workers' own plight as indentured servants in the New South. By 1913, the fresh eyes of William Randolph Hearst's politically astute staff had already spotted the muckraking opportunity awaiting their relentless yellow journalism. Hearst's paper attacked factory owners (mostly Jewish) who helped kill a state bill to raise the minimum work age to fourteen. Newsboys hawked the latest edition of the *Georgian* deploring the horrors of child labor on the same Saturday in late April of 1913 that someone dumped Mary Phagan's battered body in a dark corner of the gloomy National Pencil Company basement.

Newly arrived country folk like Mary Phagan's mother and stepfather worried whenever they sent their daughters to work in factories that the girls might be attacked or subjected to moral degradation. Egged on by lurid newspaper photos and maudlin accounts of the teenager's death, Phagan's funeral attracted ten thousand angry locals who thirsted for retribution and demanded results. The *Georgian* quoted Phagan's grandfather describing the victim as "the sweetest and purest thing on earth,"[18] an invented quote characteristic of Hearst newspapers. It was an obvious reference to its readers' beloved ante-bellum South. By enflaming public opinion, all the leading papers put heavy pressure on the police to produce results.

The police department had an abysmal track record – hardly surprising when officers had little formal education and only a week's training on the force. Seventeen black women had been murdered in the previous two years with no one arrested for the crimes. The mayor warned the police chief that he would not tolerate such incompetence when the victim was a young white girl.[19] Starting on Sunday morning when first summoned to the pencil factory, the police had done a slipshod job in analyzing and preserving the crime scene.

The basement's back door was covered with numerous bloody fingerprints that the police never analyzed. They found two notes near the body, purportedly written by the dying young girl to describe the "long tall negro black,"[20] who assaulted her. Lax oversight allowed a journalist to borrow them. Once retrieved, the notes – no longer a useful source of prints – played a major, misleading role in the trial. Fingerprints on the victim's jacket were not sent out for analysis by the city's forensic analyst. Police and reporters trampled all the footprints in the factory basement that, if preserved, could have helped identify the perpetrator. Yet, if they did not find the brute who killed innocent Mary Phagan, the entire department might lose its badges.

Hearst offered a $500 reward for information leading to the arrest of the perpetrator – more than a year and a half's wages for many locals. Other papers chipped in, bringing the total to a whopping $1800. The extraordinary bounty resulted in a flood of suggestions, most of which proved useless. At first, the police focused on Newt Lee, the Negro night watchman who reported the crime immediately after he found Phagan's blood-caked corpse covered with sawdust near the colored toilet in the basement. The police grilled Lee mercilessly for three days – amid calls for his hanging. Ultimately, they decided that Lee was telling the truth when he claimed no role in the girl's death. The murder occurred hours before Lee's shift started and his answers were so guileless he appeared incapable of having played any role in abetting the crime.

Leo Frank, the superintendent of the pencil factory, had been working that Saturday in his office. After police questioned the badly shaken
superintendent, word got out that Frank was the last person who admitted seeing the young teenager alive. On her way to the parade, Phagan
had stopped in Frank's office at mid-day on Saturday to collect $1.20
for part-time work that past week. Until Frank's arrest, he had been a
rising star in Atlanta's Jewish community, the largest in the South. His
wealthy wife, Lucille Selig Frank, descended from a co-founder of the
first synagogue in the city two generations before. Both she and Leo
had well-connected families. In 1912, at just twenty-eight, Frank was
elected president of his local chapter of the B'nai Brith, a branch so
prominent that they had just secured the organization's 1914 national
convention for Atlanta.

Frank stripped to show the police no signs of having engaged in a
struggle. Their search of his home turned up no incriminating bloody
shirt. Yet police found it suspicious that Frank had called in lawyers
before he was officially arrested; they assumed it pointed to a guilty
conscience. In fact, when officers first took Frank to headquarters for
questioning, his uncle had sent for the lawyers on his own initiative.

The *Georgian* pounced on every suspect fingered by the police. Not
having learned anything from having to retract the headline "LEE's
GUILT PROVED," it printed Frank's picture with another banner headline, "POLICE HAVE THE STRANGLER."[21] Frank did not look like a
son of the South, but the bantam-weight Hebrew number cruncher he
was: impeccably dressed, five-foot-six, with neatly parted brown hair, a
thin, angular face with a prominent, slightly hooked nose and overgen-
erous mouth. He wore thick, wire-rimmed spectacles over his dark, protruding eyes. Though raised in Brooklyn, New York, Frank was actually
born in Texas. Neither his birthplace nor Lucille's ante-bellum roots in
Atlanta impressed local white Christians. As far as they were concerned,
the tennis-playing opera buff with an engineering degree from Cornell
was an elite Yankee Jew.

Leo Frank's uncle was a part-owner of the pencil factory, and
Frank himself owned a small share. Frank's lack of warmth and sense
of self-importance irritated many people who met him. Some girls who

Source: https://www.leofrank.org/trial-and-evidence/coroners-inquest/

*Pictured here is janitor Newt Lee, who found Mary Phagan's body the morning
after she was strangled. Lee became the first suspect the press blamed for the
crime. The police grilled him mercilessly for three days — amid calls for his
hanging. Ultimately, they decided that Lee was telling the truth when he claimed
no role in the girl's death. Lee then testified at the inquest.*

Source: www.georgiaencyclopedia.org/articles/history-archaeology/leo-frank-case

The Atlanta Georgian's *new headline after Lee was cleared and Leo Frank
was arrested.*

worked at the factory came forward to claim that Frank had harassed them on occasion. Much annoyance apparently stemmed from Frank sticking his head into the ladies' dressing room to warn dawdlers to get back to their stations. But being a boor was a far cry from committing a murder. Even had Frank done everything he was accused of – which was hotly disputed – his past behavior with other employees had no legitimate bearing on whether he killed Mary Phagan. Juries are not supposed to determine guilt based on prior bad acts or because they consider the defendant a bad person, but for proof beyond a reasonable doubt that the person committed the crime of which he is accused.

The *Georgian's* headline condemning Frank produced vehement protests to Hearst from Jewish advertisers both locally and in New York. That protest, in turn, prompted an editorial instructing readers not to rely on what they read in the newspapers. It by no means undid the damage, but from then on the Hearst paper would become increasingly skeptical of the case against Frank. Yet in the three months leading up to the July trial, local coverage in the *Georgian* and other city newspapers had prejudiced the Atlanta community beyond repair.

A makeshift bed had been found in the basement storage area, which substantiated fears of the moral degradation associated with factory life, even if Frank had no knowledge of who put it there or used it. Rumors spread that Frank was a pervert with a history of improper advances toward young girls, and possibly boys too. The Jewish community rallied to Frank's defense, rejecting any such allegations out of hand. But the sensational gossip sold papers and enflamed a populace which had lynched many black men on far less provocation.

Forty-two-year-old prosecutor Hugh Dorsey badly needed a victory after two highly publicized prosecutions in which he failed to get a conviction. The owl-eyed son of a prominent Atlanta lawyer, Dorsey had high ambitions. Another embarrassing defeat like the one that had recently come at the hands of Frank's chief counsel Luther Rosser and Dorsey's political aspirations might be stymied. Fearful of being sabotaged by police incompetence, the shrewd prosecutor took the unusual step of seizing control of the investigation at the autopsy stage. Nothing was going to keep him from winning this conviction.

Although Rosser and his co-counsel were both prominent lawyers with accomplished track records, they severely misjudged the prejudice and rage being stirred up. Though later criticized for failing to request a change of venue, there may have been no city in Georgia where Frank stood a better chance of acquittal than its capital, where Jewish businessmen had long been valued members of the community. The grand jury that indicted Frank had included Jewish members who, at the time, believed there was enough evidence to indict Frank. The panel learned later that Dorsey had omitted key facts pointing to another suspect whose handwriting matched that of the notes found near the murdered girl.

The indictment of Frank depended on placing the murder on the second floor near Frank's office. Strands of hair found on a nearby lathe the Monday after the murder initially appeared to support this theory, but when analyzed under a microscope, they did not match others taken from Phagan's head. Dorsey suppressed the doctor's report and continued to assert that the hairs were Phagan's. A decade later a journalist reported another major discrepancy: the official files contained photographs and x-rays of Phagan's body that showed she had been bitten on her shoulder, leaving marks that "did not correspond with Leo Frank's set of teeth."[22] Today, prosecutors would be required to turn any potentially exculpatory evidence over to the defense before trial. Even under the prevailing standards at the time, Dorsey's concealment of key crime facts undermining his theory was indefensible.

The case went to trial in the scorching heat of July. Dubbed "the Greatest Legal Battle in the history of Dixie,"[23] it received the most press coverage of any case ever tried in Georgia. In preparation for trial, the defense team hired two Pinkerton detectives to ferret out exculpatory evidence. They were at the same time secretly reporting to the police, apparently concerned they would otherwise lose their privileges in Atlanta. One in particular made it his mission to prove Frank's guilt.

The proceedings for the Leo Frank trial took place in city hall with a huge crowd of partisan spectators. When the heat forced the windows open, the angry gathering outside could often be heard within the courtroom. The jury pool was all male and predominantly white, although a couple of eligible black men showed up for the Frank jury selection as well. The adoption of the Fifteenth Amendment precluded states from categorically excluding black men from voting and thus made them theoretically eligible for jury service. But states could still impose other voting restrictions such as poll taxes, moral character and IQ tests often used as a pretext to exclude most black men from voting lists and jury service.

Women were still rarely eligible for jury service anywhere, particularly in the South. In Southern states, even after women obtained the right to vote in 1920, legislatures would continue to protect women from jury service primarily on the grounds they were needed at home or should be shielded from hearing sordid details of crime.[24] Another concern that loomed large for Southern white men was the prospect of any white woman sitting next to a black male juror for any length of time.

In the Frank case, it was the defense team that was particularly leery of seating any black men on the jury because they needed to discredit damning testimony from a part-time Negro janitor named Jim Conley. Dorsey gambled his future career on the credibility of Conley as his chief witness against Frank. The stocky sweeper had a criminal record and reputation for hard drinking. The police had somehow waited three weeks before arresting him even though Conley had been seen attempting to wash his shirt shortly after the murder. Conley convinced the police that he was just an accessory-after-the-fact. He claimed that Leo Frank had paid him to transport the girl's dead body in the elevator to the basement from a room across from Frank's second-floor office. Conley explained that the reason his handwriting matched the two retrieved murder notes was because Frank dictated the murder notes to Conley to throw suspicion on the night watchman. All of this testimony was uncorroborated and inconsistent with Conley's earlier accounts. But Dorsey and the police erroneously considered Conley barely literate and incapable of inventing the last version of his story on his own initiative. They believed they had at last gotten to the bottom of the sordid tale. In any event, despite numerous false starts, Conley eventually told them exactly what they wanted to hear.

In preparation for trial, Conley was coached not only by Dorsey but by his own lawyer, William Smith, originally hired for Conley by the

Georgian. But Smith refused to share confidential information with the newspaper and severed their relationship. Smith stayed on as Conley's lawyer because of his belief in Conley's innocence and concern the janitor might be scapegoated, a decision Smith would later regret. Even under Smith's tutelage, Conley changed his story, embellishing his final version with claims that Frank had secret trysts on a regular basis in his office on Saturdays with female employees, including oral sex. According to Conley, Frank had frequently trusted the alcoholic ex-convict to stand guard because his office otherwise afforded no real privacy. These tales outraged spectators, even though several factory employees on the premises most Saturdays testified that Conley was never seen standing guard for Frank and they considered the stories complete fabrications.

The defense, still confident of acquittal, presented two hundred witnesses on Frank's behalf, many attesting to Frank's good character. Given the poisonous accusations permeating the city, they may have felt they had no choice. But that tactic opened the door wide for Dorsey to assassinate Frank's character rather than stick just to the facts potentially implicating him in the murder. Dorsey presented a parade of former female employees who claimed Frank was a lecher. When he summed up, Dorsey simply told the jury to disregard all evidence of Frank's good character on the theory that Frank was a Dr. Jekyll and Mr. Hyde. Looking back after the trial, an editor of the *Atlanta Journal* observed that Dorsey appeared engaged in "a cynical bid for political notoriety and power."[25]

Frank's lawyers still thought they had a convincing defense. They put Leo Frank on the stand to deny Conley's account as a tissue of lies and to swear that he had no part in causing Mary Phagan's death. By painstakingly detailing the superintendent's whereabouts on Saturday, April 26, they established that it would have been physically impossible for him to have completed detailed accounting chores, committed the murder, dictated the misleading notes, and helped transport the body as Conley asserted. Among the corroborating witnesses was a city trolley driver who testified that Mary Phagan had not yet arrived at the factory when Conley placed her there. Dorsey challenged key parts of the timeline, including browbeating the Franks' cook to sign an affidavit that her employer had cut short his lunch break – a statement she immediately repudiated.

Frank's wife Lucille was prohibited by law from taking the stand, but that did not prevent Dorsey from suggesting to the jury that Lucille's delay in visiting her husband a second time in jail evidenced her belief in his guilt. Dorsey also argued to the jury that having counsel at an early stage was further evidence of Frank's guilt. Frank's lawyers did not always raise timely objections, but even when they did, they were unable to convince the judge to declare a mistrial. The lawyers also failed to appreciate the significance of key physical evidence that would have completely disproved the prosecution's theory of where the murder took place. Worst of all, they failed to convince the trial judge to exclude the salacious charges of a history of sexual perversion. Once before the jury, these alleged outrages proved so powerful the jury never focused on gaping holes in the prosecutor's logic regarding the perpetration of the crime itself. Dorsey would then shamelessly indulge in Jew-bashing in his closing argument, even comparing Leo Frank to Judas Iscariot.

By the end of the trial, locals were so obviously out for blood against the Brooklyn-raised Jew that trial judge Leonard Roan convinced Leo Frank and his lawyers not to come to court when the verdict was read. The judge feared that if the jury acquitted Frank, the twenty courtroom deputies stationed outside could not prevent Frank and his counsel from being strung up on the spot. The judge and defense counsel had themselves been threatened with death if the "damned Jew" were not convicted; some of the jurors may have been as well.[26]

Just before closing arguments, Governor Slaton readied the National Guard for possible riots. After deliberating for four hours, the jury found Frank guilty as charged. As Dorsey exited the courthouse, men in the crowd hoisted their hero on their shoulders. The joyous multitude also applauded the judge and jurors for reaching the result they coveted and invited them all as guests of honor to a feast.

Racism played a significant but ironic role in the trial. The defense had stricken the only two blacks from the panel, leaving an all-white male jury. The ridicule heaped on a carefully groomed Conley by chief defense counsel Luther Rosser backfired. Carefully prepared by Dorsey and Smith, Conley remained unwavering on the details after sixteen hours of grueling cross-examination. Yet on any other subject he claimed lack of memory. He reeked of coaching.

The jurors willingly accepted Dorsey's claim that Conley was simply too uneducated to have fabricated the detailed allegations for which he so convincingly confessed to being a paid accomplice. Conley instantly became a hero to the black community. No jury in America had to anyone's knowledge ever convicted a white man of murder solely on the word of a Negro. In some states, like California, such reliance had once been prohibited by statute. But acceptance of Conley's charges constituted no sea change in Southern jurisprudence. As one spectator put it, "That wasn't a white man convicted by that Nigger's testimony. It was a [Yankee] Jew."[27] The implication was obvious. Had Frank been a local Protestant, he would have been acquitted in the extremely unlikely event that Dorsey prosecuted him based on Conley's word.

Judge Roan was facing reelection the following year and could ill afford to have Tom Watson as a powerful political enemy. Some observers speculated that was the reason Roan denied Frank a new trial even while taking the unusual step of expressing his personal doubt about Frank's guilt. The judge also privately opined that Dorsey's predecessor, known for his high standards, would never have brought the case to trial. When new evidence came to light implicating Conley, The *Atlanta Journal* tried its best to restore reason in the community. The *Journal* characterized the prior year as one that "unhinged" Atlanta to such a politically frenzied state that it suspended disbelief of the untrustworthy Conley to scapegoat Frank.[28]

The *Journal*'s call for calm and a new trial brought Tom Watson out swinging. He considered the newspaper still the "personal organ" of his political enemy Senator Hoke Smith.[29] Watson joined the public debate with all the vituperation he had previously aimed at the Pope. Watson's editorials proclaimed Frank guilty because Jewish men, like blacks, all had a "ravenous appetite for the forbidden fruit." One could tell just by looking at "those bulging satyr eyes, the protruding fearfully sensual lips; and also the animal jaw."[30]

Watson also attacked Adolph Ochs' *New York Times,* Hearst and other Northern journalists for instigating a national uproar over Frank's trial. Ochs had abandoned all claim to objectivity in the campaign to save Frank's life. To Watson, that was all the more reason for Georgians to dig in their heels against all Yankee interference. Watson obtained more ammunition when Frank's supporters hired the "Sherlock Holmes of America," private detective William Burns, who promised to prove Frank innocent by exposing the true murderer. Burns' tactics had always been questionable, especially when his ego was on the line. His men were caught paying for false affidavits supporting Frank. The uproar over the compromised private investigation only fueled resentment of the Jews whose money kept the case alive. Burns lost his state license; the "Great Detective" was himself driven out of Georgia, barely escaping from incensed locals.

Frank's attorneys sought both state and federal review of the fairness of his trial all the way to the United States Supreme Court. They designated one hundred and three points of error, including affidavits that two jurors had expressed strong desire to hang Frank before they were chosen for the panel. Dorsey countered with sworn statements from eleven of the jurors that they had relied solely on the evidence presented. In February of 1915, two weeks before the Supreme Court heard oral argument, D. W. Griffiths premiered his three-hour-and-ten-minute epic film, *The Clansman*, soon to be renamed *The Birth of a Nation*. The ambitious movie portrayed Ku Klux Klan lynch mobs as bands of heroes who reunited America by putting an end to the horrors of the corrupt Reconstruction Era. The revisionist epic ends with Northern and Southern veterans of the Civil War recognizing their common bond of white supremacy under a beaming image of Christ, sending a powerful anti-Semitic message.

Thomas Dixon, the celebrated author of *The Clansman*, had been a college friend of President Woodrow Wilson, who himself was raised in Georgia. The president hosted a special showing of the controversial movie in the White House. It featured a quote from his own *History of the American People*, praising the Klan for its historic role in preserving the Southern homeland. A day after the White House showing, the novelist

Source: https://commons.wikimedia.org/wiki/File:Birth-ofanation-klan-and-black-man.jpg

This scene from the 1915 blockbuster The Birth of a Nation *features a white actor in blackface with a mob about to stage his lynching. The epic ends with Northern and Southern veterans of the Civil War recognizing their common bond of white supremacy under a beaming image of Christ – sending a powerful anti-Semitic message. Author Thomas Dixon, whose 1906 book* The Clansman *gave rise to the film, had been a college friend of President Woodrow Wilson. Wilson was raised in Georgia and wrote a history book that praised the Klan. During his presidency, he ordered federal offices to be segregated. In February 1915, Dixon arranged for a special showing of* The Birth of a Nation *at the White House; the controversial film would be advertised as federally endorsed. A day after the White House showing, Dixon reportedly arranged another special viewing for the Supreme Court at the request of Chief Justice White, while the high court had Leo Frank's appeal pending.*

Source: https://en.wikipedia.org/wiki/Edward_Douglass_White

Chief Justice
Edward Douglass White
1845–1921

Edward Douglass White was one of three former Confederate soldiers to be named a Supreme Court justice. Justice White was also one of the eight men who voted in Plessy v. Ferguson *(1896) to make "separate but equal" accommodations in public transit the law of the land. In 1909 he voted to absolve Sheriff Shipp of any wrongdoing in Ed Johnson's lynching. In 1915, as chief justice, he refused to consider any of 103 points of error raised by Leo Frank's attorneys in challenging his death penalty conviction. Oliver Wendell Holmes wrote a scathing dissent, joined by Justice Charles Evans Hughes: "Mob law does not become due process of law by securing the assent of a terrorized jury."*

reportedly arranged another special viewing for the Supreme Court at the request of Chief Justice Edward D. White, the former Confederate soldier and Louisiana White League member who had voted in 1909 to absolve Sheriff Shipp of any wrongdoing in Ed Johnson's lynching.

The film generated the largest attendance of any for a generation, aided no doubt by Dixon's claim that it was "federally endorsed."[31] In many cities the showings precipitated race riots. The anti-Semitism of Griffiths' movie could only have exacerbated the uphill battle that Frank's lawyers already faced in getting the Supreme Court to take a hard look at his politically charged conviction. Not surprisingly, in April of 1915, less than two months after oral argument, the Supreme Court rejected Frank's claim that he was denied his rights to a fair trial under the Fourteenth Amendment. Oliver Wendell Holmes wrote a scathing dissent, joined by Justice Charles Evans Hughes, that "mob law does not become due process of law by securing the assent of a terrorized jury."[32]

Meanwhile, popular entertainer "Fiddling John" Carson inflamed growing numbers of Georgians with "The Ballad of Mary Phagan." Carson painted Leo Frank as a villain "with brutish heart" who laughed at "Little Mary" when she begged for her life on bended knee.[33] The three-man Georgia Prison Commission was the next tribunal standing between Leo Frank and the gallows. The record compiled by Frank's counsel now included affidavits from key prosecution witnesses that their testimony had been manufactured at the insistence of the police. Dorsey countered with new affidavits retracting these confessions, hopelessly muddling the case against Frank.

Newly developed evidence further implicated Conley, including convincing signs that Phagan was killed downstairs. In a startling turn-about, Conley's own lawyer William Smith went public with a detailed analysis of the murder notes, now convinced that Conley had authored the notes himself after he committed the murder and sought to blame it on another black janitor. When Smith first showed the evidence to Dorsey, Dorsey said it was too late.

After the trial, Leo Frank's cause had been taken up by advertising pioneer Albert Lasker, who orchestrated a powerful national campaign on Frank's behalf: "The Truth Is on the March." Nearly two million

Source of both notes: https://en.wikipedia.org/wiki/Leo_Frank#/media/
File:Conley%27s_pantomime.jpg

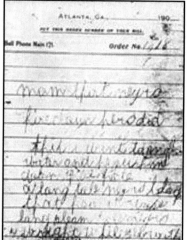

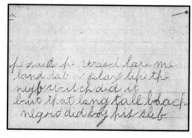

Text of note 2

he said he wood love me
land down play like the
night witch did it
but that long tall black
negro did by his slef

Text of note 1

Man that negro
hire down here did
this I went to make
water and he push me
down that hole
a long tall negro black
that hoo is wase
long sleam tall negro
it wright while play with me

Source: www.leofrank.org

The two notes introduced at Leo Frank's trial purportedly were written by murder victim Mary Phagan, blaming a long, tall Negro for her sexual assault and strangulation. Star prosecution witness Jim Conley (left), a stocky, part-time janitor testified that he wrote the notes at the direction of factory manager Leo Frank to cast blame for Phagan's death on the lanky night janitor Newt Lee. Conley was the first black man anyone had ever heard of testifying to convict a white man. A local told a surprised reporter "That wasn't a white man convicted by that Nigger's testimony. It was a Jew." Conley's own lawyer later came to believe Conley committed the murder himself and Frank was innocent.

Source: https://www.adl.org/sites/ default/files/documents/assets/ pdf/education-outreach/people-v- leo-frank-teachers-guide-the.pdf

Source: http://www.georgiaencyclopedia.org/articles/government-politics/john-m- slaton-1866-1955

Conley's lawyer, William Smith, tried to exonerate Frank after the trial, pleading with prosecutor Hugh Dorsey to reopen the case – to no avail. The ambitious prosecutor badly needed a victory after two highly publicized prosecutions in which he failed to get a conviction. Dorsey had become an instant hero after convicting Frank and won Tom Watson's endorsement for governor in 1916, serving for two terms.

Decades later, when on his death bed, William Smith scratched out on a hospital pad: IN ARTICLES OF DEATH I BELIEVE IN THE INNOCENCE AND GOOD CHARACTER OF LEO FRANK – W. M. Smith."

Gov. Slaton, like Smith, came to believe Leo Frank was not guilty. Kingmaker Tom Watson told Slaton he would support him for Senator if Slaton just let Frank's death sentence stand. Slaton's conscience would not let him do that. Instead, he wrote a 30-page decision explaining his commutation of Frank's death sentence. As a precaution, Gov. Slaton called out the National Guard to prevent angry mobs from descending on his home.

people eventually signed petitions on Frank's behalf. Unprecedented requests for commutation came from governors and legislatures of other states and prominent citizens throughout the country. Even trial judge Roan joined in the writing campaign to commute Frank's sentence. But Roan died of cancer before he could testify before the prison commission, which refused to recommend clemency by a two-to-one vote.

One option still remained. Frank's fate was placed in the hands of popular outgoing Governor Jack Slaton, who wanted to end his career with a stint in the Senate. Tom Watson made it clear to Slaton that Slaton would only get the nod for that coveted seat if Slaton did not interfere with Frank's execution. Slaton also received mountains of mail, divided between requests for clemency and letters urging him to leave the jury verdict alone. Some pointedly voiced threats that if Slaton did not let Frank hang he would face death himself.

Slaton was a law partner of Luther Rosser and thus had a conflict of interest, which the governor could have invoked to avoid making the decision and preserve his own political career. Yet Slaton harbored serious doubts about Frank's guilt and the frenzied atmosphere in which the Jewish defendant had been tried. At the urging of Lucille Frank and William Randolph Hearst, among others, the governor agreed to review the record.

Slaton was particularly intrigued by evidence that Conley had admitted to police that he defecated earlier the day of the murder on the factory's basement floor under the elevator shaft. Yet Conley insisted that, later that day, at Frank's request, Conley transported Phagan's dead body down from the second floor using the elevator. An investigative reporter pointed out after the trial that the elevator had no mechanism for stopping at the bottom except by coming to a complete rest on the basement floor. If so, it would have had to land squarely on the excrement. Police reports showed that the excrement remained untouched until they used the elevator the day after the murder. When Slaton inquired about this point at the commutation hearing, Hugh Dorsey dismissed the argument, insisting that the elevator was capable of stopping a few inches above the floor. Governor Slaton visited the crime scene to check for himself. Dorsey had misrepresented how the elevator worked. Slaton became convinced that Frank was the victim of a miscarriage of justice.

On June 20, 1915, Governor Slaton had Leo Frank secretly transferred to a state prison farm before the governor announced his decision. Slaton knew that what he was about to do could both endanger Frank's life and possibly his own. Then Slaton issued a nearly thirty-page analysis of the case, upholding the conviction but exercising gubernatorial power to commute Frank's sentence to life imprisonment. Slaton told friends at the time that he believed Frank merited a full pardon, but it would be better to wait until the situation cooled off.[34] Mobs had to be kept by state troops from storming the governor's home. Less than a week later, Slaton would face cries of "lynch him" as the outgoing governor attended his successor's inauguration.[35] Slaton and his wife quickly fled the state for a three-month vacation, hoping that would be a sufficient cooling off period.

Incensed at the commutation, Tom Watson immediately called for Frank's lynching. He told his readers point blank that clemency was bought with Jew money – one law for the rich and one for the poor: "Let no man reproach the South with Lynch law . . . let him say whether Lynch law *is not better than no law at all*. What Rosser and Slaton have together done nullifies the Code, abolishes the courts and plunges us into administrative anarchy. Shall my soul not be avenged on such a nation as this? A WONDERFUL AND HORRIBLE THING IS COMMITTED IN THE LAND."[36] Of course, the power of commutation Watson now ridiculed as lawless anarchy was the very act of clemency that Watson himself had asked Governor Hoke Smith to exercise in 1907 to save Arthur Glover. With his enemy Hoke Smith allied with Slaton and Frank's supporters, Watson could now get two for one: eye for an eye revenge for Glover's execution as well as for Mary Phagan's murder – all wrapped in the Confederate battle flag.

Former Governor Joseph Brown was then still smarting from a lost bid to unseat Hoke Smith from the Senate in 1914. In the next month, Brown acted as Watson's liaison in organizing twenty-five prominent Georgians into a lynch mob. The vigilantes included two former state supreme court justices, a sitting judge, the son of a state senator and the

Source: http://www.georgiaencyclopedia.org/articles/government-politics/john-m-slaton-1866-1955

Source: http://.com/2013/05/georgia-governor-john-briankeithohara.blogspotslaton-when-was.html

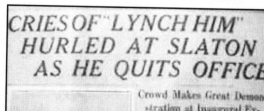

source: http://www.aboutnorthgeorgia.com/ang/Little_Secrets

Slaton mockingly hanged in effigy with sign "King of Jews." An angry crowd had to be kept in check by state troopers protecting Slaton at his successor's inauguration ceremonies. After his term expired, Gov. Slaton and his wife fled the state for their safety. The Slatons did not return to Georgia for another ten years. He resumed practicing law and ultimately served as president of the Georgia Bar Association, but never again ran for office.

Source of magazine images: http://www.georgiaencyclopedia.org/articles/history-archaeology/thomas-e-watson-1856-1922.

Georgia kingmaker Thomas E. Watson (1856–1922) published a monthly magazine and an influential newspaper, The Jeffersonian Weekly. *To incite mob revenge for the commutation of Leo Frank's death sentence, Watson told his readers that Governor Slaton's clemency was bought with Jew money. "Let no man reproach the South with Lynch law . . . let him say whether Lynch law is not better than no law at all. . . . Shall my soul not be avenged on such a nation as this? A WONDERFUL AND HORRIBLE THING IS COMMITTED IN THE LAND."*

Source: https://en.wikipedia.org/wiki/Thomas_E._Watson

Thomas Watson in 1904

Source: wikimedia.org/wiki/File:Hugh_Dorsey.jpg

With Watson's endorsement, Leo Frank's prosecutor, Hugh Dorsey, won the 1916 Georgia governor's race. After refusing to do Watson's bidding to let the state execute Frank, Jack Slaton had barely escaped with his own life in 1915.

Gov. Hugh Dorsey
circa 1917

county prosecutor, among other prominent citizens. They called themselves the "Knights of Mary Phagan." They figured that, together with
Watson, they had the political clout to engineer immunity from prosecution if they did Watson's bidding to kidnap Frank from the prison
farm and hang him. Historian Steve Oney characterized the extensive
battle plans as essentially "a rearguard action in the Civil War."[37] To the
participants it clearly was.

Just about any politician in the overwhelmingly Protestant state who
identified himself as a diehard son of the Old South could be trusted
to support this reaffirmation of enmity for Yankees in general and Jews
in particular. By now, thanks largely to Watson's relentless attacks on
Frank's character and Carson's mournful ballad, an estimated seventy-five percent of Georgians saw Frank as a monster who should die
for Phagan's murder. Key members of the legislature cooperated in
arranging a pretext for members of the lynch mob to visit the prison on
an inspection tour. It gave the conspirators ample opportunity to scout
out the premises. Given the lack of resistance they would later face, the
contingent of visitors likely informed the warden they were planning to
come back for Frank and expected only token opposition.

Before the lynch mob returned, Frank had his throat slit by another
inmate and almost died. Prompt medical care saved him. Frank had
begun to recover by the evening of August 17, 1915, when the lynch
mob carried out their mission. They cut the telephone lines and
entered the prison farm without firing a shot. They knew just where
to find Frank in a room near the warden's office. He was clad only in
a night shirt. They forced him into one of their cars and transported
him to a preselected location in Mary Phagan's hometown. The car-
avan arrived in Marietta early in the morning, by which time Frank's
kidnapping was known all over the state.

The self-appointed executioners were so proud of their role in
defending Southern womanhood that none even bothered to wear
masks. Before they strung him up, Frank impressed some of the vigilantes with his stoicism. His last request was that his lynchers deliver
to his wife a letter and his wedding ring, telling them, "I think more
of my wife and my mother than I do of my own life."[38] Then, the mob

hanged Leo Frank from a tree, slowly asphyxiating their captive with such horrible death throes that the healing knife wound on his throat reopened and bled down his shirt. He would be the only Jew in history ever recorded being lynched in the United States.

Frank's body was left twisting for a growing crowd of onlookers to gawk at his partly exposed genitals and photograph their quarry for mementoes. That morning, nearly three thousand men, women and children gathered from around Marietta and from Atlanta excited into a frenzy by what they had accomplished. In their view, they had achieved true justice for Mary Phagan in killing the murderous, perverted Yankee Jew whom the governor had wrongly spared. Some of the lynchers gave interviews to local reporters as townsmen tore off pieces of Frank's clothing for souvenirs.

One of the key planners, Judge Newt Morris, retained some sense of propriety. He convinced the revelers to let Frank's body be returned to the undertaker for burial, but only after some of the men cut Frank's body down and dragged it on the ground. One rabid attacker, Robert E. Lee Howell, repeatedly stomped on Frank's face with his boot heels. The "Knights of Mary Phagan" had deliberately left Howell out of the planning stage for fear his lack of self-control might spoil their plot.

The lynching stunned the national media and shocked citizens throughout the land. Historian Steve Oney writes that "former President William Howard Taft might well have been speaking for the country as a whole when . . . he told reporters: 'The lynching of Leo Frank was a damnable outrage. There was no excuse, no mitigating circumstances to justify the action of the Georgia mob. An action like that makes a decent man sick.'" [39] Unabashed, Watson heaped praise on the lynching in the *Jeffersonian*. Watson blamed the nation's Jews for banding together in Frank's defense. It was the fault of people like Adolph Ochs that the lynching took place – much as Tennessee politicians blamed the United States Supreme Court for Ed Johnson's murder. The local Georgia paper took a similar tack, brashly lauding the hanging as the act of law-abiding citizens.

The subsequent whitewash was easy to arrange. A conspiracy of silence enveloped the town of Marietta. Seven members of the lynch

Proud attendees posing for widely distributed photos of the lynching of Leo Frank on August 15, 1915. It was not uncommon for lynching photos in the South to be featured on postcards. Mobs had no fear of prosecution, with Protestant white supremacists holding near monopoly power. In the top lynching photo, the arrow points to one of the planners, Judge Newt Morris, on the far right wearing a straw hat. After Leo Frank slowly twisted to a painful death, his body was dragged on the ground where a particularly vengeful member, Robert E. Lee Howell, stomped on Frank's face with his boot heels. A number of the onlookers tore off parts of Frank's clothing for souvenirs. When out-of-state reporters came to investigate, a conspiracy of silence enveloped the town of Marietta. Seven members of the lynch mob were appointed to the grand jury that, for appearance's sake, had to convene to investigate the lawless act. Witnesses said they could not identify a single member of the lynch mob. The grand jury then recorded the deed as having been perpetrated by "persons unknown."

Sources of images on this page: https://www.leofrank.org/image-gallery/lynchers/https://btx3.wordpress.com/2015/08/17/lynching-not-just-black-folks

Joseph Mackey Brown (1851–1932) served two terms as Governor of Georgia, from 1909 to 1911 and from 1912 to 1913. After his death, he was named as a ringleader in Leo Frank's lynching.

"By any amoral criteria, the lynching of Leo Frank was a great success for those who incited it and for those who actually participated in it." — Alan Dershowitz

mob were appointed to the grand jury that, for appearances' sake, had to convene to investigate the lawless act. It held a perfunctory meeting in which witnesses said they could not identify a single member of the lynch mob. The grand jury then recorded the deed as having been perpetrated by persons unknown. No criminal proceedings were ever undertaken. Strangers coming to investigate from out of state were escorted out of town or met with stony silence. Federal charges against Watson for instigating the lynching were dropped following intense opposition from Georgia's Congressmen.

Not surprisingly, the anti-Semitism aroused in Atlanta and its environs resulted in extensive vandalism of Jewish stores. The Reform Jewish community retreated into scared silence, attempting to become as invisible as possible, leaving the Orthodox Jews as handier targets. This frightening display of lawless hatred prompted half the Jewish population of Georgia to flee the state. Of course, to Georgia blacks the stunned national reaction to Frank's kidnapping and death only underscored how little their own lives were valued. No similar outrage would have resulted if the case had ended abruptly at the outset with the lynching of innocent night watchman Newt Lee. He would have been just another sad casualty among hundreds of Negroes similarly dispatched in the South in the prior decade.

Among themselves, the perpetrators remained fiercely proud. Postcards of the illegal hanging would be sold in Marietta for the next two years.[40] After executing Leo Frank, the Knights of Mary Phagan regrouped as members of a renewed Ku Klux Klan. In November 1915, the Knights of Mary Phagan relaunched the KKK with a cross-burning ceremony on Stone Mountain. Plans for a confederate memorial on Stone Mountain had already been suggested a few years earlier. Sketches drawn up in 1915 by American sculptor Gutzon Borglum (who later carved Mount Rushmore) boldly proposed the world's largest bas-relief with giant images of Robert E. Lee, Stonewall Jackson and Jefferson Davis. Borglum was himself an ardent white supremicist. He originally contemplated depicting KKK figures as well.

The KKK would grow to five million nationwide in the next decade, using terror and lynching as signature tools for implementing its white racist agenda. With the local Klan's enthusiastic support, and that of its instigator Tom Watson, prosecutor Hugh Dorsey twice won election as Georgia's governor. The voters rewarded Tom Watson himself with a seat in the United States Senate taken from his old nemesis Hoke Smith. As Prof. Alan Dershowitz notes with grim irony, "By any amoral criteria, the lynching of Leo Frank was a great success for those who incited it and for those who actually participated in it."[11]

Frightened into silence, American Jews discouraged reference to the case for many years. Yet the Frank lynching generated strong interest among writers and film makers in the '20s and '30s. It also spawned two widely read historical accounts in the '60s. An inmate in a federal penitentiary later told his attorney that he had been working in the pencil factory basement on April 26, 1913, and saw Conley grappling with a girl. Afterward, Conley gave him the girl's mesh purse for a gambling debt. Attorney William Smith had planned to write a book about the trial, but never completed it. By the time Smith lay on his death bed from Lou Gehrig's Disease in February of 1949, the remorseful lawyer had lost the use of his voice. He scratched out on a hospital pad a message to his family that had been tearing at him for decades: "IN ARTICLES OF DEATH, I BELIEVE IN THE INNOCENCE AND GOOD CHARACTER OF LEO M. FRANK. W. M. Smith."[12]

Nearly four decades later, a former office boy at the pencil factory, Alonzo Mann, came forward. Then in his eighties, Mann revealed that, as a thirteen-year-old, he had seen Conley carrying the limp body of Mary Phagan on the factory's main floor – contrary to Conley's story. At Frank's trial, Mann had kept silent about what he witnessed because he and his mother both feared Conley would kill him, too. Now Mann feared going to his grave with that knowledge on his conscience. This new evidence greatly helped the Anti-Defamation League and local volunteer attorneys obtain Frank's posthumous pardon in 1986. The pardon did not address Frank's guilt or innocence; the official records had long since disappeared and the Georgia Board of Pardons felt it could no longer review the fairness of the trial. Instead, it focused on the failure of the state government to safeguard Frank's life after his conviction, as well as the injustice of its willful failure to identify Frank's lynchers publicly or hold them in any way accountable.

After a long period left half-finished, the Stone Mountain tribute to white supremacy was completed in 1972, ironically during the term of Atlanta's first Jewish mayor, Samuel Massell. The carving on Stone Mountain is now a controversial tourist attraction in a suburb 75% black.

Revived interest in the last twenty years of the century inspired new chronicles, novels and movies, including David Mamet's novel *The Old Religion* and the Broadway musical *Parade*. In 2003, journalist Steve Oney recounted the sorry details in *And the Dead Shall Rise: The Murder of Mary Phagan and the Lynching of Leo Frank*, winning the 2004 National Jewish Book Award for history and leading to Oney's collaboration the following year on a PBS reenactment of the Frank trial by award-winning documentarian Ben Loeterman. In 2008, the Jewish American Society for Historical Preservation and the Georgia Historical Society jointly engineered the placement of an official state marker near the site of the recently felled tree where Frank had been lynched. The sign explains briefly to all comers Frank's controversial trial for the murder of Mary Phagan, the anti-Semitism that fueled it, his lynching, and the posthumous pardon. The formal dedication ceremony included state officials and a local rabbi from Cobb County's revitalized Jewish community as well as several current county officials, whose predecessors were now publicly acknowledged to have been complicit in the lynching.

In June 2015, one hundred years governor Slayton commuted the death sentence of Leo Frank, an historic marker to Slaytons' heroism was dedicated at theAtlanta history center. At the ceremony, state supreme court justice David Nahmiah noted the importane of "remember(ing) those who stood tall in defense of the rule of law to inspire all of us who need to stand tall when the rule of law is again threatened, as it is in one wayor another almost every day. We need to fight for equal justice under the law, even if we do not immediately prevail." [43]

* * * * *

The virulent anti-Semitism that surrounded the Frank trial drew comparisons at the time to the infamous French Dreyfus Affair, though it ended far differently. Jewish military officer Alfred Dreyfus was framed for treason in 1894 and exiled to the Devil's Island penal colony. Dreyfus finally won exoneration in 1906 after polarizing press battles between French national security advocates and defenders of individual rights. By the time a posse of Georgian neo-Confederates hanged Leo Frank in defiance of their own governor, the focus of front-page news across country was back on France and other countries in Europe, where World War I had begun in late July of 1914. So far, the United States had remained on the sidelines.

In 1915, Woodrow Wilson campaigned for reelection on the slogan, "He kept us out of war." But, in the meantime, Wall Street bankers were heavily involved in financing the British and French, while American industrial titan U.S. Steel was supplying them with submarines and enormous quantities of ammunition. By the spring of 1917, official neutrality was no longer an option. Americans had already become incensed when the Germans sank the passenger ship the Lusitania in the spring of 1915. Germany followed up in early 1917 by having its U-boats attack every commercial U.S. ship headed across the North Atlantic. At the same time, Germany made overtures to Mexico to become its ally in order to regain land in the Southwest above the Rio Grande lost to the United States in the mid-19th century Mexican-American War.

By April of 1917, Wilson asked Congress for a declaration of war against Germany "to make the world safe for democracy." War was declared on the Austro-Hungarian empire as well by the end of 1917. A year later, after Armistice was declared, the world war was recognized as one of the deadliest in history. President Wilson called it "a war to end all wars," hoping to form an international alliance for peaceful coexistence going forward.

The year 1919 turned out instead to be a year of extraordinary domestic upheaval. Prohibition became the law of the land and Congress sent the controversial women's suffrage amendment to the states for ratification. It was also a year of record strikes, bloody racial strife and the world's deadliest flu pandemic. President Wilson spent most of the first half of 1919 in France, negotiating the Treaty of Versailles, hoping that his plan for a League of Nations would prevent another global war. By the time the World War I peace conference started, the Irish had already started a guerrilla war for independence from the British.

A month before Wilson's voyage back from France, radicals who called themselves "The Anarchist Fighters" set off bombs in seven American cities, leaving flyers warning of class war and bloodshed to "rid the world of your tyrannical institutions."[44] On the president's return, the isolationist Congress embarrassed him by refusing to ratify the treaty he had negotiated. The ailing president then crisscrossed the country by train in a doomed effort to convince the American public to support the Utopian plan that had won him the 1919 Nobel Peace Prize. In the first week of February, labor and management conflicts broke out from coast to coast, starting with the nation's first citywide general strike in Seattle.

On September 9, Boston police made history when three-quarters of the mostly Irish-American force walked off their jobs to protest unmet demands, including the right to unionize. When gangs temporarily took control of its city streets, President Wilson accused the 1,100 underpaid peace officers of "an intolerable crime against civilization."[45]

The police lost their jobs to returning soldiers. The city offered their replacements pay raises, free uniforms and more time off. Stagnating wages exacerbated by post-war inflation and outrage at corporate war profiteering had set off the strikes. Anger reached historic levels among steel workers after a Federal Trade Commission report issued in the summer of 1918 blamed the steel, oil and gas industries for acts of "inordinate greed, barefaced fraud, deceptive accounting practices and artificial price inflation."[46]

President Wilson tried to broker a deal with the intractable owners. On September 22, after the president's efforts failed, strikers shut down half the steel industry. Broken in spirit and health, back in Washington, D.C. on October 2, the president collapsed with a massive stroke – the same day that the best team in baseball appeared to be throwing the World Series.

6. THE FIX WAS IN

The Fall Guys for the Gamblers Who Rigged the 1919 World Series

"Don't be silly. It's been pulled before and it can be again."

BOSTON BOOKIE JOSEPH "SPORT" SULLIVAN REASSURING WHITESOX FIRST BASEMAN CHICK GANDIL ABOUT THE IDEA OF THROWING THE UPCOMING WORLD SERIES – SEPT. 1919[1]

The 1919 scandal took place at a time when baseball was still trying to shed its vulgar reputation – with half-hearted efforts and spotty results. In April of 1909, fans in Washington, D.C., had cheered when they recognized their three-hundred-pound, mustachioed President William Howard Taft arriving to watch the national pastime. The former sandlot catcher was the first sitting president to honor the sport with his presence. The next year, he started the tradition of throwing out a ceremonial first pitch. Enthusiasm for baseball ran in his family. Taft's half-brother Charles Phelps Taft then owned the Philadelphia Phillies and would soon buy the Chicago Cubs – the team famed for its infielders Tinker, Evers and Chance. President Taft called baseball a "clean, straight game."[2] But baseball from its inception was far from clean.

The rough-hewn teams came largely from the ranks of illiterate, hard-drinking coal miners, factory workers and farm boys. The conditions were dangerous. For decades, no one wore protective gear – no batting helmets, catchers' masks, chest protectors or shin guards. Spiking was common as were fisticuffs. In the companion book to Ken Burns' acclaimed PBS history of baseball miniseries Burns and his co-author Geoffrey Ward vividly described the cockfight-like baseball arenas of the late 19th century. In that era the Baltimore Orioles gleefully earned their reputation as "the dirtiest" team around: "They were mean, vicious, ready at any time to maim a rival player or umpire if it helped their cause."[3]

Umpires received miserable treatment from players who disputed their calls and fared even worse as disgruntled fans vented their spleens. Drunk and rowdy spectators "routinely cursed and threw things at the officials, and sometimes rushed onto the field to pummel them." On one occasion, a hapless umpire had to fend off "vicious dogs" let loose on the playing field.[1] Some umpires armed themselves for self-protection.

During the first decade of the 20th century, umpires began to command more respect, but the owners still treated the players like slaves. Once signed, the players lost control of their own destiny; the reserve clause denied them the freedom to play for any other team. They could be forced to stay with an abusive owner for their entire careers or be sold, traded or released at any time at the owner's unfettered discretion.

Yet President Taft had reason to applaud the improvements instituted by baseball's first unofficial czar, Byron Bancroft "Ban" Johnson. Johnson was almost as enormous as Taft. In his three-piece suit with his hair neatly combed, Johnson looked every bit the stern, determined businessman he was, except when he sidled up to a bar. The son of a professor, Johnson had started law school, but found himself drawn like a magnet to baseball, first as a college player and then a sports writer.

At twenty-eight, Johnson took over a low-budget minor league franchise out West and made a go of it. At the turn of the century, Johnson ambitiously renamed his franchise the American League, aiming to challenge the National League's monopoly. Johnson believed baseball could draw far more spectators if priced affordably in a setting without on-site gambling and alcohol, crude behavior and foul-mouthed fans as then characterized National League games. The *Sporting News* described major league owners as "a malodorous gang" often engaged in "mudslinging, brawling, corruption, breaches of confidence, dishonorable conspiracies [and] threats of personal violence."[5] The time was ripe for fresh leadership.

At first, National League owners refused to give Johnson an audience. Then his new American League began drawing some of the

National League fans to their games by luring away key athletes like ace pitcher Cy Young. It wasn't hard to entice star players with pay raises in 1901, when National League owners capped salaries at a relatively chintzy $2,400 a year – about $65,000 in today's dollars.[6] Still, the average worker across the country then made about $700 per year and in some cities earned only about half that.[7] The more family-oriented American League kept attracting larger crowds. After battling in the courts for two years, the two leagues declared a truce and set up a three-man National Commission to oversee owner and player disputes, minimizing public scrutiny of any internal problems. The dictatorial Johnson would domi-nate the Commission and the sport for nearly two decades.

In an era rife with corruption, Johnson's changes were largely cos-metic. No one balked at players betting on their own teams to win. Baseball executives, including Johnson, sometimes wagered on the out-comes. Chicago reporter Hugh Fullerton – then regarded as one of the best sports analysts in the country – strongly suspected fixes in at least four early World Series, though no solid proof emerged. It was also an era of exclusion. The American establishment considered white suprem-acy a given; chapters of the revived Ku Klux Klan were opening across the country. Though more than fifty blacks had endured ridicule and abuse to play on some of the early professional baseball teams, by the late 1880s white athletes increasingly threatened boycotts of integrated match-ups. Faced with overwhelming pressure, the owners made a gentlemen's agreement banning all African-Americans from organized baseball. For the next six decades, though Native Americans could play, blacks had to be light-skinned enough to pass for white or Hispanic. If their ancestry became public, owners kicked them off the team. Almost all ball players were white and overtly, and sometimes violently, racist.

Above all, it was an era of rank hypocrisy – when society's leaders championed lofty ideals as they ignored blatant double standards in the courts and on the playing field. Detroit Tigers superstar Ty Cobb was among the most notorious. What Ty Cobb got away with over his career puts the 1919 White Sox Scandal into some perspective. In April of 1907, the twenty-year-old rising star attacked a black groundskeeper at a ball field in Augusta, Georgia, who made the mistake of offering a friendly backslap. When the man's wife came to her husband's aid, Cobb tried to choke her. He didn't let the woman go until a Tiger catcher tackled him.

Two years later toward the end of the season in Cleveland, Cobb slapped an elevator operator for acting "uppity."[8] When a black night watchman intervened, Cobb wrestled him to the ground and knifed him. A little over a week before, during a game, Cobb had spiked a Philadelphia A's player in his bare hand. On owner Connie Mack's complaint that Cobb was the dirtiest player he had ever seen, Ban Johnson issued a warning to Cobb for unsportsmanlike conduct. Cobb finished the season by winning his third straight batting championship and first Triple Crown by also leading the American League in runs batted in and home runs. After the season ended, the Tigers' attorneys resolved the attempted murder charge and civil claim by having Cobb plead guilty to assault and battery, pay a $100 fine and cover the night watchman's hospital costs.

On May 15, 1912, Cobb made the mistake of allowing his explosive temper to go out of control right before Ban Johnson's eyes. Johnson came to Hilltop Park in Washington Heights to watch the Detroit Tigers finish their first series of the year against the New York Highlanders. The Highlanders looked spiffy in their new pinstripe uniforms. The following year, the team would officially become the Yankees, as they were sometimes called already. Claude Lueker was a regular Highlander fan who came to Tigers' games just to heckle Ty Cobb, then the reigning MVP. The disabled spectator sat twelve rows up behind home plate. (He had lost one hand and three fingers of the other in a printing press accident.) From Cobb's first time at bat, Lueker shouted insults, hoping, perhaps, to help the Highlanders even the series. Cobb threw insults back, but each time Cobb came to bat the heckler grew bolder. He called Cobb's mother a murderer, using ammunition available from old newspaper stories.

When Cobb was a rookie in Detroit in August of 1905, his mother had killed his father, who had sneaked home trying to surprise his wife in bed with another man. Mrs. Cobb was acquitted of murder, claiming she shot her husband in self-defense when she mistook his shadow for a burglar. Cobb looked for the Highlanders' owner to get Lueker evicted, but had no luck. In the third inning, Lueker called Cobb a "half-nigger." This time, Cobb's teammate "Wahoo" Sam Crawford pressed Cobb to retaliate. As players switched sides for the fourth inning, the misnamed "Georgia Peach" instead clambered up the stands behind home plate. Detroit manager Hughie "Eeyah" Jennings, known for his own outbursts, did nothing to stop Cobb, rationalizing that "When Ty's Southern blood is aroused, he's a bad man to handle." Cobb tackled Lueker, viciously stomping on the New York fan with his spiked shoes, even as shocked onlookers screamed that the man had no hands to defend himself.[9]

Johnson suspended Cobb pending investigation of the attack, prompting the first ever major league players' strike in defense of Cobb's reaction. His teammates claimed "no one could stand such personal abuse."[10] Each striker was fined $100; Cobb's suspension ended in eight days with a $50 fine. He remained unapologetic: "I would not take from the United States Army what that man said to me."[11] Cobb's ability to set record after record on the playing field demonstrated the raw power of unrestrained ruthlessness, mirroring the success of unregulated industrial cutthroats. Not even the fact the surly superstar packed a gun alienated his huge fan base. Only at his career's end – when evidence emerged that he once bet on a game – did a charge of misbehavior jeopardize his chances for baseball immortality. In his case, timing was everything. So it was for his rival Shoeless Joe Jackson.

The man who controlled both their destinies was a judge with the improbable name of Kenesaw Mountain Landis. American League and National League team owners got to know Judge Landis when the Theodore Roosevelt appointee presided over a major antitrust suit against them in 1914. Some wealthy businessmen formed a new Federal League and sued to get the reserve clause declared illegal to allow players to change teams. The Federal League offered pay raises and a right to free agency that attracted 81 players. Judge Landis had a reputation as a strong-minded judge. He had gained a national reputation with a whopping $29 million judgment against Standard Oil, later reversed on appeal like many of his other rulings. Critics said Judge Landis "condemned or exonerated according to whim."[12]

As it turned out, the Federal League folded while waiting for Landis to make the tough baseball call. In 1922, the Supreme Court would resolve the antitrust issue in a related case, holding that baseball was primarily local entertainment not covered by the Sherman Act – the only sport or business ever given the thumbs up to enter into agreements in restraint of trade. Baseball owners began to assume that special treatment was their due. During World War I, they drew severe criticism by seeking to exempt players from the draft as members of an essential war-time industry. Since President Wilson had played center field himself in college and remained a devoted enthusiast, they must have assumed it was worth a try.

Meanwhile, attendance sank to an all-time low. It was hard to draw fans when so many were out on the Western Front or heeded public health signs, posted all over public buildings, warning against spreading influenza. Yet throughout the summer of 1918 baseball gambling continued unabated. Cincinnati Reds star Hal Chase was so well known for padding his income with payments for thrown games that fans often shouted, "what's the odds" when he took the field.[13] But some power players were counted on to remain clean. Straight arrow pitcher turned manager Christy Mathewson gave critics hope for reform when he suspended "Prince Hal" for bribery in early August only to have their cynicism renewed when National League President John Heydler later overturned Chase's suspension.

The 1918 season ended abruptly after the War Department told all players to report for the draft or obtain war-related employment by September 1, 1918. When the boys "Over There" let it be known how much they would enjoy the World Series, the owners negotiated a special exemption for a September match-up between the teams then leading their respective leagues – the Boston Red Sox and the Chicago Cubs. Ironically, this series took place in the same arena as would the 1919 scandal. The Cubs borrowed Comiskey Park because it had nearly double the capacity of their own home field on Chicago's North Side. The million-dollar structure replaced an old South Side dump. It was dubbed "The Baseball Palace of the World" for its impressive two-story steel and concrete grandstand, free-standing roofed-pavilions and large outfield bleachers.

During the 1917 World Series, Comiskey Park had sold out; now the combination of war-time travel restrictions and the Spanish flu left nearly 13,000 seats empty. The absent fans had good reason to fear infection. An estimated 20,000 Chicagoans died in that epidemic, which killed at least fifty million people worldwide. The South Side near the stockyards was highly unsanitary, smelling of fresh animal blood, rotting carcasses and manure. Yet many genteel Cubs fans may have stayed home because they feared rowdy Sox boosters. Back in 1906, the two teams had faced each other in the first cross-town World Series. The White Sox "Hitless Wonders" had embarrassed the favored Cubs with an upset that neither set of loyal fans would ever forget.

Chicago's neighborhoods were self-segregated by race and ethnicity. Its large Jewish population lived on the West Side, Germans and Scandinavians settled to the North, Irish and blacks divided the South, and pockets of Bohemians and Poles lived closer to the middle. Built in 1910 just north of the Stockyards, Comiskey Park stood between two tough neighborhoods. To its East was a ghetto called the "Black Metropolis." To the West was Bridgeport, a rough-and-tumble district of white Catholic immigrants.

Bridgeport contained the heart of the Democratic machine that clashed with Republican Protestants, who formed the Cubs' fan base on the North Side. Diehard White Sox boosters included Bridgeport's athletic clubs, which had their own sports leagues. They also served as political clubs and enforcers of neighborhood boundaries. These glorified street gangs had names like the "Canaryville bunch," the "Hamburgs," "Ragen's Colts" and "Our Flag." Gang members might easily erupt against any Cubs' fan with a heavy German accent. The Wilson administration had recently launched a propaganda campaign demonizing the use of both written and spoken German as evidence of disloyalty.

As game one started, Red Sox ace pitcher Babe Ruth shut out the Cubs in a one-run game, scattering six hits. The heavily favored home team played lackluster defense, fostering suspicion that the Fall Classic was fixed yet again. The game's highlight came in the seventh inning stretch, when the Navy band surprised everyone by striking up Francis

Scott Key's "Defence of Fort McHenry," later renamed "The Star-Spangled Banner." Back in 1916, President Wilson had ordered the war song played at all military ceremonies. Players and spectators now doffed their hats to join in a spontaneous burst of patriotism. It was a graphic demonstration of baseball as a great equalizer, emphasizing the common bonds of a people often divided by class and ethnic differences. The band struck up the song again in each remaining game. It became the official national anthem in 1931; by World War II, the song led off all games.

By the time the Series ended in Boston, the Red Sox had scored only nine runs in six games, the fewest ever for a winning World Series team. The Red Sox had help from five Cubs' fielding errors and a slew of base-running mistakes. Rumors circulated, but no official investigation took place. Later, two Cubs and one Red Sox player in that Series were banned from baseball for fixing other games. The stage was now set for the 1919 fiasco.

Back in 1918, national attention focused on the war. By the summer of 1919, baseball's fan base had returned, but the air crackled with new tension, particularly on Chicago's South Side. Since 1910, the Illinois metropolis had experienced a "Great Migration" of blacks fleeing persecution in the South. African-American publisher Robert Abbott's widely circulated *Chicago Defender* encouraged the newcomers with glowing descriptions of job opportunities in the Windy City. By the end of World War I, the "Black Belt" could no longer hold all the newly arriving families, who then began to encroach on neighboring white districts.

When local veterans returned from overseas, they found many thousands of black co-workers at the stockyards and meat packing plants. Owners had fanned racial tension in recent years by hiring blacks as strikebreakers. Chicago's leading dailies inflamed their readers even more by exaggerating the rates of crime and disease in the black community. Politics added to the growing difficulties. Republican Mayor Big Bill Thompson, who would go down in history as one of the country's most corrupt mayors, had just been reelected in February of 1919, by a combination of German-American supporters and his lock on the black vote. That loss prompted ugly revenge.

On the evening of June 21, 1919, police found two badly beaten black corpses on Chicago's South Side. The likely suspects were not arrested. A Bridgeport gang egged on by its sponsor, Democratic Alderman Big Joe McDonough, was trying to start a race riot and then "exploit the chaos."[14] The object was to drive colored families from the city and win back control of the mayor's office. The temperature hit 96 degrees on Sunday, July 27, 1919, drawing many Chicagoans to the lakefront. Whites threw stones at blacks encroaching on the 29th Street beach on Chicago's South Side, which was unofficially segregated. One rock hit Eugene Williams, a black seventeen-year-old who had drifted into the area on a rubber raft. Williams fell into the water and drowned.

Soon full-scale riots erupted – the worst racial violence the city had ever seen. The Bridgeport gangs attacked blacks in mixed neighborhoods. They burned houses, beat pedestrians and perpetrated the first drive-by shootings recorded by Chicago police. They blocked streets to stop fire trucks from dousing the blazes. In the Loop, whites pulled colored workers off trolleys and beat them. Some blacks defended their homes with guns, fought back in the streets or attacked whites in mostly black neighborhoods. Locals blamed blacks for torching several blocks of Lithuanian homes, leaving 950 homeless. It took 6,000 National Guardsmen to restore order.

By August 3, when the violence ended, 38 men and boys were dead, including 23 blacks and 15 whites. Over 500 were injured, of whom two-thirds were black. Yet most men arrested were black and only blacks were indicted for murder. Many black families fled the area to return to the South. In 1922, the chief of police admitted to a grand jury that his officers "shut their eyes to offenses committed by white men while they were very vigorous in getting all the colored men they could get." By then, the fire department had concluded that blacks had not committed the devastating arson. The grand jury assumed that white gangs started the fire to incite "race feeling by blaming same on the blacks."[15]

Similar incidents of beatings, torture, lynching and arson occurred across the country during that "Red Summer" of 1919, which history recorded as "the greatest period of interracial strife the nation had ever witnessed."[16] But the violence in Chicago was the worst of all. A formal

commission report in 1922 blamed the Irish Hamburg Athletic Club
of Bridgeport for instigating the mayhem. Its active members included
seventeen-year-old future Democratic Mayor Richard Daley.

With powerful Alderman Big Joe McDonough as his mentor, Daley
would rise to become the club's president in 1924. In 1968, as the last
of the old-time big city bosses, Daley oversaw the Chicago police, whose
heavy-handed treatment of anti-war demonstrators, reporters and
bystanders during the Democratic Convention became etched into
American history as one of that violence-marked year's most indelible
images. When the neighborhood of Comiskey Park erupted in carnage
on the night of July 27, 1919, the White Sox had just finished a home
stand and were headed to New York on a long road trip. By the time
they returned to their Chicago field on August 14, relative calm had
been restored to the battered community.

The team had its own problems with internal feuds and simmering
resentment of owner Charles "The Old Roman" Comiskey for his impe-
rious ways and miserly attitude. The Chicago native was the son of an
Irish ward boss in Holy Family Parish. For several years, Comiskey was a
first baseman on the St. Louis Browns, the club that became notorious
as "a saloon with a baseball attachment."[17] Comiskey had fit right in
with the gutter-mouthed crowd. Later as an owner, Comiskey proved a
master at public relations. He especially endeared himself to his base
in South Chicago by building the majestic White Sox arena. Comiskey
also made sure to treat the traveling press like royalty, while stinting
players on fringe benefits.

The only gladiator paid handsomely was pitcher Eddie Collins,
whom his teammates widely despised. Unhappiness on the team did
not interfere with its playing success. It won the 1919 American League
pennant, fielding the almost identical team that had won the 1917
World Series. Its poor finish in 1918 was chalked up to a number of
key players having enlisted or taken war-related jobs. With Shoeless Joe
Jackson back, the Sox were heavily favored to win.

The two-hundred-pound, six-foot-one superstar had just turned thirty-one and was in his eleventh year in the majors. A native of Pickings,
South Carolina, Jackson had worked in the mills as a child and had

little formal education; he never even learned to read. But Jackson had played organized ball since he was thirteen and gained fame as the best natural hitter ever. He picked up his nickname in the minors when he batted in his socks because of a blister from new shoes. "Shoeless" Joe stuck because the big-eared Southerner with the boyish grin never lost his country boy naïveté. By 1919, millions of boys idolized Joe. Babe Ruth claimed he modeled his own batting technique after the White Sox outfielder, who hit .408 the season Ruth turned sixteen.

Shoeless Joe had no idea that 1919 would end his extraordinary career in ignominy. Sports reporters became suspicious when they noticed unusual betting patterns leading up to the nine-game 1919 series, lengthened to increase revenues as the fan base returned. Hugh Fullerton even warned his readers ahead of time not to bet on any games. More eyebrows rose when White Sox starting pitcher Eddie Cicotte, who had won a phenomenal 29 games during the season, hit the lead-off Cincinnati batter in the back. The favored Sox lost the first game nine to one. The catcher was not in on the fix and cursed out Cicotte for shaking off so many signs. Manager Kid Gleason was furious. Shoeless Joe Jackson had come to Comiskey before the Series started, begging to be benched, but Comiskey refused.

Comiskey raised the obvious signs of a fix with Ban Johnson the night after the second game, but Johnson brusquely dismissed any concerns. Once friends, the strong-willed pair had often locked horns over the last fourteen years and no longer respected each other. By game five, with the Reds up three games to one, Fullerton reported "more ugly talk and more suspicion among the fans then there ever has been in any World Series. The rumors of crookedness, of fixed games and plots, are thick."[18] By now, the White Sox conspirators doubted they would get their promised payments. The team rallied and won games six and seven, bringing the Series to four and three. Then, the game eight pitcher, Lefty Williams, received a late night visit from a Chicago gangster who threatened to kill him and his wife. The next day, Williams yielded three runs in the first inning before the manager pulled him out.

The Series ended with the White Sox committing a total of twelve errors, helping Cincinnati clinch its fifth win in eight games. After the game, Comiskey consulted with his corporate lawyer, Alfred Austrian, who advised Comiskey to hire a detective to collect evidence. Comiskey also held up on paying the suspected players their World Series bonuses and instructed the private eye to gather dirt on other teams as leverage against his own ouster from baseball should a scandal erupt. Without revealing what he already knew, Comiskey then met with his muck-raking friend Hugh Fullerton and suggested that the two pool any incriminating information they found before going public with it. Comiskey convinced Fullerton that his pal Commy was as interested in cleaning up baseball as Fullerton was.

Late in the Series, Shoeless Joe Jackson had tried once more to talk to Comiskey, but the owner remained unavailable. Afterward, the Old Roman made a show of publicly defending his players' honesty and offered a $20,000 reward for anyone with information to the contrary. Comiskey later reneged on the offer – even when Jackson's wife sent him a letter describing some of the sordid details.

While Comiskey dreaded exposure of his players' misconduct, he had cause to worry about his own reputation. In 1917, the owner reportedly authorized gratitude payments to the Detroit Tigers for letting the White Sox steal bases at will in a key series when the White Sox faced a tough pennant race with the Boston Red Sox.[19] That winter following the Series, Hugh Fullerton published an exposé of the unholy relationship between gamblers and ball players and urged that Judge Landis be appointed to investigate the corruption. Fullerton predicted that there would be no more World Series contests if the gambling problem remained unaddressed. Millionaire New York vice kingpin Arnold "the Brain" Rothstein reputedly bankrolled the 1919 scheme. (Rothstein, recently featured in the HBO series *Boardwalk Empire*, was also the real-life model for Nathan Detroit in "Guys and Dolls" and Meyer Wolfsheim in *The Great Gatsby*.) The *Sporting News* backed up the owners' denial of any wrongdoing and attributed the dark rumors to "dirty, long-nosed, thick-lipped" immigrant Jewish gamblers trying to subvert the American pastime.[20]

By July of 1920, White Sox manager Kid Gleason privately confirmed his own suspicions. The following month ushered in the worst days in the history of the dead ball era. On August 20, Yankee pitcher Carl Mays killed a Cleveland Indians batter with a blackened spitball – leading to a ban on the common practice of altering baseballs with foreign substances (heralding a new era dominated by home runs). A week and a half later, Cubs owner Bill Veeck hired the famous Burns Detective Agency to check out rumors his players had just conspired with gamblers to throw a home game against the last place Philadelphia Phillies.

After the story hit the headlines, state attorney Maclay Hoyne convened a Cook County grand jury. When a player mentioned that the White Sox had thrown the 1919 Series, the inquiry shifted to a far bigger target. Days later, a small-time gambler publicly claimed he'd been double-crossed after the first two games of the 1919 Series were fixed for $100,000. The scandal exploded. Pitcher Cicotte, and then Jackson, told Comiskey about the fix. He referred the two players to Austrian to prepare them to testify before the grand jury. Austrian assured the two everything would work out if they just signed immunity waivers and statements implicating themselves and the six other players. They followed his advice, with no clue about Austrian's hidden agenda to protect Comiskey.[21]

Arnold Rothstein also volunteered to testify before the grand jury. He arrived with his own lawyer and in his customary natty dress. The race-track and casino kingpin was no stranger to baseball's elite; he had several baseball executives among his wealthy clientele. Though rumor had it that Rothstein had sent the enforcer who threatened Lefty Williams, Rothstein adamantly denied any part in the scheme, claiming low level bookies had used his name without his say so. In fact, Rothstein had profited quite nicely from more than a quarter of a million dollars in bets placed on the Reds through intermediaries.[22] Rothstein emerged from the grand jury unscathed. Austrian proclaimed that the wealthy gangster "had proved himself guiltless."[23] (Seven years later Rothstein was shot to death reportedly over a gambling debt. Rothstein's records then revealed that he had indeed financed the World Series fix.)

The Cook County grand jury indicted ten professional gamblers and all eight players, who faced up to five years in jail and a fine of

Source: Library of Congress, http://chroniclingamerica.loc.gov/lccn83030193/1920-09-28/ed-1/seq-1/n/

EIGHT WHITE SOX PLAYERS ARE INDICTED
IRISH RIOTERS DISPERSED BY BAYONETS
NEW RENT LAWS ARE NOW IN FULL FORCE

The Evening World.

FINAL EDITION

STOP 100,000 EVICTIONS; NEW RENT LAWS, SIGNED BY GOVERNOR, NOW IN FORCE

FIREMAN INDICTED FOR SETTING FIRE TO SEVEN HOMES

"WIFE COMES FIRST; SHE IS HOME BOSS," WAS HUBBY'S CREED

EXTRA
GRAND JURY INDICTS EIGHT WHITE SOX IN INQUIRY INTO CHARGE OF "FIXING" GAMES

YOUTH IS CHOKED TO DEATH WORKING EXERCISE MACHINE

BELFAST RIOTING RENEWED; BAYONETS USED BY TROOPS; SINN FEIN HOMES BURNED

M'SWINEY BETTER ON HIS 47TH DAY, BUT IS VERY WEAK

The Evening World, *Sept. 28, 1920, Wall St. Final Edition*
As Ireland revolts against British rule, the top story in U.S. is the White Sox scandal.

Source: http://www.history.com/news/the-black-sox-baseball-scandal-95-years-ago

The Sporting News, *October 7, 1920*
"Eight Men Charged with Selling Out Baseball"

$10,000 each for accepting bribes to defraud the public. The fore-man noted the grave symbolism of the crime: "Baseball is more than a national game, it is an American institution, [our great teacher of] respect for proper authority, self-confidence, fair-mindedness, quick judgment and self-control."[24] That day, Comiskey suspended all seven players still on his team, pending the outcome of the criminal case, with the promise that they would be reinstated if acquitted. It was three days before the season ended; the White Sox were tied with the Cleveland Indians for first place in the American League. The suspen-sions handed the Indians the pennant. A stunned headline captured the White Sox fans' dashed faith: "Say It Ain't So, Joe." They needed to believe their hero played for the love of the game; that their idol was as irreproachable as their sainted mothers. Some heartbroken boys in the neighborhood boycotted baseball for years.

The shocking story ranked as the most serious scandal in sports his-tory, until the century ended with a mammoth steroid scandal which cul-minated in over eighty baseball players being named as abusers. What the public did not learn for almost another ninety years after the 1919 World Series scandal broke is that Cicotte's sworn testimony before the grand jury in September of 1920 included the claim that he and several other White Sox players came up with the idea to throw the 1919 Series from seeing the Cubs get away with fixing the Series the year before.[25]

Later that fall of 1920, as a cloud of corruption threatened base-ball, the owners worried most about the future of self-regulation. They realized that posting signs outlawing gambling in their parks and eject-ing known bookies hadn't worked to restore their credibility. Yet, with Babe Ruth whacking a record-smashing 54 homeruns, the 1920 season had drawn unprecedented crowds. Over Ban Johnson's strong objec-tions, the desperate owners hit upon a new plan for damage control. They voted to accept an investor's proposal to replace the National Commission with a body of outsiders to oversee the sport and repair its tattered reputation. For members of this august new body, the owners flirted with asking luminaries like former President Taft and General Pershing of World War I fame. But one of the first people they spoke with was fifty-four-year-old Judge Kenesaw Mountain Landis.

The white-haired jurist seemed typecast for the role and already had muck-raking journalist Hugh Fullerton's endorsement. A long-time fan of the game, Landis had been sickened by its association with gamblers and fixers. He made a counterproposal: he would accept a lifetime appointment if the owners empowered him as the sole com-missioner, retained no right of appeal and waived access to the courts. Only these conditions would guarantee his independence. Though Landis had a reputation as a reformer, the owners remembered his hands-off approach to the antitrust suit that fizzled three years before and acceded to the free rein the bantam-weight, five-foot-seven-inch judge demanded.

Landis later told an interviewer that he took up the challenge with his own son in mind: "Baseball is something more than a game to an American boy; it is his training field for life work. Destroy his faith in its squareness and honesty and you have destroyed something more; you have planted suspicion of all things in his heart."[26] After the owners acquiesced to his terms, the sitting federal judge moonlighted as the first Commissioner of Baseball. He would endure a year of severe crit-icism for taking on this mammoth private job while still serving on the federal bench. Only when several members of Congress moved for his impeachment did Landis retire from his judgeship.[27]

Before trial, Jackson recanted the confession that Austrian had tricked him into giving. He claimed that he had only accepted $5,000 thrust upon him after the Series was over, but had not conspired with the others and did not participate in the fix.[28] Comiskey risked becoming embroiled in the scandal. He paid top dollar for the players' criminal defense counsel. By the time of their 1921 trial, Jackson's and Cicotte's damning grand jury testimony somehow went missing from the court records. Ban Johnson accused Arnold Rothstein of orchestrating the theft. (Years later, the records turned up in Austrian's office.)[29] The trial proceeded against seven of the eight players originally accused of the fix. All seven looked out of their element dressed up in suits and ties.

It took two weeks to select a jury from a panel of 600 men. Almost all jurors chosen were in their twenties or early thirties. Cicotte and Johnson and one other player who had signed a confession never took the stand; the other four players denied any criminal conduct. The judge instructed the jury that it was not enough to prove that games had been thrown. There had to be evidence of a conspiracy against the public. The sympathetic jury acquitted both the players and the accused gamblers. Some jurors even hoisted the Sox players on their shoulders as spectators tossed their hats and threw confetti in the air. The gleeful players partied much of the night, anticipating that their suspension would be lifted. As usual, Jackson waited for others to order first so he could ask for the same plate as one of his friends and not expose his inability to read the menu.

The celebration turned out to be premature. The real impact came the next day when Landis, just a fortnight after taking office, established himself as a merciless guardian of the sport's purity – at least when it came to game-fixing. As a judge, Landis had already sent legendary black boxer Jack Johnson to Leavenworth for taking a white "sporting girl" across state lines for immoral purposes. (In 2009, Congress passed a resolution calling for Johnson's posthumous pardon that President Obama declined to act upon.)

As commissioner, Landis would never crack down on whoring and illegal boozing at speakeasies by married white players like the Yankees' notorious new "Sultan of Swat" Babe Ruth. Yet, with a missionary's zeal, the commissioner's first act banned all eight accused White Sox players, including Joe Jackson, from the major leagues for life. As a warning to all current players, Landis issued this stiff pronouncement: "Regardless of the verdict of juries, no player who throws a ball game, no player who undertakes or promises to throw a ball game, no player who sits in confidence with a bunch of crooked gamblers and does not promptly tell his club about it, will ever play professional baseball."[30]

The Draconian decision was less dramatic than it appeared. By the time Landis made his move, the owners had already ostracized all eight players. Comiskey had fired them in the spring. Landis had held no hearing and ignored individual pleas for reconsideration. Historians Robert Grant and Joseph Katz note that there was precedent for a lifetime ban in the rare instance fixing had been found but none "for lesser offenses, for agreeing to throw a game and then double-crossing the conspirators

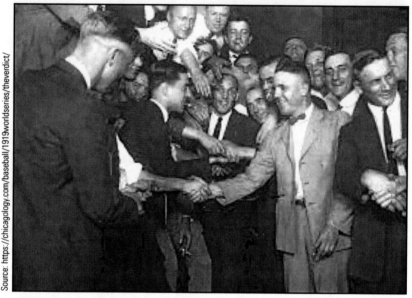

Source: https://chicagology.com/baseball/1919worldseries/theverdict/

August 1921 — It took just one ballot for the jury to vote to acquit the White Sox players and shake their hands.

Source: wikiwand.com/en/
Commissioner_of_Baseball

*The following month the eight players were banned from baseball for life by its first commissioner, Kenesaw Mountain Landis (**left**). Landis aimed to restore faith in "the squareness and honesty" of baseball after years of suspicious player conduct in key games. Yet the gambler who financed the fixing of the 1919 World Series, Arnold Rothstein, was exonerated. Ty Cobb, later accused of conspiring to throw a different game in 1919, received far less scrutiny. He wound up in the first batch of inductees to the National Baseball Hall of Fame.*

by playing honestly, or for keeping silent about a known fix."[31] Nor was Landis inclined to create any such distinctions on his own.

In 1924, Jackson sued Comiskey for payments due under his five-year contract and won a substantial jury verdict, only to see the judge overturn the award when Austrian magically produced Jackson's confession to participating in the 1919 fix. Austrian unethically used the stolen court document to protect Comiskey against the very person who relied on Austrian's advice to sign it in the first place. Though Jackson admitted to keeping $5,000 offered him after the fix went down, sports historians still debate the extent of his involvement.

In *Eight Men Out*, Eliot Asinof blames all eight players equally for conspiring with gamblers to fix the Series, but asserts that Comiskey set the stage by being such a skinflint. Jackson, regardless of his superstar status, only made $6,000 in 1919 while players on other teams earned as much as $10,000. Asinof's conclusions have since been disputed.[32] In *Say It Ain't So Joe! The True Story of Shoeless Joe Jackson*, author Donald Gropman argues that the South Carolinian was the only accused player who did not join in teammates' efforts to throw the series. Though his fielding was somewhat sluggish, Jackson had not committed any official errors and no one could deny his performance at the plate, wielding "Black Betsy" to bat an impressive .375 for the series.

Connie Mack, long-time owner of the Philadelphia Athletics, where Jackson started his major league career, called Jackson's fate "one of the real tragedies of baseball. I always thought he was more sinned against than sinning."[33] Commissioner Happy Chandler, who succeeded Landis as the second official czar of baseball, issued a far stronger statement: "I never in my life believed him to be guilty of a single thing."[34] Harvard professor and baseball fan Alan Dershowitz contends that "The real villain was Charles Comiskey. It was he who abused the game for money" and callously used his political power to sacrifice Jackson's career to protect his own reputation.[35] While Landis did get Comiskey to pay his players better wages, Landis never faulted "The Old Roman" for his cover-up, leaving Comiskey eligible for the Hall of Fame.

Looking back, most baseball insiders praise Landis for preserving public faith in America's most cherished game by his swift, punitive action against the eight Chicago White Sox players. Landis later ousted many other players of "undesirable reputation and character" who tarnished the game's image by throwing games or by hanging out with gamblers, including the infamous "Prince Hal" Chase. In 1943, Landis even tossed Phillies owner William D. Cox out of baseball after Cox admitted betting on his team. But Landis clearly played favorites. Aside from giving Comiskey a free pass in 1920, he let three Giants stars finish the season four years later while banning two lesser teammates for life for a bribery scheme to clinch the tight pennant race against the Dodgers. Ban Johnson blasted Landis for allowing the Giants to cheat their way into the World Series, which the Giants won.[36]

Landis showed his double standards again two years later when Ty Cobb was once more at the center of controversy. In 1926, Ty Cobb, as manager of the Tigers, mistreated Detroit pitcher Dutch Leonard. In retaliation, Leonard confessed to Commissioner Landis that he and Cobb had conspired with two Cleveland Indians players back in 1919 to have the Indians throw a late season game to Detroit, after which they bet heavily on Detroit to win. Just before the scandalous story surfaced, Cobb suddenly retired. By then, he had become a millionaire pitchman and investor in Coca Cola. Cobb disputed the charges and claimed that in his 22 years of baseball he had never been guilty of any "dishonorable thought or act." Congressmen, industrialists and judges wrote letters of support, lauding Cobb's honesty and integrity and long "record in baseball . . . without a blemish."[37]

Over the strenuous objections of American League President Ban Johnson – their second battle royal – Landis chose to ignore evidence implicating the superstar. Instead, Landis exonerated him with language supplied by Cobb's lawyers and convinced the owners to force Johnson out for criticizing Landis's leniency.[38]

Landis had started out aspiring to clean the game up to give Little Leaguers role models for life. But he employed selective whitewashes where he felt the truth would demoralize the public. President of the International Baseball Federation Dr. Robert Smith noted that Landis never was willing "to dig much more deeply than a finger's length into any baseball scandal." Baseball writer Glenn Stout compared Landis to a seamstress afraid to pull out a loose string because the whole garment might unravel.[39]

Ty Cobb's case showed just how far Landis fell short of his own lofty goal. Cobb biographer Don Rhodes laid bare the ugly side of the man who set ninety baseball records: "His legendary temper wasn't limited to the baseball field: at home he would beat his wife and children." His oldest daughter considered him a psychopathic Southern version of Dr. Jekyll and Mr. Hyde, claiming, "I never spent five seconds with that man that I wasn't scared pea green."[40]

Once Landis swept aside the game-fixing allegations against the superstar, it paved the way for Cobb to take his place among the first five men inducted into Baseball's Hall of Fame in 1936 – with more votes than anyone else. Meanwhile, Josh Gibson, the undisputed home run king of the Negro Leagues, wound up bashing far more round-trippers than Hall-of-Famer Babe Ruth and had a better slugging percentage than Ty Cobb. He and strikeout phenomenon Satchel Paige humiliated Dizzy Dean's Major League All-Stars of 1934 in a winter exhibition game. Hall-of-Fame pitcher Walter Johnson later said it was "too bad" Gibson wasn't white. "He can do everything."[41] In 1937, Cum Posey, co-owner of the Homestead Grays Gibson played for, claimed that Gibson was "the best ballplayer, white or colored, that we have seen in all our years of following baseball."[42] Unfortunately, the "Black Babe Ruth" never got the chance to compete in "the Bigs."

On December 3, 1943, sports writers were abuzz as they covered the annual meeting of baseball owners and general managers of all sixteen major league clubs at the Hotel Roosevelt in New York. It included an historic meeting with African-American publishers, who had chosen as their spokesman Broadway star and political activist Paul Robeson. The extraordinarily versatile singer/actor had been a former All-American football player at Rutgers University, where he graduated first in his class. Robeson had followed that up with a law degree from Columbia University, where the ambitious son of a slave helped pay his tuition by playing professional football.

Commissioner Landis effusively presented the six-foot-two Renaissance man to the gathering as a man who needed no introduction:

"Everybody knows him or what he's done as an athlete and an artist. I want to introduce him to you as a man of great common sense." Then Landis prefaced Robeson's comments with his own assurance to their black visitors: "I want to make it clear that there is not, never has been, and, as long as I am connected with baseball, there never will be any agreement among the teams or between any two teams, preventing Negroes from participating in organized baseball. Each manager is free to choose players regardless of race, color or any other condition."[43]

Robeson had just opened at the Shubert two months earlier to rave reviews as the first black man to play the Moor Othello in an American production of Shakespeare's tragedy. He told the gathering of baseball's management that his exceptionally enthusiastic reception by largely white audiences made him realize "the time has come that you must change your attitude toward Negroes and keep it consistent with the attitude of the entire country." The two-hundred-pound former athlete had experienced a number of death threats, but claimed they dropped off when he proved himself. He recalled his playing days at Rutgers when Southern teams warned they would cancel games if he was in the lineup. That was just bluster. "I can understand the owners' fears that there would be trouble if Negroes were to play in the big leagues, but my football experience showed me such fears are groundless. Because baseball is a national game, it is up to baseball to see that discrimination does not become the American pattern."[44]

With the country engaged in another world war to defend its democratic ideals, Robeson urged the owners to let players in "this very season" reflect "the best in the American spirit."[45] After the meeting, Robeson directly challenged Commissioner Landis: if there was no barrier, why were there no Negroes in baseball, as there were in all other professional sports? Landis claimed there was no prohibition, just the owners' free choice.[46] Landis' successor, Happy Chandler, unmasked Landis as a liar. Chandler read through Landis's files and reported that "for twenty-four years Landis consistently blocked any attempts to put blacks and whites together on a big league field."[47] Yet most owners felt the same way.

Newspaper editors had early on noted the absurdity of baseball's standards that excluded all blacks while allowing white "men of low birth and poor breeding" to become "the idols of the rich and cultured," with rosters including many "men of churlish disposition and coarse habits." One suggested that the owners instead "make character and personal habits the test. Weed out the toughs and intemperate men first" before drawing a color line.[48] Landis was deaf to such pleas; it was no coincidence that the Brooklyn Dodgers hired the first black player in the modern era a year after Landis died.

In retrospect, today's society rejects Landis' system of values that tolerated racist brutes and adulterous sots while excluding all African-Americans, for the "purity" of the game. Yet he was right about one thing. Destroy faith in the "squareness and honesty" of baseball and you may have "planted suspicion of all things" in the hearts and minds of the American people. Certainly, the year 1919 had put faith in law and order to the test. Even scientific truth turned topsy-turvy when, late in the year, confirmation of Einstein's theory of relativity, challenging Newton's long-accepted theory of the universe, made startling headlines. In the first two decades of the 20th century and for many years to come, on the field and in the courts, the rich and powerful wrote the rules of the game – a built-in thumb on the scales of our democracy that critics see reenergized since the United States Supreme Court decided the controversial Citizens United case in 2010 in favor of unlimited corporate contributions to political campaigns.

The landslide election in 1920 of Warren Harding illustrates how power brokers operated a hundred years ago. From a smoke-filled Chicago hotel room at the June 1920 Republican Convention, the handsome dark-horse candidate emerged as the Party's tenth round choice for two essential attributes: his willingness to do the bidding of financiers and industrialists and his likely appeal to new women voters. Only after his nomination did Harding confess to Party insiders a long-time adulterous relationship with a married lover that the Party reportedly then covered up with hush money.[19] In the first modern campaign with a media blitz and Hollywood movie stars, the Republicans capitalized on Wilson's unpopularity to crush Democrat James Cox by promising war-weary Americans a "return to normalcy." (In *They Also Ran* author Irving Stone made the case that on every objective measure Cox was the far superior candidate.)

Meanwhile, New York's politically savvy Arnold Rothstein was among the first gangsters to recognize the golden opportunity Prohibition presented. When he established his bootleg empire, Rothstein hired the son of new Attorney General Harry Daugherty as insurance. Historian Rich Cohen likened the gambling kingpin to society's more traditional robber barons of his day. The key players all appreciated "the truths of early century capitalism" – "hypocrisy, exclusion [and] greed."[50] Often, before play started "the fix" was in. Judges appointed through their ties to politicians applied stiff penalties to scapegoats or outcasts and carved unwritten exceptions for those with connections.

At the same time the 1919 White Sox team members faced trial in Illinois, two men were on trial for their lives in Massachusetts in another headline case that would start to have people around the world question whether the "fix" was in. Like the Leo Frank case, this new politically charged case would be compared to the infamous French Dreyfus Affair. This time it involved a robbery murder committed in April 1920 in the small town of South Braintree, Massachusetts. The trial of Ferdinando Nicola Sacco and Bartolomeo Vanzetti would become more deeply embedded in the American psyche as a miscarriage of justice than probably any other case in the country's history.

7. THE LEGAL LYNCHING OF SACCO AND VANZETTI

A Biased Judicial System Gives American Justice an International Black Eye

The time was on for two men
To march beyond blood into dust,
A time that comes to all men,
Some with a few loved ones at a bedside,
Some alone in the wilderness or the wide sea,
Some before a vast audience of all mankind.

— CARL SANDBURG, EXCERPT FROM "LEGAL MIDNIGHT HOUR"[1]

During War I, Galleanists rivaled Big Bill Haywood and the IWW for designation as the country's most dangerous internal threat. Some radicals had ties to both militant groups. Of 25 million immigrants who had made the United States their new home between 1860 and 1920 many remained resident aliens. Others, derisively called "hyphenated-Americans," either held dual citizenship or were naturalized citizens with strong ties to their native land and culture. Luigi Galleani was a resident alien. The Italian-born anarchist was already infamous in 1902 when he arrived in the United States at age forty-one. Galleani then made a beeline for the same community of Italian exiles in Paterson, New Jersey, from which Italian King Umberto's assassin, Gaetano Bresci, had emerged two years before. A government mole later infiltrated the radical cell and learned that several other world leaders were targeted by the Paterson group with would-be assassins.

Accused of inciting violence, Galleani soon fled to Canada. He resettled first in Vermont, among poor Italian marble cutters, and then in a similar immigrant community in Lowell, Massachusetts. From his base in these counterculture ghettos, Galleani traveled a lecture circuit to promote his revolutionary ideas of free love, atheism and the overthrow of capitalism. His speeches met with great enthusiasm from Italian émigrés suffering from social ostracism and oppressive working conditions. Galleani published a widely read newsletter – *Cronaca Sovversiva* (Subversive Chronicle) – that advocated his revolutionary agenda. For an additional 25 cents, Galleani offered thousands of subscribers a revised version of the same how-to-bomb manual that had circulated in Chicago shortly before the 1886 deadly dynamiting in Haymarket Square – only now German anarchist Johann Most's "The Science of Revolutionary Warfare" went by the innocent title (in Galleani's Italian translation) *La Salute è in voi* (Health Is in You).

Starting in 1914, Galleani's followers – like the Weathermen more than half a century later – claimed credit for planting bombs in a number of American cities. In 1915, police dramatically announced they had foiled a plot to blow up New York's St. Patrick's Cathedral by infiltrating another cell of Italian anarchists, one of whom reportedly had in his home a copy of the bombing manual. In that case, the undercover agent had helped assemble the bomb and plan the audacious attack that sent his accomplices to prison.

In 1916, an Italian chef in Chicago, who counted himself among the Galleanists, tried to poison with arsenic an entire banquet room gathered to honor Chicago's newly appointed archbishop. Other Galleanists exploded a bomb in a Boston police station; still more were suspected of planting a time bomb in San Francisco on July 22, 1916, at a parade in honor of Preparedness Day organized to build support for America's entrance into World War I. The bomb killed ten people and wounded forty more – the worst incident of violence San Francisco had ever seen. Prosecutors pinned it on labor leader Tom Mooney in a trial that drew widespread international criticism. Mooney won an eventual pardon based on evidence he had been framed.

In his much-quoted "Unification Speech," given on July 4, 1917

– three months after Congress declared war on Germany – former President Teddy Roosevelt emphatically rejected hyphenated-Americans and conscientious objectors as unpatriotic: "There can be no 50-50 Americanism in this country. There is room here for only 100 percent Americanism, only for those who are Americans and nothing else."[2] That same year many Galleanists fled to Mexico to evade the draft and await European revolution. The group included resident aliens Ferdinando Nicola Sacco and Bartolomeo Vanzetti, who had barely known each other previously. When no widespread uprisings occurred, most of them returned to the United States. Bombings resumed in Milwaukee, Wisconsin, New York City, San Francisco, Washington, D.C. and Boston, but no criminal prosecutions resulted.

The public demanded action and Congress echoed their outrage. In 1918, government agents forcibly shut down *Cronaca Sovversiva* and confiscated its mailing list. Congress passed the Anarchist Exclusion Act and Galleanists responded with anonymous threats to annihilate the ruling class "in blood and fire."[3] A series of new bomb attacks followed, including one in February 1919 that exploded too soon and killed four bombers trying to destroy a textile mill in Franklin, Massachusetts. The bombing came as labor and management conflicts erupted from coast to coast, starting with the nation's first citywide general strike in Seattle. Stagnating wages exacerbated by post-war inflation and outrage at corporate war profiteering had set off the strikes.

In late April of 1919, thirty neatly packaged bombs were addressed to political leaders, judges and prominent businessmen across the nation. The intent was to set off a gruesome fireworks display to celebrate the international workers' holiday of May Day, the anniversary of the original deadline set for achieving the eight-hour work day. Lacking sufficient postage, most of the packages were discovered by mailmen before the bombs detonated. Some injuries resulted, but no deaths. In early June, eight more bombs exploded in the homes of political officials in seven cities, causing three deaths, including one anarchist with close ties to Galleani.

At several sites investigators found a flyer, signed "The Anarchist Fighters," threatening bloody class war. The bold June 1919 attack partially destroyed Attorney General Palmer's Washington, D.C., home. Palmer immediately embarked on a strategy of prevention that ignored past concerns for civil liberties. His new methods included warrantless wiretaps on thousands of presumed radicals, many of whose names surfaced only because they subscribed to anti-establishment periodicals. His protégé, J. Edgar Hoover, headed a new "Radical Division" where Hoover eagerly collected names of suspected subversives.

Soon Boston, Massachusetts became the focal point of the establishment's attacks against unions as hotbeds of radicalism. In August of 1919, the Boston police sought to unionize and join the American Federation of Labor as police in 37 other cities had already done. By 1919, Boston officers had compiled quite a list of legitimate grievances, including salaries half of what many local skilled manual laborers made. But when 1100 mostly Irish policemen went on strike the second week of September, Boston descended into several nights of chaos, rioting and deaths. It took thousands of state guardsmen to bring order back to the city. When the strike ended, the strikers were fired amid accusations that they had acted to betray their government like soldiers who deserted or turned traitor. The strikers were also taunted as Bolsheviks and anarchists. Massachusetts Governor Calvin Coolidge famously told Samuel Gompers of the American Federation of Labor, "There is no right to strike against the public safety by anybody, anywhere, any time."[4]

As newspaper editorials across the land assailed the patriotism of the strikers, President Wilson himself condemned the Boston police strike as an act akin to treason. Three weeks later, the President literally became apoplectic when his efforts to avoid a crippling national strike in the steel industry ended in failure. Just ten days after The Great Steel Strike of 1919 commenced, President Wilson was felled by a massive stroke. The public remained unaware of his condition for months as his wife Edith concealed the truth and operated what she called "her stewardship" of the nation's highest office with help from her husband's legal assistant.[5] That crisis should have prompted passage of a constitutional amendment to provide for an unexpected presidential disability or inability to function. Instead, it took President Kennedy's assassination to provide the additional impetus for Congress almost half a century later to adopt the Twenty-Fifth Amendment to address the national emergency of a President's incapacity to carry out his duties. Since 1967, a mechanism has been in place for the Vice President to assume the highest office in the land upon a determination of the President's inability to function.

While the White House was under Edith Wilson's stewardship the Great Steel Strike continued for three months, involving over 350,000 workers. Many of the strikers were recent immigrants, making it easier for opponents to label them as subversive. Meanwhile, Palmer filled his fellow countrymen with panic that there were 60,000 terrorists in their midst poised "to bring the Russian revolution to America."[6] Starting in November of 1919 the Attorney General worked with the Immigration Department on "Palmer Raids" by which the Justice Department aggressively invoked the new Anarchist Act to arrest and deport aliens, including Galleani and eight of his followers. An associate of the deportees, printer Andrea Salsedo, died in Manhattan in May of 1920 while under interrogation in FBI offices for his connection to the publication of the anarchist threats. Officially, Salsedo's death was recorded as suicide for a fall from the high-rise building. Galleanists assumed he was pushed.

Soon Galleanists would be connected to a major crime that occurred in South Braintree, Massachusetts on April 15, 1920, the month before Salsedo died. In a bold daytime payroll robbery, a security guard and a payroll master were shot to death while bringing the company's payroll to their factory. The perpetrators took off with several other men in a stolen Buick.

The first break in solving the audacious daytime crime in South Braintree had come in early May of 1920. A garage owner alerted police that four Italian-American men came to claim from storage the presumed get-away car for both the South Braintree heist and an earlier attempted robbery in nearby Bridgewater. The heavily armed quartet were all members of *Il Gruppo Autonomo* – militant Boston anarchists with Mafia connections, also affiliated with the national Galleanist movement. Soon after their arrests, a new wave of bombings occurred, including the devastating Wall Street bombing in September 1920 that killed nearly forty people and injured hundreds more. Hand-stamped fliers found near the debris in lower Manhattan claimed they were authored by "American Anarchist fighters." The flyers demanded, "Free the political prisoners or it will be sure death for all of you."[7]

Headlines then speculated that the Wall Street bombing was the work of Galleani's followers, renewing public fear that the same anarchists were responsible for the 1919 explosions. Yet that seemed too obvious a solution to state and federal officials. They suspected the notes were intentionally misleading. J. P. Morgan's war profiteering had engendered so much Leftist outrage that the unsolved Wall Street crime had authorities also pointing the finger at labor leaders, Socialists and Bolsheviks on the assumption the historic attack on Wall Street could have been a copycat's handiwork. Even the reference to political prisoners did not narrow the field; there were so many in 1920 that no dissident group could be ruled out.

One of the four members of *Il Gruppo Autonomo* arrested trying to collect the presumed get-away car was thirty-two-year-old Bartolomeo Vanzetti. An itinerant bachelor with closely cropped, receding brown hair and a shaggy moustache, Vanzetti was a well-read intellectual who liked working outdoors with his hands. Since he arrived in America from Northern Italy in 1908, the wiry dreamer had handled various unskilled jobs while he committed himself increasingly to revolution. Vanzetti was friends with the recently deceased anarchist Salsedo. For the previous two years, Vanzetti had peddled fish in the Italian community around Plymouth, Massachusetts, where he also distributed anarchist literature.

Vanzetti first faced charges arising out of the aborted Christmas Eve robbery attempt in Bridgewater. *Il Gruppo Autonomo* anticipated strong local bias against Vanzetti for his extreme political views. The anarchists hired a prominent Massachusetts politician and trial lawyer, James Vahey, to represent the Italian fish monger. Twenty-nine-year-old Ferdinando Nicola Sacco was one of the other arrestees, but the skilled shoe craftsman had an alibi. He produced a time card that convinced the prosecutor not to charge the clean-shaven family man with the Bridgewater attempted robbery. One of the other two men originally arrested also escaped prosecution by producing a time card; the fourth fled before he could be tried.

Judge Webster Thayer eagerly presided over Vanzetti's trial, proud of the many criminal cases he had already handled involving anarchist defendants. Vahey located eleven Italian alibi witnesses who swore that Vanzetti sold them eels in Plymouth on Christmas Eve when the Bridgewater holdup was in process. Prosecutor Katzmann found five Bridgewater witnesses who instead placed Vanzetti at the crime scene. By mutual agreement, the two lawyers kept Vanzetti's anarchist views out of the trial. Vahey warned his client that if he took the stand, he would open himself up to cross-examination that might alienate the jury. Vanzetti chose not to testify and was convicted after Katzmann cast doubt on the alibi witnesses' memory of when they made their purchases. The media paid scant attention to the case. When Vahey later joined the prosecutor's law firm, Vanzetti became livid with mistrust of his former lawyer and blamed Vahey for his imprisonment.

Meanwhile, police experts tested casings and shells of bullets from the South Braintree crime scene and the victims' bodies and compared them with the guns and bullets the suspects carried when arrested. The resulting evidence was inconclusive, but appeared to implicate Sacco's pistol as a murder weapon. Police also found a hat at the scene that they believed belonged to Sacco. The heavily guarded pair were then put on trial together for the twin murders in the wealthy Boston suburb of Dedham, Massachusetts. Judge Thayer sought out this assignment as well. The irascible jurist derided Sacco and Vanzetti to members of his club and the press as "Bolsheviki" and vowed he would "get those guys hanged."[8]

This time veteran IWW lawyer Fred Moore came East to serve as Sacco's counsel. The California labor champion had helped defend Big Bill Haywood in 1917. Moore had far too much baggage to benefit his new client. A Lothario and habitual cocaine user, he dressed flamboyantly and did not seem to care that he alienated both the judge and jury. Moore associated as local counsel a competent but excitable Irish-American attorney, Republican Jeremiah McAnarney, to represent Vanzetti.

Worry about bomb threats prompted reinforcements to the Dedham courtroom. It was fitted with sliding steel doors and cast-iron

shutters painted to look like wood. Police patrolled the streets around
the building on motorcycle and horseback. The immigrant anarchists
drew no support from mainstream labor unions, and the case did not
attract large crowds. Those who did attend the trial each day were
searched. An unusually large panel of five hundred potential jurors –
more than five times that normally assembled – yielded only seven men
deemed qualified to serve. Many had read about the sensational crime
and already considered them guilty; others opposed the death penalty.
After deputies scoured the county for another hundred and fifty wor-
thy additional prospects,the judge finally seated five more men. None
had Italian surnames.

District Attorney Katzmann was again the chief prosecutor. He
focused on vilifying the two men as much for their lack of patriotism
in avoiding war service as for their alleged role in the Braintree robbery. Though careful to minimize overtly biased statements in court,
Judge Thayer likewise made his distaste for disloyal "arnuchists" like
the defendants and their "long-haired" counsel manifest. Several prominent reporters covering the case later signed affidavits attesting to
Judge Thayer's prejudice.[9] Moore, in turn, told the press that an Italian
had as little chance of receiving a fair trial in Boston as a Negro did
in the South. Looking back, Pulitzer Prize–winning columnist George
Will agreed.[10] Italians were at the time of the trial the most despised
(and least assimilated) ethnic European group of immigrants in the
Brahmin-controlled state.

The very first day of the trial came on the heels of Decoration Day
(now Memorial Day) and started off on a bad footing. The prosecutor
zeroed in on Sacco and Vanzetti's radicalism and avoidance of the war-
time draft. He invited the jury's hatred of their politics to justify finding
them both guilty of the robbery-murder. Moore repeatedly jumped up
to object; the judge glared fiercely at him and overruled every objection.

Attorney William Thompson had been a spectator at the trial. He
later described Thayer's belligerent attitude toward Moore as lead
defense counsel: "It wasn't what [Judge Thayer] said, it was his manner
of saying it. It looked perfectly straight on the record; he was too clever
to do otherwise. I sat there for a while and I told John McAnarney,

'Your goose is cooked. You will never in this world get these two men acquitted. The judge is going to convict these two men . . . and keep his records straight . . . you have no chance."[11] (Expert studies have long since concluded that nonverbal cues from tone of voice and body language account for at least sixty percent of human communication.)[12]

The trial consumed thirty-five court days, during which the two reviled defendants were placed in a cage in the middle of the courtroom. Over forty witnesses had seen the robbery, but only a handful identified either of the two men as participants. These identifications were only made after the witnesses viewed the pair of defendants in prison without a lineup – a practice that has since been disallowed. At trial, both defendants testified in broken English with help from interpreters. They adamantly defended their radical politics, but denied any involvement in the robbery. On later review of the record, Harvard Professor (and future Supreme Court Justice) Felix Frankfurter noted how often the pair appeared to misunderstand questions put to them. Sacco claimed to have been in Boston on personal business obtaining a passport, and Vanzetti peddling fish. Both alibis were supported by many defense witnesses, who disputed the prosecutor's eyewitnesses.

Key eyewitnesses for the prosecutor grew far more positive at the time of trial than they had been before. Katzmann again claimed defense witnesses were wrong about their dates and pointed out that both men had lied about their activities when first arrested. Sacco and Vanzetti explained that they lied to protect themselves from deportation or persecution, as befell many colleagues who distributed anarchist literature.

The nearly seven-week trial produced conflicting testimony from nearly a hundred and sixty witnesses. In prosecutor Katzmann's zeal to see both men convicted, Katzmann claimed that the gun Vanzetti had in his possession when arrested had been lifted from the felled payroll guard. Historians Robert Grant and Joseph Katz assert that Katzmann had to know at the time that the assertion was false – the weapon was a different caliber than the guard carried.[13] Prof. Frankfurter later noted the judge's strong bias in skirting over the massive testimonial conflict when Judge Thayer summed up the evidence. Judge Thayer also overstated the state expert's opinion regarding Sacco's gun as the possible murder weapon and invited the jurors to dwell on the two men's behavior following arrest to assess whether it demonstrated "consciousness of guilt."[14]

Most unprofessionally, Judge Thayer stressed loyalty as a virtue, which reinforced the prosecutor's focus on the defendants' lack of war service. The loyalty of the two immigrants to America had no legitimate bearing on their guilt or innocence of the charged crime. The judge then asked the jury members to do their civic duty as "soldiers" in reaching a verdict. The jury took less than a day to find the two anarchists guilty as charged. Judge Thayer was soon heard to brag, "Did you see what I did with those anarchistic bastards the other day?"[15]

Meanwhile, Moore and McAnarney worked day and night trying to publicize the case as the railroading of two innocent men based on ethnic bias and postwar anti-immigrant hysteria. The appeal resonated with prominent civil libertarians who had participated in a scathing 1920 report that condemned Palmer's 1919 raids. In 1921, a congressional committee severely criticized Palmer's aggressive post-war strategy. They accused Palmer of exceeding his authority and trampling on basic constitutional guarantees. That same year, Congress repealed the war-time Sedition Act; labor leader Bill Haywood jumped bail on appeal of his Espionage Act conviction and fled to Russia; and the year-old robbery-murder of a payroll master and guard for a shoe company on the outskirts of Boston began to attract international attention. Additional criticism of Palmer began to mount in December of 1921 after newly-appointed FBI Chief William Burns, a.k.a. "The Great Detective," triumphantly announced that the Wall Street bombing formerly attributed by the press to Italian anarchists had been planned and executed by Russian and Polish Bolsheviks. Burns was wrong. Unlike militant anarchists, Communist Party officials shunned isolated acts of terrorism like the Wall Street bombing, which Lenin considered counterproductive to achieving true revolutionary conditions.

Soon, much to Burns' embarrassment, newspapers discovered that the confessed co-conspirator was a former paid FBI informer. The tale he concocted was so unworthy of belief that Burns became a laughing stock. The Wall Street investigation was back at a standstill and

Source of both: https://en.wikipedia.org/wiki/Sacco_and_Vanzetti#/media/File:Save_Sacco_and_Vanzetti.jpg

Bartolomeo Vanzetti (left) handcuffed together with Nicolo Sacco (right) spoke only broken English but were given no interpreters at their robbery/murder trial. They sat in a cage in front of the jury while the prosecutor derided the pair as draft dodgers during World War I, which had no bearing on the charges against them. Judge Webster Thayer then asked the jurors to do their civic duty as "soldiers" in reaching a verdict. The jury took less than a day to find the two guilty as charged. Judge Thayer was soon heard to brag, "Did you see what I did with those anarchistic bastards the other day?" Their biased treatment by Judge Thayer and their ultimate execution subjected the United States justice system to withering criticism, prompting major reforms.

London 1921 post-trial protest — one of many around the world.

discredited even further by a confession from another former paid informer, Albert Bailin. Bailin asserted that Burns had directed him on a campaign of falsifying evidence to implicate Communists and labor leaders like Haywood in the Wall Street bombing. Bailin was himself caught threatening to bomb the Woolworth building in New York, using a note like the one found in a mailbox near the Wall Street bombing. Bailin told police that Burns ordered the bogus bomb threat when he was still a private detective to convince bankers to increase funding for the Wall Street bombing investigation.

The entire fiasco underscored claims that Italian anarchists like Sacco and Vanzetti were being unfairly persecuted due to political scare tactics and ethnic prejudice. After Sacco and Vanzetti's conviction and death sentence, Moore gained traction in instigating international protests against the perceived injustice perpetrated by the world's new superpower. Moore's claim was bolstered by Palmer Raid opponent Louis Post, former acting Secretary of Labor. Post wrote a 1923 memoir characterizing the American general public in 1920 as suffering from the same fear-driven "delirium" that had precipitated the 1886 Haymarket convictions, all out of proportion to any real threat to the country that the alleged revolutionaries posed.[16]

Post also pointed to the huge state, federal and private banking resources that had been expended to no avail in bungled efforts to pin the Wall Street bombing on various radicals. He joined speculation that the Wall Street bombing might have been an isolated act (like that of President McKinley's assassin) or an industrial accident. Post assumed that the bombing had been recharacterized as a sinister plot solely to justify repressive governmental policies.

Media coverage of the Sacco and Vanzetti case in the United States remained spotty. Protests elsewhere died down as the two Italian anarchists began to pursue fruitless motions for reconsideration and appeals. In contrast to the irresponsible newspaper coverage of the Fatty Arbuckle trials, in April of 1922, the *Wall Street Journal* broke a real scandal – secret leases of Navy oil reserves at Teapot Ridge in Wyoming by President Warren Harding's new Secretary of the Interior, Albert Fall. The former New Mexican Senator was a Republican crony of Ohio political boss Harry Daugherty, who had engineered Harding's improbable presidential campaign and his own appointment as attorney general. Key Democrats in the Senate, with the support of Progressive Republican leader Robert "Fighting Bob" La Follette, called for investigation of the suspicious, no-bid Teapot Dome contracts. In the spring of 1923, Harding tried to curb a related scandal by ordering the dismissal of Daugherty's aide Jess Smith, who then committed suicide. Harding himself died suddenly in August of 1923. The Senate probes continued after President Calvin Coolidge took office. Wisconsin's Senator La Follette then launched his own presidential campaign as a third-party candidate – the short-lived Progressive Party of 1924 – which garnered the Wisconsin reformer 17 percent of the vote.

In the spring of 1924, Attorney General Daugherty resigned amid accusations of another major scandal – that he and his deceased pal Jess Smith had received large bribes from bootleggers buying immunity from prosecution under Prohibition's Volstead Act. In late 1924, investigators finally found evidence that Albert Fall had been bribed to permit the secret oil leases with a $100,000 interest free loan – about $1.4 million today – and lied to a Senate committee to cover it up. The Teapot Dome scandal established both the right of Congress to compel testimony and Albert Fall's dubious place in history as the first cabinet member ever imprisoned for his official actions.

In 1924, the Justice Department made more embarrassing headlines by accusing a prominent Montana senator, Democrat Burton Wheeler, of being a Communist. The unsupported charge appeared all too obviously in retaliation for Wheeler's request that Congress investigate the Justice Department's recent abuses of power. When it came to light that the FBI had illegally searched Senator Wheeler's office and put a tail on him, President Coolidge forced the resignation of both scandal-plagued Attorney General Daugherty and Bureau of Investigations Chief Burns.

Burns' ouster elevated his zealous assistant J. Edgar Hoover to head that office, though Hoover was not yet thirty. In securing the post, Hoover falsely assured the new reform-minded attorney general that he had played only an "unwilling part" in the "misguided raids and botched investigations."[17] The idea of rounding up thousands of immigrant Communist Party members and anarchists for deportation in 1919 had, in fact, been Hoover's own brainchild. Promising to avoid intrusion on civil liberties, Hoover agreed to stop the agency from gathering its own intelligence on radicals, but surreptitiously kept collecting information from other sources. He also kept alert for opportunities to obtain express authorization to "enable the federal authorities to deal vigorously with the ultra-radical elements."[18] Hoover would ultimately convince President Franklin Roosevelt to restore extraordinary investigative power to the Bureau before America joined World War II. When Congress passed the peacetime Smith Loyalty Act, Hoover exulted in the opportunity to revive his official index file of suspected subversives.[19] Perceived radical threats to the government would remain Hoover's preoccupation throughout his long career.

The same year that Hoover assumed office as FBI director, Sacco decided to fire IWW attorney Fred Moore, with whom he had never gotten along. Sacco kept McAnarney and added highly regarded Massachusetts lawyer William Thompson. Thompson proceeded to collect additional evidence in an effort to win a new trial for the two vilified radicals. Unfortunately, under Massachusetts law at the time, these motions challenging the fairness of the death penalty trial Judge Thayer had presided over all had to be presented for decision to Judge Thayer himself. French intellectuals analogized the prosecution to their own country's notorious Dreyfus Affair. Influential writers led by Nobel Prize–winner Anatole France fanned anti-American sentiment by citing the case as proof of the frightening "soullessness" of the new world superpower. They criticized the United States as "mechanical, amoral, conformist and hypermaterialistic" with no regard for fundamental fairness or individual freedom of expression.[20] British author H. G. Wells, one of the most prominent international journalists to cover the Sacco and Vanzetti case, coined the term "Thayerism" to describe the "mental and moral obtuseness" he believed was all too prevalent in the United States.[21]

Vanzetti aided his own cause with poignant letters from prison protesting persecution for his political beliefs. Meanwhile, Europeans increasingly demonstrated hostility toward American tourists amid anxiety about the consequences of the country's world dominance. Across the political spectrum, Europeans were appalled at the extraordinary length of time the two men remained on death row pursuing apparently useless appeals.

The post-trial delays allowed Communists the opportunity to exploit the travails of the two anarchists as a propaganda tool, collecting hundreds of thousands of dollars ostensibly for the cost of Sacco and Vanzetti's legal fees. Much of the money was used for other purposes. At the same time, Mussolini's new fascist government permitted only muted pleas for clemency to emerge from the Italian press. The new dictator did not want to unduly antagonize the United States by giving full vent to his compatriots' outrage.[22] (Neither Mussolini nor Joseph Stalin would have had any compunction about executing two more dissidents as they cemented their own control.)

In 1925, Sacco and Vanzetti had begun receiving support from the newly formed International Labor Defense Committee (ILD). Composed of American Communist Party members, it included among its ranks William Patterson, a black attorney in his mid-thirties from Northern California. The mission of the ILD was to represent Communists and radical union members targeted for their politics. Wider support for the pair on death row came after a belated confession in 1926 from a jailed member of a Rhode Island crime syndicate known as the Morelli gang. The gang member claimed, improbably, that the Morelli gang had actually perpetrated the South Braintree holdup.

In early 1927, Frankfurter published a blistering attack on Judge Thayer's conduct of the trial and the doubtful evidence used to convict Sacco and Vanzetti. Ultimately, hundreds of thousands of people signed requests for clemency. Some may have been influenced by growing awareness of the unprecedented concentration of wealth among the top one percent of Americans, creating greater sympathy for the anarchists' political views at the same time that anarchism was on the wane.

Under intense pressure both from overseas and from domestic critics, Governor Fuller took the unusual step of appointing a three-man commission headed by Harvard's president, A. Lawrence Lowell. Their job was to reassure the public by conducting an independent review of the record of the two immigrant men's conviction. The move was received with great relief by critics as a sign that the miscarriage of justice would soon be remedied. Trusting in Lowell's integrity, American intellectuals who considered the case a deplorable aberration pinned their hopes on his scholarly review of the record. Lowell had previously defended the freedom of speech of Harvard professors espousing unpopular views, including Jewish scholar Felix Frankfurter, whose published criticism of the Sacco and Vanzetti case had cost the venerable university over a million dollars in donations.

Lowell was also a prominent member of the Boston-based Immigration Restriction League, formed three decades earlier to curtail the influx of undesirable immigrants whom League members accused of debasing American society. In keeping with those views, Lowell enforced strict quotas on Jews admitted to Harvard. The seventy-one-year-old Brahmin was predisposed to reject claims of unfairness by two Italian working-class radicals. Lowell was also not blinded to the far more devastating economic impact on his beloved Harvard that could be expected if he vindicated a pair of admitted anarchists. Lowell steeled himself against threats of international repercussions against Americans abroad; he viewed such attempts to influence him as the equivalent of pressure from a lynch mob.

After three weeks of closed hearings, the Lowell Commission issued its much-anticipated report on July 27, 1927. Despite their own lack of legal training, the panelists had called in no experts to advise them. Nor did the panel consider it necessary to explain in detail the reasoning that led them to conclude that the two Italians were properly found guilty. The report even noted that the evidence against Vanzetti was less certain, but validated his conviction anyway.

In reaching its desired result, the panel had a major hurdle to overcome – Judge Thayer's blatant misconduct. They solved it by noting that the jurist had engaged in "a grave breach of official decorum," but then simply refused to credit all the references to "Dagoes," "sons of bitches" and "anarchistic bastards" attributed to Judge Thayer. The report concluded that, in any event, the panel saw no signs that the jurist's out-of-court invective impugned the outcome. After all, the jurors who followed Judge Thayer's bidding thought he was fair.[23]

It is difficult to imagine a similar public whitewash occurring so readily today, particularly with heightened standards of judicial review like those instituted in Massachusetts as a direct result of this much-criticized case. Then the international outcry only reinforced main-stream support for carrying out the executions as an act in defiance of world opinion. Massachusetts Governor Fuller had his eye on national office in 1928 and dared not accede to the demand for clemency. Last minute applications to the United States Supreme Court for stay of exe-cution were also unavailing. That was unsurprising, given the extremely deferential standard of review of state proceedings then in effect and the conservative majority on the high court.

Both Justice Louis Brandeis and the "Great Dissenter," Oliver Wendell Holmes, privately expressed their belief that Thayer had conducted a prej-udiced trial. However, Brandeis recused himself from any official action because of his wife's personal involvement in assisting Sacco's family. Holmes resisted entreaties to grant a stay because he felt that federal inter-ference in the state proceeding was unwarranted under existing law.

A few days before the scheduled execution, bombs exploded in several American cities. On the night the sentence was to be carried out in Charlestown, the Massachusetts prison was cordoned off. More than five hundred peace officers patrolled the thousands of Leftists and intellectuals who kept a grim vigil in the city square. Extraordinary pre-cautions against reprisals were taken throughout the country, including the nation's capital. President Coolidge absented himself on a Western vacation as crowds gathered in protest in major cities throughout the world, some subdued, others incensed.

In New York, conscience-pricking journalist Heywood Broun quipped, "What more can the immigrants from Italy expect? It is not every prisoner who has a President of Harvard throw the switch for him."[24] Workers walked off their jobs in South America; anarchists bombed the American Embassy and two American banks in Buenos Aires; others threatened the Embassy in Japan. Rioting caused deaths in Germany and Switzerland. In Paris, the American Embassy and the Moulin Rouge suffered extensive damage. The protests even extended as far away as Johannesburg, South Africa.

Thousands of mourners accompanied the remains of Sacco and Vanzetti on a march through Boston's North End. Not long after the

Source: Everett Collection, Inc., Alamy stock photos

Funeral Procession for Sacco and Vanzetti
Boston North End, August 29, 1927

Thousands of mourners accompanied the remains of Sacco and Vanzetti on a march through Boston's North End while violent protests targeted American embassies in a number of countries around the globe. Massachusetts Governor Alvan Fuller's national ambitions were now history in the wake of the controversial executions. Judge Thayer spent the rest of his own life living in his club under armed guard.

pair's death, bombers targeted Judge Thayer's home and that of a juror and the executioner. Other prison officials were also targeted. Substantial damage occurred, but there were no fatalities. An unsuccessful attempt was also made to mail a bomb to Governor Fuller of Massachusetts, whose national ambitions were now history in the wake of the controversial executions. In 1928, a train transporting President Herbert Hoover on a trip through Argentina barely escaped bombing. Judge Thayer spent the rest of his own life living in his club under armed guard.

Many American intellectuals lost faith in the establishment following the Lowell Commission's unexpected stamp of approval on Judge Thayer's biased conduct. The knee-jerk solidarity Brahmins had shown for Thayer's conduct of the trial proved a debilitating, self-inflicted wound that engendered decades of criticism. The executions gave momentum to growing alliances among disaffected Liberals, minority groups and unions to support their own candidates and press for major reforms, many of which would be implemented in the next decade.

Ever since, the trial of Sacco and Vanzetti has become a source of reflection on the failings of the American justice system. It inspired an album by Woody Guthrie, an opera, numerous historical essays and books debating their guilt or innocence, movies, plays such as *Gods of the Lightning*, Sinclair Lewis's *Boston: A Novel*, Maxwell Anderson's *Winterset* and poetry by Carl Sandburg and Edna St. Vincent Millay, among others. For decades in the Soviet Union, a state factory churned out Sacco and Vanzetti pencils and crayons for the nation's school children. In Italian towns, streets were renamed in the pair's honor.

In the eyes of many around the world, Sacco and Vanzetti remain martyrs to this day. Yet, the evidence was preserved and later, more exhaustive ballistics tests on Sacco's gun convinced many skeptics that Sacco did in fact participate in the Braintree robbery-murder. His complicity was also confirmed by a fellow member of *Il Gruppo Autonomo*. Sacco's former lawyer, Moore, confessed to muckraker Upton Sinclair that he believed so, too, prompting Sinclair to abandon a proposed exposé of the biased prosecution for a fictionalized account.

No similar proof of Vanzetti's participation ever emerged, though he might well have been an accessory after the fact. Controversy still surrounded the Sacco and Vanzetti case on the 50th anniversary of their execution, when Massachusetts Governor Michael Dukakis proclaimed that the extreme prejudice surrounding the trial prompted him to decree that "Any stigma and disgrace should be forever removed from the names of Nicola Sacco and Bartolomeo Vanzetti. We are not here to say whether these men are guilty or innocent. We are here to say that the high standards of justice, which we in Massachusetts take such pride in, failed Sacco and Vanzetti."[25]

More controversy followed twenty years later, on the 70th anniversary of their execution, when Boston's first Italian-American mayor presided over ceremonies at which the Boston Public Library finally accepted a fifty-year-old bas-relief commemorating Sacco and Vanzetti. The memorial had been designed by the sculptor who created Mount Rushmore.

By 1991, historian Paul Avrich published his conclusion that both Sacco and Vanzetti were implicated in the April and June bombings of 1919 along with many other Galleanisti. Among them was another suspect in the South Braintree robbery, Mario Buda, a.k.a. Mike Boda. Buda had gone into hiding in New England when Sacco and Vanzetti were arrested and never stood trial. But five days after Sacco and Vanzetti were indicted, Buda showed up in New York City. His nephew later told Avrich that Buda then had plans to retaliate for his revolutionary colleagues' arrest. On the fateful day of September 16, 1920, Buda loaded a horse and wagon with explosives, set a timer for noon and then fled Wall Street to Rhode Island, where he embarked for Sicily, never to be caught for the devastating Wall Street bombing.[26]

* * * * *

As much as the general public vilified violent anarchists, at least their belief in a cause provided a rationale for robbery and murder that many could understand. The senseless murder of fourteen-year-old Bobby Franks in May of 1924 preoccupied people all over the globe. The case against teenagers Nathan Leopold and Richard Loeb provided ministers in their pulpits with fodder to condemn the godlessness and immorality of the new decade and intensified class rancor to a fever pitch.

8. TEENAGE SOCIOPATHS

Life or Death for Leopold and Loeb?

*This terrible crime was inherent in his organism, and it came
from some ancestor. Is any blame attached because somebody took
Nietzsche's philosophy seriously and fashioned his life upon it?*

– Excerpt from Clarence Darrow's closing argument

Public preoccupation with the Leopold and Loeb murder
prosecution combined elements of both the 1913 Leo
Frank trial and the 1907–08 Thaw murder prosecutions,
updated through the prism of the Roaring Twenties. For nativists who
still believed Leo Frank was guilty, Leopold and Loeb proved once
again that their anti-Semitism was amply justified; these two Jewish
intellectuals were perverts as well. The sooner they were hanged and
made an example of the better. For those who had loudly protested that
Leo Frank was framed, the sensationalized coverage of the Leopold
and Loeb case silenced their voices. As in Thaw's case, the prosecution
yielded voyeuristic glimpses into the decadent lives of two more spoiled
rich boys with severe psychological problems. Yet there was a new twist.
The two teenagers were influenced most by Prussian nihilist Friedrich
Nietzsche. Many Americans now blamed Nietzsche for inspiring the
Germans in 1914 to instigate one of history's deadliest wars.

The question whether the two college students should live or die
had millions of people at their kitchen tables outraged at the privileges
of the rich. These youths had all the advantages normally associated
with success. If they got off, what did that say about the poor nineteen-
year-old Chicago boy then awaiting hanging for participating in a robbery in which his accomplice killed a policeman? It seemed as though

everyone who read newspapers and popular magazines was talking about the "new psychology" and Freudian concepts. What behaviors are human beings responsible for, and what in their nature is predetermined and beyond their control? Wasn't this just a question of how good a defense a perpetrator could afford?

Nathan Leopold was born November 19, 1904, into one of the wealthiest families in Chicago's Southside. By the turn of the century, his grandfather had established the biggest shipping company on the Great Lakes. Leopold's father magnified their wealth by launching a successful container-manufacturing business, spending little time in the process with his youngest son. The family soon realized the sickly "Babe" was a child prodigy; they bragged that he was walking and talking before he was six months old. More thought should have been given to the question of young Leopold's schooling. Small, flatfooted and potbellied, with eyes that bulged out, the whiz kid went to two years of public elementary school where he endured constant hazing from other boys his age. What else but ridicule could his parents expect for a sensitive and unathletic mama's boy who was picked up each day after school by a governess?

In 1915, the family moved to a mansion in the city's upscale Kenwood District. Ten-year-old Nathan switched to the Harvard School for Boys. He still remained a loner raised largely by governesses, whom the other boys taunted as "Crazy Nathan" and "the flea." With the encouragement of his teachers, Leopold found intellectual escape as a young teenager by developing a passion for dead languages and ornithology. He also evinced a precocious interest in sex. By the time Leopold was twelve, it was common knowledge among the household staff that the family's thirty-year-old governess had embarked on a sexual relationship with him, just as she had already undertaken with his older brother.

Richard Loeb came from a similarly wealthy family that already lived in the same upscale Jewish neighborhood of Kenwood when the Leopolds arrived. Loeb's father was vice president of Sears, Roebuck; his mother was active in the Chicago Women's Club. The two boys were very unlike in many ways. As he matured, Leopold remained short, awkward and sickly looking, with coarse, black hair and large, gray eyes.

In contrast, Richard Loeb was tall and athletic with sandy brown hair, blue eyes and an engaging smile. Loeb made friends easily, though the relationships were often of short duration. Loeb enthusiastically joined his classmates in extracurricular activities. Though he played baseball and football, he preferred tennis to contact sports for fear of injury. Like Leopold, Loeb was fragile. He had occasional fainting spells and a nervous tic. Both youths could behave quite recklessly despite their aversion to pain.

Loeb was no genius like Leopold, but a Canadian governess prodded him relentlessly to accelerate his studies at a record pace. Both Leopold and Loeb would finish college well ahead of their peers. Leopold emerged Phi Beta Kappa from the University of Chicago at eighteen, and Loeb would have the distinction of being the youngest person to ever graduate from the University of Michigan, though with an unremarkable record. Both planned to attend top law schools in the fall of 1924, presumably bound for successful legal careers like Loeb's Uncle Jacob, who had recently served as president of the Chicago Board of Education.

The two friends had met after Leopold's junior year at the Harvard School for Boys. At the time, Loeb was already in college, though he was six months younger than Leopold. The Leopold family then considered Loeb a good influence on their son. They had no idea Loeb was an inveterate liar and corner-cutter, skating through school with as little effort as he could get away with while constantly plotting nasty bits of mischief. Nor did they realize that, at first sight, Leopold had developed a crush on Loeb.

Leopold greatly flattered Loeb with his slavish attention. They became lovers, but then Loeb backed off and spent more time with other friends. Yet Loeb was an accomplished manipulator, intoxicated by the realization that Leopold would do anything for him. Loeb had been fascinated with crime novels and detective stories since he was a child, a secret he kept from his overbearing governess. He envisioned himself as a super-criminal and soon talked Leopold into joining him on a crime spree. The inducement was a formal pact that Loeb would agree to resume sex with Leopold three times a month, which evolved into once after each illicit adventure.

For four years, the pair got away with a variety of crimes Loeb carefully planned, including arson, vandalism and burglary. Loeb may have also accomplished a few more serious crimes on his own. His successful exploits with Leopold only whetted Loeb's appetite for attempting the perfect crime just for the thrill of getting away with it. The idea appealed to Leopold as well. He believed that would prove the two were Nietzschean supermen, unbound by laws applicable to mere ordinary mortals.

After several months of planning, the pair decided to rent a car under an assumed name and kidnap a child whose parents could afford $10,000 in ransom. They figured they had several suitable targets at the Harvard School for Boys, which Loeb's ten-year-old brother still attended. They prepared an elaborate scheme for collecting the ransom. It included a typed note that ended "should you carefully follow our instructions to the letter, we can assure you that your son will be safely returned to you within six hours of our receipt of the money."[1] This guarantee was designed to ensure payment of the ransom. The pair had already decided that, by the time the anxious parents delivered the money, the two would have jointly strangled the victim. That way neither could repent – since both would be complicit in the murder – and the victim could never identify his kidnappers to the police.

On the afternoon of the chosen day, May 21, 1924, Leopold picked up a green Willys-Knight touring car from a downtown rental agency. He met up with Loeb, and the two cruised the school's neighborhood. They had almost given up hope of finding a boy walking alone when Loeb spotted his fourteen-year-old second cousin Bobby Franks headed home from umpiring a pickup baseball game. The two had just played tennis together the day before, and Franks showed little hesitation before he hopped in when offered a ride.

As the unsuspecting youth settled into the front passenger seat, Leopold drove away. Then, before Franks realized he was not being dropped off as he expected, Loeb reached over from the back seat and stifled his cousin's surprised cry. With his other hand Loeb then clubbed Franks' head several times with the blunt end of a chisel. Blood

Source: DN-0077041, Chicago Daily News negatives collection, Chicago History Museum

This family photo of 14-year-old victim Bobby Franks taken not long before his death appeared on the front pages of Chicago newspapers accompanying dramatic headlines about the killing. The gruesome crime quickly became the talk of the town with parents wondering whose child was safe from a similar kidnap-murder.

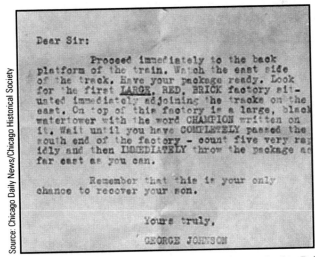

Source: Chicago Daily News/Chicago Historical Society

Ransom note proposing safe return of Franks' son delivered after Bobby Franks was killed.

streamed all over the front of the car. Franks continued to struggle and cry while Leopold somehow kept driving slowly through heavy traffic in the densely populated district. Loeb yanked Franks into the back, stuffed a rag down his cousin's throat, and taped his mouth shut, holding him until the boy went limp. Loeb then wrapped the body in a blanket.

Leopold drove for twenty miles. He had already picked out a remote spot near a forest preserve south of Chicago where he had often gone bird-watching. There, they would await darkness and hide Franks' body in a culvert. They made good time and decided to stop for hot dogs and root beer en route. In an effort to obscure Franks' identity if the body were found before it decomposed, Leopold poured hydrochloric acid on the boy's face and genitals. Back in the city, Leopold then made a call to Franks' frantic parents to tell them that their son was alive and well and being held for ransom. He penned their address on a generic ransom note he had typed before they selected the victim. Leopold then posted the letter to arrive the next morning.

Afterward, Leopold parked the rental car on a side street near Loeb's home and the pair burned Franks' clothes in the Loebs' basement furnace. They hid the bloody blanket in the side yard and headed to Leopold's home where they played cards. Loeb forgot about the blood-soaked chisel still in his pocket until Leopold drove him home later that evening. Loeb tossed it out the window on the street where it was picked up by a night watchman, who got a good glimpse of the distinctive maroon sports car as it turned the corner.

The next morning, the Leopold family chauffeur was puzzled to observe the teenage boys in the driveway. They were hard at work at the unaccustomed chore of cleaning a car, the same one he had seen them drive off in the day before. The two made up a story about spilled wine and declined any help. They then set off to complete the rest of their perfect crime by collecting the ransom. The pair had no reason to know that an immigrant worker walking home from his night shift had spotted Franks' bare feet sticking out of the culvert that same morning. Meanwhile, Leopold called the drugstore he had designated as a rendezvous to ask if a Mr. Franks was there. By then, a family member had identified the naked, battered corpse, and Bobby Franks' father was at home with his shocked family meeting with the police.

The gruesome kidnap and murder of the popular, high-achieving student was the instant talk of the town. Whose child was safe if such a brazen crime in a good neighborhood could go unpunished? The police gave the matter the highest priority, a welcome diversion from the heat they got for allowing the widespread flouting of Prohibition. Law-abiding Chicagoans were scandalized at how corrupt police let gangsters like Al Capone flourish while the Volstead Act prohibited legitimate businesses from competing in the distribution and sale of liquor.

At first, police focused suspicion on two teachers at the Harvard School for Boys. The police attempted to beat confessions out of the teachers – to no avail. The authorities then undertook a broad search for "known perverts" and harshly questioned the owners of gray Winton automobiles like the one seen by a playmate on the street just before Bobby Franks disappeared. With the attendant bad publicity, a couple of these early suspects lost their jobs, though they had done nothing wrong. A distinctive pair of horned-rimmed glasses had also been found near the site of Bobby Franks' corpse. Only one Chicago optometrist sold eyewear with that peculiar hinge. Through painstaking review of more than fifty thousand receipts, only three possible purchasers were found. The glasses were quickly identified as a pair sold to Nathan Leopold, Jr., in the fall of 1923. Police brought him in for questioning with the consent of his father and the family's lawyer Benjamin Bachrach. Neither suspected that Leopold had anything to do with the crime.

When Leopold was interviewed, he claimed to have just realized that he lost the glasses bird-watching the week before. He recited an alibi for the afternoon of the murder that he had concocted with Loeb. Soon police spoke to Loeb. Though vaguer on his whereabouts at the time of the crime, Loeb offered helpful suggestions to the police, appearing quite intrigued by the crime. Both sets of parents assumed the police had made a mistake as the two were subjected to close questioning for three days straight. The police had already found a gun in Leopold's room and a letter from Loeb that made it clear that the two were lovers. The boys' coordinated alibis seemed highly suspicious, especially when they claimed they had spent part of the afternoon cruising in Leopold's sports car looking for girls.

The Leopolds' chauffeur, Sven Englund, remembered an important piece of information which the family urged him to share with police. Nathan's sports car had been home the entire afternoon of May 21. How could Nathan have possibly committed the murder if his car remained at home? Englund had no idea the boys had told police they spent the afternoon driving Nathan's sports car. Apparently, until the police jogged his memory, Englund had also temporarily forgotten the green touring car the boys drove off in, which they had spent so much time cleaning the next morning. Their alibi in a shambles, Loeb confessed. Though disgusted with Loeb's cowardice, Leopold followed suit. Neither showed signs of remorse.

The quick-thinking county prosecutor, Robert Crowe, immediately called in three top state psychiatrists to evaluate whether the pair knew right from wrong – the legal definition of sanity. Once both answered yes, Crowe announced to the reporters present that the murder had been solved. Crowe then dramatically formed a cavalcade of police cars and invited the press to follow along as Leopold and Loeb offered to retrace their steps the day of the murder, starting with the car rental agency. Without any legal counsel, the pair were hugely flattered by all the attention.

Leopold's and Loeb's families were astounded to hear that their sons had just confessed to a capital crime. They immediately decided only the legendary Clarence Darrow could save the two from the gallows. Richard's Uncle Jacob had firsthand knowledge of Darrow's courtroom skills. Just a year before, Darrow had demolished the former school board president as the star witness for County Prosecutor Robert Crowe in a political corruption case. Early Sunday morning, Jacob Loeb and Benjamin Bachrach and two other family representatives arrived unannounced by limousine at Darrow's penthouse apartment near the University of Chicago.

By persistent ringing of the doorbell, they succeeded in rousing Darrow's wife Ruby. The men then marched past her into the couple's bedroom and begged the aged libertarian for his help, assuring him that money was no object. Jacob Loeb sat next to the bed, explaining

Nathan Freudenthal Leopold, Jr.

Richard Albert Loeb

Source: Unknown photographers, August 1924; top two photos provided to Wikimedia by the German Federal Archive (Deutsches Bundesarchiv), http://www.wikiwand.com/en/Leopold_and_Loeb. Bottom two arrest photos DN-0078242, DN-0078243 Chicago Daily News negatives collection, Chicago History Museum.

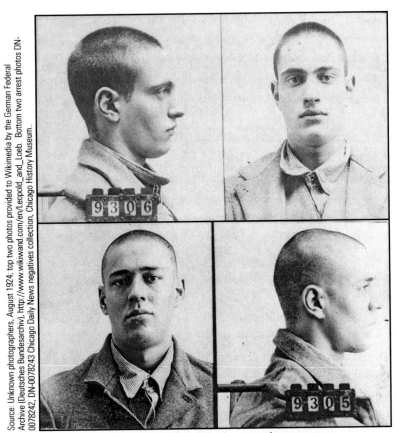

Leopold and Loeb arrest photos

the dire situation to the barely awakened lawyer. Darrow had, of course, read of the brutal crime. He felt torn between wanting to assist them and his visceral reaction to avoid such a "shocking and bizarre" case that already had so thoroughly alienated the public and press. At sixty-seven, Darrow's thinning hair was now all gray. His craggy face and loose jowls showed the ravages of time. The slump-shouldered lion of the Chicago bar was bone weary of "standing in the lean and lonely front line facing the greatest enemy that ever confronted man – public opinion."[2]

Darrow reluctantly got up and dressed to accompany his visitors down to the county jail in Loeb's limousine. As Darrow contemplated how in the world he could keep the pair from being hanged for the abhorrent crime, Prosecutor Crowe set out once more with Leopold and Loeb as his guides to locate further evidence. An even bigger media entourage accompanied the police procession. The large caval-cade attracted thousands of observers when they parked by the Jackson Park Harbor on Lake Michigan and dredged the water. The boys had led them there to retrieve the jettisoned Underwood that Leopold had used to type the ransom note the night before the murder. During the time-consuming process, reporters had free access to both youths. Leopold and Loeb basked in the limelight.

Crowe had anticipated that the sensationalized media coverage would incense the public with details of the callous crime. So did Darrow. In his experience, unlike the English ban on inflammatory pre-trial publicity, "in America, if the case is one of public interest, a cam-paign that reeks with venom is at once launched against the accused; columns of interviews and pictures are printed each day; . . . the stories grow lurid and appalling. Newspaper sales shoot up beyond belief."[3] So it immediately proved in the Leopold and Loeb case.

Darrow had expected scorn from the public for switching from a passionate defense of the poor as victims of society to a paid mouth-piece of the rich. Yet he was likely taken aback when his own friends deserted him. Many reacted in disbelief at what they considered treachery to his calling, a disgrace to the nation's criminal defense bar. Rumors circulated that the champion of the oppressed had sold out for a million-dollar fee. A Nebraskan newspaperman close to Darrow ruefully observed that "The practice of criminal law fell into its greatest disfavor and disrepute in decades."[4]

As public furor mounted, the Jewish community sat mute, while the Ku Klux Klan triumphantly added its powerful voice to the cacophony of calls for hanging the pair. Crowe exulted. He planned to use this case as a launching pad to run for mayor. Though he and Darrow remained cordial to each other, it would also be sweet revenge for losing the political corruption trial to Darrow when the two had opposed each other in June of 1923.

After the indictment issued, the arraignment on June 11, 1924, attracted the largest crowd in the history of the court. Coincidentally, the date was Loeb's nineteenth birthday. People lined up hours ahead of time for standing room only. Gangster Al Capone counted on the public distraction in choosing that day to surrender for a gangland execution. His arrest garnered far less attention. Capone would later get the charges dismissed when his accusers developed sudden amnesia.[5] In a short hearing, Leopold and Loeb pleaded not guilty to the murder and kidnapping charges, and Chief Judge John Caverly set the trial date for early August in his own courtroom. Time was short. The date was less than two months away. Yet Darrow was greatly pleased with their draw. Judge Caverly had helped establish Chicago's pioneering juvenile court system, which gave judges discretion to treat youthful offenders less harshly than adults. "Fighting Bob" Crowe worried about all the resources available to his skilled adversary, but had faith any jury would vote for death.

In newspaper interviews, Darrow gave hints that insanity would be their defense. He sent co-counsel Walter Bachrach to a national convention of psychiatrists to hire some of the most highly respected authorities in the country on mental abnormality. Together with local experts, they questioned Leopold and Loeb at length and conducted a battery of medical tests. The media ridiculed the rich boys' proposed Freudian defense, comparing these expert witnesses to those used in the successful defense of Harry Thaw for Stanford White's murder twenty years earlier.

Reveling in the prospect of stealing readers from the *Chicago Tribune*, Hearst contacted Sigmund Freud himself in Vienna. Hearst offered to charter a liner for the world's most renowned psychiatrist to come to Chicago to comment on the trial at whatever fee Dr. Freud named. The *Tribune* then cabled a counteroffer to Dr. Freud of $25,000 or more to psychoanalyze the two defendants. Feeling all of his sixty-eight years, Dr. Freud refused both offers, both for health reasons and because the circumstances would not permit any meaningful professional evaluation. As he probably anticipated, the newspapers harbored little or no respect for psychiatry. They happily substituted a phrenologist, astrologist and character analyst to study the defendants' features. The public then was entertained with pseudoscientific comments, such as that Leopold's left ear evinced a dynamic personality, while the curve of Loeb's jaw was "distinctly feminine."[6] The tongue-in-cheek publicity exacerbated populist outrage against the wealthy defendants.

Media representatives from Canada, Cuba, Argentina, Great Britain, Australia and Italy all expressed interest in attending. To go one up on the Hearst papers and other competition, the *Chicago Daily Tribune* proposed to air the Leopold and Loeb trial over the radio – a battle that later in the century would be fought over the propriety of television broadcasts of murder trials. Hearst's *Evening American* derided that idea as appealing to morons and sarcastically suggested that the trial might as well take place in a baseball stadium.[7] Darrow vigorously objected. Live radio coverage could only create even greater community prejudice against his clients. Shocked parents and clergy throughout the city voiced their strong opposition as well; they had already read innuendoes that the pair were homosexuals and wanted children in the city exposed to less coverage, not more. The *Tribune* offered to censor any lurid details, but then withdrew the idea of any live radio broadcast amid a torrent of criticism.

Darrow steered clear of his office most days to avoid harassment and the piles of hate mail. The few letters he read had been so vituperative he had no interest in the rest. It bothered him that the mere provision of a defense met with such anger and derision. Every defendant was entitled to representation, especially those most vilified. Darrow kept his defense strategy a closely guarded secret. By early July, every major paper in the country assigned a reporter to attend the trial in the 200-seat courtroom. As big a crowd as had shown up in June, it was dwarfed by the thousands of people waiting to swarm the courthouse for access to this hearing.

Crowe exuded self-assurance, striding buoyantly into the court smoking a cigar. At worst, he assumed that Darrow might challenge the two confessions, since the pair had no access to lawyers at the time. Of course, no one had read Leopold and Loeb their rights first: the law did not then require warnings. Crowe thought he had a pat hand. In contrast to the stylish prosecutor in his crisp black suit and lively bow tie, Darrow looked saggy and tired in an outdated blue suit, apparently bought when he was somewhat heavier. His younger co-counsel Benjamin Bachrach made a sharp contrast, well-tailored and exuding athletic vigor. But Darrow was playing possum. He had a surprise in store.

When Leopold and Loeb arrived, Darrow shocked Crowe and the media. With his thumbs in his suspenders, he changed their pleas to guilty, avoiding any possibility of a jury. The bailiff had to call repeatedly for quiet in the courtroom. Darrow then employed a tactic he had successfully used a decade before in another case. The savvy trial lawyer asked Judge Caverly to agree to a sentencing hearing at which psychiatric evidence could be offered to justify a lesser penalty for the capital crime. Crowe immediately derided the change of plea as a ploy to substitute a "friendly judge" for a jury. Judge Caverly rebuked Crowe for "a cowardly and dastardly assault upon the integrity of this court" and ordered Crowe's comment removed from the stenographer's record.[8] Reporters fell over chairs running for telephones to make the afternoon paper. Could this daring move possibly preserve Darrow's track record of never losing a client to the death penalty?

Preparation for the hearing was grueling. The schedule had been a whirlwind of nonstop activity and heavy pressure since early June when Darrow first agreed to participate. At the August sentencing hearing, crowds seeking to gain access to the packed courtroom at times overwhelmed the police. Crowe put on eighty witnesses to describe the callous details of the murder plot. Darrow objected that Crowe simply wanted to inflame public opinion to pressure the judge into executing them. After all, the pair had already admitted their guilt. Judge Caverly disagreed.

To Crowe's delight, the judge explained that he considered it appropriate to hear all the gory details of the kidnapping and murder. In deciding on the sentence, the judge wanted to consider all the aggravating circumstances of the crimes. But when Crowe tried to prevent any psychiatric testimony from coming in, the evenhanded judge overruled him, too. It was true that Leopold and Loeb had to be considered legally sane when they committed the crimes – that was established by their guilty pleas. Yet Judge Caverly was also interested in hearing how their mental state might cause him to reduce the penalty he might otherwise apply.

Darrow and his co-counsel proceeded with a parade of expert witnesses to show that tests of both Leopold and Loeb showed significant abnormalities. Both had long suffered from pathologically delusional fantasies: Loeb from schizophrenia and Leopold from paranoia. Each had contemplated suicide. Though they appeared normal or superior intellectually, they were emotionally immature. Loeb still talked to his teddy bear. Their courtroom demeanor bore that out. At times, the two smiled inappropriately, appearing to share inside jokes, and continued to demonstrate absolutely no remorse.

When his turn came, Crowe put on the stand the highly respected state psychiatrists who had previously vouched for the sanity of the two youths. But as eminent as these men were in their field, they had to admit their own examination of the two teenagers was hasty and exceedingly unorthodox. The trio had not seen the defendants privately, but only questioned them for a total of three hours in the presence of police, prosecutorial staff and stenographers. The circumstances were hardly conducive to a probing inquiry.

As with the Leo Frank trial, throughout the proceedings the judge and defense lawyers received multiple death threats. So did at least one of the defense psychiatrists. As a precaution, all the participants had guards provided as they came and left the courthouse for various hearings. Anonymous notes threatened to blow up the courthouse and lynch Leopold and Loeb. More comparisons were made to the ghetto youth who was about to be hanged because his companion had killed a policeman the two accidentally encountered when pulling a robbery.

Many people were incensed at the "poor little rich boys"[9] who premeditated a callous and arbitrary murder and sought a lesser penalty for their heinous crime. How fair was that?

With huge crowds outside the courtroom demanding vengeance, Darrow made an impassioned closing argument against capital punishment. Giving his emotions full sway, Darrow wept both for the victim and for the defendants, whom he claimed could not control their shocking behavior. Darrow went into such graphic detail of the hanging process that his clients lost all trace of their smirks. Loeb visibly shuddered and Leopold became hysterical. Many women in the courtroom were moved to tears. Darrow emphasized that the alternative punishment was life in prison. He argued that facing several decades behind bars would be an even harsher penalty for the youths to endure than execution. When Darrow ended, he was totally spent. He later described the strain as so extensive, "I could never do it again, even if I should try."[10]

Some observers considered Darrow's histrionics way over the top, but fans of the legendary lawyer believed he had just delivered the finest speech of his long career. Crowe still thought he held the trump card. He spent nearly two days in furious rebuttal. "Eyes blazing," he called the two a pair of "cowardly perverts" who had likely raped Franks after he died. [11] Crowe had not mentioned this sensational charge in his original presentation, probably because he knew how inconclusive the evidence was. He followed the claim of rape with unproved allegations that Loeb had committed four other serious crimes.

Crowe argued that Leopold knew about Loeb's past criminal acts and that the joint murder of Bobby Franks was intended to buy Leopold's silence. Piling on every theory, Crowe also asserted that the ransom was a major motive. Loeb had gambling debts that greatly exceeded his allowance. Crowe saved his biggest zinger for Darrow. Crowe charged that the death penalty opponent's soft-hearted approach to law and order invited the court to "strike 'a greater blow . . . to our institutions' than a thousand murders."[12] Darrow made a quick, gloomy exit after the judge announced he would take ten days to reach his decision. Crowe reveled in the moment. He smoked a cigar while accepting congratulations from colleagues for his masterful refutation of Darrow's plea for clemency.

The pressure was now all on the judge. Every day, he received stacks of letters urging him to impose the death penalty. Reporters fueled public ire with more interviews of Leopold and Loeb enjoying their celebrity status at the jail. They ate well, got plenty of sleep, played baseball in the yard and entertained visitors, including a half dozen Chicago Cubs. Around the city, heavy bets were being placed on the outcome: Darrow's past record led odds-makers to favor a life sentence over the death penalty.

The day before Judge Caverly announced his decision, the county took extraordinary security precautions. All other court business scheduled for Wednesday, September 10, 1924, was cancelled. Scores of sheriff's deputies and bailiffs were assigned to monitor the elevators and hallways. Nearly six dozen policemen on motorcycles would back up one hundred patrolmen encircling the Criminal Court Building. Another fifty mounted on horseback would patrol the street. Plainclothes men were instructed to mix into the crowds to spot any potential bomb throwers or gunmen.

On the day of the hearing, Judge Caverly's wife received a phone call that her husband had been killed. Unaware of the horrible prank, Judge Caverly arrived safely at the court building for his last case before retiring. To protect him from attack, he came in a limousine with an armed police escort. Accompanying the judge inside the car were two detectives carrying machine guns and revolvers. Crowds surged around the building into the street and up the stairs of the six-story building, but only media representatives and people connected with the case were allowed inside Judge Caverly's courtroom. For the reading of his decision, the judge also permitted live radio coverage – score one victory for the *Chicago Tribune*'s station WGN (an acronym for the "World's Greatest Newspaper"). Throughout Chicago, people stopped whatever they were doing to congregate by radios to await the judge's ruling.

Judge Caverly methodically addressed all three arguments for leniency argued by the defense team. First was the rarity of imposing the death penalty on a defendant who offered a guilty plea instead of forcing the prosecutor to prove his guilt. The elderly jurist rejected that argument out of hand. He noted that the evidence of guilt was so overwhelming, they would have been convicted anyway. The pair did not accommodate the prosecutor by pleading guilty; it was a surprise, unwelcomed, defense tactic. The second argument was based on the mountain of psychiatric evidence offered to convince the judge not to execute the pair for their compulsive crime. The judge was now convinced that Leopold and Loeb were quite abnormal, but he rejected the impact of their mental state on the sentence. "Similar analyses made of other persons accused of crime would probably reveal similar or different abnormalities,"[13] he said. By then, it seemed obvious to observers and those listening raptly to their radios that the pair would indeed be executed.

But Judge Caverly had not finished. He realized that it would be "the path of least resistance to impose the extreme penalty of the law."[14] He had saved until last the question of their age, noting that only two minors had been put to death in Illinois history by legal process. Falling in line with the thinking of modern criminologists, Judge Caverly reasoned that the penalty should never be used for minors. Despite the atrocity of the crime, he sentenced both Leopold and Loeb to life imprisonment for the murder and 99 years for the kidnap for ransom. In imposing that sentence, he expressed his strong opinion that the horrendous nature of their crime should render them permanently ineligible for parole.

Everyone was astounded. Darrow had salvaged his record and reinforced his amazing reputation. Crowe voiced his fury at the judge to the press. Adding fuel to an already outraged public reaction, Crowe declared the crime "unequaled in the criminal history of the state . . . an atrocious and cold blooded murder by [a pair with a history] of perversion . . . degenerates of the worst type [who] struck terror to the heart of every father and mother throughout the community."[15] Newspapers echoed his condemnation of the decision. The rich were judged by different standards. Money bought results. (Though most people believed newspaper accounts that Darrow had been paid a million-dollar fee, Darrow only wound up getting paid about thirty thousand dollars, the same amount as each of his two co-counsel and a fraction of the value he attributed to his services.)

Some skeptics even speculated that Darrow bribed the judge, recalling the criminal charges on similar allegations for which Darrow had narrowly escaped conviction in California over a decade before in defending the McNamara brothers' bombing case.[16] Others wondered, if the judge's ruling was based simply on their age, why had the county been forced to waste huge amounts of taxpayers' money on a lengthy hearing entertaining psychiatric evidence? Leopold put it more succinctly. Couldn't they have achieved the same result by just offering their birth certificates into evidence?[17]

Historian Simon Baatz estimates that several thousand contemporaneous articles were written about the Leopold and Loeb proceedings.[18] The case soon spawned a highly successful London play, *Rope*, ironically adapted as one of Alfred Hitchcock's least-watched movies. Accounts of the case appeared prominently in Darrow biographies and inspired several novels. One novel was turned into another movie in 1959, *Compulsion*, with Orson Welles playing the aging legal giant. Interest revived in the story in the last decade of the century with films in 1992 and 2002; a 2003 musical, *Thrill Me: The Leopold and Loeb Story;* and, most recently, Baatz's own 2008 work *For the Thrill of It: Leopold, Loeb, and the Murder That Shocked Chicago.* Throughout the 20th century and into our own, people remained captivated by the psychological motivation of two young men who threw away lives of great promise for a senseless act of extreme depravity.

One side benefit of all the publicity was that it raised awareness of the predicament of Bernard Grant, the other youthful defendant then on death row. Grant won a reprieve from the governor. Meanwhile, "Fighting Bob" Crowe's standing in the community plummeted due to his failure to stop bold gangland murders. Rumors began to circulate that Crowe must be on the take. Then in 1926, one of Crowe's chief assistants was gunned down by machine gun fire as he emerged from a Cicero bar with members of the O'Donnell gang. At the time, the Irish gang was known to be battling an Italian mob for the beer trade. The taint of corruption ruined Crowe's chances for future political office.

Once they started serving their sentences, Leopold and Loeb helped update and expand the prison library and were permitted to start a correspondence school. Loeb also used family money to bribe his jailers for favors. In 1936, he was killed by another inmate, who claimed Loeb had made sexual advances and threatened him with a razor. The evidence suggested that Loeb was unarmed and attacked from behind, but the homicide was left unresolved.

Leopold did his best to become a model prisoner. He compiled statistics to help officials evaluate parole risks. He volunteered as a guinea pig for malaria testing on the promise that risking his life for that medical experiment would be taken into account when he came up for parole. Not surprisingly, the notoriety of his crime still trumped all rehabilitation efforts the first time Leopold sought parole. Yet, after thirty-three years in prison, he applied again in 1958 and was successful.

Even after such lengthy incarceration, Leopold's release brought severe criticism to the parole board. That same year Leopold published his autobiography *Life Plus 99 Years*. By then, he had moved to Puerto Rico where he began living off his substantial inheritance and started working with the local poor. Leopold spent the remaining decade of his life married to a doctor's widow and taking time to travel extensively throughout the world. He died of a heart attack in August of 1971, just a few months shy of his sixty-seventh birthday.

Darrow followed up on his defense of Leopold and Loeb with a spirited campaign to abolish the death penalty altogether. He would have been gratified to learn that in 2000 Republican Governor George Ryan placed a moratorium on the Illinois death penalty pending recommendations for overhaul of the criminal justice system. Governor Ryan explained that he harbored "grave concerns about our state's shameful record of convicting innocent people and putting them on death row."[19] The moratorium remained in effect until 2011 when Illinois officially abolished capital punishment, following recent bans enacted in New York, New Jersey and New Mexico. Since then Connecticut and Maryland have also banned the death penalty.

Shortly after his 2015 inauguration, Pennsylvania's new governor Tom Wolf imposed a moratorium pending completion of a report on capital punishment. Governor Wolf described capital punishment as "a flawed system that has been proven to be an endless cycle of court proceedings as well as ineffective, unjust, and expensive."[20] Pennsylvania's District Attorney Association unsuccessfully challenged that moratorium as an abuse of power. As of mid-2017 it still remained in effect. Currently, the federal government, the military and thirty-one states retain the death penalty for adults. From the mid-1970s to 2005, though twenty states still permitted execution of minors, only ten in fact did so. Of the twenty-two youths executed in these states between 1976 and 2005, Texas alone accounted for thirteen, underscoring the mounting reluctance of most states to invoke capital punishment for juvenile offenders.

In 2005, by a five-to-four vote in *Roper v. Simmons*, the United States Supreme Court concluded such an extreme penalty was cruel and unusual punishment. Writing for a bare majority, Justice Anthony Kennedy relied upon a national consensus supported by medical and social-science evidence that the immaturity of teenagers made it inappropriate to impose that ultimate sanction no matter how horrendous the circumstances. He noted that "instability and emotional imbalance of young people may often be a factor in the crime." Justice Kennedy concluded, "From a moral standpoint, it would be misguided to equate the failings of a minor with those of an adult, for a greater possibility exists that a minor's character deficiencies will be reformed. . . . Our determination finds confirmation in the stark reality that the United States is the only country in the world that continues to give official sanction to the juvenile death penalty."[21] The Supreme Court's ruling spared 72 other juveniles on death row, 29 of them in Texas. The ruling applied only to those under 18 at the time of the crime. It would not have affected death sentences against teenage offenders like Leopold and Loeb, who were 19 and 18, respectively, on the date of Franks' murder.

In 2012, in *Miller v. Alabama*, the Supreme Court took the next step and declared that sentencing a juvenile to life without possibility of parole was unconstitutional under the Eighth Amendment. At the time, more than two thousand inmates were incarcerated across the country for brutal crimes committed when they were children – a draconian sentencing practice which isolated the United States among advanced nations of the world. Imposition of life without parole subjected most teenagers to longer sentences than adults who committed similar crimes, simply by reason of their life expectancy. As Justice Kagan pointed out in her majority opinion, the youthfulness of an offender should allow for the possibility of eventual release:

> Mandatory life without parole for a juvenile precludes consideration of his chronological age and its hallmark features – among them immaturity, impetuosity, and failure to appreciate risks and consequences. It prevents taking into account the family and home environment that surrounds him – and from which he cannot usually extricate himself – no matter how brutal or dysfunctional. It neglects the circumstances of the homicide offense, including the extent of his participation in the conduct and the way familial and peer pressures may have affected him. Indeed, it ignores that he might have been charged and convicted of a lesser offense if not for incompetencies associated with youth – for example, his inability to deal with police officers or prosecutors (including on a plea agreement) or his incapacity to assist his own attorneys.[22]

* * * * *

Darrow took a very unpopular stance in arguing for the lives of two privileged teenagers who cold-bloodedly committed a heinous crime. But history would not judge Darrow's astonishing performance in saving the lives of Leopold and Loeb as his most memorable case. In the summer of 1925, Darrow interrupted his lecture tour against capital punishment with an impromptu trip to Tennessee. The war horse who spent much of his forty-five-year career battling over issues of life and death would best be remembered for volunteering to defend a high school teacher for a minor infraction that involved a $100 fine. Yet everyone headed to Dayton, Tennessee, that July knew that the stakes were enormous. This show trial would engage Americans in a heated debate over the proper roles of science and religion in public education of their children on the most controversial subject then in dispute – the origins of mankind itself. Despite the carnival atmosphere of the debate, lives hung in the balance here as well. Whether observers believed in survival of the fittest or God's preordained plan, both sides drew heavy support from white supremacists using genocidal tactics to preserve their power.

9. THE DARK SIDE OF THE SCOPES TRIAL

White Supremacists on Both Sides Embrace Genocide

*I furnished the body that was needed
to sit in the defendant's chair.*

– JOHN SCOPES[1]

Darrow's most famous case was custom-designed to be an extraordinary spectacle. The Scopes "monkey" trial was, from start to finish, popular entertainment for the White majority played out in an international arena. It capitalized on front-page clashes in newspapers and sold-out lecture halls that pitted Fundamentalist believers in the literal truth of Genesis against the consensus of established academia teaching Darwin's theory of evolution. Supporters of evolution included not only agnostics and atheists, but a growing number of liberal monotheists. Darwin also had most of the media on his side, both in the United States and abroad. Less widely remembered is the moral issue that underlay the debate – the growing worldwide Social Darwinism movement among white Christians embracing forced eugenics to accomplish racial purity, a movement that would soon reach its most frightening form in Nazi Germany.

In his Pulitzer Prize–winning book, *Summer for the Gods: The Scopes Trial and America's Continuing Debate over Science and Religion*, Prof. Edward Larson argues that the Scopes trial deserves the distinction of "THE" trial of the century: "The issues raised by the Scopes trial and legend endure precisely because they embody the characteristically American struggle between individual liberty and majoritarian democracy, and cast it in the timeless debate over science and religion."[2]

The issues do endure, but they preceded and postdated the event in Dayton, Tennessee, that is more aptly described as an immensely entertaining political debate than a true trial. What made it so memorable is that it starred two men who stole the show: Darrow, the shaggy-haired legend in the twilight of his career, and another aged American giant of even greater renown, perennial presidential candidate and orator William Jennings Bryan, trumpeting his very last cause.

The famous scene of Darrow cross-examining Bryan on his belief in the literal truth of the Bible occurred outside the presence of the jury and was ruled inadmissible. In the trial itself, Scopes' lawyers never paid much attention to the nominal defendant as an individual, nor did the jury ever consider any issue of his intent to violate the Butler Act. The images imprinted in the memory of four generations of Americans – a jailed science teacher persecuted by a bombastic prosecutor who died fighting to impose creationism as the law of the land – are largely a media product of the .

It was not until its thirtieth anniversary in 1955 that the test case spawned a Broadway play, which has since been revived twice, in 1996 and again in 2007. In more than half a century, the play *Inherit the Wind* became a highly popular high school and community theater staple. Most indelibly, the trial was transformed into a classic 1960 movie, starring Oscar-winners Spencer Tracy and Fredric March as the two American titans. Since then, the movie with its irresistible lead roles was remade three more times with different actors, including the late George C. Scott as Darrow. But the first time the *Scopes* trial was performed on stage was in the summer of 1925.

Several leading townsmen of Dayton, Tennessee, including its part-time prosecutor, were excited by the prospect of a gimmick that would put their picturesque Cumberland Mountain town on a tourism map. The governor had just the month before signed the first law in the country forbidding the teaching in public schools of man's descent from primitive ancestors. One of the Dayton boosters then spotted an intriguing ad the ACLU ran in the *Chattanooga Times*: "We are looking for a Tennessee teacher who is willing to accept our services in testing [the new Tennessee anti-evolution] law in the courts. Our lawyers think a friendly test case can be arranged without costing a teacher his or her job. Distinguished counsel have volunteered their services. All we need now is a willing client."[3]

What could bring renown and an influx of cash to Dayton better than hosting a summer debate on a national hot button issue? In Dayton, as elsewhere in Tennessee, almost everyone attended church. There were nine places of worship for a population of three thousand. But uncharacteristic of the South as a whole at that time, a majority of the local adults had a high school education. Dayton had established its own high school twenty years earlier. The town also boasted some Progressives who founded a library and met regularly in a readers' club.

As Larson points out, several recent developments had pushed the issue to the forefront of American public consciousness. More than a decade earlier a major archeological "find" was reported with much fan-fare in England. The skeletal remains of what became known as "Piltdown man" were pronounced the missing link – a common ancestor of men and apes. The discovery caused great excitement. It appeared to confirm just what Charles Darwin had posited in his 1859 book, *On the Origin of Species by Means of Natural Selection, or, The Preservation of Favoured Races in the Struggle for Life.*[4]

Evolutionary theories predated Darwin by more than half a century in modern Europe, and even as far back as the ancient Greeks. But many modern scientists did not find theories of evolution irreconcilable with their belief in God. They simply treated the Biblical account of creation as allegory. Charles Darwin considered himself an agnostic. But atheists began latching onto his assumption that, rather than springing into existence at God's command, species evolved as random variations passed on over millions of years simply by the principle of survival of the fittest.

One of Darwin's most influential followers was Prussian philosopher Friedrich Nietzsche. Nietzsche insisted that there was no God. Mankind, like other animals, only progressed through brutal battles for dominance. Nietzsche's theory, which included the concept of a race of supermen, gained wide support among white supremacists in the first two decades of the 20th century. Leopold and Loeb were but extreme examples of Nietzsche's many zealous followers.

Though Leopold and Loeb were not the only Jewish intellectuals to embrace Nietzsche, the prevailing view was that his super race would be achieved through breeding of homogenous Protestants of Northern European ancestry. Jews and Catholics were considered inferior, as were persons with inherited disabilities. Though Darwin considered Negroes part of the same species as whites, he firmly believed they were lower on the evolutionary chain than Caucasians.

Darwin's theory of evolution was now supported by numerous archaeological discoveries. It posed a direct threat to literalists who interpreted the Bible to mean that God created all life in six twenty-four hour days in or about 4004 B.C.[5] Literalists firmly believed mankind was created by God in his own image, not as the result of gradual evolution from more primitive life forms. Yet for many years, these competing views occupied largely separate spheres. Fundamentalist farmers had little trouble accepting the pioneering work on plant hybrids by agriculturist Luther Burbank, even though it was premised on Darwinian theory. There was also growing acceptance of the evolution of animals traceable through fossil remains. But for over half a century, the absence of evidence of modern man's own primitive ancestors had left the issue of divine creation of humankind more debatable. That was why the discovery of "Piltdown man" in 1912 created such an uproar.

The Piltdown skull was much later exposed as a hoax: it combined an orangutan jaw with a modern human skull fragment. But at the time, world-renowned scientists were taken in. Reputable journalists turned the story into banner headlines. Its impact was compounded in 1916 when a new study of American religiosity rattled conservative Christians. The scholarly survey revealed that university students and professors now shared widespread disbelief in the fundamental Christian tenet of immortality. The author concluded that "Christianity, as a system of belief, has utterly broken down."[6]

The survey results helped galvanize the foundation of the World's Christian Fundamentals Association (WCFA) in 1919. It did not take long for the WCFA to focus on challenging the teaching of evolution in high schools as its primary focus. In the early 1920s, newspapers featured the growing controversy. Leading Fundamentalist preachers across the nation condemned Darwin as an infidel, and they ridiculed as agents of the devil those who taught that man descended from pre-historic apelike ancestors.

In February of 1925, newspapers reported another missing link – a skull of a hominid more than two million years old, found in northern South Africa. Prodded by leaders of the national Fundamentalist move-ment, within a month, Tennessee's legislature made history by becom-ing the first to adopt a statute outlawing the teaching of evolution in the public schools. The 1925 Butler Act made it a finable offense "for any teacher in the public schools of the State which are supported in whole or in part by the public school funds of the State, to teach any theory that denies the Story of the Divine Creation of man as taught in the Bible, and to teach instead that man has descended from a lower order of animals."[7]

In Tennessee at the time this new law was simply considered good politics. Few legislators in the majority assumed that the Butler Act would be rigorously enforced. Nor did the governor, who, like more than half of the state's adult population, was himself a Baptist. The ACLU had been following closely all the states considering such leg-islation and immediately set to work on challenging the new law. The ACLU's primary concern was the threat posed to academic freedom by religious fanatics whom many feared might not stop until the Biblical account of Genesis was enshrined in the Constitution.

Meeting at the local drugstore, the convivial Dayton plotters included lawyer Sue Hicks (reportedly the original "boy named Sue" after his mother who died in childbirth) and his brother Herbert who convinced a good-natured friend to volunteer for the proposed exhibi-tion contest. The young man who agreed to have his name put forward as the proposed defendant was a physics and math teacher named John Scopes. The ACLU quickly accepted Scopes as the guinea pig; it was already planning to foot the bill for the special prosecutor and defense team. No one would expect a true legal contest to have one agency offering to pay for both sides. The ACLU Board assumed the case would likely be lost at trial and won on appeal on constitutional grounds in the United States Supreme Court. The ACLU was not focused on dis-proving Fundamentalism, but on preventing political curtailment of academic freedom. The broader issue was one of the original focuses of the ACLU almost a decade earlier, when the organization was newly formed. Back then it was called the National Civil Liberties Bureau and battled for the jobs of teachers who opposed World War I.

The local judge, John Raulston, was an eager participant in the scheme to lure new visitors to Dayton. If they wanted to attract summer vacationers and get the jump on every other Tennessee town, speed was essential. So Raulston specially convened the grand jury in late May with his eye on an early July trial date. Scopes coached his students on what to say, and the indictment was issued within an hour. Word spread quickly. The Chamber of Commerce went to work on a brochure high-lighting local industry. Dayton's shopkeepers stocked up on kitschy simian souvenirs. The community weathered the scorn of neighboring townspeople for the publicity-seeking stunt. Daytonians figured other municipalities just wished they had thought of it first. They expected up to thirty thousand people to flock to their town.

Sue Hicks was one of the original prosecutors and would remain on the team as it expanded. The prosecutors were excited when one of the most prominent anti-evolutionists in the country, the "Silver-Tongued Orator" William Jennings Bryan, immediately volunteered his services. They gladly accepted, although the three-time Presidential candidate had not practiced law in over thirty-five years. His job would primarily be to make speeches and attract media attention — the actual chief prosecutor would be district attorbney Tom Stewart who, a decade plus later, would be elected Senator. Dayton hoped to entice British science fiction writer H. G. Wells to lead the defense team. The fact that Wells was not even a lawyer underscored just how little the spectacle was intended to resemble a real criminal trial. The most Scopes risked was being fined, and Bryan himself had generously offered to pay that fine for Scopes, assuming the teacher was convicted.

When Clarence Darrow read that Bryan had signed up, Darrow could not resist offering free assistance to the history-making effort. The ACLU tried its best to keep Darrow out; the organization felt that his notoriety would do the case more harm than good. But the chance to challenge his old friend Bryan directly in a courtroom in the heart of the Fundamentalist South was too tempting. Back in 1896, Darrow had vigorously campaigned for Bryan when the Populist first ran for President and Darrow ran unsuccessfully for Congress. Both had also supported the women's suffrage movement that had just succeeded in 1920 in passing the Nineteenth Amendment granting women the right to vote after more than seven decades of effort. (Yet when it came to women lawyers in the courtroom, Darrow remained a confirmed misogynist.)

The two men took opposite positions on the Eighteenth Amendment's installation of Prohibition. They also had parted ways over the recent world war. Bryan was a leading pacifist in the pre-war years. He quit his post as Secretary of State in the Wilson administration to protest the impending entry of the United States into that war. Yet once war was declared, Bryan supported the Wilson administration's persecution of war opponents. Always attracted to unpopular causes, Darrow was on the opposite side. He defended conscientious objectors, though he had personally come around to the view that the war was necessary. Yet the biggest issue that separated the two men was the one that lured both aging giants to Dayton, Tennessee, in the summer of 1925.

Though Bryan was not as deep a thinker as Darrow, "The Great Commoner" was appalled by a newly published history book that described how Nietzsche and Darwin had influenced German war mongers. Nietzsche challenged the very premise of the Judeo-Christian ethic valuing charity and compassion to those less able. Nietzsche also glorified war and ridiculed democracy as the refuge of weaklings. To Bryan, the will of the majority was sacrosanct, as was the Biblical injunction to love thy neighbor as thyself. The horrific consequences of World War I reinforced Bryan's view that old time religion was a cure for what ailed the modern world.

Though Darrow also prized democracy and compassion, he was, in contrast to Bryan, a confirmed agnostic and lifelong supporter of evolutionary theory. Darrow had made it his own personal mission to challenge traditional Christianity as a "slave religion," tolerating injustice, mediocrity and complacency.[8] In the early twenties, Bryan incorporated into his lectures the danger posed by Nietzsche's and Darwin's ideas. Bryan had new fodder from the widespread publicity surrounding the Leopold and Loeb murder trial in 1924. The God-fearing majority of Americans were horrified by the amoral consequences of Nietzsche's concept of supermen unbound by rules of behavior constraining ordinary mortals.

Fundamentalists' concern for the souls of the next generation found a ready audience among their alarmed congregations. Nationwide, public high schools had mushroomed over the past thirty years. In Tennessee, five times as many children attended high school in 1925 as had done so at the turn of the century. Didn't parents have the right to control what their children were being taught? In the 19th century, public schools had incorporated generalities from the Bible into their rudimentary science courses. But by the early 20th century, textbooks such as those used in Tennessee routinely incorporated the growing scientific consensus supporting Darwin's theory of evolution, including the concept of survival of the fittest.

Separation of church and state was interpreted to relegate religious teaching to private schools. Orators like Bryan argued that if the First Amendment prevented the teaching of the Bible in public schools, surely it was improper to force-feed the nation's children with the notion that men and apes were cousins with common ancestors that evolved over millions of years. The very idea was contrary to everything Fundamentalists learned in Sunday school. Bryan was also greatly concerned by a more sinister aspect of teaching Social Darwinism.

George William Hunter – the author of the official textbook every public high school in Tennessee had been using for the past five years – was an ardent proponent of forced eugenics. It was then a growing field which had started in Europe in the 1880s and then slowly gained adherents in the United States. Its popularity increased substantially following the publication of a book in 1916 by New York lawyer and conservationist Madison Grant. In *The Passing of the Great Race* Grant advocated sterilization and anti-miscegenation laws to preserve the Nordic race from presumed degradation.

In 1922, Harry Laughlin, the director of the influential Carnegie-funded Eugenics Record Office in New York, published a book in which he proposed a model national law for compulsory sterilization of persons chronically demonstrating social inadequacy. Included in the list of targets were those whom Dr. Laughlin labeled "criminalistic" (including the "delinquent and wayward"), inebriates, the blind and deaf (and those with severely impaired sight or hearing), persons with deformities (including crippled persons), the insane, dependents (including "orphans, ne'er-do-wells, the homeless, tramps and paupers") and a catch-all of persons labeled "feeble-minded," which encompassed persons labeled as exhibiting low moral standards.[9]

Hunter was among educators bent on convincing the next generation to accept eugenics as a necessary approach to controlling the American population going forward. His high school textbook, *A Civic Biology Presented in Problems,* describes the evolution of man from races "much lower in their mental organization than the present inhabitants." It goes on to state that:

> Even to-day the earth is not entirely civilized. The Races of Man. –
> At the present time there exist upon the earth five races or varieties
> of man, each very different from the other in instincts, social
> customs, and, to an extent, in structure. These are the Ethiopian
> or negro type, originating in Africa; the Malay or brown race, from
> the islands of the Pacific; The American Indian; the Mongolian or
> yellow race, including the natives of China, Japan, and the Eskimos;
> and finally, the highest type of all, the Caucasians, represented by
> the civilized white inhabitants of Europe and America.[10]

Bryan had no quarrel with Hunter's premise that "civilized white inhabitants from Europe and America" represented the highest form of life. But Hunter did not stop there: "If the stock of domesticated animals can be improved, it is not unfair to ask if the health and vigor of the future generations of men and women on the earth might not be improved by applying to them the laws of selection." Hunter had no qualms about teaching eugenics as the new gospel. Hunter argued that the "race should demand . . . freedom from germ diseases which might be handed down to the offspring. Tuberculosis, syphilis, that dread disease which cripples and kills hundreds of thousands of innocent children, epilepsy, and feeble-mindedness are handicaps which it is not only unfair but criminal to hand down to posterity."[11]

In a section entitled "Parasitism and its Cost to Society," Hunter went much further:

> Hundreds of families . . . exist today, spreading disease, immorality, and crime to all parts of this country. The cost to society of such families is very severe. Just as certain animals or plants become parasitic on other plants or animals, these families have become parasitic on society. They not only do harm to others by corrupting, stealing, or spreading disease, but they are actually protected and cared for by the state out of public money. Largely for them the poorhouse and the asylum exist. They take from society, but they give nothing in return. They are true parasites.

Most chilling was Hunter's suggestion to his adolescent readers of "The Remedy." He told his students: "If such people were lower animals, we would probably kill them off to prevent them from spreading. Humanity will not allow this, but we do have the remedy of separating the sexes in asylums or other places and in various ways preventing intermarriage and the possibilities of perpetuating such a low and degenerate race. Remedies of this sort have been tried successfully in Europe and are now meeting with some success in this country."[12]

Bryan objected that Social Darwinists should pay for their own private schools and keep the public schools neutral. The taxpayers who funded educational institutions should have the right to prevent proselytizing atheists from advancing the theory of evolution as established fact. Bryan at least wanted Fundamentalist beliefs like "Love thy neighbor as thyself" placed on an equal footing. Otherwise, the curriculum undermined the individual right of children raised as Fundamentalists to believe in an almighty God who created mankind directly in his own image.

In the South, the question of how Darwin's theory would be presented in public schools was one whose direct impact was almost exclusively on white students. Schools remained strictly segregated. Evolution was not taught in elementary school. Just as was true elsewhere in the South, virtually no black children anywhere in the state of Tennessee had public schooling available to them after eighth grade. Although a few black preachers openly supported the Fundamentalist position, the NAACP and deans of black universities sided with evolutionary science as the more enlightened position. Darrow was a founding member of the NAACP and one of the leading civil rights advocates of his day. But acceptance of evolution still had Darrow and the NAACP at odds with Social Darwinists like Hunter who were indoctrinating impressionable high school students on the values of maintaining separation of the races and perpetuating belief in the inferiority of blacks.

Religious leaders were equally divided on the issue of white supremacy. Liberal ministers and rabbis had led the 19th century abolitionist movement. Their successors saw no conflict between evolutionary theory and belief in an almighty God, all of whose children were entitled to equal dignity and respect. In contrast, Fundamentalist preachers claimed blacks were a separate subhuman species or descendants of Ham cursed by God to eternal slavery or subservience. Among the revived Ku Klux Klan leaders were conservative ministers who strongly endorsed the Fundamentalist viewpoint. Yet the KKK and eugenics proponents like George William Hunter and Madison Grant did agree wholeheartedly on white supremacy.

Just over a year before the Scopes trial, they collaborated to enact strict quotas on non-Nordic emigrants. The Johnson-Reed Immigration Act expressly promoted white homogeneity and would remain U.S. policy for more than 40 years. In promoting its passage, Congress turned to Madison Grant and other eugenicists to provide them with a pseudo-scientific rationale for drastically reducing the influx of European Jews and Catholics, as well as Greeks, Slavs and African emigres, while altogether excluding Asian and Arab nationals based on their countries of origin. The bill passed with overwhelming support in both the House (323-71) and Senate (94-6).

Bryan believed in white supremacy but feared where Social Darwinists were headed with their interventionist approach to racial purity. Yet, since 1896, "the Prairie Populist" had drawn strong support from white Southern Democrats. KKK backing was also essential in getting his younger brother nominated for Vice President in 1924

Source: The Chicago Defender; used with the permission of The Chicago Defender.

"Disbelievers in the Evolution Theory" – (The Chicago Defender, *June 13, 1925*)

The Chicago Defender's *African-American publisher, Robert Abbott, had an entirely different take on the Scopes trial than white supremacists did. Since 1905, Abbott had been a major influence among his black readership urging what became the Great Migration from the South northward to Chicago, Detroit and other cities across the nation. His cartoon about the Scopes trial showed an American flag over the Capitol in the background, a black man being lynched in the lower left and two apes huddled in a tree wondering if "fiends like those" in the white mob below could really be their descendants.*

on the brokered Democratic Party ticket with former Ambassador to Great Britain John W. Davies. As a trusted elder statesman, Bryan helped forge that compromise ticket by playing a key role in preventing the 1924 Democratic Party platform from condemning KKK violence. (Newspapers dubbed that New York convention "the Klanbake." On the Fourth of July, KKK-affiliated delegates took a break from the contentious gathering at Madison Square Garden to join 20,000 Klansmen across the river in New Jersey burning crosses and hanging New York Gov. Al Smith in effigy. Smith had been a frontrunner coming into the Convention and would win the nomination in 1928 as the nation's first Catholic candidate for president).[13]

The gathering in Dayton in the summer of 1925 promised a more lighthearted meeting of opposing political and philosophical camps than the raucous Democratic Convention Bryan had participated in the summer before in New York. When Darrow and his wife arrived in Dayton, they were quite surprised. It was already overflowing with competing factions, producing a carnival atmosphere, complete with live monkeys. Prominent signs throughout the town told all comers to "READ YOUR BIBLE." One of those signs was posted on the side of the courthouse itself. Hordes of reporters, atheists, scientists and radicals overflowed the hotels and boarding houses. Poorer farmers and unemployed mineworkers from nearby areas created a tent city on the outskirts of town near where Pentecostal Christian "Holy Rollers" had decided to hold a revival meeting.

The *Chicago Defender*'s African-American publisher Robert Abbott had an entirely different take on the Scopes trial. Since 1905, Abbott had been a major influence among his black readership, urging what became the Great Migration from the South northward to Chicago, Detroit and other cities. His cartoon about the Scopes trial showed a black being lynched and two monkeys huddled in a tree wondering if fiends like those in the frenzied white mob could really be their descendants. It posed a good question.

Meanwhile, in Dayton, in anticipation of record crowds, brand new public toilets and phone banks were installed in the courthouse. The courtroom itself was redesigned to allow for five hundred more seats in the gallery, a platform for a movie camera, and telegraph wires. Few paying tourists actually ever arrived, but over 200 newspaper reporters did descend upon the town from across the country. London also sent two correspondents. "In a move symbolic of the trial itself," Larson noted that microphones displaced the jury box in the center of the courtroom. The microphones enabled the proceedings to be heard simultaneously in four public halls elsewhere in Dayton and via loudspeakers for attendees on the court's own front lawn.[11]

At a banquet in his honor, William Jennings Bryan called the upcoming debate "a duel to the death." When Darrow got his chance to respond, he announced that "We will smother Mr. Bryan's influence under a mountain of scientific testimony."[15] More than a score of telegraphers would cover the drama as if it were the World Series: they disseminated play-by-play daily reports via the specially hung telegraph wires to over twenty-three hundred daily papers covering the trial. The media coverage exceeded that for any prior American event, including unprecedented transmissions during the trial to European newspapers eager to cover the spectacle for their readers.

The ACLU board had tried to get Darrow removed from the case as an unnecessary distraction, but did not succeed. So they sent their General Counsel Arthur Hays to make sure the defense stayed on track. Though Scopes had little to lose, the affable young bachelor from Kentucky liked having someone of Darrow's stature on his team. Nor was Scopes an ideal defendant for promoting the ACLU's agenda. He did not regularly conduct biology classes, but only occasionally taught the subject as a substitute. If called as a witness, Scopes would likely have had trouble expounding articulately upon either evolutionary principles or academic freedom, particularly if subjected to rigorous cross-examination. Indeed, his lack of substantial training in biology was the principal reason why Scopes assumed that his lawyers never asked him to testify.

Had Scopes been called to the stand, a major issue of criminal intent could have easily become dispositive of the trial's outcome. Before Scopes' friends asked him if he was game to submit to a symbolic arrest, Scopes had already brought to the attention of his principal that

Hunter's *Civic Biology* violated the new Butler Act. With the short time left in the spring semester, the principal – who normally taught the course himself – had told Scopes just to go ahead with teaching evolution the same as before.

At the time of the trial Hunter's *Civic Biology* was still the official textbook supplied by the state. No replacement had yet been put forward. In fact, Governor Peary, in signing the Butler Act into law, had blithely stated that he did not believe that the textbooks currently in use contradicted the Bible. The governor did not anticipate the law would be invoked any time soon. None of Scopes' students and none of their parents had raised any issue when Scopes taught a class on Darwin's theory, which Scopes wasn't exactly sure he had really covered in any meaningful detail.

Had defending Scopes as an individual been the issue – as befits true criminal trials – the focus of his lawyers in seeking his acquittal should have been on the teacher's lack of criminal intent. Scopes was using the legislatively preapproved Tennessee biology textbook at the express direction of the school's principal. But his lawyers had a different agenda and seemed almost to forget Scopes existed. On the afternoon that trial testimony was to commence, Scopes came back late. He had been cooling off with a swim at lunchtime, accompanied by a new member of the prosecution team, William Jennings Bryan, Jr. When Scopes wormed his way back to his seat, proceedings had already started without the ostensible defendant even in attendance!

Unlike the severe public reaction that had prevented radio broadcast of the Leopold and Loeb sentencing hearing, the radio station affiliated with the *Chicago Tribune* apparently had no difficulty obtaining permission to broadcast the entire Scopes trial live. The *Chicago Tribune* claimed the simultaneous broadcast was a first in the history of radio. It quashed criticism that such intrusion was unfair to Scopes: "This is not a criminal trial as that term is ordinarily understood. It is more like the opening of a summer university. . . The defendant, Scopes, is . . . a negligible factor. Nothing serious can happen to him. The contest is entirely over ideas."[16]

In a gesture of equality, Darrow and Bryan had each been feted with

Source: https://en.wikipedia.org/wiki/John_T._Scopes. (Smithsonian Institution, photographed by Watson Davis.)

*John Scopes (**left**), a month before the trial. He considered himself window dressing for a publicity stunt featuring agnostic Clarence Darrow and creationist William Jennings Bryan. In 2005, a statue of Bryan was erected at the courthouse in Dayton. In July 2017, a statue of Darrow joined the one of Bryan.*

Source: "Judge Raulston Charging the Jury at the Scopes Trial," The New York Public Library Digital Collections. 1860–1920. http://digitalcollections.nypl.org/items/510d47d9-b758-a3d9-e040-e00a18064a99

*Judge Raulston (**left**) reading to the jury. He brought his own well-thumbed Bible to court along with a statute book. Newspapers covered the trial as if they were reporting the World Series, play by play.*

The outcome of the trial was predicted when it opened with an invocation by a local minister: "We are conscious, our Father, that Thou art the source of our wisdom and of our power . . ."

More than a score of telegraphers disseminated daily reports via specially hung telegraph wires to over 2300 daily papers. The media coverage exceeded that for any prior American event and included unprecedented transmissions during the trial to European newspapers eager to cover the spectacle for their readers.

consecutive banquets by the Chamber of Commerce before the trial commenced. But Darrow knew the deck was heavily stacked against the defense team. From what it appeared, the jury pool consisted mostly of conservative Christian men whose preachers warned them in Sunday sermons that those who questioned the literal truth of Genesis would be damned to Hell. The judge himself arrived in court with both a well-thumbed Bible and a statute book. Darrow soon began to wonder why the judge bothered at all with the latter.

The very first day of trial set the tone with an invocation by a local minister that commenced, "We are conscious, our Father, that Thou art the source of our wisdom and of our power . . . . We come to Thee this morning, our divine Father, that we may seek from Thee that wisdom to so transact the business of this court in such a way and manner that Thy name may be honored and glorified among men."[17] Rev. Cartwright elicited amens from the gallery as he asked the Holy Spirit to "be with the jury and with the accused and with all the attorneys . . . [to] be loyal to God."[18]

Not surprisingly, the prosecution accepted every one of the panel of one hundred white men whose name was drawn from a hat for jury service. Darrow and his co-counsel realized they would do more harm than good by questioning the men extensively on their ability to be objective. Instead, they focused on just three basic issues. Did the jurors have preconceived ideas about evolution? Did they consider the Bible to be for or against evolution? Would they each make up their own minds based on evidence produced at the trial? It was clear from their answers that all the men relished having front-row seats at the spectacle. Only a few admitted to bias that forced their elimination. Seasoned reporters like H. L. Mencken were highly critical of the jury's pro-Creationism bias. But an East Coast African-American newspaper editor saw nothing unusual in the situation: "The Scopes' jury is typical – typical of the judgment bar before which black men and women in the bourbon south must stand when charged with crime against members of the opposite group."[19]

The defense team primarily pinned its hopes for winning the case on pretrial arguments to the judge that the Butler Act was unconstitutional. They also intended to put on testimony from several leading scientists who believed both in God and in evolution, though not the literal truth of the Bible. Darrow and his co-counsel already had the upper hand in the court of public opinion. The scientists would cement that position. Secretly, Darrow planned to back that demonstration up by destroying Bryan's credibility. The defense would call Bryan himself to the stand and force him to answer under oath how much of Genesis he really took at face value.

Though most reporters found Darrow extraordinarily effective in arguing the illegality of the Butler Act, he likely realized that he had made little headway with the conservative judge. In any event, the defense exhibited no surprise when Judge Raulston upheld the new law. Then the judge ruled out live testimony from scientific defense witnesses, upholding the prosecutors' position that the law precluded *any* teaching that men descended from lower animals even if it was consistent with theology.

The overcrowded courtroom was exceedingly hot. Judge Raulston also was concerned its floor could not hold all the extra weight. By Monday of the second week, the judge moved the proceedings to a specially built platform on the lawn in front of the courthouse where it could be viewed by thousands of spectators. As bottles of soft drinks were hawked to the thirsty crowd, the defense surprised the prosecution and spectators by calling Bryan to the stand. Bryan rose to the challenge, to the applause of many spectators. But, as Darrow had anticipated, Bryan floundered in answering pointed questions about his belief in the literal truth of the Bible, which ended with a shouting match between the two. The *New York Times* described Darrow's cross-examination of Bryan as "the most amazing courtroom scene in Anglo-American history."[20] Yet the judge had excused the jury during Bryan's questioning and the next day, Judge Raulston ruled Darrow's examination of Bryan irrelevant and struck it from the record.

Back inside the courtroom, Darrow ended the proceedings abruptly. He explained to the jury that there was no factual issue for them to decide. Since the defense did not dispute what Scopes had taught, Darrow did not want to waste the court and jury's time. He considered

Source: John Frost
Newspapers/
Alamy stock photo

THE CHICAGO DAILY NEWS.

SCOPES "GUILTY" IN APE CASE

Source: Flickr, https://c1.staticflickr.com/7/6175/6225708128_a25b0eca30_b.jpg

RHEA COUNTY COURTHOUSE

The red brick 1891 Rhea County Courthouse where the trial took place was designated a National Historic Landmark in 1977. The Scopes trial started in a courtroom on the second floor. The courthouse now houses a museum dedicated to memorabilia from the trial. The courtroom on the second floor includes the original judge's bench, four tables, railing, jury chairs and spectator seats. Fears about the weight being put on its floor by a packed courtroom led the judge to move the trial to a temporary platform outside. That is where Darrow conducted his historic cross-examination of Bryan's beliefs in Creationism before thousands of spectators. Source: http://www. rheacounty.com/attractions.html.

In 1950, looking back, a newspaper journalist wrote: "If I had been a top flight reporter 25 years ago, I would have been down in Tennessee covering the trial of a young lad charged with teaching that man is descended from the anthropoid apes. . . . Science has come a long way since that . . . day. The 'monkey trial" in July, 1925 caused more furor, got more newspaper space and created more stir than the 1950 trial of another scientist, Dr. Klaus Emil Julius Fuchs, who was sentenced to 14 years in a British prison for giving the atom bomb blueprint to Russia." (Emphasis supplied). Source: Press and Sun Bulletin, Binghamton, New York, July 14, 1950, p. 30, www.newspaperarchives.com.

A 2015 Pew research study showed 34% of Americans still reject evolution.

Scopes' conviction a foregone conclusion. As Darrow had planned, the prosecutor was then also barred under Tennessee law from making a summation. The speech Bryan had prepared to rouse the faithful in the gallery and inspire the jury would have to await another forum. The jury retired for less than ten minutes and came back with their only choice: defendant John Thomas Scopes was found guilty of violating Tennessee's Butler Act. The judge then ordered Scopes to pay a $100 fine.

Constitutional scholar Douglas Linden describes the twelve-day Scopes trial as "a symbolic struggle for America's culture between the forces of Traditionalism and the forces of Modernism . . . [T]he Scopes Trial was about what much of the 20th century has been about."[21] Prof. Edward Gaffney, reviewing Prof. Larson's book for the *Los Angeles Times,* was more cautious in assessing the impact of that trial. He credited the Scopes trial with coming "close to meriting the designation 'trial of the century,' at least for its lasting impact on American culture."[22]

The jury itself was never asked to grapple with either modernism versus traditionalism or individual rights versus majoritarian rule. As a consequence of the court's rulings and the defense strategy, the jury only heard about two hours of testimony, and almost no argument. In the end, it had no real decision-making role at all. The case ended anti-climactically with a conceded verdict of guilty that the ACLU could then appeal on constitutional grounds.

Bryan died while napping less than two weeks later, to be eulogized as a martyr to the cause. Darrow argued the appeal the following year before the Tennessee Supreme Court. Much to the ACLU's dismay, the Tennessee Supreme Court reversed the conviction on a technicality that precluded further appeal of the constitutional issue to the United States Supreme Court.[23] The result in the case itself was thus a draw. In the meantime, Hunter's biology text was revised to delete the word "evolution" and almost all discussion of its related concepts.

The book did mention that man was a vertebrate and a mammal and included Charles Darwin as one of the "Great Names in Biology." The category of Caucasians was expanded to include Hindus and Arabs of Asia, but was no longer described as "the highest type of all." What still remained largely unchanged was the advocacy of forced eugenics.

To the passage on "Parasitism and its Cost to Society" was now added, "It is estimated that between 25% and 50% of all prisoners in penal institutions are feeble-minded."[24] In a much-awaited test case in 1927 the United States Supreme Court upheld Virginia's sterilization law, which was based on the 1922 model promoted by the Eugenics Records Office.[25] Only one justice dissented. Among those impressed with the United States experiment over the next decade was Adolf Hitler, who praised Madison Grant's book as his Bible.[26] With the Supreme Court's endorsement of eugenics, states were then encouraged to adopt or expand their own programs to modify the gene pool, resulting in the forced sterilization of more than 62,000 people nationwide by the 1960s – mostly women.[27]

Meanwhile, Creationists, buoyed by their successful defense of the Butler Act, were able to convince legislatures in a number of states – primarily in the South – to pass laws like Tennessee's against teaching evolution in the public schools. The Butler Act itself remained on the books for another forty years until the Supreme Court of the United States ultimately ruled in favor of the ACLU's original position – that state bans on teaching evolution were unconstitutional violations of the Establishment Clause of the First Amendment.[28]

Although Fundamentalists considered their crusade a holy war, the nation's fear of losing the Cold War won out. Creationists controlling public school curricula began to be perceived as undermining the country's standing as a world power. When the Russians launched Sputnik in the fall of 1957, concern that the Soviet Union was surpassing the United States in scientific advances prompted Congress to pass the National Defense Education Act. Among other changes, that 1958 law financed revised high school textbooks highlighting Darwin's theory of evolution as a key biological principle underlying the modern science of genetics. Yet in the Deep South, local officials pasted disclaimers in the inside cover of some public school textbooks, disputing the scientific evidence that supported the theory of evolution.

For the last half of the 20th century the actual issue tried in Dayton greatly diminished in real world significance just as the theatrical 1925 confrontation hit Broadway and began its enduring reincarnation in theaters and movies. Yet certain pockets of American school systems persisted in their strong resistance to Darwin's theory. Preachers in the pulpit, Sunday school teachers, home schooling parents and conservative Christian religious schools continue to wage war against a scientific principle that they dismiss as untested. The cause espoused by populist William Jennings Bryan in the celebrated 1925 Scopes trial still sparks considerable interest today. Indeed, the Dayton businessmen gathered at Robinson's drugstore who dreamed up the public relations campaign for the historic Scopes trial would be delighted at the long lasting fruits of their labor. Now the Rhea Heritage Preservation Foundation hosts an annual summer Scopes Trial Festival for folks to debate the contrasting views of Bryan and Darrow.

In 1999, the Fundamentalist Christian battle against the teaching of evolution hit headlines once again when creationists on the Kansas state school board succeeded in temporarily removing the big bang theory from mandatory coverage in the state's science classes. When the religious right reemerged as a major political player at the turn of the 21st century the teaching of evolution faced increased opposition. In 2005, the *Scopes* trial had its sequel in a widely-publicized Dover, Pennsylvania, case. The ACLU again played the lead role when several parents challenged the local school board's decision to require the teaching of intelligent design as an alternative to evolution. A six-week trial took place before District Judge John Jones, a recent Republican appointee who was himself a devout Lutheran. Judge Jones studied the evidence and concluded that intelligent design was clearly a religious belief, not a scientific principle, and that teaching it in public schools violated the First Amendment.

* * * * *

After his dramatic confrontation with William Jennings Bryan over the teaching of evolution, Clarence Darrow wanted to retire and vowed to take no more cases. Instead, he traveled the lecture circuit. But in October of 1925, Darrow could not resist returning to the forefront of the civil rights movement. A contingent from the NAACP begged

Folks in Dayton mostly enjoy being part of history – as focused now on attracting hordes of tourists to town as their ancestors were in 1925.

Source of photo and quoteshttp: http://scopesfestival.com/about-the-trial/WWW.TNHISTORYFORKIDS.ORG

Modern reenactment of the Scopes Trial

Today, the Rhea Heritage Preservation Foundation hosts an annual Scopes Trial Festival in Dayton, Tennessee, highlighting the contrasting views between Bryan and Darrow:

> "All the ills from which America suffers can be traced to the teaching of evolution." —William Jennings Bryan

> "Just think of the tragedy of teaching children not to doubt." — Clarence Darrow

Dayton, Tennessee, 2017 – Controversies Today

In 2004, a statue of William Jennings Bryan was erected in Dayton, a town with a Christian college named for Bryan since 1930. In 2014, the President of Bryan College made the news for taking the same stance on Creationism as Bryan. ("CHRISTIAN UNIVERSITY PRESIDENT UNDER FIRE FOR AFFIRMING BELIEF IN BIBLICAL CREATION," Beginning and End, April 7, 2014, http://beginningandend.com/christian-university-president-under-fire-for-affirming-belief-in-biblical-creation/.)

More public disagreement on the issue surfaced in Dayton in mid-summer 2017 when the Freedom From Religion Foundation donated a $150,000 statue of Clarence Darrow to stand on display with Bryan's in front of the Scopes Trial Museum. (Richard Faussett, "At Site of Scope's Trial, Statue of Darrow Belatedly Joins Bryan's," The New York Times, July 14, 2017.)

him to come to Detroit to help defend a black doctor, his family, and friends on murder charges. Eleven people altogether were accused of the shooting death of a spectator when a white mob tried to prevent the doctor's family from moving into their neighborhood. Darrow saw an extraordinary opportunity to expound upon the nation's sorry history of racial discrimination, with stakes as high as they could get. The challenge was to convince an all-white jury that a black man had the same right to occupy his own home in peace as the jurors themselves did.

10. A BLACK MAN'S CASTLE

The Sweet Murder Trials Launch the NAACP Legal Defense Fund as the KKK Collapses

"The case is won or lost now. The rest is window dressing." [1]
— CLARENCE DARROW'S whispered aside after selecting
a jury for the first Sweet murder trial

ladys Sweet spent the spring of 1925 scouring Detroit for a home for herself, her husband of three years and their toddler Marguerite, whom they called Iva. Gladys's goal was to find an attractive bungalow at least as big as her parents' three-bedroom house on the city's northeast side. Like most young mothers, Gladys wanted a safe neighborhood, a decent school and a small yard where Iva could play. Housing prices had risen dramatically in the past year. Even so, if the family had been white, her quest would have posed little difficulty. Bungalows of the kind Gladys had in mind sold for around $12,000 to $13,000.

Gladys was a strikingly poised twenty-three-year-old, raised with impeccable manners and a fine appreciation for culture. She had long, dark hair with auburn highlights that she kept in a neat chignon and alluring brown eyes with dark lashes. A self-assured only child, Gladys was too thin and toothy to be considered beautiful, but had about her a quiet sophistication and charm that disarmed most people and held her husband in awe.

Gladys and Ossian had just returned from a year abroad where he had the much-envied opportunity to study for a year with Nobel Prize–winner Dr. Marie Curie. The only discrimination the pair had faced overseas was when the American hospital in Paris had refused to allow Gladys to give birth there. Fortunately, Iva's health wasn't jeopardized. The Sweets had lost their first born, a premature baby son, in the summer of 1923. Back in Detroit in June of 1924, Dr. Sweet resumed his gynecology practice and took a position at Dunbar Hospital, the city's first black hospital. The couple and their daughter Iva then spent a cramped year living again with her parents.

Gladys was born in Pittsburgh when her mother was only seventeen; Gladys never knew her father. In Detroit, where they moved when Gladys was seven, her stepfather Benjamin Mitchell made a good living as a piano teacher and orchestra musician – enough to afford a car. Yet he and his wife Rosella had to take in a boarder to pay the mortgage. The family regularly attended St. Matthew's Church, the congregation to which the best black families belonged.

Unlike her husband, Gladys was light-skinned. Her mother's father was white. Gladys could almost pass for white, too. In looking for her own home, Gladys checked out communities on the East Side and got repeatedly turned down. She did not shrink from being the first black family on the block. On the street where she grew up, there had been only one black couple besides her parents. Gladys had been the only black child in her elementary school class and among the few in her high school.

Ossian Sweet had spent many summers in Detroit as a bellhop and at other low-paying jobs before he returned to the city in 1921 with his long-sought medical degree. By age thirty, Dr. Sweet had saved enough and earned enough that, if he were white, he would have had no trouble making a down payment on their dream house and covering a bank mortgage. But banks would not lend to blacks trying to buy homes in white districts, and sellers quoted black buyers a hefty premium, if they made any proposal at all. Some newer developments had restrictive deeds preventing sales to Negroes. Gladys did not appreciate how racially charged the city had recently become. Her mistake turned out to be fatal.

In the late 19th century, Detroit had both thriving boat engine factories and high-quality carriage builders. The combination made it ideal turf for the new automobile industry. Since 1900, the city's population had grown almost fivefold, emerging as the country's fourth largest metropolis. Henry Ford's wildly popular Model T prompted the need for many thousand assembly line workers. His competitors Chrysler, General Motors, the Dodge brothers and their suppliers also advertised widely for their ever-expanding labor requirements.

Back in 1910, when Gladys was new to Detroit, white families did not feel threatened by their rare black neighbors. There were fewer than six thousand Negroes in the whole city, mostly living in three central districts near the railroad tracks where poor Russian Jews, Italians, Greeks and Syrians had located. That area had long been called Black Bottom for the darkness of its soil. Starting in 1915, a surge of new employees, both black and white, migrated from the South, lured by Ford's offer of $5 per day – twice the going wage. By 1925, Detroit boasted 1,250,000 residents, including 82,000 Negroes. Most blacks new to Motor City crammed into the same three disease-plagued city districts where less than a tenth as many lived in 1910. Accommodations were so scarce some fleabag hotels rented beds in eight-hour-shifts. Only half of Black Bottom had running water.

In 1921, when the Ku Klux Klan first organized in Detroit, just 3,000 people identified themselves as members. By the spring of 1923, 22,000 people claimed membership in the rapidly growing political movement. Most white Southerners had moved into Detroit's working class neighborhoods on the West Side, anxious to keep their women and daughters from mixing with black men and foreigners. The transplanted Fundamentalists found the urban culture of the Roaring Twenties particularly disturbing. They steered clear of the swarthy, Mafia-connected, Sicilian community and shunned Jewish bootleggers, Irish and Polish Catholics, Greeks, Russians and other immigrants on the city's East Side. Indeed, as in Chicago and New York, ethnic and racial groups formed their own protective clusters where similarly self-identified newcomers commonly made their own home.

The newly arriving whites from the South mostly blamed Detroit's decadence on the influence of degenerate blacks. In fact, anyone looking to indulge in their favorite sin could find thousands of beer joints, drug sellers, prostitutes and gambling dens throughout the city. Yet it was easier to focus on Black Bottom. It featured jazz and blues, speak-easies, gambling, pool halls and rampant crime. Transplanted Southern whites feared this loose behavior would spread if they did not remain vigilant; they joined forces with anxious Protestant locals to prevent any Negroes from moving onto their blocks.

Henry Ford had spearheaded a reform government in Detroit, which officially became a dry city two years before the Eighteenth Amendment went into effect. The Ku Klux Klan had a tee-totaling, moralistic image and isolationist message. By the early 1920s, the KKK emerged as a powerful political machine in Detroit, electing several city council members. Opponents got a frightening look at its sinister side in November of 1923, when members stormed an anti-Klan rally and 50,000 robed Klansmen gathered with flaming torches in nearby Dearborn. By 1925, the white supremacist organization boasted that Detroit had become its largest urban base in the nation.

In the fall of 1924, the KKK sponsored a hand-picked unknown, Charles Bowles, as the write-in "American values" candidate for mayor. Bowles barely lost out in a three-way race to Johnny Smith, the street-smart Polish Catholic candidate supported by immigrants, Catholics and blacks. Had misspelled ballots been counted, Bowles would have won. The KKK was bent on revenge. Its marketing tool was neighbor-hood improvement associations, a civic-sounding name for racial exclu-sion. The KKK argued that black neighbors drove down property values and should be forced out by any means, legal or not.

Gladys Sweet's exhaustive search included small black middle-class neighborhoods on the East Side which would pose a long commute for her husband. She found real-estate agents resistant to showing her anything in white neighborhoods, but she remained determined to suc-ceed. By late May, Gladys thought she had found an excellent choice. It was a well-built brick cottage on Garland Avenue at the intersection of Charlevoix, a major boulevard with a streetcar line on the East Side, four miles from the city's center.

Gladys noticed that across Charlevoix were an elementary school and a grocery store, several two-story flats and an apartment house. The neighborhood was a mix of renters and owners of diverse Northern

European ethnicity. The men mostly held high-level blue collar jobs. Some had spent many generations in Detroit. Others had moved recently from other cities in the north. The women were housewives or ran boarding houses. Many men who owned their own homes were barely hanging on with two or three mortgages, fearful of what would happen if they missed a paycheck.

Gladys enjoyed at first sight the shaded front porch of the arts-and-crafts style bungalow and appreciated how well-kept it looked with its newly painted shingles. The narrow lot was 125 feet deep, with a small, fenced-in backyard for Iva. Once inside, Gladys fell in love with the special touches that the Belgian builder had created for his own family. The living room was trimmed in polished oak and had leaded glass windows along one wall. It also included a fireplace with inlaid Dutch tiles. The dining room was trimmed in matching oak. It had an attractive chandelier, a handsome, built-in china cabinet on one end and bookcases on the other. Best of all, Gladys noticed that an adjacent alcove could later fit a piano. Upstairs, there were four bedrooms so Iva could have her own, even if they rented out two to boarders.

Gladys took heart from the fact that the sellers were an inter-racial couple. Yet, Mr. Smith was so light-skinned he normally passed for white. He had taken advantage of his appearance to establish a thriving real estate practice where no other black agents were permitted to compete. His neighbors had never been sure of Mr. Smith's pigmentation. It appeared that the appraisers and banks had not either. If a new black family moved in, property values could easily plummet and the chance of refinancing any house on the block evaporate.

Though Ossian liked the idea of owning the best house on the block with its own attached garage, unlike Gladys he remained quite nervous about the transaction. Gladys had heard her cousins' account of the bloody Chicago riots of 1919, targeting mainly blacks who moved into white neighborhoods. She also was aware that similar violence against black families erupted in other American cities and towns that summer and fall. For Gladys, these events happened to other people. Ossian tried not to show the fear that gnawed at him. When Ossian was in medical school in Washington, D.C., in the Red Summer of 1919, he

"MAN'S HOUSE HIS CASTLE"
ARGUES COUNSEL FOR SWEET

Headline, The Chicago Defender *Nov. 21, 1925*

Used with the permission of *The Chicago Defender.*

Source: http://www.jurist.org/wayback/trials9.htm

*Ossian Sweet's home in 1926 (**top left**) that had its windows broken by a mob throwing stones to try to force the Sweet family out of the neighborhood. An errant warning shot (likely from either a policeman protecting the home or Sweet's younger brother) killed a bystander, resulting in all of the occupants being prosecuted for murder. The NAACP brought Clarence Darrow in to defend them. The trial judge was deeply moved by Darrow's closing argument. He told a friend at the trial's end, "This is the greatest experience of my life. . . . Clarence Darrow at his best. I will never hear anything like it again. He is the most Christ-like man I have ever known." The case launched the NAACP Legal Defense Fund. Dr. Sweet's house became a Michigan state historic site in 2004 following renovations (**top right**).*

Below: *Dr. Ossian Sweet and his wife Gladys (**left**) who scoured the city looking for suitable housing. A map of Detroit in 1925 (**right**) shows the density of the black population and the location of the Sweet house in a mostly white neighborhood.*

Sources: https://roaring20scush8.wikispaces.com/Ossian+Sweet; Famous Trials, Sweet Trials, https://en.wikipedia.org/wiki/Ossian_Sweet; http://www.famous-trials.com/sweet/132-images

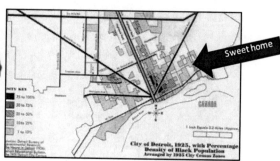

Sweet home

City of Detroit, 1925, with Percentage Density of Black Population Arranged by 1925 City Census Zones

had witnessed men in uniform pull a black man from a trolley and club him senseless. In the next several years, he saw plastered over the front pages of the *Chicago Defender* many other gory stories of race violence, each of which sent chills down his spine.

Ossian had been particularly appalled at the New Year's Day 1923 murders and destruction of Rosewood, Florida, by a white mob searching for a black rapist. Rosewood was like the Florida town in which he had been raised. Ossian still vividly recalled with horror the scene he had witnessed as a five-year-old child hiding in a bush by a bridge in Bartow, Florida. A frenzied mob of whites lynched and set fire to his neighbor's sixteen-year-old son, who had been accused of raping and murdering a white woman. Ossian could still hear the teenager's shrieks of agony and picture the laughing crowd of respectable white townspeople taking Fred Rochelle's charred bones home as mementoes.

In March of 1925, a black woman who moved with her baby into a white neighborhood in Detroit had her house stoned. When she fired a shotgun over the assailants' heads, she was arrested, though charges were later dropped. Other black families long ensconced in white communities suddenly faced harassment. But Gladys wanted Iva to grow up in a decent neighborhood like the one Gladys had enjoyed. She convinced Ossian that he had earned that right. Most Detroit physicians lived in even better neighborhoods than the one Gladys coveted.

Ossian felt self-righteous. When he was just thirteen, his parents had sent him North from his segregated Florida hometown on a scholarship to a black Methodist school in Xenia, Ohio. The scholarship never materialized. Rather than admit defeat, he had taken backbreaking menial jobs to pay his way while pursuing an almost unheard-of college degree and professional career. Ossian's parents had drilled in him the duty to lead by example. It was second nature to help his next brother Otis become a dentist and assist Henry with college. Ossian's training placed him among the "Talented Tenth" that W. E. B. Dubois encouraged to advance the Negro race with their coattails.

The two-story brick house Gladys found was only a few miles from where she had been raised and presented a short commute for Ossian Sweet. Dr. Sweet was cautiously optimistic after he sat with the sellers several times on their porch and no neighbors seemed to take offense. He had deliberately taken over negotiations because Gladys was so light-skinned. Wearing his tailored suit and tie, pressed shirt, horn-rimmed glasses and a well-trimmed moustache, Ossian probably thought he reassured his neighbors. Mr. Smith said he believed that his neighbors knew that he was black; none had ever bothered him. His wife swore that no Klansmen lived in the area. Ossian felt better.

The negotiations were extremely lopsided. Mr. Smith took advantage of the Sweets' lack of options and priced the bungalow about fifty percent higher than it would have sold to a white buyer. At $18,500, Ossian could just barely afford it. The Smiths further gouged the Sweets by insisting on eighteen percent interest. They would retain title to the property for ten years while Dr. Sweet paid off the balance. Ossian saw little choice but to accept the harsh terms. His brother Otis, a dentist, could rent one bedroom and the Sweets could find another boarder. Ossian Sweet swallowed his fears and decided to embrace the challenge. He closed the deal on June 7. The Smiths would vacate by the end of July.

In late June, a mob attacked the new home of Dunbar's chief of surgery in an upscale white neighborhood. Dr. Turner was one of the city's most venerated physicians. He treated both white and black patients, but that mattered not a whit to the hooligans who stormed his house, pulled out the telephone lines and destroyed his furnishings. Fearful for his life, Dr. Turner deeded his house to a KKK-backed neighborhood association that same night.

Dr. Sweet now agonized over his decision. Although he disliked confrontation, he knew that blacks had fought back in Washington, D.C., in 1919. Emboldened black newspapers touted "The NEW NEGRO" for whom the "time for cringing is over."[2] Ossian was not part of the movement for a separatist African Black Brotherhood or, for that matter, a member of Detroit's NAACP. He simply embraced the principles of the NAACP's Talented Tenth to achieve integration by persistence and example.

Before the summer of 1925, Ossian's only public protest consisted of joining the lone table of black professionals at a banquet for Detroit

Tigers superstar Ty Cobb. Their aim had been to discomfit the white supremacists in attendance and perhaps get a rise out of baseball's most virulent racist. Dr. Sweet now spent long hours talking to Dr. Turner and other colleagues. Most encouraged him to go ahead. More than pride was at stake, Dr. Sweet had already paid the down payment. He knew what standing his ground meant. Guns were the only equalizer. Ossian had received weapons training in the Student Army Training Corps in medical school during World War I and kept a .38 Smith and Wesson a patient had traded him for medical care.

The atmosphere got even uglier in early July, when 10,000 members of the KKK rallied under a burning cross on Detroit's West Side. They had gathered to lobby for a proposed law limiting the districts where black residents could live – an ordinance that might run afoul of the Constitution. The United States Supreme Court had handed the NAACP a victory in 1917 by unanimously striking down a Kentucky segregation ordinance for violating the Fourteenth Amendment. But the high court ruling did not apply to discrimination by private citizens. Direct action felt far more satisfying to KKK members anyway. Several hundred armed men stormed the home of another Negro who moved into an all-white neighborhood. On July 10, thousands of whites wielding bricks and stones forced yet another colored man and his family to flee his new home amid cries of "lynch him."[3] Mayor Smith responded by warning against riots, which only spurred the KKK to further defiance.

By early July, the neighbors of 2905 Garland Avenue all knew about the Sweets' impending arrival. On July 12, posters appeared throughout the neighborhood announcing a meeting on July 14 for "self-defense" at the Howe elementary school. More than six hundred white residents – many only renters – came to the auditorium to join the new Waterworks Park Home Improvement Association. The guest speaker was the same man who had spearheaded the assault on Dr. Turner's residence. His biggest applause line was "Where the nigger shows his head, the white must shoot."[4]

Dr. Sweet told his two brothers, "I have to die like a man or live a coward."[5] So he prepared as best he could. He postponed the move

Source: nexgenacademy.com/more-than-laissez-faire/african-native-american/african-native-american-photos/the-klu-klux-klan

*The photo (**above**) shows one of many KKK rallies in the South. In early July 1925, 10,000 members of the KKK rallied under a burning cross on Detroit's West Side to lobby for a law limiting where black families could live. That December KKK members rallied under a cross in Washington, D.C.*

Source: https://commons.wikimedia.org/wiki/File:Klan-sheet-music.jpg

The KKK was gearing up to run a candidate for president in 1928 until a major scandal derailed that ambition. Pictured here is the cover of sheet music for the song "We Are All Loyal Klansmen" copyright, 1923, by William Davis, William M. Hart, Charles E. Downey and E. M. McMahon.

In July 2017 the Ku Klux Klan rallied in Charlottesville, Virginia, to protest the removal of a statue of Robert E. Lee. The event drew far more counter-protesters than KKK supporters.

to September 8, the first day of school. His brother Otis contacted the police for protection. Otis and Henry agreed to join Ossian in defending the home for the first several nights. Twenty-one-year-old Henry was in Detroit only for the summer before entering his senior year in college. Dr. Sweet also pleaded with a few other good friends and business associates to help him ward off any invasion. The Sweets left Iva with her grandparents for the time being.

Dr. Sweet had hired a driver and handyman to help with the moving van. It did not take long to settle in because the Sweets had not yet accumulated much furniture. Within an hour of their arrival, a policeman knocked on the door and let them know he and four other officers were stationed outside to protect them. Dr. Sweet did not tell the officer that he had brought into the home a satchel full of newly purchased guns and rounds of ammunition.

More than a hundred people gathered outside the first night, surprised to see police protecting the sidewalk in front of the Sweets' property. Many in the crowd wondered whose side they were on. The Detroit police force included many Klansmen, for whom such an assignment would have been anathema. A few rocks hit the house around 3 a.m., but otherwise the night was eerily quiet. The Sweets and their guests ate an uncomfortable dinner that lasted past dark, not daring to turn on lights when they had no curtains yet. They spent a sleepless night with the guns by their sides in case of attack. The next morning a neighbor warned that the Sweets better abandon their home before dark because an even bigger crowd was coming back.

Ossian again asked his brothers and friends to join him the night of September 9. That morning, Gladys and Ossian Sweet optimistically went furniture shopping, but returned to hear more warnings that neighbors intended to force the "niggers" out that night. As promised, a dozen police were stationed outside, but they never tried to disperse the menacing gathering on the street corner. Around 8 p.m., Otis arrived in a taxi with a friend. Someone shouted, "Here's niggers! There they go! Get them! Get them!"[6] The pair made it safely into the dark house as someone began throwing stones. Then others joined in, breaking a window. The police did not stop the hailstorm of rocks.

Inside the house, panic reigned. Ossian again passed the guns out among the men.

As the pelting continued, shots rang out from the second floor window and back porch. Outside, a man screamed in pain, shot through the back. Another sustained a minor leg injury. Officers called for reinforcements. Then they arrested all eleven people in the Sweets' home, marching them out a back alley and into a paddy wagon while waving their guns to hold back the seething crowd, now growing into the thousands. The Sweets realized their situation was dire; someone had died.

The men called their lawyers at the first opportunity. Detroit cops were notorious for beating confessions out of arrested black men, keeping them from access to lawyers and sometimes killing them with impunity. This time, the chief prosecutor sent an assistant to ensure a civilized interrogation. Yet the lawyers were denied access to their clients. As questioning proceeded into the night, the Sweets learned that the dead man was a neighbor named Leon Breiner. He was not a member of the new neighborhood association, but had only stopped to watch the goings on.

At first, all of the defendants denied that they had gathered in the house in anticipation of violence, but a friend of Ossian's soon confessed the truth in hopes of leniency. Henry then admitted that he had fired a rifle from the second floor window. He was aiming just over the heads of the mob to get them to leave the family alone. A policeman later said he had also emptied his gun. More shots had been fired, but it was unclear by whom.

A reporter for the *Detroit News* had happened on the scene. He saw the large, menacing crowd, the rain of stones pelting the cottage and the shooting. After taking his family home, he raced to the office with his story, which the *Detroit News* never printed. Instead, all three leading Detroit papers, including William Randolph Hearst's recently purchased *Detroit Times,* filed lock step accounts that exonerated the neighbors and the police. The police inspector on site had been adamant: no mob had gathered; no stones were hurled; the black occupants opened fire without provocation upon peacefully clustered neighbors. Other details emerged. The blacks had moved in with almost no furnishings, but plenty of ammo, ready to precipitate trouble.

The story became an angry call to action as threats of race violence unnerved the city. The KKK held a huge rally and demanded murder prosecutions. It looked like the issue that could clinch them the mayor's office. The next day the district attorney's office announced first degree murder charges against all eleven people in the house since it could not tell who fired the fatal bullet. Gladys had never even held a gun.

By Saturday, the Detroit NAACP had agreed to defend the case, and the lawyers actually met with their clients. A three-day preliminary hearing was scheduled for the following week. As rumors spread of impending race war, Mayor Smith spoke out for the first time since the shooting. Rather than criticize the police in any way, he lambasted both the Invisible Empire and black people who moved into white neighborhoods. He accused people like the Sweets of being tools of the KKK. Mayor Smith urged all Negroes to remain voluntarily segregated rather than insist on a right to move into "districts in which their presence would cause a disturbance."[7] The NAACP was furious to see their white allies beating a hasty retreat for fear of violence.

The NAACP brought five hundred supporters to the preliminary hearing. Police in plainclothes spread out through the crowded gallery in case any trouble broke out, but there was none. Rather than focus on the behavior of the defendants, Assistant Prosecutor Lester Moll brought witness after witness to describe in similar coached fashion how peaceful the folks on the street had been at the time a Negro in the newly purchased house shot and killed a neighbor. It worked. The judge ordered all of the defendants to stand trial for murder without bail. At least the death penalty was not an option. The state of Michigan had never executed anyone; its Legislature had the distinction of being the first in the nation to officially abolish capital punishment some eighty years earlier for all crimes except treason.

The new presiding judge, thirty-four-year-old Democrat Frank Murphy, assigned himself to try the politically explosive case. He drew the KKK's wrath when he released Gladys Sweet from the women's ward on October 2 on $10,000 bail. It was none too soon; the shocking ordeal of jail had destroyed her appetite. The KKK held another giant rally the next day. On Tuesday, October 6 its candidates for city council won the primary by a huge margin. The KKK expected to take over the entire city government in November, riding high on these murder prosecutions.

Trial was set to begin in mid-October. The men remained in the Wayne County Jail with pimps and burglars, drug addicts and thugs. Overhearing bets among the jailers about their case beat down the men's spirits – the bets overwhelmingly favored conviction. At the same time, a turf battle raged between the local NAACP and its national office. With over three hundred branches, the powerful organization could cherry pick the few cases across country each year that framed race issues most dramatically. The Sweet prosecution focused on the most widespread problem blacks faced in the North. It appeared to be the perfect vehicle for a national campaign to create a NAACP Legal Defense Fund. The national office wanted to replace the three black lawyers already on the case with a high-powered white attorney.

An impasse had been reached between the local and national offices of the NAACP before Henry Sweet, Sr., arrived from Florida to visit his three sons behind bars. He came to reassure his sons of how proud he was of their principled stand. Otis Sweet then sent telegrams to both the Detroit and national NAACP offices urging the national office to take the case over: "This is a case in which more is involved than the liberties of the eleven persons concerned; it is a case that boldly challenges the liberties, the hopes, and the aspirations of fifteen million colored Americans . . . to live without molestation and prosecution."[8] Soon word came to the defendants that the national NAACP leadership had talked Clarence Darrow into taking over the lead role for the defense team.

Darrow had frequently defended impoverished blacks and agreed to handle this case for a steep discount. He and his wife Ruby were themselves charter members of the NAACP. Yet Darrow made NAACP Board members apprehensive by sitting with black students in a segregated train car and giving speeches advocating miscegenation. Some feared his radical views would backfire, but the publicity the most famous lawyer in America would bring outweighed the risks. Darrow was now sixty-eight years old and semi-retired. But the case energized him. Darrow sensed an unparalleled opportunity for a full-bore attack on the history of racism.

Darrow made his dramatic public debut in the case at a hearing to request a two-week continuance of the trial. His first pleasant surprise was Judge Frank Murphy, a redheaded, tee-totaling bachelor. The ambitious Irish lawyer had run for judge as a reform candidate on a slate against entrenched conservatives. Murphy's 1922 election campaign emphasized that the current criminal justice system benefited "political grafters, exploiters of the poor, and profiteers" and left "the friendless and the penniless" with "less than an equal chance of justice." Murphy vowed that, upon election, he would "try to have a temple of justice, not a butcher shop."[9] He had taken the Sweet case himself because every other judge was afraid to handle it.

Prosecutor Robert Toms also impressed Darrow with his civility. Toms was a good-natured public servant, several years older than the judge. Toms normally prided himself on not chasing convictions as a numbers game. He felt honor-bound only to prosecute those cases where he felt he had solid evidence of guilt. But then again the Republican did not want to commit political suicide. That was what facing down the KKK would have meant in 1925, particularly on the eve of the hotly contested mayoral election.

The same day Darrow was named lead defense counsel, the NAACP's chief publicist Walter White released to major newspapers the Sweets' version of the assault. It resulted in a wave of favorable front-page press. Suddenly, the Sweets were celebrities and the betting odds changed. Yet only the black press continued to follow the case closely as one affecting "every Negro in America." It raised the "question whether prejudice and hatred shall rule our nation or whether a pure democracy shall prevail." *The Chicago Defender* warned "if the police cannot protect us from mob violence, then we must be prepared to protect ourselves." *The Amsterdam News* trumpeted it as "possibly the most important court case the Negro has ever figured in."[10] W. E. B. DuBois lauded Ossian Sweet as a role model.

The trial began on October 30, 1925. As in the Scopes trial, Darrow worked with ACLU General Counsel Arthur Hays. Darrow kept the original three attorneys as a support team and added another white Detroit attorney, for a total of six lawyers. Darrow was never one for handling the nuts and bolts. He liked to focus on the big picture, the critical work of jury selection, and the closing argument. He filled many evenings with speech engagements and political discussions over drinks, leaving most trial preparation to his co-counsel.

Unlike his laid-back appearance in the heat of Dayton, Tennessee, Darrow came to court neatly groomed with his suit freshly pressed. The risk of life imprisonment demanded formality. Picking the jury for eleven defendants in a murder case gave the defense counsel thirty challenges per defendant, 330 opportunities to strike jurors. It was the main reason they opted to have all eleven defendants tried together. Yet Darrow left most of the challenges unused. The judge was determined to seat open-minded jurors and readily excused for cause three admitted members of the KKK.

Neither Darrow nor the prosecutor wanted the few women who showed up – a phenomenon galvanized by the recent passage of the Nineteenth Amendment. In many places women had to preregister for service to opt in to jury panels, while men were automatically eligible to serve. Of course, few women signed up. Darrow believed the civic-minded feminists who navigated their way into the jury pool were too fastidious in applying the law and thus less susceptible to his emotional closing arguments. He practiced mostly in Chicago where – until the Supreme Court nixed the practice in 1941 – women could only serve on criminal juries if they were on a League of Women Voters list limited to those who completed a jury-service course taught by the local prosecutor.

Darrow also avoided rich men, Presbyterians, Prohibitionists and Baptists. Seven of the twelve selected were Catholics. Most were fathers with minor children, but the defense included one man past seventy and one just twenty-one, who had not yet left home. The jurors resided all over Detroit. Some owned their own homes; some were tenants. Darrow's selections mostly favored workers with family ties to foreigners. He considered that a sign that they more likely supported Detroit's mayor than the Invisible Empire.

By the time they finished selecting the jury, prosecutor Toms had been far more choosy. To observers, Darrow seemed to be gambling that it was better to set the panel at ease than to give them the impression that only persons of a particular background would see the case his way. He conveyed the notion that all men with reasonably open minds were acceptable, while risking failure to discover entrenched prejudice. Some observers feared Darrow had been too hasty.

Hays opened the trial by reminding the jury of the age-old British right to self-defense: "The poorest man may in his cottage bid defiance to all the forces of the Crown; it may be frail, its roof may shake, the wind may blow through it; the storm may enter, the ram may enter; but the King of England cannot enter; all his forces dare not cross the threshold of that ruined tenement."[11] Michigan law favored the defense. If the Sweets had good reason to fear imminent danger, they could protect their home with deadly force even if no invasion was actually contemplated. Justifiable belief that a dangerous mob was about to descend upon them was enough. Under state law, a mob could be proved in one of two ways: a dozen or more armed persons or thirty unarmed persons gathered to intimidate or cause harm. The minimum standard of harm was $25, which the window breakage easily met.

Toms had his work cut out for him to deny the existence of a mob. Yet the jury could be expected to blame the Sweets for deliberately forcing the issue, arriving heavily armed and firing into the crowd even though they had police protection. When examined by the defense, some of the neighbors reluctantly admitted to a crowd far in excess of thirty, which kept growing larger and more ominous. Then a thirteen-year-old boy admitted what the adults would not – that four or five teens started throwing stones and broke at least one window before the shooting happened.

Fortunately for the defense, by the time of trial, KKK influence had already passed its peak. Liberal supporters rallied to the incumbent mayor's defense with backing from William Randolph Hearst's *Detroit Times* and the far more conservative *Detroit Free Press*. Three days into the trial, Mayor Smith won reelection by a thirty-thousand-vote margin in his rematch with KKK candidate Bowles. In fact, KKK influence nationwide had just taken a major blow due to a front-page scandal that enveloped one of its two most powerful leaders, Grand Dragon David Stephenson. Stephenson, who referred to himself as "the law in Indiana," was so influential in other states that he had his sights on securing nomination as the 1928 Republican presidential candidate. That was before the thirty-four-year-old demagogue's wild private life caught up with him.

Stephenson had been indicted in Indiana in the spring of 1925 following the death of a twenty-seven-year-old state employee named Madge Oberholtzer. His murder trial started on October 12, 1925, spreading salacious details over the front pages based largely on a sworn statement Oberholtzer had made shortly before she died. With the help of two aides, the drunken Grand Dragon had lured her from her parents' home under false pretenses. He then abducted and drugged Oberholtzer and took her captive on a private train car.

During the train trip, Stephenson savagely raped and bit Oberholtzer. She then attempted suicide by ingesting poison. Stephenson returned her home near death. Doctors who then examined the young woman said she looked like she had been "chewed by a cannibal."[12] She died a few weeks later from infections in her left breast. On November 14, Stephenson's murder trial ended with a second-degree-murder conviction and life sentence, just before Ossian Sweet took the stand in Detroit. By then, the crowded gallery at the Sweet trial was filled with mostly black spectators. When the trial began, many more whites flocked to the proceedings.

Though it is always risky for a defendant to testify in a criminal case, the benefits here far outweighed the downside. Dr. Sweet had a golden opportunity on the stand to educate the all-white jury about his Horatio Alger life story. Most particularly, the defense team planned to have Dr. Sweet detail for the jury all of the fear factors that affected his state of mind as he holed up with his wife, his brothers and other recruits to defend his new home.

When Dr. Sweet began to describe the neighbor he saw burnt alive when he was a child in Florida twenty-five years earlier, Toms jumped up to object to its relevance. Darrow rose to respond: "What we learn as children we remember – it gets fastened to the mind . . . this defendant's actions were predicated on the psychology of the past . . ."[13] It was a variation on Darrow's Leopold and Loeb defense the year before. Here, the difference between judges like Chattanooga, Tennessee's Samuel McReynolds and Massachusetts Judge Webster Thayer, on the one hand, and Chicago's Judge Caverly and Detroit's Frank Murphy, on the other, was quite evident. Judge Murphy overruled Toms' objection.

Darrow then ceded the floor to Hays, who elicited from Dr. Sweet one horrid event etched in his mind after another: the trolley passenger he saw beaten in Washington, D.C.; the murder of a black surgeon in Tulsa, Oklahoma; the killing of two Negro professionals in Arkansas; the destruction of the town of Rosewood; and other acts of race violence, culminating in the June and July 1925 attacks on black home-owners in Detroit. All formed the context in which Dr. Sweet acted to defend his family from the menacing crowd stoning his home on September 9, 1925. Journalists noted the whole courtroom's silence at the riveting details.

In his closing argument, Darrow invited the jury to take a close look at the eleven defendants, including demure Gladys Sweet and the well-groomed professional men who had come to the aid of her beleaguered husband. They presented a stark contrast to the inarticulate neighbors the prosecution had placed on the stand, who fidgeted in response to questions whether they harbored any ill will toward their new black neighbors, why they joined the neighborhood protection association, and exactly what such a huge number of them were doing on the street that night.

Darrow challenged the all-white jury to put themselves in his clients' shoes. "I know that if these defendants had been a white group defending themselves from a colored mob, they never would have been arrested or tried. My clients are charged with murder, but they are really charged with being black. . . . You are facing a problem of two races, a problem that will take centuries to solve. . . . Every policeman knew that the crowd was after the Negroes. But no one batted an eye. . . . Draw upon your imagination and think how you would feel if you fired at some black man in a black community, and then had to be tried by them. . . ."[14]

When the jury retired to deliberate on November 25, the aged war horse was exhausted. The jurors' muffled voices carried outside the room as they argued with each other into the night until 2 a.m. They resumed all Thanksgiving Day, except for a break ordered by the judge for an elaborate turkey dinner. At 11 p.m. they reported they were deadlocked; the judge ordered them to deliberate again the next day. Darrow and a few close friends shared some scotch while they waited. By his side was Josephine Gomon, a married local activist less than half his age whose friendship Darrow had cultivated when Ruby wasn't looking. By the trial's end, the irrepressible flirt had decided Jo Gomon was a kindred spirit. (Gomon would win recognition as "the City's Conscience" during the Depression, when she turned Detroit's welfare system into a model of compassionate efficiency.)

After forty-six hours, the jurors came back to court bedraggled and exhausted, unable to reach a verdict. Judge Murphy declared a mistrial on November 27 and the following day ordered the defendants released on bail. Word had it that ten jurors voted for acquittal of all the defendants except Ossian and Henry Sweet, and five would have acquitted them as well. Seven jurors had voted to convict both brothers of second degree murder or manslaughter. None voted for first degree murder.

During the fall, police had guarded the Sweets' home from vandalism. A week before the trial ended, an officer saw someone running away after throwing rags soaked in gasoline into the Sweets' garage. The fire was extinguished with only minor damage. Yet no arrest followed. The police inspector announced plans to withdraw as soon as the Sweets resumed occupancy. Instead, the NAACP helped Dr. Sweet with monthly payments on the empty home while he joined Gladys and Iva in a small apartment a mile away in another neighborhood. Dr. Sweet worried about the two of them coughing so much all winter. Yet mostly he reveled in his new celebrity status, feeling immensely self-important.

Not unexpectedly, Prosecutor Toms announced his intention to retry the eleven defendants for murder. The defense had the right to demand separate trials. This time, they did so. Darrow had concluded that the jury had too many options for assigning guilt with everyone tied together. He wanted to confront them with making a decision on one man's freedom or imprisonment, thumbs up or thumbs down. Darrow exuded confidence, as did Ossian Sweet. But Prosecutor Toms surprisingly decided to start with his younger brother Henry, the only one to admit that he fired a rifle in Breiner's general direction. If Henry was convicted then the others would be tried in turn. If acquitted, no further prosecutions would take place.

By spring the political climate had shifted. The national KKK leadership had terminated the head of its Detroit branch in a messy exchange of accusations plastered all over the newspapers. Mayor Smith made amends for backing off from support for the Sweets in the fall by naming a Blue Ribbon Commission to make concrete recommendations to improve race relations in the city. The retrial of Henry Sweet was scheduled for April 1, 1926. Darrow returned to Detroit, but learned in mid-March that Arthur Hays would not rejoin him. Instead, Darrow asked Thomas Chawke to serve as co-counsel, a sharply dressed Irish mob lawyer, reputed to be the best in Detroit.

Chawke had no strong interest in the NAACP cause, but would sign on if the price was right. He bargained with the NAACP for higher compensation than Darrow and equal say in handling the case. The NAACP worried about Chawke's gangland affiliations, but agreed to his terms. They also kept Julian Perry on the defense team, one of the three original lawyers hired by its local branch. Though given no active role before the jury, Perry was well known in Detroit. He had run a quixotic campaign as a Republican candidate for the Michigan legislature.

The trial was delayed in part by the death of Judge Murphy's father. It wound up starting on April 19, 1926, the day after Darrow's sixty-ninth birthday. Spectators again packed the courtroom, including nationally known figures specially invited by the NAACP to add their dignity to the proceedings. The gallery of the sixty-by-fifty-foot courtroom seated about a hundred on benches. On many days it was standing room only for the mostly black observers.

A hundred and sixty-five potential jurors were asked the same general questions about their family background, religion and politics as in the first trial. But Darrow also had a new tack: "Well, you've heard about this case, I suppose? Read about it? Talked about it? Formed an opinion? Got it yet? And it would take evidence to change it? Well, I s'pose you're right. Challenge for cause." Both he and Chawke focused on ferreting out prejudice: "Ever had any association with any colored people? No? Understand Dr. Sweet's a colored man – bought a house in a neighborhood where there were no colored people. . . . He was in the house at the time of the shooting. One of eleven. Now you wouldn't want not to be fair. You just tell me yourself whether any views you have or surroundings you have would handicap my clients or the state."[15]

The two defense lawyers were using their preliminary questions to educate the panel in advance on the merits of their case. When Darrow asked the judge to dismiss a juror because he did not want a Negro to move near him, assistant prosecutor Moll jumped to object that "This is not a trial of race prejudice." Darrow responded, "I think we're try- ing the race question and nothing else." Judge Murphy continued to give the defense broad scope in their questions, agreeing that the jury should be free from prejudice.[16]

It took a week to select the all-male white jury. Darrow found it much easier going with one trial already under his belt. The youngest juror was in his mid-twenties, the oldest over eighty. There were three others over sixty, three middle-aged and the rest in their twenties. To a keen-eyed reporter, all seemed "straight forward, average men," none of clearly superior intelligence, none below normal.[17]

The prosecution team did not worry about proof that Henry Sweet actually killed Breiner; its theory was that Henry either fired the fatal bullet or aided and abetted whoever did. The bullet itself had passed through Breiner and had never been recovered, so there was no way to ascertain from which gun it had been shot. Toms had learned lessons from the first trial. He piled onto the table in front of the jury all of the guns that police had confiscated from the Sweets' home, one of which was the likely source of the bullet that killed Breiner.

Darrow did not flinch. He stood up and casually admitted to the jury that the bullet may well have come from the gun Henry Sweet used. But that did not make him a murderer; the culprits were those who created the dangerous situation – the people about to testify for the prosecution. Toms then presented seventy-one witnesses – policemen, neighbors and others on the street that night – who all downplayed the crowd's size and threatening nature. Though subjected to fiercer cross-examination than in the first trial, none would admit seeing a single stone thrown. Yet the police confirmed that they brought in reinforcements because they anticipated violence. By the end of the second week, Darrow was fighting a heavy cold. Yet he finally got a witness to say that the principal speaker at the July 14 meeting had urged the crowd to drive the Sweets out by violence.

Then the defense put on its own witnesses to establish that several hundred people had gathered in an angry mob, some hurling stones. Ossian Sweet testified again, but the defense team wisely kept Henry off the stand. Darrow had already conceded that Henry came to the house to help his older brother defend his home with guns and his life, if need be. The twenty-two-year-old did his part by just sitting at the defense table in his suit. Day after day the jury observed the defendant as an appealing, very serious young man of average height, short curly hair and a moustache – a younger version of his much-admired older brother.

Assistant Prosecutor Moll ridiculed the defense for its focus on all of Ossian Sweet's experiences leading up to September 9 rather than just the events of that night and the death of Leon Breiner. Chawke responded with an appeal to the jury's recollection of Detroit's history of tolerance and the risks that people like the jurors and their families also ran: "Have we come to a point in the history of our city when a majority can ride roughshod and ruthlessly over the rights of a minority?"[18] By day's end, the disappointed spectators still had not seen Darrow get up to speak. The next day, the gallery was crammed as tight as could be with onlookers, both white and black, while a huge crowd filled the hall, hoping to catch some glimpse of the proceedings or hear part of Darrow's argument. They were excited just to be part of history in the making.

Darrow talked for seven hours, directly challenging the jury to admit their own prejudice and set it aside. He dissected the prosecution's case and pointed out that it would never have been brought against a white man in similar circumstances: "Life is a hard game, anyhow. But, when the cards are stacked against you, it is terribly hard.

And they are stacked against a race for no reason but that they are black." Darrow seemed ready to stop more than once, but resumed out of fear he had not yet convinced his targets. "I would like to see a time when man loves his fellow man, and forgets his color or his creed. . . . I believe the life of a Negro has been a life full of tragedy, of injustice, of oppression. The law has made him equal – but man has not." Finally he apologized for taking so much time, explaining "this case is close to my heart. . . . I ask you, in the name of progress and of the human race, to return a verdict of not guilty in this case!"[19]

Toms had the last opportunity to speak the next morning, but it was anti-climactic. Judge Murphy gave the jury a special instruction that "Real justice does not draw any line of color, race, or creed or class. All charged with crime, rich or poor, humble or great, white or black, are entitled to the same right and the same full measure of justice."[20]

The lawyers assumed that deliberations would take nearly as long as the first time, but it was only four hours later that they learned the jury had reached a verdict. A packed courtroom watched the jurors enter one at a time, looking solemn and inscrutable. When the clerk asked for their verdict, the foreman answered in a faltering voice, "Not guilty." Toms, in disbelief, asked for the verdict to be repeated. Ossian Sweet was overcome with emotion. Henry Sweet, Chawke and Darrow could not help shedding tears of gratitude, nor could the judge. As he stepped off the bench, he told a friend, "This is the greatest experience of my life. That was Clarence Darrow at his best. I will never hear anything like it again. He is the most Christ-like man I have ever known."[21]

In his autobiography, Darrow called his closing argument one of the most satisfying he had ever given. He interpreted the jury's message as "simply that the doctrine that a man's house is his castle applied to the black man as well as to the white man. If not the first time that a white jury had vindicated this principle, it was the first that ever came to my notice." Both Robert Toms and Lester Moll later told Darrow they thought "the verdict was just and did a great deal of good in Detroit."[22]

Toms followed through on his promise that he would hold no further trials against the other defendants. Yet Ossian could take small comfort from the news. Both his wife and daughter had been diagnosed with tuberculosis, which they assumed stemmed from Gladys's three weeks in jail. Dr. Sweet sent them to Arizona for the summer, hoping the heat and dry climate would benefit their lungs. Iva died in August. Gladys brought her body home for burial by their infant son. At the cemetery, a white custodian tried to redirect the funeral procession to the rear entrance for colored folks. Ossian pulled his equalizer out and obtained access through the main gates.[23]

Gladys returned to Tucson to try to recover while Ossian stayed in an apartment in Detroit. He moved back into his house in mid-1928, after it had stood vacant for almost three years. Gladys's health continued to decline. She came back to Detroit in early November of 1928 to die at home and be buried with her children. Noting this sad outcome, Darrow did not resent the people who "grievously wronged" his clients, but rather blamed "the bitterness bred through race prejudice. . . . So long as this feeling lives, tragedies will result."[24]

Ossian's younger brother Henry earned a law degree and rose to prominence in the Michigan NAACP, but he, too, caught tuberculosis and died in 1940, only thirty-six-years old. By then, the clout of the Ku Klux Klan had all but disappeared. From a height of five million members in the 1920s, by 1930 a host of scandals starting with Grand Dragon Stephenson's murder conviction reduced its numbers to 30,000. The KKK continued to dwindle further year by year to near extinction as a national political party in the 1940s. Yet the KKK would rise again in the '60s in the Deep South and spread once more to other states as it intermingled with Neo-Nazis and other vigilante groups embracing terrorism as a tactic.

David Cunningham, author of *Klansville, U.S.A.: The Rise and Fall of the Civil Rights-Era KKK,* observed in January of 2015 that a "greater number of KKK organizations exist today than at any other point in the group's long history." He noted that the Southern Poverty Law Center Hate Map cites KKK-affiliated chapters in four states out of five. Cunningham notes that "nearly all of these groups are small, marginal, and lacking in meaningful political or social influence" but they bear close watch as potential "breeding grounds for unpredictable violence," particularly since the KKK historically has ebbed and surged in waves.[25]

* * * * *

Supported by a coalition of minorities, Judge Murphy later became Mayor of Detroit and then Governor of Michigan and U.S. Attorney General. He ended his career as President Franklin Roosevelt's appointee to the United States Supreme Court. Justice Murphy joined the high court in 1940, just in time to participate in the landmark decision in *Hansberry v. Lee* that opened the door nationwide to constitutional challenges to discriminatory housing covenants.

Four years later Justice Murphy introduced the word "racism" into the Supreme Court's vocabulary in his scathing dissent in *Korematsu v. United States,* the controversial six-to-three decision upholding the validity of California's war-time internment camps for Japanese-Americans. California's Republican Attorney General Earl Warren was a primary instigator of the internment policy. He had since become the state's popular governor. Unlike the majority of his brethren on the high court in the 1940s, Justice Murphy could not accept the deadly attack on Pearl Harbor as an excuse for racist internment. He saw absolutely no defensible distinction between California's forced relocation of Japanese-American families and Nazi Germany's "abhorrent and despicable treatment of minority groups."[26]

Justice Murphy died in 1949, four years before President Eisenhower named Governor Earl Warren the new Chief Justice of the United States. Justice Murphy would doubtless have been surprised and delighted to see Chief Justice Warren forge a unanimous landmark civil rights decision in 1954, just months after he was sworn into office. The historic decision in *Brown v. Board of Education of Topeka, Kansas* overturned *Plessy v. Ferguson* and flatly rejected the "separate but equal" doctrine used to justify racial segregation for over half a century. Justice Murphy would likely have been even more amazed and gratified when the Chief Justice again spoke for a unanimous high court in 1967 to invalidate the nation's remaining anti-miscegenation laws. In *Loving v. Virginia,* Warren expressly found "White Supremacy" an unconstitutional reason for states to criminalize interracial marriages.[27]

After Warren retired, he also became conscience-stricken over his role in establishing Japanese-American internment camps during World War II. Like Justice Murphy nearly three decades earlier, Warren concluded he was wrong to assume all those of Japanese descent had suspect loyalties. Warren particularly felt guilty for uprooting children from their homes, schools and friends. On reflection, he deemed his conduct at the time "not in keeping with our American concept of freedom and the rights of citizens."[28] The 2017 documentary film "And Then They Came for Us" starring Star Trek actor George Takei revisits that bitter civics lesson. As fear of terrorists gives rise to proposals for registering all Muslim citizens and blanket travel bans, veteran documentarians Abby Ginzberg and Ken Schneider provide our nation with a timely reminder that respect for individual rights is a cornerstone of our democracy.

Like Earl Warren, Sweet prosecutor Robert Toms likely also absorbed lessons from Justice Murphy's example. Toms later became a judge, surprisingly devoted to civil rights. In 1947, Toms spent a year in Nuremberg presiding over Nazi war crime trials under the direction of Supreme Court Associate Justice Robert H. Jackson, on leave from the high court. Jackson had been one of Justice Murphy's two colleagues who also dissented in the *Korematsu* case.

Historian Kevin Boyle researched and retold the story of the Sweet trials in *Arc of Justice: A Saga of Race, Civil Rights, and Murder in the Jazz Age*. His prize-winning 2004 book inspired Arthur Beer's 2007 play *Malice Aforethought: The Sweet Trials*. What was so ground-breaking about that early 20th century trial then – and still riveting today – was that an exceptionally persuasive lawyer managed to get a white male jury to acquit a young black man on a homicide charge that no white man would have had to defend in court under similar circumstances.

Today, violent self-defense is on the rise as fear of violence mounts. Harvard University Director of Undergraduate Studies Caroline Light has researched the alarming rate at which "Stand Your Ground" laws are spreading – with disparate consequences depending on the shooter's race, gender and social status. Whether a shooting is justifiable homicide or murder depends on the motivation the police, prosecutor and ultimately a jury decide the shooter acted upon. Was it hate or fear for personal safety or that of others? When police face rare prosecution for shooting minority male suspects, the officers are overwhelmingly exculpated.[29]

White male vigilantes are benefitting from similar benign assumptions about their motives. In Light's new book, *Stand Your Ground: A History of America's Love Affair with Lethal Self-Defense,* Light points out, "The American legal system's handling of violent self-defense has long favored white, property-owning men. Nonwhite, female, poor or gender-nonconforming people have always been more likely to be punished for defending themselves and less likely to see the courts come to their aid when they are harmed."[30]

Light calls special attention to a recent study by the *Journal of Personality and Social Psychology* reinforcing the stereotype used to justify lynching for more than half of the last century. The study documented "the way in which people [still] perceive black men as larger and stronger and thus more threatening than they actually are." Light concludes: "We live in a country with more guns than people, and laws like Florida's help us justify a culture of anxiety and intimidation where conflicts that might have been settled peacefully end in tragedy. The burden of this shift falls on people who are already marginalized. While some Americans enjoy growing legal protections around the use of deadly weapons, too many are left out in the cold and more vulnerable than ever to the deadly impulses of their fellow citizens."[31]

* * * * *

While the Sweet trials ended favorably to the defense, the family itself experienced trauma and tragedy. Following his wife and young daughter's deaths, Dr. Ossian Sweet tried to move on with his life, with some success. From 1928 on, Dr. Sweet lived in his bungalow in his white neighborhood unmolested. He stayed there for twenty-five years while his practice in Black Bottom flourished. His patients called him "Big Doc." He bought more land and dabbled in politics, remarried and divorced twice. Yet in the end, his finances foundered. Dr. Sweet sold his home to another black family and moved to an apartment above his office in the slums. Overweight and in deteriorating health, he became bitter and disillusioned.

Ever since Ossian and Gladys Sweet had decided to pursue their dream house, he had likely never been without his equalizer. On March 20, 1960, Ossian picked his gun up and held it to his head, firing one shot to end his misery. Soon afterward Black Bottom itself was condemned and replaced in a major urban renewal project. During the July 1967 Detroit riots, vandals destroyed his brother Otis Sweet's dental office, forcing Otis out of practice. Detroit remains highly segregated to this day, suffering from severe economic problems exacerbated by white flight and the collapse of the automobile industry that brought so many blacks to the city for the promise of a better life.

* * * * *

Darrow joined the NAACP board and stepped up his lobbying for civil rights as he wound down his practice. But after he closed his doors for good, the Depression nearly wiped out Darrow's assets once again. In 1931, the NAACP convinced him to represent nine black teenagers in a compelling Alabama death penalty case involving dubious charges of gang rape. A full quarter of a century since a blood-thirsty Chattanooga lynch mob kept the high court from deciding Ed Johnson's claimed denial of a fair trial, the Ku Klux Klan's political clout had plummeted. The time looked ripe to convince a reticent Supreme Court to tackle the mockery that often passed for justice in capital cases against black defendants. This time the NAACP had fierce competition from the Left as to whose voice would champion the rights of the Scottsboro Boys.

11. ALABAMA STAND-OFF

The Railroading of the Scottsboro Boys Prompts Two Landmark Supreme Court Decisions

Southern trees bear strange fruit,
Blood on the leaves and blood at the root,
Black bodies swinging in the southern breeze,
Strange fruit hanging from the poplar trees.

— ABEL MEEROPOL[1]

When Clarence Darrow wrote his autobiography, he considered his summation to the jurors in the Sweet case the highlight of his career. Nothing challenged Americans to reexamine their own souls the way that the cancer of racism repeatedly did throughout the century. In 1855, two years before Darrow's birth, French philosopher Alexis de Tocqueville had focused on the Achilles' heel of the United States: "An old and sincere friend of America, I am uneasy at seeing Slavery retard her progress, tarnish her glory, furnish arms to her detractors, compromise the future career of the Union which is the guaranty of her safety and greatness, and point out beforehand to her, to all her enemies, the spot where they are to strike."[2]

Not much had changed in Darrow's lifetime. In the 1920s, the NAACP reported an average of two lynchings in the Deep South each week. Only a federal law against lynching could be expected to be enforced. Yet not until the fall of 1921 did any sitting president ever dare endorse such a bill. Even then, Warren Harding's support won little respect. It had been whispered for years that one of his own great-great-grandfathers in the West Indies was black. Ignoring the president, Southern Democrats readily blocked passage of the proposed new federal anti-lynching law. Eagerly casting one of his first no votes was Tennessee's freshman Congressman Samuel McReynolds. The former judge still likely recalled with fondness his front-row seat at Ed Johnson's abduction from the Chattanooga jail, frustrating Supreme Court review of the travesty of a rape trial over which McReynolds had presided.

It took another decade before serious national attention turned to ending lynch mobs. One catalyst for action was a ghastly photograph of two black men, Thomas Shipp and Abram Smith, taken in August of 1930 in Marion, Indiana. The two men had been arrested for robbery and murder of a white factory worker and alleged rape of his girlfriend. The following night, local police collaborated with an angry crowd that broke the two men out of jail and strung them up. The haunting photograph prompted New York school teacher Abel Meeropol to write the poem "Strange Fruit," which he later set to music. (Two decades later Meeropol, a Communist friend of accused Cold War spies Julius and Ethel Rosenberg, would adopt their orphaned sons.)

The Tuskegee Institute kept a grim tally: 1,837 documented lynchings in the United States from 1900 to 1930, of which 182 were white men and 1,655 blacks. A recent review indicates these figures were understated.[3] Civil rights activists focused not only on eliminating vigilante justice, but on attacking the thornier problem of "legal lynching" by kangaroo court proceedings. In Cotton Belt states, white men convicted of raping white women were almost never executed, and white men who raped black women were seldom, if ever, prosecuted. At the same time, black men accused of raping white women customarily received the death penalty from all-white juries. The most famous of these cases arose in the spring of 1931 and became a continuing legal saga through the next decade.

The incident on March 25, 1931, started with racial taunts by a white teenager who stepped on the hand of a black nineteen-year-old clinging to the side of a rail car. Soon a race fight broke out among a score of unemployed youths riding hobo on the freight train. As the slow train crossed into Paint Rock, Alabama, from Tennessee, some black teenagers took over a gravel car occupied by white boys and forced all but one of them off the train. The dispossessed boys complained to the station master, who called the sheriff. He quickly deputized a posse to "capture every Negro on the train."[4] When the sheriff arrived at the next station with fifty armed men, they searched all forty-two cars and hauled off nine black youths they found on board, threw them all on a flatbed truck, and took them to the local jail where the terrified teenagers were held for assault with intent to commit murder. In fact, several blacks involved in the fight had already left the train, never to be arrested.

The posse had only found five boys in gondola-shaped gravel car number 16. Searching the entire length of the train the posse found four more boys, who, by their account, were each found in a different car: numbers 21, 23, 37 and 39. The posse had also found in car number 12, dressed in overalls, twenty-one-year-old Victoria Price and seventeen-year-old Ruby Bates.[5] Both tried to run away and were arrested and jailed, too.

Only after the sheriff asked Price and Bates if the colored boys had bothered them, did the pair make rape accusations. Price told an elaborate story in which she claimed she and Bates had earlier been in the gravel car (no. 16) where six boys attacked them. She identified three of the defendants. Bates could not decide whom to blame. Doctors confirmed that both Price and Bates had recently had intercourse, though all the sperm were dead and not likely the result of sex in the last half hour of the train ride as they both claimed.

Bates later confessed that Price, a known prostitute in their home town of Huntsville, Alabama, made up the rape story to fend off prosecution under the Mann Act for transporting Bates across state lines for immoral purposes. All of the boys taken from the train were charged with rape. They were from out of state and broke. None was allowed to contact his family or a lawyer. Locals instantly spread false rumors that one girl had her breast bitten off. A lynch mob gathered at the jail and demanded the boys be turned over for hanging. Officials led by County Sheriff Matt Wann only dispersed the angry crowd by threatening to kill anyone who tried to grab one of his prisoners. To appease them, Wann promised a quick trial "to send them to the chair."[6] Still, the sheriff

The Scottsboro Boys

Source: Pamphlet by Angelo Herndon (New York: Scottsboro Workers Library Publishers, Inc., 1937). https://wikimediafoundation.org/wiki/. See also: History: The Scottsboro Boys: Communist Party Involvement, https://sites.google.com/site/historyscottboys/communits-party-involvement

Haywood Patterson

Clarence Norris

Ozie Powell

Willie Roberson

Charlie Weems

Andy Wright

Roy Wright

Eugene Williams

Montgomery Olen

Determined Alabama prosecutors subjected the Scottsboro Boys to more retrials than in any other criminal proceeding in American history. Finally, in 1937, the state agreed to drop charges against four of them. Four others received lengthy prison terms. Only Clarence Norris was sentenced to die. After the Supreme Court declined any further review, Alabama's governor commuted Norris's sentence to life in prison. In 1948, Patterson was still serving a 75-year sentence under his fourth conviction when he escaped to Michigan, where the governor refused to extradite him. In 1976, at the instigation of the NAACP, Alabama Gov. George Wallace pardoned Clarence Norris, the last of the Scottsboro Boys over whom the state still had jurisdiction.

Source: http://famoustrials.com/scottsboroboys/1605-diagram; Images from rail_freight_transport#/media/file

Price and Bates claimed they started out holding onto tank car 22 and moved to gondola car 16 at prior stop

Andy Wright found here on only flat car, car 21

DIAGRAM OF THE SOUTHERN RAILWAY FREIGHT TRAIN IN MARCH 1932 ON WHICH THE SCOTTSBORO BOYS WERE ARRESTED FOR ASSAULTING WHITE BOYS AND LATER CHARGED WITH GANG RAPE OF TWO YOUNG WOMEN (Competent counsel ordered by the Supreme Court created a 32-foot model train for use at the first retrial).

Montgomery Olen found here in box car 37

Willie Roberson found here in box car 39

Gondola car 16 where inter-racial fight occurred and white boys all left the train. Only after Price and Bates faced arrest did Price claim the two were in car 16 and were gang raped by all remaining black boys on the train, including 3 found in cars 21, 37 and 39.

gondolas

Gondola car 12 where Price and Bates were found outside and their snuff box was found inside the gondola.

Source: https://en.wikipedia.org/wiki/File:Bates,_Ruby_%26_Victoria_Price.jpg

Victoria Price (left) and Ruby Bates (right)

Both 21-year-old Victoria Price and 17-year-old Ruby Bates tried to run away from the Alabama sheriff and his posse of 50 armed men who had just begun searching the Tennessee freight train on March 31, 1932, "to capture every Negro" for allegedly assaulting some white boys thrown off the train. The posse found Price and Bates dressed in overalls in car 12, apart from the nine teen-age boys they rounded up in five different cars. Price and Bates were arrested and jailed, too. Only after the sheriff asked the pair if the colored boys had bothered them, did Price tell an elaborate story about being in car no. 16 a half hour before the train stopped where the two were gang raped by six boys. She identified three of the nine Scottsboro Boys as her assailants. Bates could not decide whom to blame. Doctors confirmed that both Price and Bates had recently had sex – not surprising, since they were both making what living they could as prostitutes – but likely had no sex in the time frame they claimed. It was only after the first trial, in which eight of the nine Scottsboro Boys were convicted and sentenced to die, that Bates confessed Price had made up the rape story to fend off prosecution under the Mann Act for transporting Bates across state lines for immoral purposes. In getting Bates to change her story, the Scottsboro Boys' new counsel had the benefit of a detailed report by an ACLU social worker named Hollace Ransdall, who thoroughly investigated the sad back stories of both Price and Bates. (See http://www.famoustrials.com/images/ftrials /ScottsboroBoys/documents/Scottsbororeport.pdf); see also "Why did they lie?" https://prezi.com/x9ewprcvj01f/why-did-they-lie/.)

feared the accused teenagers would be kidnapped and killed before trial. He called in the National Guard for reinforcements. Five days after
their arrest, armed reserve units transported the boys to the county seat
of Scottsboro where they were promptly indicted by an all-white jury.

Barely a week later, the Scottsboro Boys faced trial – the same day
as a county fair. The governor again sent armed guards to protect the
prisoners with machine guns and bayonets. Permits to enter the gallery became the hottest ticket in town as a standing-room-only crowd
of white men filled the garrisoned courthouse. Some 10,000 defenders of Southern womanhood gathered outside awaiting the results. A
Tennessee real estate lawyer named Stephen Roddy volunteered to ask
for a change of venue on the boys' behalf in light of the lynch mob
atmosphere. The trial judge denied the motion based on the testimony
of the sheriff and another state's witness, who characterized the swarming crowd as just friendly and curious. Under continuing armed guard,
the prosecutor then conducted four separate trials back to back that,
together, took all of five days.

Though Roddy told the judge he was unprepared and unfamiliar
with Alabama law, the judge asked him to act as co-counsel for the boys
along with a sixty-nine-year-old local volunteer. The Alabama lawyer,
Milo Moody, had not been to trial in many years. In fact, Moody was
exhibiting signs of senility and Roddy showed up in court the first day
"so stewed he could hardly walk straight."[7] The two were given less than
half an hour to consult with their clients before the first trial started.
They made no objection to the defendants being tried in groups despite the grave risk of guilt by association rather than proof that each
of them participated in the capital crime. The train had 42 cars plus
a caboose. The boys, who ranged in age from twelve to nineteen, had
not all been traveling together. A few had not even met each other on
board or seen Price or Bates. One was nearly blind and crippled from
syphilis. He had been sitting alone in car 39, the furthest location of
any of the boys accused of rape.

In the very first trial, one of the two defendants, Clarence Norris,
caught his lawyers by surprise when he testified that he had witnessed
the other eight rape Price and Bates. Norris later claimed that this was

false testimony coerced by the police. They had taken him from his cell the night before and beaten him into helping convict all the others on the promise that his own life would thereby be spared. Two other defendants later tried the same tactic in a futile effort to avoid being sentenced to death – promises that the police apparently never intended to be honored. The dumbfounded lawyers should have moved to withdraw and request mistrials. They could not represent all of the defendants with such a basic conflict in their stories. Instead, the lawyers solved their dilemma by failing to make any closing argument at all, even to ask the jury to use its discretion to send one or more of the youths to prison instead of the electric chair.

When the first two teenagers were sentenced to die, the elated gallery burst into applause. Outside, a band struck up, "There'll be a Hot Time in the Old Town Tonight."[8] Each of the next three trials lasted only a day. The trial of twelve-year-old Roy Wright was last. All but one juror voted for the death penalty against Wright even though, in view of his age, the prosecutor only asked for life imprisonment. The judge had no choice but to declare that one a mistrial.

As eight of the teenagers endured the miseries of death row, national newspapers reported the outrageous details of their prosecution. The Scottsboro Boys immediately became a cause célèbre for civil rights advocates. The ACLU sent an investigator to gather facts. The Communist Party saw great recruiting potential in embarrassing the American system of justice as they had done through the martyrdom of Sacco and Vanzetti just four years before. Their International Labor Defense Committee (ILD) immediately sent lawyers to sign the boys up as clients.

The NAACP was at first reticent to champion the controversial cause, but talked Clarence Darrow into coming out of retirement to argue the appeal and represent the defendants on retrial. By then, the ILD had already obtained the consent of the Scottsboro Boys and their parents to represent them. When Darrow arrived in Alabama, a telegram signed by all nine prisoners awaited him. The obviously ghost-written message informed Darrow that he could only join the defense team if he severed his connections with the NAACP and let the ILD control the litigation strategy. For the first time in his long career, the seventy-four-year-old warhorse quit a case in disgust. He felt the ILD lawyers "cared far less for the safety and well-being of those poor Negro boys than the exploitation of their own cause."[9]

On appeal to the Alabama Supreme Court, the convictions were affirmed over the lone dissent of the state's Chief Justice that the defendants had not received a fair trial.[10] On review in *Powell v. Alabama*, the United States Supreme Court agreed with the dissent. It found that there had been a clear denial of due process in the trial judge's failure to allow enough time for the defendants to obtain competent counsel. The high court cited as key factors "the ignorance and illiteracy of the defendants, their youth, the circumstances of public hostility, the imprisonment and the close surveillance of the defendants by the military forces, the fact that their friends and families were all in other states and communication with them necessarily difficult, and above all that they stood in deadly peril of their lives." For the first time ever, the high court held that "the necessity of counsel was so vital and imperative" that if the defendants could not obtain their own lawyers, the trial court had to make its own "effective appointment of counsel" to comply with the federal Constitution.[11]

On remand, the cases were moved from Scottsboro to Decatur, Alabama. To quell criticism following Darrow's ouster, the ILD recruited as head of the defense team another nationally known defense lawyer, New Yorker Samuel Leibowitz. Leibowitz was a master of cross-examination reputed to nearly match Darrow in his prime. He agreed to work for free and, with the help of investigative work by the ACLU and ILD, amassed substantial evidence that the two women were lying. Bates admitted that none of the accused rapists had even so much as spoken to her on the train. She agreed to testify for the defense at trial.

The atmosphere in Decatur was again extremely hostile. One local diner owner quipped to a journalist, "There shouldn't be any trial for them damn niggers – thirty cents worth of rope would do the work and it wouldn't cost the county much."[12] Indeed, while the convictions had been pending on appeal, Jackson County Sheriff Matt Wann was murdered.

The official story was that, shortly after midnight on May 3, 1932, Wann and three deputies sought to arrest a young man named Harry

Hambrick for failure to pay court-ordered support. Wann mistakenly put the cuffs on the man who answered the door, who was Hambrick's brother. Harry Hambrick then pulled out a shot gun and killed the sheriff. He then evaded all three deputies and took off for parts unknown, never to be seen again. No county records corroborate that story. Instead, rumors immediately began to circulate which attributed the sheriff's death to the KKK bent on revenge for Wann's courage in thwarting the mob that wanted to lynch the nine boys just after their arrest.[13] Next time they wanted a lynch party, no maverick law enforcement officer had better stand in their way.

In the first retrial, the lead defendant was Haywood Patterson. The chief prosecutor, Thomas Knight, Jr., was the son of the Alabama Supreme Court justice who wrote the decision affirming their original convictions. Knight's assistant aroused the jury's anger with anti-Semitic rhetoric like that used in Atlanta against Leo Frank: "Is justice going to be bought and sold in Alabama with Jew money from New York?"[14] Liebowitz immediately called for a mistrial, which was denied. The jurors quickly reached a guilty verdict and sentenced Patterson to death.

Yet in this case Judge James Horton had been troubled by the evidence. Himself the proud descendant of Confederate soldiers, Horton did not let that stand in the way of doing justice. He set aside the jury verdict and postponed the remaining trials, writing, "The testimony of the prosecutrix in this case is not only uncorroborated, but it also bears on its face indications of improbability and is contradicted by other evidence . . . ."[15] The incensed prosecutor demanded that Horton be replaced. (Horton lost his seat at the next election for his courageous handling of these cases.) The new assigned judge refused to request state troops to protect the defendants, and Alabama's governor declined to order any. Panicked, Liebowitz cabled President Roosevelt to urge federal intervention to prevent the "extremely grave" risk of a massacre.[16] The judge and prosecutor also received hate mail and threats that they attributed to Communists.

The next judge showed open hostility to the Northern lawyers. Each of the defendants was again convicted by an all-white jury and all except one sentenced to die. More protests followed in Washington,

Photo source: Everett Collection/Alamy stock photo, http://www.alamy.com/stock-photo-prosecution-at-the-scottsboro-trial-attorney-general-thomas-knight-52435415.html

Scottsboro Boys' prosecutor Thomas Knight, Jr. (right) and his assistant Thomas Lawson (left), photographed on Nov. 23, 1933. Knight led the Alabama legal team in the long battle to convict the Scottsboro Boys of rape. This photo was taken during the first appeal. Prosecuting the Scottsboro Boys played a major role in furthering Knight's legal career. Knight later became Attorney General and then an Associate Justice of the Alabama Supreme Court like his father, who authored the original opinion affirming the Scottsboro Boys' convictions.

The atmosphere in Decatur for the retrial after Judge Horton was removed from the Patterson case was again extremely hostile. One local diner owner quipped to a journalist, "There shouldn't be any trial for them damn niggers – thirty cents worth of rope would do the work and it wouldn't cost the county much." Indeed, while the convictions had been pending on appeal, Jackson County Sheriff Matt Wann was murdered. Rumors quickly spread that it was KKK revenge because Wann **(right)** had protected the Scottsboro Boys from a lynch mob immediately after their arrest. Clarence Norris assumed to his dying day that the nine boys owed their lives to the sheriff. Norris viewed Wann as a civil rights martyr betrayed by his own deputies in collusion with the KKK for daring to try to ensure the Scottsboro Boys a jury trial, as the Constitution requires.

Officer Down Memorial Page www.odmp.org/officer/reflections / 13823-sheriff-matt-wann

Sheriff Matt Wann, Jackson County 1931–1932. This photo hangs in the Sheriff's Office lobby in the Jackson County Courthouse, where the Scottsboro Boys were first tried.

Source of images in left column: https://www.flickr.com/photos/. Seelye http://amanilove.blogspot. com/2009/09/remembering-scottsboro-boys.html

Source: https://en.wikipedia.org/wiki/File:HORTON.jpg

*Demonstrators (**above**) including Janie Patterson, mother of defendant Haywood Patterson, march in front of the White House in May 1933. The flyer (**top**) was distributed for one of many other protest marches.*

Above: A headline in a black newspaper following Haywood Patterson's conviction in his second retrial in Decatur, Alabama.

Judge James Horton, a proud descendant of Confederate soldiers, was agreed upon by both sides for the first retrial after the Supreme Court sent the Scottsboro case back down. Judge Horton instructed the jury, "So far as the law is concerned it knows neither native nor alien, Jew nor Gentile, black nor white. This case is no different from any other. We have only to do our duty without fear or favor." When the jury came back with a guilty verdict against Patterson, the judge rejected it, finding the rape testimony simply not credible. Judge Horton was removed from further proceedings in the case by the Alabama Supreme Court and lost his next election, ending his judicial career. A plaque with his jury instruction now hangs on the wall of the courthouse where he tried the Patterson case.

D.C. and cities in the North. In 1934, Liebowitz had a falling out with the ILD after Price accused three ILD attorneys of trying to bribe her to change her testimony. In 1935, the United States Supreme Court again reversed the convictions for denial of due process. In another landmark ruling in *Norton v. Alabama*, the high court for the first time found a violation of the Fourteenth Amendment based on a determination that qualified black citizens were systematically excluded from the jury panel even though state law supposedly permitted their service.

In the war of attrition, the state had the upper hand. Determined Alabama prosecutors subjected the Scottsboro Boys to more retrials than in any other criminal proceeding in American history. Finally, in 1937 they agreed to drop charges against four of them. Four others received lengthy prison terms. Only Clarence Norris was sentenced to die. After the Supreme Court declined any further review, Alabama's governor commuted Norris's sentence to life in prison.

In 1948, Patterson was still serving a seventy-five-year sentence under his fourth conviction when he escaped to Michigan, where the governor refused to extradite him. In 1976, at the instigation of the NAACP, Alabama's Governor George Wallace pardoned Clarence Norris, the last of the Scottsboro Boys over whom the state still had jurisdiction. That same year the story became a TV movie. It had earlier inspired folk singer Leadbelly to put their ordeal to music,[17] and Langston Hughes to write the poem "Scottsboro" with the powerful opening lines, "8 BLACK BOYS IN A Southern JAIL. WORLD, TURN PALE! 8 black boys and one white lie."[18] Two documentaries appeared at the century's end (1998 and 2001). The travesty of justice inspired the 2006 movie *Heavens Fall* and a short-lived Broadway musical in 2010. That same year, a blogger dug back into the suspicious circumstances of the murder of Sheriff Matt Wann and urged an official reinvestigation.[19] Clarence Norris assumed to his dying day that the Sheriff was a civil rights martyr – betrayed by his own deputies in collusion with the KKK for daring to try to ensure the Scottsboro Boys a court trial before a jury as the Constitution requires.

Of all the cases promoted as trials of the century, those against the Scottsboro Boys likely had the greatest impact – not for their outcome, but for twin landmark rulings: that due process requires defendants in capital cases to receive competent counsel and that black citizens cannot be systematically excluded from the jury pool. By 1963, in *Gideon v. Wainwright,* the Supreme Court unanimously extended the right to effective counsel to all indigent defendants facing charges that could result in a year or more in prison. That decision finally prompted the widespread creation of public defenders' offices seven decades after creation of such offices to represent indigent criminal defendants were first proposed.

Back in 1939, when lynching was still common and the fight for the lives of the Scottsboro Boys remained a relatively fresh memory, jazz singer Billie Holiday appeared at Café Society in Greenwich Village – the first integrated nightclub in New York. As the staff dimmed all but one spotlight, she closed each performance with an emotional rendition of "Strange Fruit." It became Holiday's signature song, often moving listeners to tears. Her Grammy Hall of Fame recording wound up prominently featured on the Recording Industry of America's list of 365 historically significant hits of the century. In 1999, *Time* magazine singled out "Strange Fruit" as "THE" best song of the century, surpassing in significance, in its estimation, the top three listed by the National Endowment of the Arts: Judy Garland's "Over the Rainbow," Bing Crosby's "White Christmas" and Woody Guthrie's "This Land is Your Land."[20]

Despite the power of "Strange Fruit" in the rest of the country, in the South lynching remained a defiant tradition for decades. After World War II ended, peace representatives of fifty countries came to San Francisco to draw up the charter for the United Nations to promote human rights and fundamental freedoms. To the embarrassment of the United States, both the National Negro Congress and the NAACP immediately filed petitions with the U.N.'s Commission on Human Rights to protest America's history of barbaric treatment of their race. In this effort, the NAACP and the ILD's were temporary allies.

The United States used its clout to prevent the charges from gaining an official audience. Actor Paul Robeson and Patterson embarked on overseas lecture tours criticizing the genocidal policies of their homeland. The long history of racial atrocities belied the United States' carefully nurtured foreign image as the champion of democracy and greatly undermined America's claim of superiority to totalitarian governments like the Soviet Union and Communist China.[21] The government responded by taking away both men's passports for eight years.

In July of 1946, a Georgia mob hauled two black World War II veterans and their wives from their car, tied them to a tree and riddled their bodies with bullets. No state investigation occurred. The incident followed on the heels of news that a black sergeant had returned from combat as a decorated hero only to be beaten blind by South Carolina police on his way home through the state by bus. President Truman ordered a federal investigation of both chilling incidents and vowed to make civil rights a priority.

Public awareness of the need for national reforms had escalated after publication in 1944 of an in-depth study funded by the Carnegie Foundation, *An American Dilemma: The Negro Problem and Modern Democracy* by internationally acclaimed economist Gunnar Myrdal. By 1946, the Navy had already begun desegregating its units. Jackie Robinson had just broken the color barrier in modern baseball and made the cover on *Time* magazine as National League Rookie of the Year – after ten years of lobbying by a New York sports reporter for the American Communist press.[22]

Truman's newly appointed Commission on Civil Rights issued an historic report the following fall, criticizing the doctrine of separate but equal and recommending new laws and regulations "to end immediately all discrimination and segregation based on race, color, creed or national origin in . . . all branches of the Armed Services."[23] The panel recognized that continued state-sponsored racism was America's own worst enemy in the court of world opinion. In the 1948 presidential race, the Republican platform included a long-overdue federal anti-lynching law. When the Democrats met for their Convention in July of 1948, Minneapolis Mayor Hubert Humphrey made an historic speech urging the party to shift from states' rights to human rights and adopt a civil rights plank in its platform. Birmingham Police Chief "Bull" Connor was among the dyed-in-the-wool segregationists ready with their own agenda; he and thirty-four other Mississippi and Alabama delegates walked out.

After President Truman endorsed the Democratic Party's civil rights plank, South Carolina Governor Strom Thurmond joined the insurgent white supremacists in Birmingham, Alabama, where they organized the States' Rights Democratic Party, dedicated to maintaining Jim Crow laws. Their official motto was "Segregation Forever!" The splinter group of Dixiecrats nominated Thurmond for president and Governor Fielding L. Wright of Mississippi as his running mate. Thurmond campaigned with a line-in-the-sand message, "All the laws of Washington and all the bayonets of the Army cannot force the Negro into our homes, our schools, our churches."[24] (At the time, the forty-six-year-old governor was secretly supporting an illegitimate biracial daughter, Essie May Washington, almost the same age as his twenty-one-year-old bride. Washington's mother, a Thurmond family maid, was just fifteen years old at the time she gave birth. The avowed segregationist never publicly acknowledged that relationship.)

The Dixiecrats were incensed when President Truman desegregated the United States military by executive order. In most states, Dixiecrats ran as a third party. But in Alabama, Louisiana, Mississippi and South Carolina the Thurmond-Wright ticket replaced the official Democratic Party ticket. As Dixiecrats tried to cost Truman the presidency on the right, on the left former Democratic Vice President Henry Wallace headed a new Progressive Party ticket for president, with Idaho Senator Glen Taylor as his running mate. When Taylor boldly accepted an invitation to speak in Birmingham, Alabama, at an integrated gathering sponsored by the Southern Negro Youth Congress, Police Chief "Bull" Connor gloated, "There's not enough room in town for Bull and the Commies."[25]

Senator Taylor arrived at the church hosting the anti-establishment event, only to be arrested for using an entrance that Connor's police force had just temporarily marked "Negroes." The liberal Idaho Senator was convicted of disorderly conduct for bypassing the door for "Whites." While Dixiecrats branded Liberals as Communists for supporting African-Americans, Communists were using every opportunity to exploit on the world stage flagrant civil rights violations in the United States as evidence of the superiority of Communism. In 1948, Mississippi obliged with a mockery of a death penalty trial that lasted only one day. An all-white jury took less than three minutes to declare black truck driver Willie McGee guilty of raping a white woman. Like so many other blacks before him, McGee was slated for execution, though no white man had ever been executed in the state for that crime. Just as Communist lawyers raced to represent the Scottsboro Boys in the '30s, top Leftist constitutional lawyers volunteered to handle McGee's appeals.

Both the United States Supreme Court and President Truman faced intense pressure from prominent figures throughout the world urging clemency for McGee, though Truman had no constitutional authority to pardon a state convict. Despite the flagrant due process problems, in the height of the Cold War mainstream American commentators considered open Communist support for McGee "the kiss of death."[26] When the high court declined review, McGee was executed in 1951 for a crime he likely did not commit and for which no white man would have received such a Draconian sentence. On the eve of electrocution, McGee wrote to his wife: "Tell the people the real reason they are going to take my life is to keep the Negro down in the South. They can't do this if you and the children keep on fighting."[27]

Yet it was not just in the South that interracial rape charges drove the populace to a frenzy, nor only Negroes who excited irrational fears. Shortly after the Scottsboro Boys rejected the NAACP as their counsel, Clarence Darrow received an invitation to fight murder charges arising out of another sensationalized rape case. This time he was asked to represent four people in Honolulu indicted for a claimed "honor" murder. Practically everyone in America had heard of the lustful Hawaiian brute killed on January 8, 1932, in retaliation for a reported sexual attack on the wife of a white Navy officer. The perpetrators quickly became the darlings of a wide spectrum of high-powered politicians, the press and the public. Many conservatives who had ridiculed Darrow as a radical in the past now welcomed him as an ally. Civil rights activists compared the kidnap/murder to lawless mainland lynchings. Darrow received stacks of outraged letters from friends and supporters who could not fathom how he could represent vengeful white racists.

Darrow had second thoughts. Trying to bow out gracefully, he forwarded a copy of his closing argument in the Sweet case to show his commitment to civil rights. Yet Darrow's astounding success in the face of the hostile political situation in Detroit only made his assistance in Honolulu that much more coveted. Darrow shocked the NAACP by accepting the challenge. Tired of bitter winters in Chicago, Darrow admitted he could not pass up the chance to visit the balmy island of Oahu and earn a $40,000 fee for defending the year's highest profile trial. Top movie stars then commanded no more per film than he would get for his role in this wildly popular real life drama. Like his recent co-counsel in Detroit, Thomas Chawke, Darrow had represented scores of amoral clients. The thick-skinned Chicago lawyer endured both piles of hate mail and death threats when he represented Leopold and Loeb; why balk here?

Ruby dutifully packed their bags, unsure why her husband took this offer on the opposite side from the Scottsboro Boys case. Perhaps this platform would allow him to establish "a bridge between the white and brown folk, a new understanding, a better code of conduct," but she felt "dreadfully uncomfortable about it all."[28] The infamous "Massie Affair" would prove a most ironic end to Darrow's long career.

12. THE EXPLOSIVE MASSIE AFFAIR
False Charges of Gang Rape Set the Stage for Hawaiian Statehood

"Life is a Mysterious and Exciting Affair, and Anything Can Be A Thrill if You Know How to Look For It and What To Do With Opportunity When It Comes"

– FAKE SUMMONS USED TO LURE JOE KAHAHAWAI TO HIS DEATH[1]

By December of 1931 when the "Massie Affair" ignited mainland fears of a Hawaiian civil war, the islands had officially been a United States territory for thirty-three years. That annexation simply acknowledged a coup years earlier, effectively rendering the islands an American colony. Starting in the late 18th century, native Hawaiians had been decimated by new maladies: measles, influenza, leprosy, whooping cough, venereal diseases and intestinal diseases. All had been introduced by British sailors accompanying explorer Captain Cook in his discovery of "The Sandwich Islands." Not until 1795 – sixteen years after Cook died in a skirmish on the Island of Hawai'i – were all the islands forcibly unified under one monarch, Kamehameha I, with firearms obtained from British seafarers.

By 1819, Kamehameha II abolished the traditional worship of gods who demanded human sacrifices, leaving the populace receptive to New England missionaries bent on converting heathens to Christianity. By the 1840s, King Kamehameha III, himself a born-again Christian, was convinced to adopt a constitution and to reverse his father's edict forbidding foreign ownership of Hawaiian land. All too soon, a handful of Europeans and Americans would own more than seventy-five percent of island real estate in a parliamentary monarchy modeled after that of Great Britain. To work their sugar, rice and pineapple plantations, the owners began to import Chinese labor. When Congress barred that practice by the Chinese Exclusion Act of 1882, first Portuguese men, then Japanese and other Asians were imported to work the fields. (Chinese immigrants would remain banned for six decades.)

The plantation owners grew wealthy when the price of sugar skyrocketed during the American Civil War. In 1875, the owners negotiated an even more lucrative exclusive trade agreement with the United States. Then, in 1887, to solidify their power, the businessmen threatened to depose King Kalakaua at gunpoint unless he adopted a new constitution that disenfranchised all Asians; set literacy, property and income thresholds that kept most native Hawaiians from voting; and limited the king himself to a largely ceremonial role in the parliamentary government. The move paralleled successful efforts on the mainland to disenfranchise blacks in the South. Over time, five companies – four owned by British and American investors and one German company – dominated the island's politics as their virtual fiefdom.

In 1893, when Queen Liliuokalani sought to reform the much-despised "Bayonet Constitution," the sugar plantation oligarchy forced her from power, with naval support from the U.S.S. Boston. A hundred years later President Clinton would make history by formally apologizing for the illegal removal of Hawai'i's queen. The coup in 1893 installed the Big Five's leader, missionary descendant Sanford Dole, as president of Hawai'i's new government and paved the way for the United States to annex the territory in 1898. That same year the United States fought the Spanish-American War, acquiring further-flung Pacific islands, the former Spanish colonies of the Philippines and Guam.

At the time Hawai'i became a territory, Caucasians constituted barely five percent of the population. Native Hawaiians called them haole, "foreigners." Congress established a bicameral territorial government with the governor serving at the pleasure of America's President. All other officials were elected locally. Dole became the first governor of Hawai'i. The Hawaiian language was banned in favor of English. Uneducated workers remained largely segregated by ethnicity, with each group developing its own pidgin English dialect.

By the end of World War I, ownership of the "Big Five" was all Anglo-American, with cozy interlocking boards drawn from families that had long since intermarried. This Republican oligarchy controlled the banks, warehouses, major exports and imports and the territorial senate. The plantation owners had always found it hard to find cheap, compliant labor. When congressional exclusionary acts curtailed Asian immigration, the owners turned to Portuguese, Spanish, Eastern Europeans, Puerto Ricans and, on rare occasions, African-Americans and poor non-Hispanic or Portuguese whites. While Hawai'i still recognized members of its prior monarchy as symbolic figures of authority, they were now closely aligned with the Republican elite, and propertied Hawaiians held many governmental and teaching positions.

Tension grew within the brutally suppressed majority Asian population. The United States Department of the Interior likened plantation workers to slaves. Most had no hope of leaving the land. Despite postwar inflation, in 1920, the men earned only 77 cents per ten-hour day for their grueling field labor. The women only 58 cents per day – substantially less than child laborers in Atlanta's mills seven years before. In early 1920, island-born Japanese and Filipinos banded together in Hawai'i's first major multicultural strike. Three-quarters of the labor force on sugar plantations refused to work for five months, demanding $1.25 per day. The owners instead paid $3 to $4 per day to Chinese, Portuguese, Hawaiian and Korean scabs hired to quash this "anti-American" rebellion.

In June of 1920, when the owners finally broke the costly strike, someone dynamited the home of a Japanese interpreter at a leading sugar plantation. It was the same tactic anarchists and labor militants had used for years on the mainland. The Japanese strike leaders were blamed for the bombing, tried and found guilty. The territorial government then reported to Congress that the risk of Japanese laborers unionizing rendered them an ongoing menace. By 1924, Congress passed its most restrictive immigrant exclusion act, precluding further Japanese immigrants.

Since 1893, the United States had established both naval and army bases in Hawai'i in recognition of its strategic defensive location in the

Pacific Ocean, two-fifths of the distance from California to Japan. The Russo-Japanese War impressed the American government with Japan's military strength. In the 1920s, the American Navy and Army greatly expanded their bases on Oahu and practiced war games, readying for an attack. The build-up resulted in a dramatic increase in the Caucasian population, consisting mostly of bachelor soldiers and sailors from farming and working class backgrounds – many from the South.

The high proportion of diehard racists among the newcomers only increased the friction that had always existed between nonwhite islanders and heavy-drinking military personnel on shore leave in and around Honolulu. Unlike long-established haole, the navy men commonly referred to the dark-skinned native Hawaiians as "niggers." The Navy men were even more disdainful of Japanese islanders, who were considered potential enemies. Other minority islanders fared little better. Locals did their best to avoid any interaction with the dreaded Navy police.

Any crimes committed by whites received far less punishment, if any, than crimes by locals against haole. The disparity caused political turmoil in November of 1928 after the kidnap and murder of a ten-year-old white boy named George Gill Jamieson. All pretense at civility disappeared as tabloids egged on Oahu's white community to a "lynch mob" mentality against the Japanese community.[2] The police caught the perpetrator spending marked ransom money.

Myles Fukunaga had wanted to save his parents from eviction. He modeled the crime after newspaper accounts of Leopold and Loeb's 1924 murder of Bobby Franks. Fukunaga had a history of serious mental problems. Yet he received only a two-day trial before being sentenced to death. In contrast, a haole who robbed and killed a Japanese cab driver received only a five-year sentence. In fact, out of seventy-five convicts executed in Hawai'i in more than a hundred years, only one had been white. But appeals of Fukunaga's death sentence proved fruitless, and Governor Lawrence Judd refused to prevent the execution. The memory of that racist episode grated.

By 1930, there were 368,000 residents of Hawai'i, of which only about 15 percent were native Hawaiian. Fewer than 25 percent were

Caucasian; almost sixty percent were non-Hawaiian Asian and Pacific Islanders or persons of mixed race, and just 563 were blacks. Within the broad category of Asian and Pacific Islanders, citizens were identified by country of origin. Japanese and Okinawans numbered nearly 140,000; 63,000 were Filipinos; and 27,000 Chinese. The Caucasians included nearly 27,000 Portuguese, 6,700 Puerto Ricans and 1,200 Spanish citizens, all considered of lesser status than Anglo-Saxons.

At the turn of the century, Honolulu businessmen began heavily promoting tourism. The first luxury hotels built along Waikiki Beach attracted rich Americans arriving by steamship from San Francisco. A spectacularly successful Hawaiian pavilion at the 1915 San Francisco exposition introduced millions more Americans to the exotic Hawaiian Islands. Through the 1920s, Hawaiian music and movies filmed in Hawai'i became hugely popular across the mainland. As a result, increased numbers of nouveau riche tourists were lured to the land of hula dancers, bronzed surfboarders, coconut palms, luaus and ukuleles.

A major renovation project spearheaded by industrialist Walter Dillingham at Waikiki Beach spawned several new opulent hotels just a few years before the bubble burst in the stock market and Hawai'i suffered the effects of the Great Depression. In 1930, visitors declined 15.9 percent and continued to drop at a similar rate in 1931. Soon ugly news hit the headlines, giving the racial situation a frightening image that panicked Honolulu hoteliers even further about the prospects for future Hawai'i-bound pleasure cruises.

The marital deception that snowballed into an international uproar all started on the evening of Saturday, September 12, 1931, when a twenty-six-year-old lieutenant stationed at Pearl Harbor brought his twenty-year-old wife to the weekly "Navy Night" dance at the Ala Wai Inn in Honolulu. The four-year-old marriage of Tommie and Thalia Massie was already teetering on the brink of divorce. When they married, Thalia was an attractive brunette with stylish bobbed hair and a cupid's bow mouth. But she was no longer in good health and looked it, including weight gained in a recent failed pregnancy. Thalia suffered from Grave's disease, which caused her eyes to protrude; she drank too much, walked with a list to compensate for a misaligned eye and had

for some time exhibited severe emotional problems. Thalia was also a
total misfit as a dutiful Navy wife. She considered herself far superior to
the other women stationed in Hawai'i with their husbands; others saw
Thalia as an ill-mannered loner.

Thalia had come from a quasi-privileged background that placed
high value on appearances. Her estranged father, Granville Roland
"Roly" Fortescue, was an adventurous, illegitimate younger cousin of
President Teddy Roosevelt. Her mother, Grace Fortescue, was a socialite born to a wealthy banker cousin of Alexander Graham Bell. Roly
dissipated all of his own inherited wealth. Yet the Fortescues had sent
all three of their daughters to boarding school, likely funded through
the generosity of their extended family. With little parental supervision,
Thalia had developed a reputation for wildness as a teenager before she
met Kentucky-born Tommie Massie in 1927. Rumor had it that Thalia
began having flagrant affairs within a year after she married the dimin-
utive Annapolis Naval cadet. Since Tommie joined the submarine corps
in Hawai'i in 1930, Thalia had degenerated. Neighbors in the white
district of Manoa gossiped about Thalia, often seen parading around
half-dressed and drunk. They noticed that she entertained male friends
overnight during her husband's absences at sea.

In the summer of 1931, the marriage hit bottom. Tommie threatened divorce, but agreed to put Thalia on probation for three months.
Thalia had no marketable skills and desperately wanted to stay married.
Even so, she had been loath to attend the Waikiki dance with Tommie
on the night of September 12, 1931. He had invited two other Navy
couples to their home for drinks before they left for the dance. The
three couples consumed a fair amount of bootleg whiskey and beer
before they headed off in two cars to the Ala Wai Inn on the outskirts of
Waikiki Beach, arriving after 9:30 p.m. Tommie joined other submarine
buddies at the bar and abandoned Thalia largely to her own devices.

Around 11:30 p.m. Thalia got into an argument and slapped a
drunken skipper. Other guests summoned Tommie to intercede in
yet another embarrassing scene caused by his wife. Tommie went back
to his friends, only realizing sometime later that Thalia had left without telling him, as she had done on a number of other occasions. He

stayed until the dance ended at 1 a.m. and went to a friend's home to party some more. When Tommie called to check on Thalia, she told him "something awful has happened" and urged him to come home.[3] On Tommie's arrival around 1:30 a.m. he could see that Thalia's jaw was swollen and bruised. Thalia told him she had been walking alone when she was kidnapped, beaten and raped. Over Thalia's objections, Tommie insisted on reporting the crime.

The police came right out. They knew the address; they had responded to calls from irate neighbors when the couple engaged in loud fights. Initially, Thalia provided few details to the police except that she had left the inn around midnight and had been picked up by several Hawaiian men in an old black Ford or Dodge. She said they drove her to the former animal quarantine station on Ala Moana Road, where they raped her repeatedly in the bushes. Thalia doubted that she could identify them again, but did not tell the police she had left her glasses at home on Saturday night. Without them, Thalia's vision was so poor that she had not even been able to tell the race of the people with whom she hitchhiked home. Against her wishes, Thalia was taken to a hospital for examination.

The allegation was powerful. No one could recall a Hawaiian ever being accused of raping a haole. Police drove to the site on Ala Moana Road that Thalia had described as the scene of the crime and found a soda bottle that smelled of alcohol and a few items from a woman's purse. They quickly linked the claimed rape with another crime report that night. Around a quarter-to-one, a heavy-set Hawaiian woman named Agnes Peeples had shown up at the police station. Peeples complained that just minutes earlier four locals in their twenties had almost collided with her husband's car. The incident ended in a shouting and shoving match. One of them took a poke at Peeples and bloodied her ear. She took down the license number and gave it to the officers, who sent it out over the police radio.

Police soon traced the tan 1929 Model A Ford to a young Japanese woman living in one of the city's worst slums, a rundown neighborhood called "Hell's Half Acre." The car owner's brother, Horace Ida, at first denied using the car. Then he admitted he had driven it to a wedding luau and then to a dance party with four friends: boxer Joe Kahahawai, another well-known boxer and football player named Benny Ahakuelo, David Takai and Henry Chang.

Within hours, police returned to interview Thalia again, now under sedation at the hospital. With their prompting Thalia changed her story. She now recalled that the Hawaiians had driven up behind her in a fairly new tan Ford and that she caught a glimpse of the license plate. When brought in for questioning early Sunday morning, Ida thought the police wanted to arrest his friend Kahahawai for taking a swipe at Peeples after she insulted Ida's driving skills. When Thalia was discharged from the hospital, police immediately brought her to the station to see if she could identify Ida. Ida, whose nickname was "Shorty," was a small Japanese man, not a large, dark Hawaiian as Thalia had described. Thalia was noncommittal about Ida, but impressed Chief Inspector McIntosh with her recollection of most of the numbers matching the license plate on his car.

McIntosh was now on a mission to prove Thalia had been gang raped by the same rowdy bunch of hooligans that gave Peeples a hard time. What a coup if he already had the sensational case solved! The Irish police inspector had two decades of experience working on British colonial police forces before he arrived on Oahu. He had leapfrogged over officers with more experience on the force based on his ruthless work as a field overseer on an Oahu plantation. McIntosh flaunted his connections to Honolulu businessmen. Most of the police who worked under him were minorities whom he openly mistrusted. He preferred to work with his white subordinates.

Handed this extraordinary case, McIntosh took the initial responders off the case. He had already made up his mind. Two of the arrested men had prior criminal records. Mixed-race gangs posed the greatest threat to white supremacy on the islands. Unlike their parents, who often kept to their own kind, the next generation showed far less respect for the ruling oligarchy. McIntosh subscribed to the same philosophy as Los Angeles Detective Mark Fuhrman, the infamous star witness for the prosecution in the O. J. Simpson trial: "Even if you get the wrong guy, this guy's done something before, or he's thought about doing something."[1]

After Thalia and Tommie returned home, she was examined by her own doctor. Like the hospital staff, Dr. Porter found her claim of rape highly dubious. He knew that Thalia was almost blind without her glasses. He tried to convince Tommie to drop the prosecution and take Thalia off the islands. On Monday morning, McIntosh drove Ida's car to Thalia's home. She now claimed it looked similar to the one her abductors used. In fact, Thalia owned a Model A similar to Ida's and had driven a Model T in her teens. No one that familiar with both models would mix the two up even had they been of similar color. Ford had stopped manufacturing the Model T with its wood-spoke wheels in 1927, the same year the company debuted the modernized Model A, with its substantially wider chassis and far greater speed capability, among other easily contrasted features. Of course, Ida's siser's new car was also tan, not black like the older car Thalia had first described to the police. On the way back to the station, McIntosh and one of his underlings, Officer Sato, took Ida's Model A Ford. They drove to the old quarantine station and then repeatedly drove the car through the mud before they called in Officer Claude Benton, to analyze the car track "evidence."

Navy men passed around ugly rumors that Hawaiian thugs had violated Thalia Massie every way possible in all "three orifices . . . And they kicked her and broke her pelvis and they bit the nipple practically off one of her breasts. . . They broke her nose. Blackened both of her eyes . . . [and stomped on her face]."[5] The outspoken Naval Commandant, Rear Admiral Yates Stirling, Jr., was livid with rage. He proposed that the honor of his young lieutenant's wife be avenged by stringing the accused men up without a trial.

Stirling's public comments escalated the reported crime to a power play, which was soon backed by Honolulu's Big Five and wealthy industrialist Walter Dillingham. Truth was secondary to symbolism. The nonwhite majority needed to be sent a strong message to keep them in their place. Stirling had another agenda. Maybe this crime would galvanize Congress to restructure the government into quasi-military rule, which he greatly preferred to the uncertainties of civil government. Stirling placed no faith in any democratic institutions when the majority were

Asians or mixed race, and he much preferred court-martials to jury trials.

After police arrested Ida and his four friends and charged them with rape, Honolulu's Republican-owned dailies ran banner headlines about the gang of "thugs," "degenerates" and "fiends" who attacked "a white woman of refinement and culture."[6] The inflammatory language did its trick. Yet one Japanese-owned newspaper ran against the tide, pointing out major problems of proof, some of which had been leaked by the first policemen to interview Thalia Massie. Those who read its English-language edition or its Japanese version had a totally different take on the alleged crime, a divide that only increased over time.

At Dillingham's instigation to solve the crime and help reassure skittish tourists, Honolulu's businessmen quietly offered police several thousand dollars for use in developing evidence against the five Pacific Islanders. The police then made an offer to David Takai, whom Thalia had never identified. Charges would be dropped and he would get the reward money if he testified against his friends. When that ploy did not work, they offered the same deal to the other defendants. None wanted to turn against his companions.

All five arrestees supplied detailed accounts of their whereabouts on the night of September 12, along with the names of corroborating witnesses from the wedding luau and the dance, all of which checked out. The police could trace the travels of the defendants from 11:30 p.m. on September 12 through 12:40 a.m. on the 13th, when Benny had already walked home and the other four had almost run into Agnes Peeples and her husband at the corner of King and Lilia Streets. That intersection was located some six miles from the site of the alleged rape. By 12:45 a.m., Peeples had reported the near collision to the police. Thalia had hailed a ride home from Ala Moana Road shortly before 1 a.m. The five islanders simply could not have committed the crime in that time frame.

No evidence of semen had been found on Thalia's dress, which had not been torn or even wrinkled in the purported ordeal. Nor was any semen found in the five accused men's underwear. When the police fingerprint expert found no prints belonging to Thalia in Ida's car, Detective McIntosh insinuated that was because the expert was

Japanese. Thalia had by now identified Kahahawai and Chang as two of her assailants, but remained unsure about Ida. Even Takai faced prosecution and the same lengthy prison term as the others, if convicted.

At the request of Ahakuelo's mother, Hawai'i's Princess Kawananakoa arranged for the island's top lawyer to interview the defendants. The lone Democrat in the territorial senate, Chinese-Hawaiian attorney William Heen, first wanted to assure himself of the defendants' innocence. The princess then lent her name to fund-raising efforts. Native Hawaiians raised money for the defense of Kahahawai and Ahakuelo, the Japanese community dug deep for Ida and David Takai, and the Chinese community raised funds for Henry Chang, who was half-Chinese and half-Hawaiian.

Heen figured that, if he was to take on this highly politicized defense, he wanted a Caucasian co-counsel. He asked another political outsider, transplanted Mississippian William Pittman, who was then eyeing a seat on the county board of supervisors. They each grilled two of the defendants and compared notes. Heen and Pittman concluded the four were telling the truth. David Takai obtained his own lawyer, Robert Murakami, who had represented Myles Fukunaga on his unsuccessful appeal of the death penalty three years before.

Tension between whites and other racial groups escalated. Rumors circulated that Thalia had been seen walking unsteadily down the John Ena Road past midnight in the company of an unidentified white man. Whatever happened to Thalia in the next half hour – possibly just an argument that ended with a punch to her jaw – she wound up alone on Ala Moana Road before she flagged down a carload of five Caucasians to get a ride home between 12:50 a.m. and 1 a.m. If a sexual assault had actually occurred, the timeline developed in the course of the investigation should have alerted the police that they had jailed the wrong men.

The trial began on November 16, 1931, before Judge Alva Steadman, the very same judge who had overseen the rush to judgment in the Fukunaga murder trial. Of critical importance was the jury composition. To Rear Admiral Stirling's dismay, the case proceeded under controlling civil law. Since 1900, the Hawaiian territory had required jury panels to be chosen from all literate male citizens, but expressly prohibited a jury comprised solely of one race. (Caucasians feared bias against a haole defendant.) Because of the skewed population base from which the panels were drawn, half the jurors usually wound up being haole, and the remaining jurors tended to be far more conservative than the non-Caucasian island population as a whole.

The defense had twice as many challenges allotted as did the prosecutor. They peppered potential jurors with questions on their backgrounds and politics. Both sides together used all forty-five challenges, but still managed to complete the selection of the jury in two days. Only one juror was an Anglo-Saxon white. Four others had Caucasian surnames, but were among six jurors who were half-Hawaiian. Two were Chinese; two were Japanese. The last one was Portuguese. All of them worked for the city of Honolulu or a major company. Three had jobs with the Big Five.

The courtroom was packed, though Tommie Massie was conspicuously absent. He had requested active duty and put out to sea for the duration of the trial. So much for lending his wife moral support. Exhibiting far more interest were some of Honolulu's top businessmen. They took prominent seats to stare at the jury. The defendants thought the message was clear – jurors working for companies in the Big Five likely had their jobs on the line. Others might also expect retaliation against themselves or family members if they did not vote to convict. The jury was not sequestered, though warned against reading newspapers. The attorneys wrangled in court over the prosecutorial bias in most of the coverage. It was hard to imagine that news reports did not reach the jurors when they returned home every night. Judge Steadman apparently assumed his instructions to ignore such influences sufficed.

Deputy City Attorney Griffith Wight, who prosecuted the case, was already in his early forties. He had only practiced law for a short time before he received this extraordinary assignment. The business community provided him behind the scenes help from a private firm used by the Big Five. Wight put on his case in just over three days, including a trip to the alleged scene of the crime. The prosecution started off strong.

Thalia Massie gave a tearful account of the rapes and her broken jaw. With information since obtained, Thalia described the clothing worn by two of her assailants, their Model A car, the partial license number she had memorized, and the nicknames she heard them call each other. She was now sure it was defendant Kahahawai who punched her in the face. She claimed she had become pregnant and had to undergo an abortion at the hospital, which even in those days doctors did have limited authority to perform. (Thalia's doctor did perform a precautionary dilation and curettage procedure, but determined she was not pregnant.)

Under Hawaiian law, to prove rape, Wight needed to show corroboration for Thalia's account. The hospital physician who had examined Thalia took the stand and left it ambiguous whether she could have been gang raped without any sperm being found. The skeptical defense attorneys feared that questioning whether any rape occurred might backfire. Instead, they focused on proving Thalia was confused as to the identity of her assailants.

Thalia's original statement to police that she left the Ala Wai Inn at about midnight contradicted the notes Inspector McIntosh took at the station that she left the party at 12:30 or 1 a.m. At trial, Thalia claimed she left the party at "about 11:35" and that she had walked "five or ten minutes" along John Ena Road when two of the defendants jumped her from their car. That now placed the start of the crime at 11:45 p.m. when defense witnesses saw the quintet at the Honolulu dance party on the other side of the city.[7]

Thalia had originally claimed it was too dark to see her assailants, but identified the car as old and black. At trial, she insisted it was the tan 1929 Model A driven by Ida, still in nearly pristine condition. Thalia's belated recall also had Ida wearing a suede jacket during the rape. Actually, he wore it only when arrested on Sunday, a fact noted in one of the police reports. Thalia said she was raped several times for "perhaps twenty minutes."[8] Her time table had the crime ending just after midnight when many people saw the defendants in the dance hall parking lot across town.

A detective testified that Ida made a key admission at the police station – he already knew of an assault on a white woman before police ever told him about the crime. Yet Ida denied making the statement, which the policeman admitted was never recorded in any of several detailed police reports. The defense was even more effective in destroying the testimony of Officer Claude Benton, the designated expert on tire tracks. Prodded by Wight on direct examination, Benton described how he had identified the make of the tires from markings in the mud at the crime scene early on Sunday morning, before any suspects had been apprehended.

On cross-examination, however, Benton admitted that he did not investigate the tracks until Monday morning after police already had possession of Ida's car. Benton had no expertise on tires of recent vintage like Ida's. Benton also admitted that his original report of the crime scene – written on Sunday morning – made no mention of any tire tracks at all. Later in the trial, the defense produced Officer Sato, who admitted manufacturing the track marks with Inspector McIntosh early Monday morning before Benton's second visit to the site.

The defense produced a total of fifty-two witnesses, including a parade of credible alibi witnesses of different ages, race and ethnicity. They not only established the defendants' whereabouts during all critical times from 11:45 p.m. to 12:40 a.m. – miles from the alleged rape scene – they testified that they had also given the police similar sworn statements. Most telling were three witnesses who had seen someone dressed in a long green evening gown on the John Ena Road just after midnight on September 13. One was a Japanese hair salon worker. The other two were a couple, Mr. and Mrs. Goeases, who were headed toward a food stand. All three testified that the young woman resembled Thalia and had stumbled along drunk, talking to herself, with a white man trailing after her.

One of O. J. Simpson's lawyers called "the Fuhrman tapes," in which Los Angeles Detective Mark Fuhrman infamously revealed his own blatant racism, "the most devastating evidence ever presented in an American court of law to completely destroy the credibility of a police officer."[9] The unmasking of Honolulu's Chief Inspector McIntosh more than rivals Fuhrman's courtroom demolition. Much of the undoing of McIntosh came from his staff's own grudgingly produced police reports. Departmental witnesses also testified that they had suppressed evidence at his direction. In rebuttal, Wight tried to salvage his case with surprise testimony of a man who said he and three friends had actually witnessed the abduction. But on cross-examination, the four companions admitted that the people they saw did not look at all sinister and may have just been a group of guests leaving the Navy party together.

The whole trial took just two weeks to reach closing arguments. Prosecutor Griffith Wight still lacked any cohesive theory as to when the crime occurred or any evidence at all implicating David Takai. Wight raced through his argument in little over half an hour, happy to let the jury choose any version of the story Thalia told that suited them. Murakami and Pittman took the rest of the morning dissecting the flaws in the prosecutor's case. Murakami was low key, Pittman emotional: "If you convict [these men] you have got to have no conscience, you have got to have no soul, you have got to be cowardly. I know these men are innocent. . . ."[10]

After the luncheon recess, Heen spoke for nearly two hours ridiculing the prosecution's impossible alternate theories of the crime's timeline. As he started to sum up, the city attorney received a message from a bailiff and went out into the hall. Spectators became distracted as Wight's boss returned to huddle with Wight, who then scribbled a note he gave to another bailiff to hand to the judge. Judge Steadman then surprisingly declared a break in the proceedings and invited the lawyers into his chambers.

For two hours the packed courtroom sat in puzzlement as the lawyers argued over a request to reopen the trial to present important new evidence. The defense team must have been livid. A well-known civilian Navy contractor and his wife now offered to testify that they were on the John Ena Road just after midnight on September 13. The McClellans had been at the Navy party, and Mrs. McClellan had worn a long green dress. The prosecutor wanted to show that the eyewitnesses had seen Mrs. McClellan, not Thalia, that night.

Judge Steadman had already demonstrated prosecutorial bias in his prior rulings, but granting this motion over the objections of defense counsel was simply outrageous. Once the prosecutor rested his case, he should have been precluded from reopening it absent a compelling showing. Wight had no good reason for the delay in locating the pair. They were regulars at the weekly Navy dance. Yet Judge Steadman reopened the trial the next morning. By the time defense counsel put on its rebuttal, the ploy had backfired. A friend at the dance recalled seeing Mrs. McClellan wearing a white gown that night, not a green one. All three people who had seen the drunken woman after midnight on the John Ena Road testified there was no way they could have mistaken Mrs. McClellan for Thalia Massie. The Goeases were well-acquainted with the McClellans and would have recognized them instantly.

When finally allowed to complete his closing argument, Heen minced no words. He told the jury that the police were "caught red-handed in framing the tire evidence to send innocent men to jail." He urged the jurors to "be courageous" and "return a verdict of not guilty on your first ballot."[11] Wight had a final opportunity in rebuttal again, asking the jury to vindicate Thalia by convicting these "lust-sodden beasts." He regretted that the death penalty was not available. He blamed turncoat police who were traitors to their own department and asked the jury to find that the rape happened well before midnight. Under his latest theory, the young men raced back from their crime to establish alibis at the dance. He reminded them grimly of her injuries and intoned, "Death is preferable" to what Mrs. Massie had gone through. Blustering along to the finish, Wight implored the panel to "justify your manhood" and "protect our women."[12]

The jury asked to review portions of Thalia's testimony while an impatient crowd waited outside. As deliberations entered a second day, Honolulu tabloids tried their best to whip the white community into a lynch mob frenzy as they had done after the murder of the Jamieson boy three years earlier. One paper highlighted a recent lynching of a Negro in Maryland by a mob of 4,000. Under the tense circumstances, reporters were surprised at the calm demeanor of the defendants, who were out on bail and resting on the lawn. The islanders said they were innocent and had faith the jury would acquit them.[13]

The jurors cast a number of ballots before they reported to Judge Steadman that they were hopelessly deadlocked. Rumor had it that the vote was ten to two for conviction. Judge Steadman, as jurists commonly would do at that early stage, sent the panel back to continue deliberating to avoid a hung jury if at all possible. On Friday, new rumors spread that a verdict was near, with only one hold-out preventing conviction. Then two jurors engaged in a heated argument, only stopping short of fisticuffs when a bailiff intervened. The defense lawyers moved for a mistrial, to no avail.

On Saturday night the jurors reported they were at an impasse that no further rereading of the law or review of any evidence would resolve. The judge still advised them to keep meeting one more day. He later admitted he was trying to force a conviction despite qualms about the guilt of the defendants. Like other haole of his class, Judge Steadman viewed them as dispensable, second-class citizens worth sacrificing to resolve the ugly political situation.

After a record-setting 97 hours of deliberation, the worn-out jurors reported to the judge on Sunday evening that they simply could not agree. Judge Steadman then declared a hung jury. They ended in a six-six tie, never having had a ballot that was more lopsided than seven-to-five either way. Contrary to rumor that the voting split on racial lines, the lone haole had voted for acquittal on every ballot. Commandant Stirling still refused to believe the result reflected anything other than race bias.

Honolulu's leading tabloids displayed similar views. One paper called the result "The Shame of Honolulu." Taking his cue from *New York Post* muckraker Lincoln Steffens, the reporter recharacterized a number of minor Honolulu crimes over the past year as a wave of violence and predicted the jury verdict would just encourage more rapes of white women "by gangs of lust-mad youths."[11] No white-owned papers discussed the evidence of a frame-up.

Prominent white women in Honolulu reacted to the unexpected verdict by vowing to replace the mixed-race police force with white men whom they could trust to protect their safety. The women lobbied the governor, who immediately appointed a citizens' "Advisory Committee on Crime." That body then recommended stripping the sheriff's office of almost all investigative authority and creating a new Honolulu Police Department with a police commission appointed by the mayor and board of supervisors. Governor Judd then convened a special session of the legislature. By the end of January 1932, the new law was in place, and the commission appointed Dillingham's personal secretary and chief lobbyist as the first chief of police. His total lack of law enforcement experience proved no impediment.

At the same time, the Legislature followed recommendations to revise the rape law to make the crime punishable by death, with no corroborating evidence required. Having a politically connected chief of police in place, they could assume no minority woman victim would be allowed to invoke that law against a white man. The prospect that claims against islanders might be false did not bother them.

Following the hung jury, Navy men ran riot in the streets. Emotions were running so high that Commandant Stirling once again had to cancel all shore leave. The Pacific fleet avoided Hawaiian ports for the time being as Stirling sought authority to impose martial law to maintain order.[15] Of course, under martial law, as would be enforced in Hawai'i during World War II, citizens' right to habeas corpus would be suspended, as well as the right to jury trial.[16] The Navy could then rearrest and detain the alleged rapists and conduct its own proceedings with impunity, including summary execution. But try as he might, Stirling could not get enough support for that Draconian suggestion.

Under the laws of the territory – as was true of laws in the mainland United States – after a hung jury, the prosecutor was free to retry defendants. The Chamber of Commerce raised $5,000, which it now openly offered as a reward for anyone who came forward with evidence implicating the defendants. To ensure conviction, several sailor friends of Tommie Massie kidnapped Ida at gunpoint and severely beat him to obtain a confession. Ida was rescued by a passerby and taken to the hospital "lucky to be alive."[17] The welts on Ida's back were photographed as proof of his ordeal.

Tommie Massie quickly learned from a lawyer that the confession the men had beaten out of Ida would be useless in establishing his guilt. Back in October, Thalia Massie's mother, forty-eight-year-old Grace Fortescue, had arrived from the states. Unlike Tommie, she sat through the rape trial. Afterward, the socialite found all the ugly innuendoes about her daughter intolerable. Fortescue instigated a plan by which she and Massie could vindicate the family honor. They decided to kidnap Joe Kahahawai and get him to confess at gunpoint, leaving no telltale marks to ruin his confession. They recruited two sailors to help them, Deacon Jones and Edward Lord.

Kahahawai reported regularly to a probation officer. Early in the morning of January 7, 1932, Tommie put on a chauffeur's outfit and took Jones to the courthouse in a rented Buick sedan. There, Grace Fortescue was waiting to point out Kahahawai as he came for his appointment accompanied by his cousin Edward Ulii. Jones jumped out of the sedan and showed the islander a crudely faked summons, purportedly from the sheriff. Jones waved his gun and forced Kahahawai into the car. Grace followed the kidnappers in her own automobile, accompanied by Lord. Ulii witnessed the abduction and reported it immediately to the police.

A couple of hours later, a detective spotted Fortescue speeding in the blue Buick sedan on Oahu's south shore. She was headed out to a remote cliff overlooking the Halona Blowhole. The detective gave chase. When he forced the sedan off the road, he arrested Fortescue and two passengers: Tommie Massie and Lord. In the back was Kahahawai's naked body wrapped in a bloody sheet. The trio had been on their way to dump the corpse over the cliff into the sea.

Other police arrived at Fortescue's rental home where they found Jones, who had just wiped the room of blood. Jones had handed off the gun to Thalia and her younger sister to hide. He still had a .32 cartridge in his pocket. Nearby was a rope used in the abduction, Massie's chauffeur costume and a bloody towel. Jones later commented, "We were in a peck of trouble and we knew it."[18]

Thousands of islanders flocked to Kahahawai's funeral. Islanders considered the slain boxer like the most revered royalty, while whites painted his shameful death as an honor killing. Rear Admiral Yates Stirling received permission to house the defendants in plush accommodations onboard a ship at Pearl Harbor rather than have them spend time in jail. There, the co-conspirators received baskets upon baskets of flowers and thousands of letters of support. Commandant

Source: Everett Collection, Inc. Alamy stock photo

Hawaii "Honor Killing" principles: Mrs. Granville Fortescue with her daughter, Thalia Massie, and son-in-law, Lt. Thomas H. Massie.

When charged with the kidnap/murder of boxer Joe Kahahawai for the alleged gang rape of her daughter, Thalia's socialite mother, Grace Fortescue, lured the legendary Clarence Darrow to Hawaii to take a case that shocked his friends at the NAACP. He defended Fortescue, her son-in-law and two of his Navy buddies on murder charges. She was right that they needed the most highly skilled lawyer they could afford given overwhelming evidence of their guilt. Off the record, Fortescue told a New York Times reporter that "she came from the South and that in the South they had their own ways of dealing with 'niggers.'"

Source: Honolulu Star Bulletin, Jan. 8, 1932, headline, reprinted with permission; photo of Joe Kahahawai, Find A Grave, https://www.findagrave.com/

Boxer Joe Kahahawai
(1909–1932)

The purported "honor killing" of 22-year-old Joe Kahahawai on January 8, 1932, in the territory of Hawaii drew national attention. The vengeance taken against the Hawaiian boxer had been prompted by a hung jury the prior fall on charges Kahahawai and four friends gang raped Thalia Massie, wife of Navy Lieutenant Tommie Massie, stationed in Honolulu.

Source: Will Straw, United states Broadway Sbrevities(1930-35),https://willstraw.com/united-states-broadway-brevities-1930-1935/

Brevities *billed itself as the first national tabloid. It featured this racist cartoon on its front page two months before the four white co-conspirators faced trial in Honolulu for the kidnap and murder of Joe Kahahawai. Hearst-owned newspapers, among other popular dailies and magazines, had already inflamed the public with a grossly distorted picture of dangers faced by white women in Hawaii.*

Journalists from across the country flocked to the Hawaiian islands to cover every day of the trial. New underwater cables also allowed direct radio transmissions to the mainland for the first time. The compromise jury verdict of voluntary manslaughter made headlines from coast to coast. Here, an Albany, New York, paper focuses on the fear of reprisals. The exaggerated dangers were the work of a Navy Rear Admiral bent on gaining Congressional support for instituting a quasi-military government in the islands.

MASSIE JURY CONVICTS FOUR, HONOLULU TENSE; REPRISALS ARE FEARED

Source: Timothy Hughes Rare and Early Newspaper

The Hawaiian State Flag dates back to its territorial history reflecting prior British control. It includes stripes for each of eight islands.

The Massie Trial's Key Role in Hawaii Becoming a State

Darrow argued that Tommie Massie had shot Kahahawai while suffering from temporary insanity. Somehow, Darrow claimed that the defense might also exonerate Tommie's three co-conspirators to the kidnapping and attempt to dispose of the body. Like the rape charges themselves, the notion that Tommie pulled the trigger was fabricated. Tommie's co-defendant Deacon Jones later bragged that he was the one who shot the "black bastard," not Massie. (Two decades later, when the public learned all the sorry details, including a political cover-up by the Republicans in power, the truth swept out so many incumbents that the Democratic landslide was dubbed "The Revolution of 1954." Five years later, Democrats in Hawaii worked with Senate Majority Leader Lyndon Johnson to bring Hawaii in as our 50th state.

Stirling wasted no time writing up an inflammatory report that became a principal source of mainland newspaper accounts of the crime. Tabloids in New York carried explosive headlines: "Honor Killing in Honolulu Threatens Race War"; "Bayonets Rule Honolulu as Races Boil In Killing." *The New York Times* ran front-page stories highlighting the urgency of congressional action to safeguard the Navy. All this alarm was prompted by Stirling's reports.

Newspapers from coast to coast focused on the sensational story. Nearly a quarter of all newspaper readers subscribed to one of William Randolph Hearst's thirty-five papers. On national issues, all of the Hearst papers spoke with only one voice, that of their owner. Hearst echoed Rear Admiral Stirling's call to arms:

> The situation in Hawaii is deplorable. It is becoming or has become an unsafe place for white women. Outside the cities or small towns the roads go through jungles and in these remote places bands of degenerate natives or half-castes lie in wait for white women driving by. At least forty cases of such outrages have occurred and nobody has been punished. . . . The whole island should be promptly put under martial law and the perpetrators of outrages upon women promptly tried by court martial and executed. Until such drastic measures are taken, Hawai'i is not a safe place for decent white women and not a very good place for self-respecting civilized men.[19]

On January 21, 1932, prosecutor Griffith Wight convened the twenty-one member grand jury. Most seemed eager to whitewash the boxer's kidnapping and death with no indictment. But conservative Republican Judge Albert Cristy kept the panel deliberating for four days, emphasizing the critical role of the rule of law in all civilized societies. The panelists needed "to lay aside all race prejudice" in doing their duty or resign.[20]

Judge Cristy managed to convince a dozen members of the grand jury to indict the four on charges of second degree murder. The editor of the *Honolulu Times* then printed up 3500 copies of his next incendiary column. He sent them in bulk to Navy personnel, asking them to forward the news to family and politicians in the States. The story included a long list of minor crimes that falsely painted the Honolulu situation as an epidemic of native violence. Picked up by papers nationwide, the barrage of shocking reports outraged the public at the supposed hideous treatment of American women by savage Hawaiian islanders. *Time* magazine wrote that the islands were not a safe destination due to the territorial government's inability to restrain "the yellow men's lust for white women."[21]

Rear Admiral Stirling continued to inflame the American public with speculation that an officer under his command and his gray-haired mother-in-law might spend the rest of their lives in "a disgusting and revolting Hawaiian prison" for avenging their family's honor.[22] Congress made it a priority to look into the indictment as Stirling lobbied to suspend all privileges of nonwhites in the territory and intimated that Hawai'i was edging closer to civil war. Yet a few Congressmen were appalled at the race-based hysteria and skeptical of its factual basis. Among the harsh critics of the fear-mongering was the lone black in the House of Representatives. Oscar DePriest's parents had fled Alabama when he was seven, after his father saved one friend from a lynch mob only to see another die at his door. The Illinois Congressman noted that the Scottsboro Boys still faced death for false accusations of rape while a white Navy man remained at liberty, his rank in the Navy unaffected. "Murdering a Hawaiian did not even rise to the level of 'conduct unbecoming an officer and a gentleman.'"[23]

Despite the defendants' widespread political support, the murder trial was going forward. With such open and shut evidence of her complicity, Grace Fortescue wanted the best criminal defense lawyer in America. Arguably, that was still Clarence Darrow, though he had retired for good back in 1928. Broke again, Darrow was tempted, but not eager to travel that far and afraid his brain would not "click with its old-time vigor."[24]

He insisted on a $40,000 fee and assuaged his conscience with the assumption that he might help calm the extraordinarily volatile situation more than any other defense attorney could do. The defendants had become such a cause célèbre that contributions to their defense poured in from Grace Fortescue's wealthy society friends and from Navy families. For assistance, Darrow recruited a young New York lawyer, George Leisure, who had tried a case in Honolulu and was so excited about working with Darrow that he offered his services for free.

Grace Fortescue proved an extraordinarily difficult client. To her lawyers' dismay, she proudly gave out damaging interviews, including one to *New York Times* reporter Russell Owen. Fortescue said she only wished they had done a better job of getting rid of Kahahawai's corpse. Owen left out of his printed interview Grace's candid rationale for the murder: "She said that she came from the South and that in the South they had their own ways of dealing with 'niggers.'"[25]

Tommie, no doubt, had similar memories of regular lynchings from when he grew up in Kentucky. Darrow arrived with much fanfare on March 24, ten days before trial. He quickly learned that local defense lawyers from the same firm that had helped with the rape prosecution had already prepared much of the defense. Judge Cristy was now off the case, challenged by the defense lawyers for bias. His replacement was another conservative, Judge Charles Davis. The upcoming trial was the talk of Honolulu, rivaled only by guesses on the contents of a pending report from Justice Department investigators charged with making recommendations to Washington on the future government of the island.

The Richardson Report was issued on the first day of trial, on April 4, 1932. As locals were afraid, it suggested shifting to greater federal control of the territory to meet military defensive concerns. Yet the report fell far short of accepting Stirling's call for martial law. Appended to the report was his letter describing the urgency of the islands' current situation with its potentially "traitorous Orientals" and morally degenerate and otherwise inferior mixed-races.[26] Walter Dillingham then wrote to top Pentagon officials challenging the need for the report's governmental changes, revealing an even more pronounced rift between the island's powerful families and Rear Admiral Stirling on the issue of the continued rights of Asian citizens. When the full Richardson Report became public, Stirling's racist comments to the federal investigators incensed islanders.

The most remarkable accomplishment of the Richardson Report was its professionalism in shedding light on the hysterical atmosphere surrounding the Massie Affair. Conducted in just two months of exhaustive research, the investigation's results included fifteen volumes of interviews with hundreds of knowledgeable island professionals and another volume of compiled statistics. The federal team concluded that Hawaiians showed no propensity for sexual crime and that Hawai'i had "no organized crime, no important criminal class" and no crime wave of any substance. "Serious crimes . . . seem few in number and wholly sporadic." They found no evidence "of the supposed racial turmoil that has filled countless mainland newspaper headlines for the past three months." The report also questioned the wisdom of making rape a capital offense solely on the word of an alleged victim.[27]

The Richardson Report did little to change entrenched public opinion supporting the four defendants accused of murdering Joe Kahahawai. Journalists flocked to the islands to cover the story. New underwater cables allowed direct radio transmissions to the mainland for the first time. Seats were at a premium. The judge refused to grant privileges. Among the many people denied admission to the packed courthouse the first day was Hearst's society reporter. Honolulu matrons soon realized they could secure seats by having servants wait all night to hold their place in line.

The prosecutor, John Kelley, was considered among the island's best lawyers, when he wasn't on a bender. In this case, he faced mountains of hate mail for doing his job. Kelley intended to try the case on the theory of felony murder. That meant the four defendants who kidnapped Kahahawai were equally guilty of his murder no matter which one pulled the trigger. Judge Davis took the death threats against Kelley seriously and had everyone, including the lawyers, searched daily for weapons before they entered the courtroom.

It took a week to select seven whites, three Chinese, and two Hawaiians for the jury after a number of potential panelists showed eagerness to be dismissed, much as those jurors not chosen for the internationally watched 1968 death penalty trial of Black Panther leader Huey Newton in Oakland, California, would later be seen practically skipping out of the courtroom with undisguised relief. Six jurors were college graduates, four worked for the Big Five, including the foreman, while three others worked for Dillingham or affiliates.

Prosecutor Kelley went first. He put on evidence of the abduction and the arrest of three of the co-conspirators attempting to dispose of Kahahawai's body. Then he offered the incriminating evidence at Grace Fortescue's rental home, where the fourth defendant was arrested. Analysis of the bullet wound in the corpse showed that Kahahawai had been sitting at the time he was shot. The jury heard that police found buttons from his shirt in Fortescue's bathroom. A gun vendor matched the fatal bullet to the cartridge found in Jones's pocket and identified Jones as the man to whom he had sold the .32 Colt that was the likely murder weapon. Joe's mother identified her son's bloody clothing.

Clarence Darrow wasted no time calling Thomas Massie to the stand to change the focus. Darrow then launched into the events of September 12, 1932 – the night of the alleged rape of Thalia Massie. Over the prosecutor's objection, the judge allowed that line of questioning to establish Darrow's defense of temporary insanity. Darrow argued that what Massie had learned from his wife about the gang rape affected his mental state months later when Kahahawai was kidnapped, and that Massie shot Kahahawai without being aware of what he was doing.

The defense mirrored the "brain storm" theory that allowed Harry Thaw's lawyers to have Evelyn Thaw retell all the details of her seduction years earlier by Stanford White in her husband's 1906 murder trial. Darrow was far more audacious. He claimed that, if the defense of temporary insanity applied to Tommie, it would also exonerate his fellow kidnappers. Though Kelley strongly suspected Jones had actually pulled the trigger, he had no proof. Darrow was allowed to proceed.

Massie then described to the jury how distraught he and his wife had become after the gang rape. Thalia was suicidal. She greatly feared that she might be pregnant, which he claimed proved true and that she then underwent an abortion. Court ended that day with women brushing back tears. The next day, proceedings were unexpectedly cancelled due to Darrow's ill health. He claimed an attack of gastritis; according to others, he was suffering from a hangover. Perhaps Darrow needed liquid courage to complete his key role in this rewrite of history.

Many years later, Jones would reveal that it was Darrow's idea to claim Massie did the shooting so the quartet could all hide behind the defense of temporary insanity. Jones told an interviewer that Darrow had never asked which of them pulled the trigger, but Jones told him anyway before the end of the trial. Massie never held the gun. It was Jones who shot the "black bastard."[28]

After one day's delay of the trial, Darrow led Massie to say that Massie picked up Jones' gun and got a confession from Kahahawai: "Yeah, we done it."[29] With those words – which were not phrased the way locals spoke – Massie said his mind had been overcome with the image of his wife when this brute broke her jaw. Massie claimed he did not recall what he did next. Two defense psychiatrists testified that Massie was temporarily insane at the time of the shooting. (In Jones's version, unlike the one Massie told in court, Kahahawai never confessed. Jones impatiently pulled the trigger when the Hawaiian leaned forward in his chair as Massie questioned him.)[30]

Darrow was quite pleased with Tommie's performance and even more so with Thalia's when she took the stand to elaborate on the alleged rape. This time she claimed Kahahawai both hit her and swore at her. On cross-examination, Kelley confronted Thalia with a questionnaire she had filled out when she sought marital counseling in the summer of 1931 detailing her ongoing troubles with her husband. Thalia tore it to pieces and refused to answer any questions challenging her devotion to Tommie. She ran over and hugged her husband. Her courtroom histrionics even impressed Darrow, himself a past master.

In rebuttal, two psychiatrists testified that Massie acted like an angry spouse, but not someone who could not control his actions. Kelley also put on compelling evidence that undermined the entire theory that temporary insanity absolved the quartet of Kahahawai's murder. The autopsy revealed that Kahahawai was not killed instantly. He died of internal bleeding that may have taken twenty painful minutes. None of the defendants had made any effort to call a doctor to attempt to save Kahahawai's life after he was shot; they had dragged him bleeding to the bathroom, where he died. Both sides then rested.

For the entire month of trial, American newspapers printed detailed reports from Honolulu that had readers on the mainland

totally invested in its outcome. Darrow's emotional four-hour summation was then broadcasted nationally on radio. Darrow pleaded to
the jury to put an end to racial strife by acquitting the defendants. He
argued that to act otherwise would only increase civil unrest and com-
pound the suffering of the devoted mother and husband who stood
accused before them. Prosecutor Kelley derided the "serpent of lynch
law" that the defense would sanctify and reminded the jurors: "We
must abide by the law or descend into chaos."[31] Fans of Darrow's performance in the Sweet trial could only cringe at his turnabout.

Judge Davis instructed the jury that their duty was to apply the law
as written, emphasizing that no one had the right to take it into his own
hands. The vast majority of Americans following the case disagreed: if
the law called for conviction, the victim's presumed participation in the
gang rape of Thalia Massie cried out for the law to be ignored. Navy
personnel stationed at Pearl Harbor were adamant that Massie should
go free or they might seek their own revenge upon the populace.
Shore leave remained suspended. Islanders seethed at the injustice of
Kahahawai's murder, but they still showed no propensity for revolt. It
would only have given the Navy excuse for mass reprisals and possibly
bring on martial law.

The jury deliberated for almost forty-eight hours without reaching
a result. Then, after returning briefly to the courtroom, they only took
another half hour before announcing they had reached a verdict. When
they returned to the packed courtroom, Darrow anticipated acquittal.
That proved too optimistic. The jury compromised on a manslaughter
verdict with a recommendation of leniency. Top officials in the Navy and
powerful Hawaiian business leaders immediately demanded full pardons
for all four. The judge sentenced each defendant to ten years' hard labor.

In Washington, D.C., Congressmen immediately denounced the
result, the jury, Judge Davis and Judge Cristy and demanded that all four
defendants be pardoned. A House Committee voted to investigate the
territorial government with the threat of removing local control altogether. Stirling now requested that Hawai'i be run by a quasi-military
commission headed by both civilians and representatives of the Army
and Navy. The plan still contemplated taking away voting rights and

other privileges like jury service from almost all non-whites.

The twelve jurors seemed eager to repudiate their verdict. They told the defense team that they had been forced to vote guilty under the judge's instructions. Darrow vowed to appeal the case to the Supreme Court. Then the attorney general surprised Darrow with a visit to his hotel room. The chief prosecutor confided that he now faced a major dilemma. If he tried to jail the defendants, he might well cause a furor that could topple the government. Instead, defense counsel were summoned to the office of Republican Governor Lawrence Judd, where the sheriff had just brought their four clients. According to the lawyers, the governor then received an urgent call from President Herbert Hoover pressing for the defendants' release.

Governor Judd risked subjecting the territory to a quasi-military government if he allowed Massie and his mother-in-law to spend time in a Honolulu jail. In the alternative, Governor Judd faced islanders' wrath if he granted a full pardon for the murder. Instead, the governor commuted the sentence of the four defendants to one hour in the Old Palace on Darrow's promise to get his clients to leave Hawai'i as soon as it could be arranged. When Darrow and his wife Ruby boarded a luxury liner for the mainland a few days later, the Massies, their mother-in-law and the two sailors departed with them. Tommie and Thalia would divorce within two years.

Princess Kawananakoa reacted with controlled outrage to the slap on the wrist for cold-blooded murder that the commutation represented: "Are we to infer from the Governor's act that there are two sets of laws in Hawai'i – one for the favored few and one for the people generally?"[32] The answer to her question was an emphatic yes. Hawai'i was a U.S. territory where the minority of whites intended to remain supreme. Back in Washington, D.C., Congress was incensed that the judgment of the defendants' guilt remained intact, depriving them of the right to vote. Congress reduced the eligibility of nonwhites for the territory's public service jobs and made it more difficult for them to hold local political office on the islands.

Governor Judd knew whom he blamed for exacerbating tensions on Oahu to the boiling point. He wrote to the Secretary of the Interior, excoriating Rear Admiral Stirling for his bigotry and racial insensitivity. At Judd's request, Stirling was reassigned elsewhere. Governor Judd also requested the Pinkerton Detective Agency to thoroughly reinvestigate the gang rape allegations. Six months after the Massies emigrated from Oahu, the agency issued a nearly 280-page report exonerating the accused rapists and finding no evidence Thalia had been raped. The double negative conclusion exposed the strong prosecutorial bias with which the agency had undertaken its charge: "It is impossible to escape the conclusion that the kidnapping and assault was *not* caused by those accused."[33] Based on the report, Kelley asked the court to dismiss all charges against the remaining four defendants.

At Dillingham's instigation, the governor suppressed publication of the complete Pinkerton report to forestall political upheaval. Yet Princess Kawananakoa had already galvanized a few prominent white Hawaiians to chip away at the old order with a vision of how they might achieve even greater success. Leaders of the Chinese and Japanese communities and Native Hawaiians recognized how much more influence they had when they teamed up to address issues affecting them all. It offered a model for future concerted action in pushing for statehood, which would receive a further boost from the demonstrated heroism of Japanese-American soldiers from Hawai'i in World War II.

When the detailed Pinkerton findings were finally publicized two decades later, they produced the powerful effect Dillingham had originally feared. Dissemination of the truth about the baseless 1931 rape prosecution swept so many Hawaii Republicans out of office that the Democratic landslide was dubbed "The Revolution of 1954." In the summer of 2006, the American Bar Association used the information contained in the Pinkerton report to reenact the rape trial at the Hawai'i Convention Center, where the Ala Wai Inn once stood. This time, a jury of volunteer lawyers voted unanimously for acquittal.

* * * * *

In his acclaimed 2005 book *Honor Killing: How the Infamous "Massie Affair" Transformed Hawai'i,* historian David Stannard analyzes how the case prompted ethnic groups in the territory to identify themselves all as local islanders rather than by their country of origin. It also caused them to recognize how that sense of unity magnified their political clout. Ironically, the man who organized the Japanese and Filipino grassroots campaign to establish the modern Democratic Party in Hawai'i was a white police officer. Montana-born John Burns had bonded with the people on his beat oppressed by the Republican territorial government. With the overwhelming support of nonwhite Hawaiian citizens, Burns was elected the territory's congressional delegate in 1956. He then convinced Senate Majority Leader Lyndon Johnson to engineer Hawai'i's acceptance as America's fiftieth state in 1959. Burns became its second governor.

Progressive Democrats would dominate the state for the next half century, most notably Japanese-American World War II veteran Daniel Inouye. The medal-of-honor-winning son of immigrants lost his arm volunteering to fight the Nazis in a segregated Nisei unit stationed in Italy. Inouye and other Nisei in his unit relished the opportunity to demonstrate their patriotism while other Nisei and their immigrant families were forcibly removed to internment camps as suspected enemies. Inouye never lost an election in nearly sixty years, first serving as a territorial representative and then the new state's first Congressman in 1959. Three years later, he became the first Asian-American to join the United States Senate. (Hawaii Representative Patsy Mink would become the first Asian-American woman elected to Congress.)

Inouye started his illustrious career in Washington before Barack Hussein Obama was born in Honolulu and served with great distinction through almost the entirety of Obama's first term as President. From 2010 until his death in 2012, Inouye was President Pro Tem of the Senate, third in line to the presidency. At Senator Inouye's funeral, President Obama acknowledged how Daniel Inouye – a member of a despised minority given the chance to rise to extraordinary political heights in a democracy "whose values he had bled for" – had inspired Obama as a young teen. President Obama explained:

> Now, here I was, a young boy with a white mom, a black father,

raised in Indonesia and Hawaii . . .. [T]o see this man, this senator, this powerful, accomplished person who wasn't out of central casting when it came to what you'd think a senator might look like at the time, and the way he commanded the respect of an entire nation – I think it hinted to me what might be possible in my own life. . . . It gave me a powerful sense – one that I couldn't put into words – a powerful sense of hope.

[Watching Daniel Inouye at the nationally televised Senate Watergate hearings that led to President Nixon's impeachment and resignation,] I learned how our democracy was supposed to work, our government of and by and for the people; that we had a system of government where nobody is above the law, where we have an obligation to hold each other accountable, from the average citizen to the most powerful of leaders, because these things that we stand for, these ideals that we hold dear are bigger than any one person or party or politician.[34]

Senator Inouye's extraordinary opportunity to represent his state and serve the nation over six decades could, in turn, be traced back to the public outrage in the mid-1950s over the truth about the made-up gang rape that had prompted four white supremacists to murder Hawaiian boxer Joe Kahahawai two decades before. Yet that historic chain of events enabling Inouye's stellar career and Obama's presidential aspirations still depended on multitudes of motivated Hawaiian citizens seizing the opportunity to assert their voting power at the polls.

For every generation in the last sixty years, the Massie cases have provided a powerful lesson. Seven years after Hawaii became a state, author Peter Van Slingerland published the historical account, *Something Terrible Has Happened*. In 2002, Oahu newspaper columnist Cobey Black penned *Hawai'i Scandal*. Fictionalized versions of the two sensational cases include the 1986 miniseries "Blood & Orchids" and the novel *Damned In Paradise*. In 2005, the true story aired as a dramatic PBS movie, the same year Professor Stannard's definitive look back at the explosive Massie trials hit the book stores. Today, we still experience its lasting impact through the key figures it helped thrust into our national political arena.

* * * * *

In his autobiography, Clarence Darrow gave himself credit for helping resolve the Massie Affair peacefully. Darrow did play a major role
in deescalating the extraordinarily polarized situation. He kept his big-
oted clients under a tight leash during the trial and helped minimize
race-baiting. Most importantly, he convinced the Massies to leave the
territory, which forced the prosecutor to drop plans for a retrial of the
baseless rape charges. That compromise resolution, coupled with the
governor's success in getting Rear Admiral Stirling reassigned, defused
the situation enough for political processes to begin to address the
underlying racial tension. But none of that justified Darrow's unethical conduct at trial or explained why he still publicly defended Thalia
Massie's veracity after the summary of the Pinkerton report came out.
Darrow had befriended her physician during the Honolulu trial and
likely knew that Thalia was lying when he put her on the stand.

* * * * *

By the time the Massies fled the islands, the public had a new drama
to replace their fascination with the alleged honor killing. Despite the
thousands of stories written about the two Hawaiian trials, by mid-May
of 1932, the saga had already been eclipsed by news of a shocking kidnapping and murder in New Jersey, the third decade's "crime of the
century."

13. THE LINDBERGH BABY KILLING

Law Enforcement Helps Cover Up "The Crime of the Century"

*I am glad that my life in a world which has not understood me
has ended. . . . I am dying an innocent man. Should, however,
my death serve the purpose of abolishing capital punishment
– such a punishment being arrived at only by circumstantial
Evidence – I feel that my death has not been in vain. . . .
[translated from the German]*

– Bruno Richard Hauptmann's last statement, April 3, 1936[1]

In the depths of the Depression, the *New York Times* ran feature stories on a lucrative wave of kidnappings, averaging more than two a day nationwide since 1929. Worried Hollywood stars signed up for ransom insurance from Lloyd's of London. Then came startling radio announcements late on the evening of March 1, 1932, that Charles Lindbergh, Jr. – the toddler son of America's most revered hero – had just been snatched. The public was stunned. It seemed that no child in America was safe. The astounded global reaction was like the one that would occur at the century's end to news of Princess Diana's sudden death.

Charles Lindbergh had burst into international public consciousness with an historic solo transatlantic flight in May of 1927, heralding a new geopolitical era. His achievement – flying for more than thirty-three hours from New York to Paris nonstop in a monoplane – was a remarkable feat of endurance. Far more renowned competitors had died attempting the journey, but as planes improved it was just a question of time before some daring aviator was bound to succeed.

Source of poster: https://wikimedia.org/wikipedia/commons/c/ce/Lindbergh_baby_poster.jpg

WANTED

INFORMATION AS TO THE WHEREABOUTS OF

CHAS. A. LINDBERGH, Jr.

OF HOPEWELL, N. J.

SON OF COL. CHAS. A. LINDBERGH

World-Famous Aviator

This child was kidnaped from his home
in Hopewell, N. J., between 8 and 10 p. m.
on Tuesday, March 1, 1932.

DESCRIPTION:

Age, 20 months Hair, blond, curly
Weight, 27 to 30 lbs. Eyes, dark blue
Height, 29 inches Complexion, light
Deep dimple in center of chin
Dressed in one-piece coverall night suit

ADDRESS ALL COMMUNICATIONS TO
COL. H. N. SCHWARZKOPF, TRENTON, N. J., or
COL. CHAS. A. LINDBERGH, HOPEWELL, N. J.

ALL COMMUNICATIONS WILL BE TREATED IN CONFIDENCE

COL. H. NORMAN SCHWARZKOPF
March 11, 1932   Supt. New Jersey State Police, Trenton, N. J.

This widely distributed wanted-poster accompanied a nationwide hunt for Lindbergh's toddler son. Even the notorious gangster Al "Scarface" Capone, serving time for tax evasion, offered to use his gangland connections to find the culprits.

The night the baby disappeared, the Coast Guard and all airports were alerted, and police stopped all drivers headed into New York. Gov. Harry Moore of New Jersey immediately sent telegrams to other governors in the region seeking their help in hunting for the suspected gang of kidnappers. President Hoover offered full support from the federal government. Within hours, police set up a temporary headquarters in the Lindberghs' garage, yet they did not prevent hundreds of newsmen from swarming the estate, destroying valuable clues underfoot. FBI Chief J. Edgar Hoover sat frustrated on the sidelines. Shortly after the baby's body was found, Hoover persuaded Congress to pass a new "Lindbergh Law," making kidnapping across state lines a federal crime. Despite an unprecedented dragnet, enormous publicity, a $25,000 reward and many false leads, no real progress in the murder case was made for two-and-a-half years. Only then did the police focus on a sole German immigrant found with some marked ransom money he claimed was left by a friend who never told him its source.

Winning that lottery transformed the former barnstorming stunt man into the most celebrated individual on the planet. Congress gave the lanky Minnesotan its first civilian medal of honor. He inspired an outpouring of poems, songs and even a new dance craze – the Lindy Hop.

The American public was not alone in eating up details about this tee-totaling, sandy-haired mama's boy with a passion for flying, all things mechanical and crude practical jokes. He was *Time* magazine's first man of the year, acing out homerun phenomenon Babe Ruth. Tall and handsome, the socially awkward Minnesotan received a flood of endorsement offers. Every city he visited honored their blue-eyed Scandinavian hero with a parade. He drew record-breaking crowds. Roads and lakes were named in his honor; his face adorned new airmail envelopes. Real and imagined accounts of his exploits filled books, magazines and newspapers until he was sick to death of reporters.

Most importantly, Lindbergh became the spokesperson for new airlines. He promoted government subsidies of much-needed airports at a critical time in the fledgling industry's development. Embracing Lindbergh as a national hero allowed top brass in the military to save face after their hugely embarrassing confrontation with Colonel Billy Mitchell in 1925. Just two years before Lindbergh's historic intercontinental flight, turf-defending Neanderthals in the military had stubbornly ignored Mitchell's plea to develop an independent air force. After they ignored his dire warning, the World War I hero bluntly accused the Navy and War departments of "almost treasonable" negligent administration of our national defense.[2]

President Coolidge instigated a military "trial of the century" in October of 1925, charging Mitchell with insubordination. Mitchell was then drummed out of the service and ridiculed for his predictions: the need for a unified department of defense (presaging the future Pentagon), protection of Pearl Harbor's fleet from a Japanese air attack (which caught Americans by surprise 16 years later) and preparation for future wars in which unmanned missiles and planes would unleash bombs and chemical weapons on civilian populations.

Ironically, Colonel Mitchell's proposals played a pivotal role in bringing Charles Lindbergh together with his future wife, Anne

Morrow. Mitchell had enough political support for his ideas to convince a congressional committee to propose an umbrella department of defense and an independent air force. To stymie that movement, in 1925 President Coolidge appointed his own special board, headed by his college friend Dwight Morrow, then one of the top movers and shakers in the Republican Party. The general counsel for J. P. Morgan's bank had served as the top American civilian aide to General Pershing in France in World War I. The Morrow Board's far more conservative proposal for military airplane usage left the Secretaries of both the Army and Navy with their powers undiminished, but elevated the status of the air service to an Army Air Corps.

In June 1927 Morrow remained a key player in American aviation policy. Not surprisingly, he was one of the first dignitaries to greet Lindbergh on his triumphant return from Paris with an extravagant military escort to Washington, D.C. The uncouth Minnesota barnstormer was thrilled when the fabulously wealthy and influential power broker took him under his wing. That same month President Coolidge appointed Morrow ambassador to the first relatively stable Mexican government since its 1910–20 revolution. Morrow instantly realized Lindbergh's value as a one-man ambassador of good will to the nation's southern neighbor.

By the 1920s, Mexico was the world's leading exporter of oil products, mostly through fields developed and exploited by American companies. At the time Morrow arrived in Mexico in October of 1927, the relationship between the two countries was extremely tense. Persecuted Catholics were in armed revolt against President Plutarco Calles, and American oil companies were demanding federal action to protect their pre-existing rights to oil fields that had been nationalized along with American landholdings in Mexico by the radical changes adopted in the 1917 Mexican Constitution.

While involved in treaty negotiations with President Calles, Morrow engineered a public relations coup that December: Morrow convinced Lindbergh to accept an invitation from the Mexican president to fly to Mexico City. Lindbergh added to the drama by flying through the night to make the first nonstop flight from Washington,

D.C., to Mexico's capital. On his arrival Lindbergh once again received an elaborate hero's welcome. It was while staying with the Morrow family in the ambassador's residence in Mexico City over Christmas that the rough-hewn mid-Westerner first met Morrow's three daughters. Now America's most eligible bachelor, Lindbergh seemed taken by Elisabeth, the beautiful but fragile eldest daughter. He paid far less attention to her shyer younger sister Anne. Constance was still a young teen. Like Lindbergh's myriad other female admirers, all three Morrow daughters found the invitation to fly in the celebrity's modern magic carpet thrilling beyond belief.

Amid speculation that a romance had begun between Lindbergh and the delicate Elisabeth Morrow, paparazzi pursued the Flying Eagle relentlessly as he spent more time with the Morrow family and their four children in the United States. At the time, many believed that Dwight Morrow might become the Republican Party's next presidential nominee. Meanwhile, Lindbergh delighted in hiding from the press his courtship of Morrow's middle daughter Anne, circumventing press coverage of their unannounced wedding at her parents' home, and – with less success – their honeymoon destination.

Meanwhile, Lindbergh trained Anne to be his co-pilot and radio operator, intoxicating the Smith graduate with the opportunity to take to the skies on daring expeditions by his side. Together, they set new flight records and were featured regularly in movie theater newsreels and the tabloids. In a welcome change for Americans from the enormous negative publicity generated by the Sacco and Vanzetti case, record crowds all over the globe had greeted Lindbergh as a hero from the day he landed outside Paris. Heads of state welcomed first Lindbergh and then Lindbergh and his bride as American royalty and showered them with gifts – enough to fill a museum in St. Louis soon built to house most of them.

By the summer of 1930 Lindbergh had fathered a son and namesake. A strong proponent of eugenics, Lindbergh later claimed that he chose his wife in part for the superior offspring he expected that the two would produce. (Certainly Anne was far sturdier a prospective life partner than her sister Elisabeth, who would die in her early thirties from heart failure.) The papers called the blond, blue-eyed boy the "Eaglet" and vied for stories and pictures to feed the public's insatiable appetite. But photo opportunities remained few and far between as the Lindberghs shielded Little Charlie from cameras while living with Anne's parents at the Morrows' lavish estate in Englewood, New Jersey. So few pictures emerged that rumors circulated something was wrong with the boy, perhaps birth defects from his mother being deprived of oxygen on a harrowing cross-country flight when she was seven-months pregnant.

By the morning of March 2, 1932, the whole nation was feasting on mysterious details surrounding the snatching of the "Eaglet" the night before. The Lindberghs had just completed building a much-publicized new home near Princeton, New Jersey, on the sparsely populated "Sourland Mountain" ridge that was the highest promontory in rugged territory known as "The Sourlands." The famous couple still spent most of their time at the Morrows' Englewood estate and had only begun to spend every weekend at Highfields in January.

Though the ridge jutted up less than 570 feet above sea level, there was no highway access to the Lindbergh's new home. Visitors could only reach it on back roads, some of them unpaved. In the daytime, celebrity seekers got lost in the Sourlands trying to find the estate for a glimpse of its reclusive owners. At night, the narrow unlit roads were far trickier to negotiate.

Normally, by Monday morning the couple and their young son would have been back at Englewood with Anne's recently widowed mother. But both Anne and Little Charlie had a cold. Since the weather remained windy and rainy, the Lindberghs decided at the last minute to stay at Highfields through Tuesday night. By Tuesday morning, Anne was exhausted from three long nights with her sick child and summoned the boy's Scottish nurse, Betty Gow from Englewood. That evening both Gow and Anne put Little Charlie to bed at 7:30 p.m. Following strict rules laid down by Lindbergh against coddling his son, no one was to check on the toddler again until 10 p.m.

Lindbergh himself arrived at Highfields around 8:30 p.m. for a late dinner with his wife. At ten o'clock, Gow went to check on the twenty-month-old baby. By then, Anne was getting ready to retire in the couple's bedroom, separated only by a short passageway from the nursery. Lindbergh sat reading in his downstairs study. When Gow went to the crib, the toddler was gone. Gow first asked Anne if she had her son. Both women then accused Lindbergh of taking the toddler.

Lindbergh was notorious for pranks and had once panicked the Morrow household by hiding his eight-month-old son in a closet for almost half an hour before the baby was found. But Lindbergh swore otherwise. He bolted upstairs, peeked at the empty crib and ran for his rifle, announcing that it must be a gang of kidnappers. He then dashed outside. His butler joined him. When the two came back, Lindbergh called his lawyer. At Lindbergh's direction, the butler called the police and then drove off in the dark toward Hopewell to buy some flashlights so they could explore the property.

The women fruitlessly searched the nursery for clues to Little Charlie's disappearance and then explored the rest of the house as well, to no avail. Lindbergh came back, went to the nursery and summoned Gow to show her a plain envelope sitting unopened near the center of the foot-wide inner sill of the closed window to the right of the second-story-fireplace. He instructed her that it should remain sealed and untouched until the police arrived.

The local Hopewell police chief arrived soon afterward. The chief later told a journalist how unlike a crime scene the room looked. All the windows were closed and all but the one with the sealed envelope in the center of its sill remained locked. On one end of that same sill rested an antique beer stein, which managed not to have been dislodged. Most surprisingly, on the floor up against the wall under the unlatched window sat a wooden chest with a suitcase on it. On top of that lay undisturbed a roof piece of Little Charlie's toy Noah's Ark.

It was hard to see how a gang of kidnappers could have climbed in and out of the one unlocked second-story window, snatched Lindbergh's son and hurriedly departed the same way, while leaving the stack under that window unmoved. It was equally difficult to envision a brutal kidnapping when the toddler's crib sheets and blanket remained pinned in place the way they were fastened when he was put to bed.

Police carefully opened the envelope with a knife. It contained a misspelled ransom note demanding $50,000. Outside, with the aid of flashlights supplied by the police, Lindbergh showed them marks in the sod under the nursery window and, some twenty-five yards from the house, a crudely fashioned sectional ladder lying on the grass in two pieces. When checked against the impressions by the house, the foot of the sectional ladder fit precisely. Lindbergh immediately insisted on taking charge of the official investigation himself, joined by his attorney, Henry Breckinridge, who had just arrived from New York. Together, they directed the efforts of Colonel Norman Schwarzkopf (the father of the Gulf War General), who headed the New Jersey State Police.

The Coast Guard and all airports were alerted, police stopped all drivers headed into New York. Governor of New Jersey immediately sent telegrams to his counterparts in every state in the region seeking their help. President Hoover offered full support from the federal government. Within hours, police set up a temporary headquarters in the Highfields garage with a bank of telephones installed to receive tips. Yet they did not prevent hundreds of newsmen from swarming the estate, destroying valuable clues underfoot.

When Lindbergh announced his theory that the kidnapping was the work of organized crime, the first police responders were nonplussed. If professional kidnappers had executed such an audacious home invasion, why wouldn't they have cut the telephone wires? None of the five adults at home from 8:30 p.m. to 10 p.m. had reported seeing anyone else near the premises that night. Anne said she heard a noise around 8:15 p.m. Lindbergh reported that he heard a cracking sound shortly after 9 p.m. that he thought came from the direction of the kitchen on the far side of the house from the nursery.

The State Police fingerprint expert arrived at midnight. He found no usable prints in the nursery and remarked that it looked like someone had wiped all fingerprints from the walls and furniture, including the crib. Lights were on in rooms near the nursery most of the evening in a house that still lacked curtains and shades. It seemed extraordinarily bold for a stranger to climb in the nursery window and risk discovery while the adults were all still up. Police assumed the kidnappers had to know in advance about the household rule that the baby was not to be disturbed between 8 p.m. and 10 p.m. Gow told the police that the toddler hated to be touched by anyone but her and his mother. Yet the police noted that he had not cried out and no one smelled any odor of chloroform.

The skittish family dog uncharacteristically never barked that night to warn of strangers approaching the home. Most baffling was the question why the kidnappers chose to enter the estate at all on a Tuesday night when the family routinely left by Monday morning at the latest. Police also found the ladder odd. Instead of standard spacing for the rungs, it looked specially built for a very tall man. Yet its rungs could barely hold an average man's weight.

The police openly wondered if the ladder might be a decoy from an inside job with a member of the household staff handing the baby out the front door to an accomplice. The police focused first on Betty Gow, who had not reported seeing the envelope when she first searched the room. They grilled Gow's illegal immigrant boyfriend and issued a warrant for his deportation (later rescinded without explanation). They questioned other household staff to no avail. Colonel Schwarzkopf suggested subjecting the staff to lie detector tests, but Lindbergh refused; it would "humiliate and insult innocent people."[3]

J. Edgar Hoover, head of the FBI since 1924, chafed at his inability to control the investigation or even pry information from the resistant New Jersey State Police. The FBI found particularly interesting the report taken from a neighbor's teenage son, Ben Lupica, who came forward the day after the kidnapping. Lupica described a man wearing an overcoat and fedora, driving a 1929 Dodge with a local county license plate near the Highfields driveway at around 6 p.m. on March 1. He told investigators the man had a sectional ladder in the back seat.

The FBI listed the unknown Dodge driver as suspect "number one." Yet the New Jersey police inexplicably dropped that lead among others the FBI considered promising, including reinvestigation of an anonymous threat the Morrow family had received in 1929 that Constance Morrow would be kidnapped if $50,000 ransom were not paid. In private, FBI Director Hoover also heaped criticism on the ineptitude of the local police in failing to preserve the crime scene, including footprints found outside the nursery window and tire prints in a nearby abandoned lane.

New Jersey's Governor Moore wanted to see the matter solved as expeditiously as possible. The cost of the investigation was running $15,000 per day. That did not count federal and other states' expenditures for a nationwide manhunt for the kidnappers and the baby. Even the notorious gangster Al "Scarface" Capone, serving time for tax evasion, publicly offered to use his gangland connections to assist in bringing the culprits to justice. A follow-up ransom note was soon posted in Brooklyn, followed by a third. Over the course of a little more than a month a total of fifteen communications were received, including the one found in the nursery. One expert opined that the unusual number of notes with repeated assurances of the baby's health had all the earmarks of an elaborate wild goose chase for a child that was already dead.

A week after his son's disappearance, Lindbergh opened negotiations with the alleged kidnappers through a volunteer named John Condon, a retired teacher from the Bronx. Condon met a mysterious contact twice in local graveyards. The press dubbed the man "Cemetery John." Cemetery John reportedly told Condon that the kidnappers were a gang of six, four men and two women. To prove they had the toddler, they sent Condon a pair of freshly washed gray Dr. Denton pajamas, which Lindbergh quickly identified as the ones his son wore the night he disappeared. Schwarzkopf remained unsure that was so.

Lindbergh then accompanied Condon to St. Raymond's Cemetery in the Bronx, where Lindbergh sat in his parked car while Condon delivered $50,000 in small bills to Cemetery John. In exchange, Condon received a note that said the boy was on a boat called "The Nelly" off the Massachusetts coast. By Lindbergh's specific request, the New Jersey Police did not tell the New York Police about the cemetery rendezvous, and the New Jersey Police undertook no surveillance either. Cemetery John disappeared with the ransom money after his conversation with Condon.

The offshore location where "The Nelly" was supposed to hold Little Charlie was where the Lindberghs had honeymooned four years earlier. Lindbergh quickly followed that lead, but found nothing. He then took off to pursue other suggested aerial and sea searches for his kidnapped son, while police continued to stop any cars or pedestrians with small children who resembled the missing child, even little girls. Parents of toddlers became paranoid about leaving home. The editor of a crime magazine criticized the investigation as a "monumental fizzle . . . Miserably bungled from every angle."[4]

Meanwhile, the family started receiving huge stacks of mail, all screened by the police. Some letters expressed sympathy; others were the work of cranks and hucksters. A number even accused the Lindberghs themselves of the crime, based on rumors that the child had serious health problems that the perfectionist father could not abide. The police rejected such accusations out of hand. They did not even consider it appropriate to check Lindbergh's alibi before he arrived home at 8:30 p.m., late for dinner, having uncharacteristically failed to show up as a featured guest at a Manhattan fund-raiser.

All efforts nationwide ended abruptly on May 12, 1932, when an African-American trucker accidentally found the toddler's badly decomposed body. William Allen had been traveling with a co-worker on a road a few miles south of Highfields, when they stopped so Allen could walk a short way into the woods to relieve himself. That was when Allen spotted a toddler's head poking out of a pile of leaves. The body was so mutilated that it was hard to tell if this really was Little Charlie. Most of his internal organs were missing; even the child's sex could not be determined. Yet he still wore his diaper and hand-made tee shirt and a burlap bag was found close to the nearby road.

Police summoned Dr. Phillip Van Ingen, the Lindbergh's pediatrician. Dr. Van Ingen had seen the toddler in mid-February when he diagnosed the boy with rickets. Dr. Van Ingen brought his medical records with him, but told the coroner that he could not identify the remains "if someone were to come here and offer me ten million dollars."[5] Betty Gow was brought to the morgue where she recognized the shirt she had sewn for Charlie the night he disappeared. It was still stained with Vapo-Rub. She also recognized Charlie's overlapping small toes. The coroner and county physician preliminarily concluded that death had occurred by a severe blow to the head at least two months' before, but took no photographs. The next day, Lindbergh hastily identified the corpse and then ordered the baby's remains cremated without any further tests.

The police thought they were about to break the case open on June 10, a month after finding the child's remains. They drove out to the Englewood estate to question one of the maids again. They had already spoken at least once to all twenty-nine household employees at the Morrow mansion and were concerned about discrepancies in Violet Sharp's prior interviews. The morning of March 1, Sharp had taken Anne Lindbergh's telephone call asking for Betty Gow to go to Hopewell. Police thought Sharp might have tipped off the kidnappers.

Before they could talk to Sharp again, the butler told them Sharp had just fallen violently ill. Within minutes, Sharp was dead. A can of cyanide, normally used for cleaning household silver, was found in her room. Schwarzkopf announced that Sharp's apparent suicide "strongly tends to confirm the suspicions of the investigating authorities concerning her guilty knowledge of the crime" and identified a companion named Ernest Brinkert as "her associate on the night of the kidnapping." Condon thought Brinkert's picture looked like Cemetery John, but later decided he was too short.[6] Anne Morrow publicly criticized the investigators for their heavy-handedness, refusing to believe Sharp had anything to do with her son's murder. Sharp's role, if any, would remain forever unknown.

Within a week after Sharp died, Congress passed a new "Lindbergh Law" making kidnapping across state lines a federal crime. J. Edgar Hoover's men could now legally pursue suspects with or without local cooperation. Police alerted tellers nationwide to the serial numbers of the ransom money and turned up several gold certificates in circulation the year after the kidnapping. The police also uncovered several scams and beat many kidnapping suspects only to release them later when their alibis proved ironclad. Despite an unprecedented dragnet, enormous publicity, a $25,000 reward and many false leads, no real progress in the murder case was made for two-and-a-half years.

After President Roosevelt withdrew gold certificates from official currency in 1933, it became easier to trace gold certificates that had been included in the ransom money. In the fall of 1934, a German immigrant by the name of Bruno Richard Hauptmann used a few of the small denomination gold certificates in New York. By then the police and FBI were desperate to solve the infamous case. Hauptmann, who still only spoke broken English, turned out to have entered the country illegally a decade before. When arrested, he lied about having no criminal record as a youth in Germany. Americans still remembered Germans as their hated enemy in World War I. Hauptmann had served as a machine gunner and had older brothers who died fighting against the Allies. Police believed they finally had their man. The press thought so, too.

Hauptmann professed his innocence of the kidnapping from the day he was arrested. Yet he had originally lied about how many gold certificates he possessed and how he obtained them. Only after police found nearly $14,000 in certificates still hidden in his garage, did Hauptmann explain that he had recently found the stash in a shoebox left behind by a friend named Isidor Fisch who owed him money. Hauptmann claimed to know nothing of the origin of the certificates or about the kidnapped Lindbergh baby. Attempts to beat a confession out of Hauptmann got nowhere. He denied even knowing where the Lindberghs lived.

Initially after his arrest, police isolated Hauptmann in a small, brightly lit cell and deprived him of reading materials and mail, or even conversation with his guards. Fighting insanity, he still refused to confess. Soon, his wife Anna was allowed to visit twice a day, two or three times a week so the police could secretly monitor their German conversations in hopes of obtaining some type of admission. Instead, the couple blamed his friend Fisch for getting them into this predicament and joked that the police were using Hauptmann as a fall guy for their own ineptitude. Fisch was in fact a known scam artist who had bilked a number of people. He had returned to Germany in December of 1933 and died a few months later of tuberculosis. The police undertook no serious effort to determine if Fisch might have been the mysterious Cemetery John, even though Condon had originally described the unknown man to whom he gave the ransom money as having a persistent cough.

Hauptmann reconstructed his whereabouts two-and-a-half years earlier. He insisted that he was employed on a job in New York the day of the March 1 kidnapping and used his car to pick his wife up at the bakery where she worked that night, as he always did on Tuesdays. He and his wife produced witnesses to prove it. Hauptmann's first lawyer was James Fawcett, a hard worker who believed in Hauptmann's innocence and began marshaling corroborating evidence. But Hauptmann's funds were confiscated by the police and the couple could little afford the high cost of a murder defense. New Jersey would not fund a public defender's office until the late 1960s, but it spent lavishly on getting this conviction.

Hearst reporter Adela Rogers St. John cultivated Anna Hauptmann's trust and persuaded the distraught woman that the Hearst papers would support her and her son during the trial if she just switched lawyers. The offer should have seemed too good to be true. William Randolph Hearst had befriended Lindbergh back in 1927 when he first became a media star. The wealthy publisher would foot the bill only for a flamboyant Irish criminal defense attorney from Brooklyn named Edward Reilly.

What neither Anna nor her husband knew was that Hearst wanted to make sure Hauptmann was convicted, and cynically expected "the Bull of Brooklyn" to help inflame the public against his own client.[7] The Hauptmanns were impressed with misleading news of Reilly's success in a difficult case. It never occurred to them that the pompous, flashy dresser would alienate a rural New Jersey jury. Nor did they realize Reilly was an alcoholic on a downhill trajectory whose recent failures had earned him the nickname "Death House."

Reilly accepted a flat fee of $7500 from Hearst, for which he and his client agreed to provide the Hearst newspapers exclusive defense stories through trial. Today it would be highly unethical for an attorney to make such an agreement, compromising a lawyer's loyalty to his client with a promise to feed a newspaper sensational stories. But Reilly had worse conflicts of interest. He was an unabashed fan of Lindbergh and proudly displayed a photo of his hero on his desk. During the proceedings, Reilly told an FBI agent that he "knew Hauptmann was guilty, didn't like him, and was anxious to see him get the chair."[8]

Source: New Jersey State Archives. http://www.nj.gov/ state/archives/slcsp001.html

Evidence in Lindbergh trial. **Above left:** *Lindbergh house;* **above right:** *close up of ladder propped up against the house by police in an effort to reconstruct the crime. It was actually found in two pieces in the yard. At trial, Hauptmann criticized the ladder's shaky construction as the work of an amateur, not a master carpenter like himself.*

Source: Flemington Police Dept. photographic records

Mug shot of Bruno Hauptmann taken following his arrest

Hauptmann quickly became demoralized when Reilly only met briefly with his client four times before trial. The consultations totaled less than forty minutes and each time Reilly reeked of alcohol. Hauptmann placed far more faith in the local attorney who sat as second chair, C. Lloyd Fisher. Fisher came to the jail often and believed in Hauptmann's innocence.

The case went to trial in the Hunterdon County Courthouse in the small town of Flemington on January 2, 1935, less than four months after Hauptmann's arrest. The atmosphere in the New Jersey town was little different from the carnival-like celebration in Southern towns eager for a lynching, which Northerners had long since ridiculed as barbaric. Reporters booked every hotel and motel room for miles around. Prostitutes flocked there, too. (For two decades, from 1990 to 2010, an annual reenactment of "Lindbergh & Hauptmann: The Trial of the Century" again highlighted the small town's claim to fame.)

The actual trial was full of larger than life characters. Reilly, who suffered from syphilis, would often party at night with a prostitute and show up in court with a hangover. A number of reporters did the same. Scalpers hawked trial tickets. Bettors gambled on the trial's length, not its outcome. When potential jurors were questioned, practically the entire pool had been tainted by prejudicial pretrial publicity. One said he had not made up his mind about the case, "not more than anybody else."[9] He became the foreman. Though Hauptmann spoke English only haltingly, no inerpreter was provided. In the thirties, prosecutors could still play their case close to the vest with impunity. Although the New Jersey State Police had compiled 90,000 pages of documents during their investigation, Hauptmann's lawyers never saw any of it. Fisher requested access to the crime scene and Hauptmann's apartment. Both requests were denied.

In 1963, in *Brady v. Maryland*,[10] the Supreme Court rejected the historic practice of prosecutors to conceal information that might lead to acquittal. It found that such a strategy of winning at all costs was incompatible with the prosecutor's role to seek justice and violated due process guarantees. From then on, the Constitution was interpreted to require prosecutors to turn over evidence important to the defense of the case. Failure to do so could result in overturning convictions many years later. But Richard Bruno Hauptmann was among countless accused criminal defendants prior to *Brady* to whom the high court showed no empathy at all.

With all of the conflicting witness accounts and suspects in the New Jersey police file, ample ammunition existed to raise reasonable doubts of Hauptmann's guilt that never surfaced before the jury. Despite the long-held police view that Cemetery John headed a gang of six, the prosecutor went to trial on the theory that Hauptmann acted alone. Ninety witnesses were called for the state. None were subjected to pre-trial depositions by the defense team or even interviews. The defense had little clue how to proceed at trial and feared alienating the jury by cross-examining either Lindbergh or his wife.

When Reilly conceded that the mutilated corpse was that of Charles Lindbergh, Jr., his co-counsel Fisher left the courtroom in disgust, convinced that their one hope for saving Hauptmann from execution had just been thrown away. Throughout the trial, Lindbergh dominated the proceedings. He sat glaring at the defense from a prominent seat directly behind the prosecution table, wearing a gun in a shoulder holster. Lindbergh only took it off when he took the stand briefly to testify. The jury got the message how much the conviction meant to their hero.

An accountant gave elaborate testimony demonstrating how Hauptmann could have spent the missing bulk of the $50,000 ransom. J. Edgar Hoover monitored the trial from afar. He considered the reconstruction totally unconvincing, but stayed silent. The prosecutor then set out to prove that Hauptmann was Cemetery John through three witnesses: John Condon, a cab driver and Lindbergh himself. But police thought Condon mentally unstable. He and the cab driver had already misidentified a number of other men as Cemetery John.

The jury paid rapt attention when Lindbergh claimed to recognize Hauptmann's voice from hearing the defendant repeatedly recite in court on command the words "Hey Doctor, here Doctor! Over here!" Lindbergh said he heard the mystery man shout more than two-and-a-half years before. The jury did not learn that there was a dispute over whether Lindbergh had previously told the police the phrase he heard while sitting in his parked car a block away from the rendezvous was "Hey Doc, over here," and that Lindbergh doubted he could ever identify who said it.[11]

Prosecutor Wilentz also put on evidence that Hauptmann's closet had Dr. Condon's telephone number and address inscribed in it. Hauptmann denied writing it, though at some point during his earlier grilling, he had told police interrogators that he must have written what they found there. The coerced confession made little sense. Why would Hauptmann write Condon's number in his closet when Hauptmann did not even have a telephone in his home? A reporter later claimed the note in the closet was his own prank, written after Hauptmann's arrest when free access had been afforded the press to Hauptmann's apartment.

Wilentz presented two neighbors of the Lindberghs as witnesses. Millard Whited identified Hauptmann as the stranger he saw near the property twice during the month before the 1932 kidnapping. Amandus Hochmuth placed Hauptmann in the area of Hopewell, New Jersey, on the day of the kidnapping. Whited had originally told police he saw no one unusual that day, and Hochmuth had not come forward until two-and-a-half years after the crime.

Neighbor Ben Lupica was never called by the prosecutor. He testified for the defense that he saw a dark blue or black 1929 Dodge with ladder sections in the back by the Highfields driveway on the evening of March 1. Lupica recognized the New Jersey plates and noted they had an "L," signifying the same county where he lived. He was sure that the car was not green like Hauptmann's New York sedan. Yet, on cross-examination, Wilentz confronted Lupica with a newspaper article that claimed Lupica had previously identified Hauptmann. It was false. Flustered, Lupica testified that Hauptmann resembled the driver.

Two types of expert testimony provided further damning evidence. Trial lawyers all know that, if both sides have money, they can almost always find experts to support their client. The state hired eight handwriting experts to say they were sure Hauptmann wrote all of the ransom notes. At least two had privately told police they were convinced at one point that Hauptmann did not author the ransom notes. In fact, their original report concluded that the first note found in the nursery had been written in a disguised hand; the rest appeared to be copycat notes by a forger. Only after police told the experts they had found gold certificates in Hauptmann's home did the men shift gears and identify Hauptmann as the author of all the notes.[12]

Hauptmann could only afford one handwriting expert to dispute the state's eight witnesses. Yet doubts should have been raised. Hauptmann's handwriting samples resulted from police instructions to rewrite notes many times in different styles. As evidence of his authorship, the experts relied in part on similar misspellings which should have had no weight. Hauptmann testified, "I was told to write exactly as it was dictated to me and this included writing words spelled as I was told to spell them."[13] Even Schwarzkopf would later concede that Hauptmann – without any attorney to object – had been given spelling "help" by one or more officers.[14]

Lastly, the prosecutor produced Arthur Koehler, a wood expert, who testified that he traced some of the wood used for the ladder to a Bronx lumber yard. Koehler also identified a missing floor board in Hauptmann's attic as the source of one small piece of the ladder. Hauptmann thought the ladder evidence was the most bizarre. The workmanship of the ladder was not that of a master carpenter like himself. He weighed one hundred eighty pounds and was of only average height. He would not have built a makeshift ladder with rungs spaced for a tall, light man that might collapse under his own weight.

Hauptmann also questioned the assumption that he would have bypassed the pile of spare wood in his garage to remove a plank from his landlord's attic and cut it to size to use in making a ladder. In fact, no one had noticed any missing plank in Hauptmann's attic until a week after his arrest – even though fifteen police had searched the house high and low before then.

At trial, Hauptmann had his own volunteer fingerprint expert who had assisted the prosecutor early on in the investigation. When no suspect had yet been identified, Erastus Mead Hudson had carefully taken the ladder apart and used a new technique employing silver nitrate to reveal hundreds of usable prints, not visible through standard procedures. Some of the prints were on the ends of the rungs that Hudson had just disassembled. No one could have touched them to make those prints but the person who handled the pieces of wood before they were put in place to construct the ladder. Dr. Hudson testified that he had been quite surprised not to be contacted when Hauptmann was arrested. It prompted him to call a New Jersey police officer, who said, "We got our man." When asked if Hauptmann's prints were found anywhere on the ladder, the officer said, "No."

Hudson responded "Then you'll have to look further."

The officer said "Good God, don't tell us that, doctor!" Shortly afterward, an extraordinary order issued from State Police headquarters to wash off *all the fingerprints* – no evidence of any fingerprints on the ladder remained by the time of trial.[15]

Wilentz originally argued that Hauptmann took the toddler from the house as a kidnap for ransom and then the boy died accidentally falling from the ladder. But when the defense lawyers focused on the infant's failure to cry out, Wilentz switched theories in his closing argument and argued that the child had his life brutally snuffed out inside the nursery before Hauptmann ever descended. This presented a quite different scenario – with no corpse or autopsy to back it up. Nor was any blood found in the nursery or on the ground outside.

Hauptmann was seriously prejudiced in trying to address the shifting charge. His lawyers would not have emphasized that the toddler never cried out as an argument that no stranger kidnapped him had the prosecutor claimed from the outset that the child had been murdered in the nursery. The new theory horrified the jury. The prosecutor now had them convinced that the ransom note planted in the room – and the fourteen more that followed – evidenced a cruel hoax from the outset perpetrated by the heartless fiend at the defense table.

Despite huge inconsistencies in the prosecutor's case, Judge Thomas Trenchard left little doubt what he thought the jury should do. Spectators commented on the judge's sarcasm when he summarized defense claims and asked the jury, "Now, do you believe *that?*"[16] Such obvious bias paralleled that of Judge Webster Thayer in the Sacco and Vanzetti case.

A crowd of ten thousand outside the courthouse kept yelling, "Kill Hauptmann," while the jury deliberated.[17] When the guilty verdict was announced eleven hours later, they erupted in celebration. It turned out that the jurors had immediately voted to convict, but had taken time to consider whether to recommend leniency. After Hauptmann's sixteen hours on the stand, despite his bristly nature, some jurors found him sympathetic.

Hauptmann's appeals proved fruitless. Clarence Darrow counted himself among the skeptics. From the accounts he had read, the nation's most famous criminal defense lawyer called the evidence flimsy and urged New Jersey Governor Harold Hoffman to delay Hauptmann's execution and allow him a new trial.[18] Governor Hoffman was greatly troubled by the evidence and the manner in which the case had been investigated. Like Governor Jack of Georgia in the Leo Frank case twenty years before, Hoffman gambled with his political future and delayed the execution for thirty days.

Hoffman forced Colonel Schwarzkopf to retire and started reinvestigating the case in an attempt to determine what really happened. The governor originally assumed Hauptmann might have been part of a gang. Yet, after visiting the Hauptmann's former home himself, Hoffman became convinced of the Hauptmanns' claim that the police had manufactured the evidence of the attic plank after the force took control of their apartment.

The governor also revisited the damning testimony of neighbors Millard Whited and Amandus Hochmuth. The two had provided no useful information at all to police when the case was first investigated in 1932. They only came forward in 1934 after Hauptmann's picture circulated in the newspapers and the huge reward was offered. Whited told Governor Hoffman he was paid for his testimony. Hochmuth was 87, had cataracts in both eyes and was legally blind. The disgusted governor tested Hochmuth's vision and found that the old man could not tell a vase from a woman's hat at ten feet. Many years later, Ben Lupica recalled the trial as a sham. He knew the other neighbors received money for fingering Hauptmann. He had been offered money, too, if he changed his testimony. Lupica had refused. He told investigators that the only similarity between Hauptmann and the driver was that Hauptmann was also white.[19]

Before Lindbergh and his family could be questioned further about the many unresolved aspects of the kidnapping/murder, they were gone. In late December of 1935, immediately after newspapers announced that Governor Hoffman was reopening the case for further investigation, Lindbergh abruptly told his wife to pack up to leave the country. With their second son, Jon, they secretly boarded a ship to England. Lindbergh gave a *New York Times* reporter an exclusive interview on his promise not to publish the fact they had departed until after their ship sailed. Lindbergh told the reporter that they were fleeing out of fear for his son Jon's continued safety. They would not come back for three years. The public blamed Governor Hoffman for prolonging their hero's ordeal.

Despite his own misgivings, the governor could not convince the New Jersey Court of Errors to commute Hauptmann's death sentence. Yet Hauptmann did gain more supporters when he turned down a $90,000 offer from a Hearst newspaper for his confession. The condemned man obtained even more converts to his cause when he refused the prosecutor's last-minute offer of a life sentence in exchange for revealing the names of the co-conspirators with whom he was assumed to have worked. A confirmed Christian, the death-row prisoner told the governor that he believed in salvation and could not offer a false confession even to obtain much-needed support for his loyal wife and baby.

The state of New Jersey executed Hauptmann on April 3, 1936. He professed his innocence to the end. All the evidence was circumstantial. As author James Fisher states, "No one saw Hauptmann snatch the baby from his crib and no one, save the killer, witnessed the child's death."[20] To this one could add no reliable witness ever placed Hauptmann anywhere near central New Jersey on the day or evening of the toddler's disappearance. No cause of death or even date or place of death was reliably established. No murder weapon was ever found, no one ever saw Hauptmann with the Lindbergh baby, and no fingerprint evidence ever placed him at the Lindbergh home.

The O. J. Simpson Dream Team would have made much of the inconsistencies in the evidence used in court and the extensive evidence withheld from the Hauptmann trial. Once the police caught

Source: iconicphotos, https://iconicphotos.org/2009/05/21/the-trial-of-hauptmann/

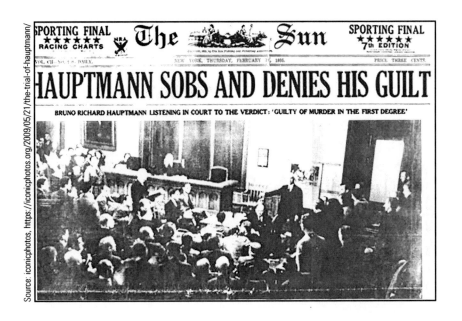

SPORTING FINAL
RACING CHARTS

The Sun

SPORTING FINAL
7th EDITION

NEW YORK, THURSDAY, FEBRUARY 14, 1935.   PRICE THREE CENTS

HAUPTMANN SOBS AND DENIES HIS GUILT

BRUNO RICHARD HAUPTMANN LISTENING IN COURT TO THE VERDICT: 'GUILTY OF MURDER IN THE FIRST DEGREE.'

Clarence Darrow thought the evidence against Hauptmann quite flimsy. He urged New Jersey Gov. Harold Hoffman to delay Hauptmann's execution and allow him a new trial. Hoffman gambled with his political future and delayed the execution for 30 days while he began reinvestigating the case. He became convinced the police had manufactured key evidence and that at least one witness was paid for his testimony. Before the Lindberghs could be interviewed again, Lindbergh left the country with his wife and second son and did not return for three years. In the meantime, the New Jersey Court of Errors refused to commute Hauptmann's sentence. Hauptmann was executed on April 3, 1936, professing his innocence to the end.

Harold G. Hoffman,
Governor of New Jersey
1935–1938

Source: Alton H. Blackington Collection (PH 061), Special Collections and University Archives, University of Massachusetts Amherst Libraries.

Hauptmann in a lie and found that he had hidden thousands of dollars of the ransom money in his home, they settled on him as the culprit. When they learned he was an illegal alien with a prior criminal record in Germany, nothing could convince them otherwise. Even with all the problems that surfaced, they assumed he was at least complicit. At that point, the police did whatever it took to prove their case to a jury.

In their book *Actual Innocence,* co-founders of the Innocence Project Barry Scheck and Peter Neufeld detail serious flaws in 135 death penalty trials where juries convicted men who were later exonerated on death row. Many other inmates have proclaimed their innocence right up to their executions. A *Stanford Law Review* article, "Miscarriages of Justice in Potentially Capital Cases," counts the much-discussed Hauptmann conviction as a "classic case" among hundreds of documented examples of wrongly convicted defendants with their life on the line.[21]

* * * * *

Experts estimate that wrongful convictions occur each year in roughly one to three percent of felony cases nationwide. They point to mistaken eyewitness identifications, false confessions, ineffective assistance of counsel, police or prosecutorial misconduct and other causes. On April 3, 2015, a 58-year-old African-American man was freed after spending half of his life on Alabama's death row when ballistics tests by the state's own experts confirmed that bullets from the scene of the 1985 fast food robbery-murder did not in fact match his family's revolver. Unlike O. J. Simpson, Anthony Ray Hinton could not afford a competent expert witness at trial to dispute the only evidence purporting to link him to a capital crime. The state should have been forced to pay for one. It took Equal Justice Initiative Director Bryan Stevenson 16 years to obtain Hinton's release, triggered by a decision of the United States Supreme Court in 2014 that Hinton's defense did not meet the minimal competence standards first established in the death penalty prosecution of the Scottsboro Boys over 80 years before.

Stevenson described Hinton's horror story as a "case study" in disparate treatment under our American justice system: "We have a system that treats you better if you are rich and guilty then if you are poor and innocent and this case proves it. We have a system that is compromised by racial bias and this case proves it. We have a system that doesn't do the right thing when the right thing is apparent," Stevenson said. "Prosecutors should have done this testing years ago."[22] The state attorney general did not respond to his criticism.

Criminologist C. Ronald Huff argues we must do better: "In societies that value the freedom of their citizens . . . it is arguable that being convicted of a crime that one did not commit, and being incarcerated with criminals or even put to death, represents one of the worst nightmares imaginable."[23]

As Barry Scheck of the Innocence Project points out, for each wrongfully convicted felon, the true perpetrator likely stayed on the streets. In 2014, a wrongly convicted felon was released somewhere in the nation on average every three days. Thousands of other inmates likely are making truthful claims of innocence to no avail, lacking irrefutable evidence to prompt their release.

* * * * *

Periodically over the decades following the execution of Bruno Hauptmann for the kidnap-murder of the Lindberghs' first child, someone would surface claiming to be the real Lindbergh baby and that the corpse belonged to another child. Continued fascination with the kidnapping has spawned movies, novels and various conspiracy theories implicating various members of the Lindbergh and Morrow family. Convinced that the execution of the German immigrant was a travesty of justice, British muckraker Ludovic Kennedy aired a documentary on the Hauptmann trial in 1982. In 1985, with the full cooperation of Anne Lindbergh, Kennedy published *The Airman and The Carpenter: The Lindbergh Kidnapping and the Framing of Richard Hauptmann*. Kennedy claimed that the aviator's widow assured him "that if in fact a miscarriage of justice did take place, and notwithstanding any difficulties this might create for her and her family, it should not be glossed over."[24]

In 1993, New Hampshire legislator and criminal defense attorney

Gregory Ahlgren collaborated with his sometime adversary, local police chief Stephen Monier, in authoring *Crime of the Century: The Lindbergh Kidnapping Hoax*. The book hypothesized that Charles Lindbergh accidentally killed his son in a failed prank and sought to cover it up with a false report of a kidnapping. Other authors argue that a sibling of Anne Morrow – her jealous older sister Elisabeth or her schizophrenic younger brother Dwight – killed the baby. Under each of these theories, Lindbergh was accused of covering up the crime and misdirecting the investigation that led to Hauptmann's conviction. A website has been devoted to exploring the "Lindbergh kidnapping hoax."[25] There is certainly ample evidence that Lindbergh obstructed the investigation, intentionally or otherwise.

In 2004, in *The Case That Does Not Die: The Lindbergh Kidnapping*, historian Lloyd Gardner also reached the conclusion that Hauptmann was wrongly executed. Gardner did not rule out the possibility Hauptmann played some lesser role, such as constructing the ladder used in the crime or laundering the ransom money. In 2005, the true-crime documentary program "Forensic Files" aired a review of key Hauptmann trial evidence. Experts used advanced technology to reexamine the ladder and reanalyze the ransom notes. They reaffirmed that a ladder piece came from Hauptmann's attic, but that did not solve the question of whether the police planted that evidence. The results on the ransom note were mixed, as they had been previously.

The 2005 documentary did not address claims that Hauptmann never got a fair trial with all the prejudicial publicity, circuslike proceedings, compromised physical evidence and perjured testimony. Most of all, the Hauptmann trial, like the Leo Frank and Massie cases, suffered from an atmosphere electric with the desire for revenge, and a setting where the prosecutor had similar latitude in suppressing facts that did not fit his theory. There is no doubt that a modern investigation and trial of Hauptmann would proceed quite differently.[26] Among other things, the crime scene would be cordoned off, the corpse would undergo a proper autopsy to determine exactly how and when the baby died, and key evidence such as the fingerprints on the ladder, would likely be far less susceptible to charges of tampering. Prosecutors would be required to provide the defense with potentially exculpatory evidence, the judge would be required to take far more precautions against prejudicial publicity tainting the trial, the jury panel would not exclude those with general reservations about the death penalty, and that issue would be addressed in a separate sentencing hearing only if guilt was first determined.

Yet some criminologists still defend the prosecution and conviction of Bruno Richard Hauptmann. Chief among them is former FBI agent Jim Fisher, who reinvestigated the case at the behest of the New Jersey State Police. In *The Lindbergh Case,* first published in 1987, Fisher set out to refute accusations of Ludovic Kennedy and other vocal critics of how the case was handled. In the introduction to his book, Fisher lists his assumptions in concluding that Hauptmann was guilty as charged, all of which are questionable.

First, Fisher states as a given that the New Jersey State Police conducted a thorough investigation – failing to address the FBI's own serious criticisms. As J. Edgar Hoover realized at the time, while the New Jersey state investigation was extraordinarily extensive, it had major gaps stemming largely from the fact it was controlled from the outset by a parent. By April of 1932, the FBI suspected Lindbergh of holding back information. Under Lindbergh's watch, key evidence was lost and crucial leads never pursued thoroughly, including determining who owned the 1929 Dodge sedan with local plates seen at the Highfields driveway that night with a sectional ladder in the back.

The FBI has since documented that a parent is ultimately found to blame for more than half of all reported infanticides; of those committed at home, nine out of ten are perpetrated by a family member.[27] Nowadays, even millionaire parents reporting a child's abduction and death at the hands of mysterious strangers remain prime suspects. That was what happened in the still unsolved kidnap-murder of JonBenet Ramsey, which generated a similar media circus in 1996 as the Lindbergh baby kidnapping.

Second, Fisher assumes that no evidence was fabricated or materially altered to implicate Hauptmann, discrediting the claim that police pulled up the plank from Hauptmann's attic. Yet there was no question that hundreds of fingerprints on the ladder were eradicated while that crucial piece of evidence was in police custody before trial. The timing also appears highly suspect: the ladder was not wiped clean until after their own expert told police the prints might prove Hauptmann's innocence.[28]

Third, Fisher defends the trial as being "as fair as could be expected under the circumstances," while others cite shocking deficiencies. (See, e.g., Robert R. Bryan, "The Execution of the Innocent: The Tragedy of the Hauptmann-Lindbergh and Bigelow Cases" ["Surrounded by a hostile atmosphere, the proceeding featured mistakes, fraud, concealment of evidence, witness intimidation, and false testimony"][29] and Gilbert Geis [past president of the American Society of Criminology] and Leigh B. Beinen ["Whatever else, the untainted evidence did not support a verdict of guilt beyond a reasonable doubt of the charge against him"]).[30]

Fisher also reports confidence that "the small, mutilated corpse discovered a few miles from the Lindbergh estate more than two months after the crime" was that of the missing Lindbergh toddler without acknowledging that the police fostered doubt by their inexcusable negligence.[31] Even before identification, the body was immediately recognized as that of a crime victim. A full autopsy could have provided key information. The police should never have allowed Lindbergh to prevent full tests from being conducted and to cremate the remains, precluding definitive identification and analysis of exactly how and when the baby died.

Even reasonable doubt about Hauptmann's guilt of the kidnap/murder would have been enough to save the carpenter's life. All that was really proved beyond a reasonable doubt was that he hoarded and spent some of the gold certificates whose source as ransom he may not have known. It should not have taken a Clarence Darrow to defend Hauptmann from execution had the illegal immigrant been afforded a fair opportunity before an impartial tribunal.

Old Smokey

Source: Dennis K. Johnson/Alamy stock photos

The electric chair, nicknamed "Old Smokey," that was used to execute Bruno Hauptmann on April 3, 1936, is now on display at the New Jersey State Police Museum, Trenton, New Jersey, where this photo was taken. Many scholars who have made studies of wrongful executions consider Hauptmann's trial a classic example of a miscarriage of justice.

CONCLUSION

The deeply problematic handling of the Lindbergh kidnapping case from start to finish provides a classic example of the "hard truths" FBI director James Comey broadly acknowledged in his speech at Georgetown University in February 2015. Once the public learned that Bruno Hauptmann was an illegal German immigrant, few cared about the patent unfairness of his death penalty trial. J. Edgar Hoover harbored serious questions about that botched investigation, yet kept silent for the remainder of his life. Indeed, the FBI kept Hoover's misgivings about Lindbergh's own suspicious behavior secret long after Hoover's death – another hard truth.

Owning up to past misdeeds is essential if America is to reform its criminal justice system, which still too often discriminates not only based on wealth and power, but race, ethnicity, sexual orientation, religion and political affiliation. Bruno Hauptmann's execution, thwarting New Jersey Governor Harold Hoffman's efforts to reinvestigate the kidnapping, shows how easily in the past law enforcement favored the rich and powerful. Ironically, Comey's 2015 speech heralding a new era of accountable law enforcement came just two years before resident Trump abruptly terminated Comey's own tenure. The president's dismissal letter cited the need to "find new leadership for the FBI that restores public trust and confidence in its vital law enforcement mission."[1] Comey's replacement at the head of the FBI needed to assure the Senate that he would avoid both the appearance and reality of thumbs on the scales of justice.

As we have seen time and again in the early 20th century trials recounted in this book, progress can take place at a slow crawl, especially when it comes to social justice. In 1915 black military veterans first dared lobby for a museum on the National Mall dedicated to African-Americans who defended their homeland with life and limb.

That same year the Ku Klux Klan reemerged with renewed vigor after the virulently racist three-hour blockbuster *Birth of a Nation* broke box office records in cities where the controversial epic was not banned. Over time, Senator Tillman's express call for stepped-up lynching at the beginning of the 20th century evolved into 1960s editorials in the Cotton Belt which openly ridiculed "the Rev. Dr. Extremist Agitator Martin Luther King junior" and "the miserable 'non-violent' street rabble led by the unspeakable Martin Luther King, and his ilk."[2] Southern elected officials spewed similar vitriol.

These unwavering opponents of the campaign for racial equality did not act in a vacuum. At FBI Director Hoover's direction, from December of 1963 through King's assassination in April of 1968, federal agents waged an intensive campaign against the civil rights leader. As a key part of that effort, the FBI leaked stories to the press seeking to convince the public that the nonviolent Southern Christian Leadership Conference Dr. King led was a "Black Nationalist Hate Group" and that Dr. King was "the most dangerous Negro" in America, threatening the nation's future with Communism. A 1976 Senate Committee investigation revealed Hoover's explicit instructions "to remove King from the national picture," which FBI agents understood meant "no holds barred" tactics like those they had employed against Soviet agents during the Cold War.[3]

The FBI Director was particularly incensed by the announcement that Dr. King would be awarded the 1964 Nobel Peace Prize. To prevent his acceptance of that international honor, FBI agents attempted to blackmail Dr. King into committing suicide by threatening to reveal illegal audiotapes of his sex life.[4] (The secret dossiers Hoover amassed on public figures over his lengthy tenure figured prominently among his many abuses of power that prompted Congress in 1968 to limit all of Hoover's successors to a single ten-year term.)

In the 1960s, white Southern newspaper publishers and politicians openly encouraged local police and vigilantes to attack civil rights protesters. When the bodies of murdered activists were found, there was no hope that state law enforcement agencies in the Deep South would conduct proper homicide investigations and prosecutions. The

FBI was little better. Its investigations often moved slowly, if at all, and might result simply in suspects being turned over to state officials, who would dismiss all the charges.

In June of 1964, national media riveted public attention on the suspicious disappearance in Philadelphia, Mississippi, of Congress of Racial Equality (CORE) workers Michael Schwerner, James Chaney and Andrew Goodman. The FBI came under heavy pressure from President Johnson and Attorney General Robert Kennedy to solve the case. Even after a tip-off led to discovery of their buried bodies, it took the FBI three years to bring charges for civil rights violations against the KKK members involved, including the Neshoba County sheriff, a deputy and nearly a score of accused co-conspirators. Though fewer than half were convicted, the occasion was historic. As the *New York Times* later reported: "that 1967 verdict in Meridian was the first time a white Mississippi jury had voted to convict a white official in a civil rights killing, finally acknowledging the horrors that most white Southerners had long denied."[5]

Two of the three civil rights martyrs were Northern whites, whose lives Freedom Summer planners gambled the nation would value much higher than those of local black volunteers like James Chaney. Instead of reducing Chaney's risk as he sought to register voters, all three instantly became marked for death. Although the historic prosecution that followed produced some convictions, the longest sentence was six years. It would take decades before new evidence induced state officials to prosecute state homicide charges against KKK recruiter Edgar Ray Killen, the part-time minister who helped plan that ambush. In 2005, Killen was convicted and sentenced to three consecutive twenty-year prison terms, which he is currently serving.

Yet it was not just in the South that the white community historically signaled to police and the press the message that black lives don't matter. At the same time national media vilified Mississippi and Alabama officials for their brutal treatment of civil rights activists, less overt discrimination also pervaded supposedly liberal enclaves such as the San Francisco Bay Area and New York. *Ramparts* magazine editor Warren Hinckle recalled in a 1973 book the rule of thumb he learned as a Bay Area cub reporter: "Whether a homicide would be reported at all depended largely upon the neighborhood in which it was committed. Ghetto murders, being regarded as natural black events, were rarely considered newsworthy."[6] Journalist Bob Herbert still vividly remembers that double standard when he arrived as the first black deputy city editor at the *New York Daily News*: the editorial staff assigned breaking crime stories priority levels depending on the color of the victim's skin – even if the killing involved an innocent baby.[7]

In 1986 the United States Supreme Court had under consideration a detailed statistical analysis of racial disparities in capital punishment.[8] Known by the name of its most prominent author, the Baldus study was offered by lawyers for death row inmate Warren McCleskey to prove that if a Georgia victim of homicide were white and the suspect was black, the prosecutor was more than four times as likely to seek and obtain the death penalty. By a five-to-four vote, the high court concluded that the remarkable disparity did not show a "constitutionally significant risk of racial bias affecting the Georgia capital sentencing process."[9]

Justice Lewis Powell, Jr., authored the majority opinion in *McCleskey v. Kemp*. After he retired, he wished he could take those words back and cast his swing vote the other way.[10] Not only might the Virginian have prevented McCleskey's execution, and that of many other black men, but such a change of heart could have had much broader consequences. That lone jurist's second thoughts could have created a precedent for defense lawyers across the country to cite time and again in a wide range of criminal cases where much harsher punishment had been imposed on minorities than on white defendants.[11]

The Baldus study also demonstrated that the Georgia criminal justice system showed far less concern for black homicide victims than for murdered whites. That was just another manifestation of how black lives did not matter. Indeed, black war heroes had no national monument to their valor until the late 1990s, when a "Spirit of Freedom" sculpture and museum opened in Washington, D.C., memorializing more than 209,000 "Colored Troops" of Union soldiers and sailors, 40,000 of whom died in the Civil War. By the end of the century, a thirty-foot statue honoring Dr. Martin Luther King, Jr., was in the planning stages to be located at 1964

Independence Avenue near the Franklin Delano Roosevelt Memorial in West Potomac Park. Since 2011, that extraordinary granite memorial to the civil rights icon has towered over hordes of awed visitors from all parts of the country and the world.

* * * * *

In 2000 a powerful collection of photographs of early 20th century lynchings drew record crowds to a New York gallery. It prompted a traveling art show, many educational programs and a haunting book, *Without Sanctuary: Lynching Photography in America*. In 2002, these gruesome images came home to the region where most of the atrocities took place. The temporary exhibit in the Martin Luther King, Jr., National Historical Site in Atlanta, Georgia, drew over 175,000 visitors during its eight-month run. As visitors walked the halls, they could hear Billie Holiday's soulful rendition of "Strange Fruit" playing over a sound system. Amid great controversy, the National Center for Civil and Human Rights in Atlanta bought the collection for display as part of its permanent holdings, and to loan out on request to other museums. African American Studies Professor Leigh Raiford noted in her 2011 book *Imprisoned in a Luminous Glare*, "It is a strange century that opens and closes with images of dead black bodies at center stage."[12]

Yet in 2008, then Newark Mayor Cory Booker noted how little progress our society had made in valuing black lives: "The reality is we're still in a place and a time where everybody knows who JonBenet Ramsey is [a six-year-old blonde beauty queen found strangled in her parents' basement in 1996], or who Natalee Holloway is [a blonde Alabama teenager who went missing in Aruba in 2005]. But so many people . . . cannot name a black child that died . . . in an unsolved murder. So you still see a world in which there [are sometimes] . . . different degrees of horror or response, or . . . persistent and insidious divisions between black and white."[13] Cory Booker is a living example of progress in race relations. The rising star in the Democratic Party won election in 2013 as the first African-American senator from New Jersey – a state that is two-thirds white.

Every step toward equality in our society inevitably engenders a backlash. We are witnessing today the return of "the Angry White Man" as a powerful voting bloc.[14] Militant groups and lone actors have found inspiration in a 1978 book, *The Turner Diaries*, by white supremacist William Luther Pierce. Writing under the name Andrew MacDonald, Pierce envisioned an apocalyptic race war in the 21st century and advocated preemptive strikes through bombing and other guerilla warfare tactics. Over the years since it was published, devotees of the book carried out a number of hate crimes, including the 1995 Oklahoma City bombing – the country's worst terrorist act of the 20th century.

In 1999, James Von Brunn published *Kill the Best Gentiles* in which he similarly asserted that the white race was being destroyed by "hordes of non-Whites and mongrels." On June 10, 2009, he murdered a black security guard at the Holocaust Museum in Washington, D.C. When police arrested Von Brunn, they found in his pocket a list of Congressional leaders, fueling speculation they were also intended targets.[15] Like Oklahoma City Bomber Timothy McVeigh, Von Brunn considered *The Turner Diaries* his bible. Others today undoubtedly do, too. The book can easily be downloaded from the Internet.

* * * * *

In 2003, with support from President George W. Bush, Congress finally overcame entrenched opposition, led by white Southern members, to fund a National Museum of African American History and Culture on the National Mall, near the Washington Monument. The new museum's director, Dr. Lonnie Bunch III, realized that the board had a daunting task before them: "grappling with fundamental questions about the museum's soul and message." He sought to achieve a unifying purpose: "to make sure people see this is not an ancillary story, but it's really the central story of the American experience."[16] The Smithsonian opened the doors to that ambitious project in September 2016 to record crowds. Then eight years out of office, former President George W. Bush was invited to speak at the dedication ceremony. In just a few well-chosen words, he captured why that museum mattered so much to the world's leading democracy: "A great nation does not hide its history. It faces its flaws and corrects them."[17]

When Bush left office in 2008, the nation had just reached a milestone by electing its first biracial president, 12 years after Republicans surfaced General Colin Powell's name as a potentially viable candidate. During his first term, President Obama received more death threats by far than any other American president. Yet in 2012 he was reelected by a wide margin and voiced optimism in his second inaugural address: "What binds this nation together is not the colors of our skin or the tenets of our faith or the origins of our names. What makes us exceptional – what makes us American – is our allegiance to an idea, articulated in a declaration made more than two centuries ago: 'We hold these truths to be self-evident, that all men are created equal, that they are endowed by their Creator with certain unalienable rights, that among these are Life, Liberty, and the pursuit of Happiness.'"[18]

President Obama added: "History tells us that while these truths may be self-evident, they have never been self-executing." He pointed out that if our aim as a nation is to treat all men and women as created equal – with liberty and justice for all – "our journey is not complete."[19] Indeed, the 2016 documentary "13th" makes the case that the Thirteenth Amendment freeing slaves did not accomplish its aim. It simply led to a different form of slavery in modern society. Today, African-American men are disproportionately arrested, incarcerated, executed or eventually released on parole with a virtual scarlet letter "F" (for felon) severely hobbling their chances for success in life. Celebrated author Michelle Alexander points out the irony in her best seller, *The New Jim Crow: Mass Incarceration in the Age of Color Blindness*. More African-Americans are now "in prison or jail, on probation or parole – than were enslaved in 1850, a decade before the Civil War began." Alexander argues that convicted felons have become a "permanent undercaste . . . relegated by law to a second-class status." Among other restrictions, "they can be denied the right to vote, automatically excluded from juries, and legally discriminated against in employment, housing, access to education, and public benefits, much as their grandparents and great-grandparents were during the

Jim Crow era."[20]

One of the enduring symbols of discriminatory felonization of black men is heavyweight champion Jack Johnson, convicted over a hundred years ago of taking a white woman across state lines in violation of the new Mann Act. A groundswell of pressure from influential sports figures won bipartisan support for Johnson's posthumous pardon as the centennial of the historic Johnson-Jeffries 1910 fight approached. Nevertheless, President Obama declined to risk any political capital by granting that request. As one commentator noted, "[Obama] would likely not be hailed for righting a historic wrong but for playing race with a deceased black man who in his day flaunted the law and the moral code of society. Race and politics simply can't be separated even when the recipient of justice is a dead man."[21]

To be sure, the vast majority of convicted felons are guilty of illegal conduct. But the word "felon" conjures up an image of a dangerous criminal: a murderer, rapist, armed robber or kidnapper. Violent crimes have actually fallen off significantly in recent years. Most felons are convicted of nonviolent crimes. In fact, the exponential increase in the American inmate population is primarily for possession of illegal drugs. Ironically, despite a prolonged "war on drugs" since the days of President Nixon, the United States reports the highest rate of illegal drug use in the world – in 2014, nearly 24 million users over the age of 12. Use is reportedly most prevalent among those in higher income brackets, whom studies show are least likely to be prosecuted.[22] There but for the grace of law enforcement's discretion and priorities go millions more potential "felons."

In *A Colony in a Nation*, Emmy-winning political analyst Chris Hayes observes that the discretion of law enforcement personnel is routinely applied in opposite ways depending on which of two Americas the suspected criminal is from: a nation of largely white haves who are presumed not to threaten the status quo, or an occupied territory of largely black and brown have-nots controlled by aggressive policing. Hayes took the title of his 2017 book from Republican presidential candidate Richard Nixon's acceptance speech in the summer of 1968 when Nixon ran on a law and order platform proposing to have government come down hard on growing inner city unrest.

Hayes observes: "American history is the story of white fear, of the constant violent impulses it produces and the management and ordering of those impulses."[23] He adds: "Through our shared cultural inheritance, Americans convert white fear into policy. When the system receives a shock . . . our collective response is punishment, toughness and violence . . . . White fear is one of the most singularly explosive forces (if not *the* most explosive force) in American politics."[24] That fear does not just motivate those who overtly identify as white supremacists, on a subliminal level it permeates society in ways we mask with loftier goals.

Reducing nonviolent prison populations is a "Right on Crime" goal shared by both Democrats like California Senator Kamala Harris and stalwart Republicans like Newt Gingrich, Grover Norquist and Reagan's Attorney General Edwin Meese.[25] Analysts on both the Right and Left recently pointed to successful reforms implemented by Republican Governor Nathan Deal of Georgia as a model for other states to follow to reduce prison populations and minimize the likelihood of recidivism.[26]

These reformers now face headwinds from Washington following the 2016 election. Candidate Trump's renewed tough-on-crime rhetoric has emerged as unbending policy under our new Attorney General, Jefferson Beauregard Sessions. In May 2017, Sessions issued a directive to all U.S. attorneys to seek maximum sentences for all crimes, eliminating their discretion to reduce charges for low-level crimes if they could be charged as felonies.[27] What that accomplishes is to transfer enormous power of exercising discretion over whom to charge as "felons" from prosecutors to the federal agents deciding to make or forego arrests – decisions which have historically reflected race bias.

Despite this federal about-face on drug crimes, further reforms at the state level are likely. The *New York Times* Sunday Review in late March 2017 featured this trend in an article by Yale Law Professor James Forman, Jr., which he titled "Justice Springs Eternal." Professor Forman – the son of '60s black activist James Forman – noted the "movement to reduce the prison population and make our prison system more humane . . . is stronger than ever." He pointed out that nine crimes out of ten are prosecuted in state courts. "The same election that produced

Mr. Trump and Mr. Sessions also saw widespread criminal justice reform victories at the state level through ballot initiatives." Professor Forman noted his surprise that some Republicans as well as Democrats campaigned for election as prosecutors on promises to "charge fewer juveniles as adults, stop prosecuting low-level marijuana possession and seek the death penalty less often."[28]

Many reform-minded prosecutors in 2016 won their elections – and now face a predictable backlash. Yet the reform movement currently gaining strength on the state level appears likely to survive such renewed attacks. Indeed, with opiate addiction at historic levels among whites, outgoing New Jersey Governor Chris Christie is a leading voice for treating it as a disease rather than a crime. President Trump himself has tasked Governor Christie with leading the charge on this health crisis. Unfortunately, it is an illustration of how the power structure's empathy tracks the skin color of the user. The recent directive of Attorney General Sessions to charge drug crimes to the maximum extent the law provides is a move in the opposite direction. Republican Senator Rand Paul of Kentucky is among the reformers who have publicly denounced the new policy, noting that the drug laws have "unfairly and disproportionately incarcerated too many minorities for too long. Attorney General Sessions' new policy will accentuate that injustice."[29] Senator Paul's implicit assumption is the same as that of political analyst Chris Hayes – law enforcement will continue to bypass most white addicts while arresting and prosecuting to the maximum black and Latino drug users.

* * * * *

How can this nation heal the divide when many Americans today appear more polarized than ever? Bullying on school playgrounds is on the rise, as is violent hate crime – even killing Good Samaritans for daring to intervene. Such a horrific incident occurred on Friday, May 28, 2017, when 35-year-old Jeremy Christian launched a verbal assault on two teenage girls on a Portland, Oregon, commuter train. The 17-year-old was apparently targeted with taunts for wearing a hijab;

her 16-year-old girlfriend was black. Three chivalrous strangers jumped to the girls' defense and were knifed in the throat. Rick John Best, 53, and Taliesin Myrddin Namkai-Meche, 23, died of their wounds. Micah David Cole Fletcher, 21, came within a millimeter of suffering the same fate. Two days later President Trump tweeted that the violent attacks against men who had simply sought to "stand up to hate and intolerance" were "unacceptable."[30]

At Christian's arraignment the following Tuesday, the unremorseful white supremacist called his murderous rampage an act of "patriotism."[31] Tell that to the family of recent Reed College graduate Taliesin Namkai-Meche, whose bright future with an economics degree Christian had just cut short. Tell that to the four teenaged children of Army vet Rick Best, a dedicated father whom his family now grieves as a fallen hero. Tell that to surviving college student Micah Fletcher and the two teenage girls whom Fletcher described in a moving Facebook video just days after the assault as "the real victims here."[32] The deadly incident prompted both an outpouring of peaceful protests and violent confrontations between activists on the Left and Right necessitating Portland police intervention – just one of many cities where racial tension has long simmered.[33]

These emerging phenomena raise the question for us all – if we are silent in the face of acts of extreme disrespect for our fellow men, women and children, does that connote consent? Do we as a democratic nation have as our aim equal justice for all, or do we prefer some races and religions over others, men over women, straights over gays, the wealthy classes over the poor, some immigrants over others?

Historically, as Chris Hayes points out, "white voters had (and continue to have) little appetite" for "making racial equality a genuine, lived economic reality in America."[34] Meanwhile, inequality of opportunity for most Americans now closely resembles the Gilded Age. Poor whites increasingly share the same dismal life prospects of poor black and brown communities. In his 2017 book, *The Broken Ladder: How Inequality Affects the Way We Think, Live, and Die,* University of North Carolina Professor Keith Payne posits that extreme economic inequality "makes us superstitiously cling . . . to the world as we want it to be rather than as it is. Inequality divides us, cleaving us into camps not only of income but also of ideology and race, eroding our trust in one another."[35]

Commentator Nicholas Kristof suggests that "to uncover the root of our national dysfunctions we must go deeper than politics, deeper than poverty, deeper than demagoguery, and confront the inequality that is America today."[36] In today's skewed society, it ill serves those who occupy the bottom rungs to vent their anger at each other. We all need to speak up for the equal opportunity this country should stand for and rein in the abuses of power that hold us back.

* * * * *

On March 7, 2015, President Obama and former President George W. Bush joined thousands of marchers in Selma, Alabama, to celebrate the 50th anniversary of a civil rights milestone – "Bloody Sunday," March 7, 1965. Congressman John Lewis never expected to live to see an African-American president when he and other activists joined Martin Luther King, Jr., that day in Selma to march for voting rights. In 1965, the young civil rights leader was clubbed near to death by police as he crossed the Edmund Pettus Bridge – a bridge proudly named by local politicians in 1940 for a Confederate General, Senator and Grand Wizard of the Ku Klux Klan who was buried in Selma. Pettus had been a staunch opponent of the Reconstruction Amendments that gave former slaves citizenship rights.

President Obama's stirring message on the 50th anniversary of that attempt to march across the Edmund Pettus Bridge also applies to lessons from some early century prosecutions where law enforcement, judges and lawyers made history:

> What greater expression of faith in the American experiment .
> . . what greater form of patriotism is there; than the belief that
> America is not yet finished, that we are strong enough to be self-
> critical . . . . The success of our experiment in self-government
> rested on engaging all our citizens in this work. . . . America is a
> constant work in progress. . . . With such effort, we can make sure
> our criminal justice system serves all and not just some. Together,

> we can raise the level of mutual trust that policing is built on – the idea that police officers are members of the communities they risk their lives to protect . . . . We do a disservice to the cause of justice by intimating that bias and discrimination are immutable. . . . Of course, . . . we know the march is not yet over, the race is not yet won, and that reaching that blessed destination . . . requires admitting as much.[37]

On June 26, 2015, President Obama drew international attention to Charleston, South Carolina, as he eulogized Reverend Clementa Pinckney, the pastor among nine black church members massacred the week before by a young white supremacist who had just been welcomed to join Pinckney's Bible study meeting. Dylann Roof opened fire on the unsuspecting worshippers as their eyes were closed in prayer. Survivors recounted that Roof shouted as he reloaded: "You all are taking over our country. Y'all want something to pray about? I'll give you something to pray about." When caught, Roof boasted that he was attempting to start a race war. He considered it his mission.[38]

Reverend Pinckney's funeral drew huge crowds. He was a long-time state legislator, highly beloved and respected by colleagues in both parties. His casket arrived by horse-drawn cart for viewing at the state capitol, where cameras captured the American and South Carolina state flags at half-mast. On a separate pole still flying high was the Confederate battle flag – the same flag killer Dylann Roof had posed with for his racist website.

Governor Nikki Haley had previously defended the Rebel flag's continued location at the capitol, but, in a surprising reversal after the Charleston Church massacre, she endorsed renewed calls to remove the controversial flag from the seat of state government. In his eulogy, President Obama noted that Reverend Pinckney once said, "Across the South, we have a deep appreciation of history – we haven't always had a deep appreciation of each other's history. What is true in the South is true for America. . . . justice grows out of recognition of ourselves in each other. . . . That history can't be a sword to justify injustice, or a shield against progress, but must be a manual for how to avoid repeating the mistakes of the past – how to break the cycle. A roadway toward a better world."[39]

Amazingly, on July 10, 2015, that Rebel flag came down following a 37 to 3 vote in the South Carolina Senate – where Senator Pinckney had been a popular colleague – and a heated 13-hour debate in the House. There the tide was turned in favor of its immediate removal by an impassioned plea from a descendant of Confederacy President Jefferson Davis. The final vote in the House was 94 to 20. The truth was that no such rebellious flag had flown at the state capitol during the first hundred years after the Union won the Civil War. The Confederate flag was first raised there in 1964 as a defiant message of entrenched opposition to the civil rights movement. By 2015, the time had long since come for the state of South Carolina to stop embracing that secessionist symbol of white supremacy. Nevertheless, some diehards vowed they would never forgive Governor Haley for endorsing its removal.[40]

New Orleans Mayor Mitch Landrieu made a similar courageous decision in the wake of the 2015 Charleston Church massacre. He arranged for the removal of four long-standing Confederate monuments from city plazas and parks after overcoming fierce opposition from those who insisted on the monuments' historic value. In his remarks at the ceremonies following the removal of General Robert E. Lee's statue from its pedestal on May 19, 2017, Mayor Landrieu refused to sugarcoat the purpose of such longstanding tributes to white supremacy: "There are no slave ship monuments, no prominent markers on public land to remember the lynchings or the slave blocks; nothing to remember this long chapter of our lives; the pain, the sacrifice, the shame. . . ."[41]

Mayor Landrieu added, "These monuments that we took down were meant to rebrand the history of our city and the ideals of a defeated Confederacy. . . . [They] purposefully celebrate a fictional, sanitized Confederacy, ignoring the death, ignoring the enslavement and the terror that it actually stood for . . . ." He noted that those urging him to keep the monuments in place "are eerily silent on what amounts to this historical malfeasance, a lie by omission. For America . . . it has been a long, winding road, marked by great tragedy and great triumph. But we cannot be afraid of our truth. . . . This [reconciliation] process can move us towards healing and understanding of each other."[42]

Mayor Landrieu eloquently reminded us that it takes will power and courage on the part of political leaders, law enforcement and individuals from all segments of society to keep moving us forward. The opposite is also true. A partial answer to Mississippi Federal Judge Reeves' question about what transformed "genteel, God-fearing, God-loving Mississippians into mindless murderers and sadistic torturers" is tacit or explicit community and governmental support for devaluing the lives of others.

Dylann Roof has been sentenced to die for murderous acts inspired by racist lies he learned via the Internet. He was motivated in part by reading wildly false "statistics" blaming more than four-fifths of murders of white people on black perpetrators. The truth is whites kill by far the most white victims, just as homicides against blacks, Latinos and Asian-Americans are mostly committed by people of their own race. (Of all homicide victims in the nation, blacks number a whopping eight times as many as whites.)[43] Roof confessed that most of what incensed him about black Americans came from the website of a South Carolina hate group called the Council of Conservative Citizens.[44] At his competency hearing, Roof spoke on his own behalf: "I am not going to lie to you. Other than the fact that I trusted people I shouldn't have . . . there's nothing wrong with me psychologically."[45] Had Roof been incited to kill fellow Americans by ISIS propaganda, he undoubtedly would not have been treated by officials as a lone wolf.

Instead of condemning the primary source of Roof's misinformation, as a candidate for president, Donald Trump courted the same Council of Conservative Citizens.[46] Indeed, as Roof awaited trial for his horrific crime, Trump retweeted to his millions of followers similar false and inflammatory "crime statistics." That tweet earned Trump an immediate "Pants on Fire" rating from *Politifact*[47] even as the inflammatory tweet found a scarily receptive audience among some members of his base.

Trump has zeroed in on the strategy that has worked phenomenally well for demagogues in the past. That strategy not only exacerbates white anger, it has succeeded in instilling in many young black Americans the feeling of the hunted. Author Ta-Nehisi Coates movingly described that deep anxiety in his recent best-selling book *Between the World and Me.* As political commentator Chris Hayes notes, exploiting the enduring myth that most violent crime against whites is committed by blacks predictably operates at a visceral level . . .. It is "primal and primary . . .."[48]

Also operating today at a heightened level is rage against political enemies. By 2016 a Pew research poll measuring levels of partisanship and polarization revealed that 45% of Republicans and 41% of Democrats believed that members of the opposite party were a threat to the nation – up from a third of both parties who held such strong views two years before.[49] One could easily put killers Dylann Roof and Jeremy Christian in that category. On June 14, 2017, the nation reeled from yet another murderous rampage of a lone man with a political agenda.

This time the violence was committed by a white 66-year-old follower of Bernie Sanders who had volunteered for the Vermont Senator's 2016 presidential campaign. James Hodgkinson had recently retired from his small business in Belleville, Illinois. Incensed at the results of the November election, in the spring of 2017 he drove to Alexandria, Virginia, just outside the nation's capital, where he camped out for two months. Just before he planned to head back home, Hodgkinson showed up at an early morning practice for a charity baseball game between Republicans and Democrats. After learning that the men on the field were all Republicans, Hodgkinson positioned himself behind the third base dugout and fired volley after volley from an assault rifle and a 9mm handgun, wounding several players and compelling others to run for cover.

Two African-American special agents of the Capitol police assigned to protect Minority Whip Steve Scalise were among the wounded. Yet agents David Bailey and Crystal Griner quickly returned fire, killing Hodgkinson. Scalise was hospitalized in critical condition. Both agents were lauded as heroes, some reportes noting with irony that Griner is married to a woman and saved the life of a Congressman leading efforts to ban gay marriage. On the Fourth of July, 2017, the Sons of the American Revolution would award both officers medals in recognition of their heroism.

Immediately upon hearing news of the rampage, Senator Sanders strongly condemned the violence. The mass shooting hit home among all of Washington's political leaders. Democrats prayed for the victims as Minority Leader Nancy Pelosi expressed the group's solidarity with their Republican colleagues: "On days like today, there are no Democrats or Republicans. Only Americans. We will use this occasion to bring us together."[50] Speaker of the House Paul Ryan declared in a moving speech on the floor at the Capitol, "An attack on one of us is an attack on all of us."[51] President Trump responded similarly: "We can all agree that we are blessed to be Americans, our children deserve to grow up in a nation of safety and peace, and that we are strongest when we are unified and when we work together for the common good."[52] Presidential counselor Kellyanne Anne Conway added, "You can't attack people personally, rather than on policy, and think tragedies like the Virginia shooting won't happen."[53] That commitment among our country's leaders to model civility in political behavior lasted just one news cycle before it started to unravel. Unless renewed efforts are made to strengthen that resolve, it will likely resemble the short-lived impact on partisan venom following the attempted assassination of Democratic Congresswoman Gabby Gifford in 2011.

Just as activists on the Left have sometimes let their political rage erupt, throughout the presidential campaign and since the 2016 election, reporters have noted instances where some combative Trump supporters have done the same. The federal judges in Seattle, San Francisco and Honolulu who imposed temporary restraining orders on President Trump's two travel bans against a handful of predominantly Muslim countries have been assigned extra protection in response to death threats.

It is difficult not to see a correlation between these threats and President Trump's incessant ridicule of federal judges who interpret the Constitution differently than he does. He mocked President George W. Bush's appointee James Robart in Seattle as a "so-called judge," and publicly ridiculed for "judicial overreach" the unanimous Ninth Circuit panel in San Francisco who affirmed Judge Robart's order – jurists who were appointed by three different Republican and Democratic Presidents. Then he roused a crowd at a rally by venting anger at Hawaiian Judge Derrick Watson's similar order, which the president characterized as "unprecedented" and likely made "for political reasons."[54] (This appeared to be a thinly veiled allusion to the fact Judge Watson was appointed by President Obama.)

The white supremacist animosity that President Trump has tapped into makes it easier to envision how South Carolina Senator and Governor "Pitchfork Ben" Tillman roused mob anger in his day. Tillman's statue still stands outside that state's capitol, even though the Confederate flag he venerated has been taken down. At an alt-right conference in Washington, D.C., in late November 2016, some white supremacists in attendance excitedly hailed President-elect Trump with Nazi salutes.[55] During the first week of January 2017 – just two weeks before he left office – President Obama shared his reasons for maintaining optimism despite such open displays of bigotry:

> We don't benefit from pretending that racism doesn't exist. We don't benefit from not talking about it. The fact that these things are being surfaced means we can solve them. But over all, what I've seen as President traveling around the country is, particularly the next generation, young people, their appreciation of people who are different than them, come from different places, have different backgrounds. . . . They're far more sophisticated about race, far more tolerant and embracing of diversity. So I think over the long arc, America will keep on getting better.[56]

One sign that President Obama was right is the recent action of the Southern Baptist Conference – the largest Protestant denomination in the country, which originally split with Northern Baptists in the mid-19th century over their strong opposing views on slavery. In 1995, the Conference apologized for its historic defense of both slavery and racial segregation.[57] In 2012, the increasingly diverse body elected its first African-American president. A year after the South Carolina mass murder by Dylann Roof, the Southern Baptist Conference condemned the flying of the Confederate battle flag in its churches or by its members. And on June 14, 2017, 5,000 attendees of the Conference voted overwhelmingly to repudiate "every form of racism, including alt-right white supremacy, as antithetical to the Gospel of Jesus Christ."[58]

Another extraordinarily hopeful sign that America continues to make progress "over the long arc" is the powerful nonpartisan message of collaboration toward a more inclusive democracy that HBO aired on Independence Day 2017. In "The Words That Built America," director Alexandra Pelosi, daughter of House of Representatives minority leader Nancy Pelosi, created a star-studded patchwork quilt of patriotism composed of a who's who of prominent Americans of different races, ethnicities, genders, political parties and sexual orientations.[59] The cast included the president and vice president and all their living predecessors, the leaders of Congress, the chief justice, our ambassador to the United Nations, several governors, Hollywood legends, and television commentators, among other household names. The film begins with narration by Pulitzer-Prize-winning historian David McCullough as we see images of our country's white-male founding fathers. Then each of the diverse film participants simply reads in turn a sentence at a time from the Declaration of Independence and Constitution. The film is capped by a reading of the Bill of Rights by members of the next generation of potential leaders – middle-school students from the United Nations International School in New York. Taken as a whole, the documentary makes a strong point – patriotic Americans come in all stripes to form "We the People."

* * * * *

Four years before the historic 1965 march in Selma, John Lewis was one of the first Freedom Riders to endure beatings and arrests for attempting to integrate interstate bus stops throughout the South. In one early incident in South Carolina, several young white men assaulted the civil rights activists when they entered a "whites only" waiting room. In 2009, "Good Morning America" brought one of the leaders of that assault, Elwin Wilson, together with Congressman Lewis so that Wilson could offer Lewis a public apology. Visibly moved, Lewis forgave Wilson and the two elderly men hugged. Lewis then told the reporter: "I never thought this would happen. It says something about the power of love, of grace, the power of the people being able to say, 'I'm sorry,' and move on. And I deeply appreciate it. It's very meaningful for me."[60]

Two years later, in 2011, on the fiftieth anniversary of the 1961 Freedom Rides, Republican Governor Haley Barbour of Mississippi officially extended an olive branch to thank the civil rights activists his predecessors had jailed for "your courage, commitment, your sufferings and your sacrifices." Governor Barbour added pointedly, "It is good we are rid of segregation, and we are right grateful for the role you played in helping us get there."[61]

What Governor Barbour demonstrated mirrored the epiphany experienced by '60s white supremacist Elwin Wilson – that the people they once scorned had a righteous cause.[62] Everyone willing to reexamine our cultural heritage in a new light is helping diverse elements of our society move toward mutual respect and to champion "justice for all." The unbiased standard that Detroit judge Frank Murphy instructed an all-white-male jury to apply in the 1926 trial of Henry Sweet bears repeating for its timelessness: "Real justice does not draw any line of color, race, or creed or class. All charged with crime, rich or poor, humble or great, white or black, are entitled to the same right and the same full measure of justice."[63]

It is to the members of the judiciary that we repeatedly turn to uphold our constitutional rights against government overreach. We have made great strides in the nine decades since Judge Murphy urged his jury to dispense the same justice regardless of race, but we still have plenty of work to do to institutionalize that standard throughout our nation. We also have reason for optimism. Though our government's founding principle of equality has never been fully realized, it has always served as a beacon to guide our democratic republic moving forward.

ENDNOTES

Abbreviations Used in Notes

AC *The Atlanta Constitution*
BG *The Boston Globe*
LAT *The Los Angeles Times*
NYT *The New York Times*
OT *The Oakland Tribune*
SFC *The San Francisco Chronicle*
SFE *The San Francisco Examiner*

The endnotes include original publishing information, including original digital sources, for all references when first mentioned.

INTRODUCTION

1. Nia-Malika Henderson, "FBI Director James Comey gave a bold speech on race and police. Now what?" *The Washington Post*, February 12, 2015, 1, http://www/washingtonpost.com/blogs/the-fix/wp/2015/02/12/fbi -director-james-comey-gave-a-bold-speech-on-race-and-police-now-what/; James Comey, full speech, February 12, 2015, C-Span, http://www/c-span .org/video/?c4528067/james-comey-full-speech. Accessed February 24, 2015.
2. NPR, "A Black Mississippi Judge's Breathtaking Speech to 3 White Murderers." NPR, February 13, 2015, www.npr.org/blogs/codeswitch .2015/02/12/385777366/a-black-mississippi-judges-breathtaking-speech -to-3-white-murderers/. Accessed February 24, 2015.
3. *Ibid.*
4. The complaining witness, known also as Madame Black, was a blackmailer incapable of telling the same story twice. Rappe herself had told the hotel doctor that the shy comedian had made no advances whatsoever. She arrived at the party, feeling poorly, to borrow money from her old friend Arbuckle for an abortion – her sixth. Two doctors who examined Rappe confirmed she had advanced gonorrhea. No witness at trial ever testified to seeing or hearing Arbuckle assault Rappe. Recognizing how poor a witness Delmont would make, District Attorney Brady never called her to the witness stand. Instead, Brady pressured two other women at the hotel party to swear they heard Rappe accuse Arbuckle of hurting her, contrary to their original statements when interviewed by the police. Recently, *Hollywood Crime* reporter Denise Noe reviewed the Arbuckle case and suggested that Rappe may have actually died from complications of a hushed-up illegal abortion. Denise Noe, "Fatty Arbuckle and the Death of Virginia Rappe: How Did She Die?" *TruTV*, http://www.trutv.com/index .html. Accessed June 28, 2011.
5. Robert Grant and Joseph Katz, *The Great Trials of the Twenties: The Watershed*

Decade in America's Courtrooms (New York: Sarpedon, 1998), 91.

6. The Motion Picture Production Code of 1930, https://www.und.edu / instruct/cjacobs/ProductionCode.htm.

7. Gregory D. Black, *Hollywood Censored: Morality Codes, Catholics, and the Movies* (Cambridge University Press, 1996), 340.

8. Wanda Felix, "The Trial of Fatty Arbuckle," *Ralph Magazine*, http://www .ralphmag.org/fatty.html. Accessed June 28, 2011.

9. Garry Morgan, "Sheriff Matt Wann, a Brave Man and Untold Story," *Scottsboro Boys Blog Site*, http://scottsborostories.blogspot.com/2010/10 /sheriff-matt-wann-brave-man-and-untold.html. Accessed March 10, 2013.

10. Edward Bennett Williams, *One Man's Freedom* (Atheneum Press: New York, 1962), 7.

11. Mark Curriden and Leroy Phillips, Jr., *Contempt of Court: The Turn-of-the-Century Lynching That Launched a 100 Years of Federalism* (New York: First Anchor Books Ed. 2001), xiv.

12. The Gallup Poll conducted after the O. J. Simpson murder trial ended found that 42 percent of whites who were interviewed agreed with the acquittal, while 49 percent thought he was guilty as charged. In contrast, 78 percent of blacks thought the acquittal was the right verdict and only 10 percent disagreed. See Linder, "Famous Trials: The O.J. Simpson Trial." http://www.law.umkc.edu/faculty/projects/ftrials/Simpson/polls .html. An NBC news poll ten years after the verdicts came in found that 87 percent of whites thought Simpson had been guilty of the murders, but only 29 percent of blacks ("NBC News Poll 10 Years after Simpson verdict: Issue of Race still figures prominently in public opinion"). http://www .msnbc.com/id/5139346/. Accessed June 30, 2011.

13. "Most Black People Now Think O.J. Simpson Was Guilty," *FiveThirtyEight .com.* http://fivethirtyeight.com/features/most-black-people-now-think-oj -simson-was-guilty/. Accessed June 9, 2016.

14. Gerald Uelmen, *Lessons From the Trial: The People v. O. J. Simpson,* (Kansas City: Andrews and McMeel, 1996), 208–209.

15. The Stanley Nelson quote from his remarks upon receiving a lifetime achievement award from DoC NYC on November 10, 2016, is taken from a Firelight Media e-mail blast on November 29, 2016. Nelson included a differently worded message, urging more documentaries on previously untold stories of diverse members of American society, in "Our Stories Matter – More Than Ever" Events, Stanley's Corner, *Firelight Media,* Nov. 11, 2016, http://firelightmedia.tv/our-stories-matter-more-than-ever/.

16. Meredith Simons, "FBI watching for 'homegrown' terrorists," *Houston Chronicle,* Washington Bureau, Sept. 30, 2009, http://www.chron.com / disp/story.mpl/metropolitan/6645914.html. Accessed June 28, 2011.

17. "Radical-right terror plagues nation: Hatemongers migrating online to spread ideology," *Southern Poverty Law Center Report,* 1, 3 (quoting Mark Potok, editor of the *Intelligence Report*).

18. *Southern Poverty Law Center Report,* "SPLC fights back against bigotry in White House," p. 1.

19. Jeff Guo, "If white America is in 'crisis,' what have black Americans been

living through?" *The Washington Post*, Wonkblog Analysis, April 4, 2017, https://www.washingtonpost.com/news/wonk/wp/2017/04/04/if-white -america-is-in-crisis-what-have-black-americans-been-living-through/?utm _term=.1652d25183c1&wpisrc=nl_rainbow-anewssubs&wpmm=1.

20.   Joseph Stiglitz, *The Price of Inequality: How Today's Divided Society Endangers Our Future* (New York: W.W. Norton & Company, 2012), preface to the paperback edition, Kindle Edition., (2013), loc. 413–428.

21.   *Ibid.,* loc. 428.

Chapter 1
A BITTER TEACHING MOMENT
President McKinley's Assassination

1.   William McKinley quote, http://ourwhitehouse.org/prespgs/wmckinley .html. Accessed March 25, 2015.

2.   William Jennings Bryan, "Cross of Gold" campaign speech, PBS *The American Experience,* http://www.pbs.org/wgbh/amex/1900/filmmore /reference/primary/crossofgold.html. Accessed March 29, 2015.

3.   "*The New York Journal* and the Assassination of William McKinley," novelguide .com, http://www.novelguide.com/a/discover/adec_0001_0001_0 /adec_0001_0001_0_00202.html. Accessed June 29, 2011.

4.   Eric Rauchway, *Murdering McKinley: The Making of Theodore Roosevelt's America* (New York: Hill and Wang, 2003).

5.   *Ibid.,* 171.

6.   Emma Goldman, "The Tragedy at Buffalo," *Free Society*, October 6, 1901, 1.

7.   Jane Addams, *Twenty Years at Hull House* (New York: The MacMillan Co., 1910), 403. Addams (1860–1935) was a pioneer social worker, suffragette and pacifist who was best known for founding Hull House in Chicago as one of the first settlement houses in the United States. She later became the first woman to head the National Conference of Social Work, which established the National Federation of Settlements. Addams also became president of the Women's International League for Peace and Freedom. In 1931, she was honored as a co-recipient of the Nobel Peace Prize.

8.   Rauchway, *Murdering McKinley,* 61.

9.   *Ibid.,* 77 and fn. 45, citing Booker T. Washington, letter to the editor of the *Montgomery Advertiser,* September 23, 1901. Also see *The Booker T. Washington Papers,* 14 vols., ed. Louis R. Harlan and W. Smock with Barbara S. Kraft (Urbana, Ill.: 1972–1989), 6:217.

10.   *Ibid.*

11.   *Ibid.,* 78.

12.   *Ibid.,* 3, 16–17.

13.   *Ibid.,* 53.

14.   *Ibid.,* 78 and fn. 48, citing Leon F. Litwack, *Trouble in Mind: Black Southerners in the Age of Jim Crow* ((New York: Alfred A Knopf, 1998), 284.

15.   Deborah Davis, *Guest of Honor: Booker T. Washington, Theodore Roosevelt and the White House Dinner That Shocked a Nation* (Atria Books: New York, 2012), 227; Edmund Morris, *Theodore Rex* (Random House: New York, 2001), 227.

16.   *Ibid.,* 227, 238, 254–55.

Chapter 2
DEMENTIA AMERICANA
A Dramatic Murder Brings the Curtain Down on the Gilded Age

1. Douglas O. Linder, "Famous Trials: The Trials of Harry Thaw for the Murder of Stanford White," umkc.edu/faculty/projects/ftrials/thaw /Thawaccount.html. Accessed June 25, 2011.

2. Paula Uruburu, *American Eve: Evelyn Nesbit, Stanford White, the Birth of the "It" Girl and the Crime of the Century* (New York: Riverhead Books, 2008), 11.

3. Linder, "Famous Trials: The Trials of Harry Thaw," *op. cit.*

4. *Ibid.*

5. Uruburu, *American Eve*, 282.

6. The quotes from Evelyn and Harry Thaw on the night of the killing are from the front-page story, "THAW MURDERS STANFORD WHITE: Shoots Him on the Madison Square Garden Roof," *NYT,* June 26, 1906, 1–2.

7. Uruburu, *American Eve*, 287.

8. The term was already in use in the late 19th century. Historians Gilbert Geis and Leigh Bienen point out that, in 1898, author Henry Hunt published *The Crime of the Century: Or the Assassination of Dr. Patrick Henry Cronin,* which described the physician's ambush murder in Chicago in 1889 by members of his Irish secret society. Dr. Cronin had created a political maelstrom by publicly accusing leaders of the radical political group of embezzling funds solicited for Irish freedom fighters. Geis and Beinen *Crimes of the Century* (Boston: Northeastern Univ. Press, 1998), 4. The assassination of President McKinley in 1901 was described in print as "the greatest crime of the century," but Czolgosz received short shrift at trial. The salacious nature of the 1906 Stanford White murder case gave reporters much more fodder. So it became the first widely hyped as the "trial of the century," a claim that other journalists would repeat in covering other sensational trials in each of the ensuing nine decades.

9. Linder, "Famous Trials: The Trials of Harry Thaw," quoting reporter Irvin S. Cobb.

10. Uruburu, *American Eve*, 318.

11. "D. Delmas, Legal Napoleon of San Francisco: Character sketch of the Californian who's conducting the Thaw Defense and will settle in New York," *NYT,* Feb. 10, 1907.

12. "EVELYN THAW TELLS HER STORY; Accuses Stanford White of Causing Her Fall; CONFESSED IT TO THAW; Lays Bare Her Life in Court to Save Husband; HE SOBS AS HE LISTENS; She Will Tell More Today – Then Cross-Examination – Letters of Thaw's Love Read," *NYT,* Feb. 6, 1907, 1.

13. Linder, *op. cit.*

14. Francis Russell, *Sacco and Vanzetti: The Case Resolved* (New York: Harper & Row, 1986), 210, fn. 20, citing Louis Adams, *Dynamite: The Story of Class Violence in America,* 149–50.

Chapter 3
UNDESIRABLE CITIZENS
Two Lethal Bombings Focus Americans on Labor Wars

1. J. Anthony Lukas, *Big Trouble* (Touchstone Books: New York, 1997). Hapgood is quoted at 477–78.
2. "Rioting and Bloodshed in the Streets of Chicago," *NYT*, May 4, 1886.
3. Peter Carlson, *Roughneck: The Life and Times of Big Bill Haywood* (New York: W.W. Norton, 1983), 48.
4. Lukas, *Big Trouble*, 226.
5. Douglas O. Linder, "Famous Trials: Big Bill Haywood," http://www.law.umkc.edu/faculty/projects/ftrials/haywood/HAY_BHAY.HTM. Accessed June 30, 2011.
6. Lukas, *Big Trouble*, 145, 150.
7. *Lochner v. New York*, 198 U.S. 45, 56 (1905).
8. William Cahn, *A Pictorial History of American Labor* (New York: Crown Publishers, 1972), 126
9. James D. Horan and Howard Swiggett, *The Pinkerton Story* (New York: G.P. Putnam's Sons, 1951), 126.
10. Joseph G. Rayback, *A History of American Labor* (New York: The Free Press, 1966), 133.
11. Carlson, *Roughneck*, 96.
12. Elizabeth Gage, *The Day Wall Street Exploded: A Story of America in its First Age of Terror* (Oxford: Oxford Univ. Press, 2009), 79, fn. 19.
13. Lukas, *Big Trouble*, 278.
14. Carlson, *Roughneck*, 98.
15. Kevin Boyle, *Arc of Justice: A Saga of Race, Civil Rights and Murder in the Jazz Age* (New York: Henry Holt & Co., 2004), 231.
16. Irving Stone, *Clarence Darrow for the Defense* (New York: Doubleday & Co. Signet Books,1941, 1969), 220–221.
17. Carlson, *Roughneck*, 109.
18. *Ibid.*, 108.
19. Child labor was common in late 19th century America. The Children's Crusade followed a number of other efforts to call attention to the exploitation of poor children, who often only had a few years of schooling. Many never learned how to read or write before they were compelled into the work force. Author Susan Campbell Bartoletti described this history in a well-researched book written for children which includes a timeline of Federal Child Labor Laws, *Kids on Strike* (Houghton Mifflin Company: New York, 1999).
20. See Chapter XV. Moyer, Haywood and Pettibone, *The Autobiography of Mother Jones*, http://digital.library.upenn.edu/women/jones/autobiography/. Accessed March 4, 2015.
21. Lukas, *Big Trouble*, 387.
22. *Ibid.*, 521.
23. *Ibid.*
24. *Ibid.*, 524.
25. Irving Stone, *Clarence Darrow for the Defense*, 191.

26. Carlson, *Roughneck*, 112.

27. Stone, *Clarence Darrow for the Defense*, 191.

28. Gage, T*he Day Wall Street Exploded*, 81 and fn. 24.

29. John E. Nevins, Scripps-McRae News Service, *Milwaukee Journal*, June 6, 1907, 1.

30. Linder, "Famous Trials: The Trial of William 'Big Bill' Haywood," http://www.law.umkc.edu/faculty/projects/ftrials/haywood/hay_acct.html. Accessed June 28, 2011.

31. Oscar King Davis, "Orchard Tells About Murders," *NYT*, June 6, 1907.

32. Stone, *Clarence Darrow for the Defense*, 280.

33. Lukas, *Big Trouble*, 703, citing *The Boston Globe*, July 20,1907.

34. *Ibid.*, 704.

35. *Ibid.*, 705.

36. "Darrow's Speech in the Haywood Case," *Wayland's Monthly*, No. 90, 110, Oct. 1907 (Girard, Kansas; J. A. Wayland, Oct. 1907), http://darrow.law.umn.edu/documents/Darrow_Speech_Haywood_Case.pdf. Accessed June 28, 2011.

37. Stone, *Clarence Darrow for the Defense*, 274.

38. Carlson, *Roughneck*, 139.

39. *Ibid.*

40. Howard Blum, *American Lightning: Terror, Mystery, the Birth of Hollywood, and the Crime of the Century* (New York: Crown Publishers, 2008), 20.

41. Stone, *Clarence Darrow for the Defense*, 329.

42. Gage, *The Day Wall Street Exploded*, 71.

43. Maria Pascualy, "Witness to History: The Life and Times of Ralph Chaplin," Columbia: Summer 2001; Vol. 15, No. 2, http://columbia.washingtonhistory.org/magazine/articles/2001/0201/0201-a2.aspx. Accessed June 29, 2011.

44. Jack Phillips [pseudonym of Carl Sandburg],"Haywood of the I. W. W.," *International Socialist Review*, 18.7 (Jan. 1918), 343.

45. Murray B. Levin, *Political Hysteria in America: The Democratic Capacity for Repression* (New York: Basic Books, 1971), 29.

46. Lukas, *Big Trouble*, 753–754.

Chapter 4
SHOWDOWN WITH THE SUPREME COURT
The Lynching That Gave Teeth to the Fourteenth Amendment Right to a Fair Trial

1. "The Trial of Sheriff Joseph Shipp et al.: An Account by Doug Linder," 2000, http://law2.umkc.edu/faculty/projects/ftrials/shipp/trialaccount.html. Accessed June 26, 2011.

2. Thomas Dixon, Jr., "Booker T. Washington and the Negro," *Saturday Evening Post*, Aug. 19, 1905, 1.

3. Glenda Elizabeth Gilmore, *Gender and Jim Crow: Women and the Politics of White Supremacy in North Carolina, 1896–1920* (Durham, North Carolina: Univ. of North Carolina Press, 1996), 66–70.

4. Eric Foner, *Reconstruction: America's Unfinished Revolution*, (New York: Harper & Row, 1988), 608.

5. James M. Dormon, "Shaping the Popular Image of Post-Reconstruction American Blacks: The 'Coon Song' Phenomenon of the Gilded Age," *American Quarterly*, 40: 450–471 (1988); Richard A. Reublin and Robert L. Maine, "Question of the Month: What Were Coon Songs?" Jim Crow Museum of Racist Memorabilia website, Ferris State Univ. (May 2005), http://www.ferris.edu/jimcrow/. Accessed June 30, 2011.

6. Samuel K. Roberts, "Kelly Miller and Thomas Dixon, Jr., on Blacks in American Civilization," *Phylon* (1960), Vol. 41, No. 2, 202.

7. Curriden and Phillips, *Contempt of Court*, 36.

8. Chris Hayes, *A Colony in a Nation* (New York: W.W. Norton & Company, 2017), 87.

9. Douglas O. Linder, "Famous Trials: The Trial of Sheriff Shipp," http://www.law.umkc.edu/faculty/projects/ftrials/shipp/chronology.html. Accessed June 28, 2011.

10. Curriden and Phillips, *Contempt of Court*, 39.

11. *Ibid.*, 48.

12. *Ibid.*, 49.

13. *Coffin v. United States*, 156 U. S. 432, 15 Supreme Ct. Rptr. 394, 403 (1895).

14. Linder, *op. cit.*

15. Curriden and Phillips, *Contempt of Court*, 76.

16. *Ibid.*

17. *Ibid.*, 83.

18. Linder, *op. cit.*

19. Curriden and Phillips, *Contempt of Court*, 109.

20. *Ibid.*, 118.

21. *Ibid.*, 192, citing an article in *The Chattanooga Times*, March 19, 1906.

22. Curriden and Phillips, *Contempt of Court*, 214.

23. Hayes, *A Colony in a Nation*, 68–69. Looking back in 2017 at the way Ferguson police left Michael Brown's corpse on the street in the hot August sun for over four hours, Hayes observed, "The inert, uncovered, disrespected body was the perfect symbol of the Ferguson police's contempt. . . ."

24. Leigh Reiford, *Imprisoned in a Luminous Glare: Photography and the African American Freedom Struggle* (Chapel Hill: Univ. of North Carolina Press, 2011) 38–39, 46 (quoted language at 46, citing historian Winfield H. Collins' 1918 pamphlet, "The Truth About Lynching and the Negro in the South").

25. Curriden and Phillips, *Contempt of Court*, 231.

26. *Ibid.*, 232–233.

27. "Sheriff Shipp Talks of Government Action," *AC*, May 29, 1906, 3.

28. *United States v. Cruikshank*, 92 U.S. 542 (1876).

29. The five consolidated civil rights cases were *United States v. Stanley; United States v. Ryan; United States v. Nichols; United States v. Singleton; Robinson et ux. v. Memphis & Charleston R.R. Co.*, 109 U.S. 3 (1883).

30. Douglas A. Blackmon, *Slavery by Another Name: The Re-enslavement of Black Americans From the Civil War to World War II* (New York: Anchor Books, 2009), 93.

31. See, eg, Judge L. H. Perez, "The 14th Amendment Is Unconstitutional," http://www.sweetliberty.org/fourteenth.amend.htm. Accessed March 6, 2015.

32. *United States v. Shipp*, 214 U.S. 386, 29 Supreme Ct. Rptr. 637, 644 (1909).

33. Curriden and Phillips, *Contempt of Court*, 318.

34. *United States v. Wade*, 388 U.S. 218, 229 (1967), quoting Wall, *Eye-Witness Identification in Criminal Cases.*

35. Kevin Johnson, "States change police lineups after wrongful convictions," Sept. 19, 2009, *USA Today*, http://www.usatoday.com/news/nation/2009 -09-16-police-lineups_N.htm. Accessed June 30, 2011.

36. Ed Johnson Memorial Project, "Connect Chattanooga," quoting Mayor Andy Berke, http://connect.chattanooga.gov/edjohnson/.

37. Sean Phipps, "Ed Johnson Commemoration Day remembers 1906 lynching on Walnut Street Bridge," March 15, 2017, http://nooga.com/175497 /ed-johnson-commemoration-day-remembers-1906-lynching-on-walnut -street-bridge/.

38. Joseph L. Hoffmann and Nancy J. King, *Rethinking the Federal Role in State Criminal Justice*, 84 N.Y.U. *Law Review*, 791, 797 (2009).

39. Steven Reinhardt, "The Demise of Habeas Corpus and the Rise of Qualified Immunity: The Court's Ever Increasing Limitations on the Development and Enforcement of Constitutional Rights and Some Particularly Unfortunate Consequences," *Michigan Law Review*, Vol. 113:1219, 1240. May 2015, http://michiganlawreview.org/the-demise-of-habeas-corpus/. Accessed June 3, 2015).

40. *Ibid.*, 1221, fn. 8 and 1225.

41. *Ibid.*, 1222–23 and fn. 13, citing Justin D. Levinson, "Forgotten Racial Equality: Implicit Bias, Decisionmaking, and Misremembering," 57 *Duke Law Journal*, 345, 350 (2007); Eva Paterson, "Implicit Bias and the 14th Amendment," *L.A. Daily Journal*, Sept. 8, 2014, at 6.

42. *Ibid.*, at 1229.

43. *Ibid.*, 1251, fn. 164.

44. Charles J. Ogletree, Jr. and Austin Sarat, *From Lynch Mobs to the Killing State: Race and the Death Penalty in America* (New York: New York Univ. Press, 2006), 3. See also Charles J. Ogletree, Jr., ed., *When Law Fails: Making Sense of Miscarriage of Justice* (New York: New York Univ. Press, 2009).

Chapter 5
MURDER BEGETS MURDER
Two Tragic Deaths in Atlanta Launch the Modern KKK and the Anti-Defamation League

1. Steve Oney, *And the Dead Shall Rise: The Murder of Mary Phagan and the Lynching of Leo Frank* (New York: Pantheon, 2003), 511, quoting the governor's comments at a luncheon for his successor.

2. *Ibid*, 7.

3. *Ibid.*, 15–16, citing C. Vann Woodward, *Origins of the New South* (Baton Rouge: Louisiana State Univ. Press, 1951), 418.

4. *Ibid.*, 6.

5. History Place: Child Labor: Newsboys, http://peachtree-online .com/printer/newsboys.htm; http://www.historyplace.com/unitedstates /childlabor/. Accessed June 28, 2011.

6. Oney, *And the Dead Shall Rise*, 42, citing Herbert Asbury, "Hearst Comes to Atlanta," *American Mercury*, Jan. 1926.

7. "Race Voting Rights and Segregation Techniques of Direct Disfranchisement," http://www.umich.edu/~lawrace/disenfranchise1.htm.

8. "Atlanta Race Riot of 1906," *New Georgia Encyclopedia*, http://www.georgiaencyclopedia.org/nge/Article.jsp?id=h-3033. Accessed June 30, 2011.

9. James C. Cobb, *Georgia Odyssey: A Short History of the State* (2nd ed.) (Athens, GA: Univ. of Georgia Press, 2008), 43–44.

10. Michael Perman, *Struggle for Mastery: Disfranchisement in the South, 1888–1908* (Chapel Hill, NC: Univ. of North Carolina Press, 2001). The issue of black disenfranchisement became a major focal point again in the 2000 election. On its review, the Civil Rights Commission found that many thousands of African-Americans in that close contest were improperly disenfranchised in Florida, Missouri, and Ohio. http://www.usccr.gov/pubs/vote2000/report/ch9.htm. Accessed June 30, 2011.

11. "Glover Not Affected: Failure of Intervention by Supreme Court Does Not Affect Him," *AC*, Dec. 22, 1907, C9.

12. Peter N. Carroll and David W. Noble, *The Free and the Unfree: A Progressive History of the United States* (3rd rev. ed.) (New York: Penguin Books, 2001), 294.

13. Ken Burns, *Unforgivable Blackness: The Fight of the Century*, PBS, www.pbs.org/unforgivableblackness/fight/. Accessed June 30, 2011.

14. See Dr. Renford R. Reese, "The Socio-Political Context of the Integration of Sport in America," Cal Poly Pomona, *Journal of African American Men* (vol. 4, no. 3, Spring 1999), http://www.csupomona.edu/~rrreese/integration.html. Accessed June 28, 2011.

15. Michael Walsh, "Great Expectations," *Smithsonian*, June 2010, 54.

16. Colin Linneweber, "The Black Boxer No White Could Beat Fairly," *Bleacher Report*, April 7, 2009, http://bleacherreport.com/articles/152523-the-black-man-no-white-fighter-could-beat-fairly. Accessed June 29, 2011.

17. In his appeal to Congress, Roddenberry argued that: "Intermarriage between whites and blacks is repulsive and averse to every sentiment of pure American spirit. It is abhorrent and repugnant. It is subversive to social peace. It is destructive of moral supremacy, and ultimately this slavery to black beasts will bring this nation to a fatal conflict," quoted at http://www.nbjcoalition.org/news/inter-racial-marriage-bans-vs.html. Accessed June 29, 2011.

18. Leonard Dinnerstein, *The Leo Frank Case* (Atlanta: Univ. of Georgia Press, 1987), 9 and fn. 27, citing the *The Atlanta Georgian*, April 28, 1913, 3.

19. *Ibid.*, 16 and fn. 60, citing Charles and Louise Samuels, *Night Fell on Georgia* (New York: Dell Publishing Co., 1956), 20.

20. *Ibid.*, 3, citing Henry A. Alexander, "Some Facts about the Murder Notes in the Phagan Case" (privately published pamphlet, 1914), 5, 7.

21. Oney, *And The Dead Shall Rise*, 97–98.

22. *Ibid.*, 617.

23. *AC*, July 27, 1913, 1.

24. *Laughlin McDonald, March 18, 2011, "A Jury of One's Peers."*

25. Dinnerstein, *The Leo Frank Case*, 151 and fn. 10. Linder, "Famous Trials: The Trial of Sheriff Shipp," http://www.law.umkc.edu/faculty/projects /ftrials/shipp/chronology.html. Accessed June 28, 2011/.
26. Dinnerstein, *The Leo Frank Case*, 60.
27. A. M. Dershowitz, *America on Trial: Inside the Legal Battles That Transformed Our Nation* (New York: Warner Books, 2004), 220.
28. Oney, *And The Dead Shall Rise*, 381.
29. Dinnerstein, *The Leo Frank Case*, 97
30. Carroll and Noble, *The Free and the Unfree: A Progressive History of the United States*, 294.
31. Thomas Clough, "Hoodwinked: The Legacy of Robert Byrd, The Birth & Rebirth of the Ku Klux Klan," August 29, 2010, http://www.weirdrepublic .com/episode114.htm. Accessed June 29, 2011.
32. *Leo Frank v. C. Wheeler Magnum* (1915) 237 U.S. 309, 347 (Justice Holmes dissenting).
33. Linder, "Famous Trials: The Leo Frank Trial 1913," http://www.law.umkc .edu/faculty/projects/ftrials/frank/frankballad.html. Accessed June 30, 2011.
34. Dinnerstein, *The Leo Frank Case*, 129 and fn. 37.
35. "CRIES OF LYNCH HIM HURLED AT SLATON AS HE QUITS OFFICE" (photo of contemporaneous newspaper headline), http://upload .wikimedia.org/wikipedia/en/c/ce/Leo-frank-slaton-headline.jpg. Accessed June 29, 2011.
36. Oney, *And the Dead Shall Rise*, 508.
37. *Ibid.*, 520.
38. "Leo Frank lynching site recognized with historical marker"(video), http:// marietta.granicus.com/MediaPlayer.php?publish_id=45. Accessed June 27, 2011.
39. Oney, *And The Dead Shall Rise*, 574.
40. Dinnerstein, *The Leo Frank Case*, 145.
41. Dershowitz, *America on Trial*, 221.
42. Oney, *And The Dead Shall Rise*, 643.
43. Katheryn Hayes Tucker, "A Lesson for Judges in Memory of the Governor Who Granted Clemncy to Leo Frank," *The Daily Report*, June 18, 2015, http://www.dailyreportonline.com/search-results-layout-page?query=A+L esson+For+Judges+in+Memory+of+the+Governor+who+granted+Clemen cy+to+Leo+Frank&source=nylitnews%2Clawdecision%2.
44. "Plain Words," History Is a Weapon, http://www.historyisaweapon.com /defcon1/plainwords.html.
45. "Wilson Denounces Police Strike That Left Boston a Prey to Thugs," *NYT*, Sept. 12, 1919.
46. Lawrence, M. Salinger (ed.), *Encyclopedia of White-Collar and Corporate Crime* (Thousand Oaks, CA: Sage Publication, Inc., 2005), Vol. 1, 868.

Chapter 6
THE FIX WAS IN
The Fall Guys for the Gamblers Who Rigged the 1919 World Series

1. Marty Gitlin, "The White Sox Give Baseball a Black Eye," *The Sports Post,* May 29, 2017, https://thesportspost.com/the-white-sox-give-baseball -a-black-eye/. Excerpted from his new book, *Powerful Sports Moments: The Most Significant Sports Events in American History* (New York: Rowman & Littlefield, 2017).

2. "President William Taft's Baseball Related Quotations," Baseball Almanac, http://www.baseball-almanac.com/prz_qwt.shtml.

3. Geoffrey C. Ward and Ken Burns, *Baseball: An Illustrated History* (New York: Alfred A. Knopf, 1994), 52.

4. *Ibid.*

5. *Ibid.,* 55.

6. Michael Haupert, "MLB's Annual Salary Leaders Since 1874," sabr.org; *Cy Young: A Baseball Life* (Amherst, Massachusetts: U. Mass Press, 2003), 218. Cy Young reputedly made $3000 in the National League when Johnson lured him away with a $3500 offer. (The National League salary likely included a bonus over the announced cap.) Johnson offered a similar $500 increase to lure other players. Ward and Burns, *Baseball: An Illustrated History,* 65.

7. William J. Craig, *A History of the Boston Braves, A Time Gone By,* chapter 3 (Charleston, South Carolina: Arcadia Publishing and The History Press, 2012.) As discussed in chapter three of this book, Chattanooga's workers in 1906 often made less than $375 per year.

8. Ty Cobb, *The New Georgia Encyclopedia,* http://www.georgiaencyclopedia .org/nge/Home.jsp.

9. Don Rhodes, *Ty Cobb: Safe at Home* (Guilford, Ct. Lyon Press, 2008), 58.

10. Ken Burns, "Baseball: Second Inning, Something Like a War, 1900 to 1910" (The Baseball Film Project, Inc., 1994), Vol. 2.

11. Ward and Burns, *Baseball: An Illustrated History,* 109–110.

12. Grant and Katz, *The Great Trials of the Twenties,* 65.

13. John Stravinsky, "Hall Chase, Major League baseball 1905–1919," June 8, 1999, http://www.villagevoice.com/1999-06-08/news/hal-chase-major -league-baseball-1905-1919/.

14. "1919: Race Riots," Deaths, Disturbances, Disasters and Disorders in Chicago, Chicago Public Library, http://www.chipublib.org /cplbooksmovies/cplarchive/ chidisasters/raceriots.php.

15. Both quotes in this paragraph were obtained from "Gangs and the 1919 Race Riot," http://www.uic.edu/orgs/kbc/ganghistory/Industrial%20 Era/Riotbegins.htmlhtm.

16. Douglas O. Linder, "Before *Brown*: Charles H. Houston and the *Gaines* Case," http://www.law.umkc.edu/faculty/projects/ftrials/conlaw/houstonessay .html.

17. Ward and Burns, *Baseball an Illustrated History,* 56.

18. *Ibid.,* 139.

19. Lowell Blaisdell, "Mystery and Tragedy: The O'Connell-Dolan Scandal,"

Society for American Baseball Research (SABR) Journal Archive.

20. Ward and Burns, *Baseball: An Illustrated History,* 142.

21. Harvey Fromer, *Shoeless Joe and Ragtime Baseball* (Lincoln, Nebraska: Univ. of Nebraska, 2008), 140.

22. Douglas O. Linder, "Famous Trials: The Black Sox Trial: An Account of the 1919 Black Sox Scandal and the 1921 Trial," http://www.law.umkc.edu /faculty/projects/ftrials/blacksox/blacksoxaccount.html.

23. Robert Grant and Joseph Katz, *The Great Trials of the Twenties: The Watershed Decade in America's Courtrooms* (New York: Sarpedon, 1998), 62.

24. Ward and Burns, *Baseball: An Illustrated History,* 142.

25. Scott Deveney, "Did the 1918 Cubs throw the World Series?" *The Sporting News,* April 19, 2008, http://www.soundopinions.org/forum/index .php?showtopic=16355. Accessed June 9, 2011. See Deveney, *The Original Curse: Did the Cubs Throw the 1918 World Series to Babe Ruth's Red Sox and Incite the Black Sox Scandal?* (New York: McGraw Hill, 2010).

26. "Kenesaw Mountain Landis," Baseball Statistics, http://www.baseball -statistics.com /HOF/Landis.html.

27. "Landis Quits Bench for Baseball Job," *NYT,* Feb. 18, 1922, 1.

28. James Kirby, "The Year They Fixed the World Series," *ABA Journal,* Feb. 1, 1988, 65; Joe Jackson as told to Furman Fisher, "This is the Truth," *SPORT* magazine, October 1949, http://www.blackbetsy.com/theTruth.html.

29. Grant and Katz, *The Great Trials of the Twenties,* 68.

30. Bruce Lowitt, "Black Sox scandal: Chicago throws 1919 World Series," *St. Petersburg Times,* Dec. 22, 1999, http://www.sptimes.com/News/122299 /news_pf/Sports /Black _Sox_scandal_Ch.shtml.

31. Grant and Katz, *The Great Trials of the Twenties,* 53.

32. Daniel J. Voelker and Paul A. Duffy, "Black Sox: 'It ain't so, kid, it just ain't so,'" *Chicago Lawyer,* Sept. 1, 2009, http://www.chicagolawyermagazine .com/2009/09/01/black-sox-it-aint-so-kid-it-just-aint-so/.

33. Shoeless Joe Jackson official site, http://www.shoelessjoejackson.com /about/quotes.html. Daniel J. Voelker and Paul A. Duffy, "Black Sox: 'It ain't so, kid, it just ain't so,'" *Chicago Lawyer,* Sept. 1, 2009, http://www. chicagolawyermagazine.com/2009/09/01/black-sox-it-aint-so-kid-it-just -aint-so/.

34. Alan M. Dershowitz, *America on Trial: Inside The Legal Battles That Transformed Our Nation* (New York: Warner Books, 2004), 239.

35. *Ibid.*

36. Timothy M. Gay, *Tris Speaker, The Rough-And-Tumble Life of a Baseball Legend* (Kearney, Nebraska: Morris Book Publishing, 2007) 227–339.

37. Rhodes, *Ty Cobb: Safe at Home,* 102–103.

38. Mark Alvarez, "Say It Ain't So, Ty," Mr. Baseball, http://www.mrbaseball .com/index 720.php?option=com_content&task=view&id=43&Itemid=61.

39. Both quotes are from Gay, *Tris Speaker, The Rough-and-Tumble Life of a Baseball Legend,* 243.

40. Rhodes, *Ty Cobb: Safe at Home,* 63, 67.

41. Patrick Butters, "Meet the Unknown Slugger," *Insight on the News,* Vol. 14, Sept. 21, 1998, http://encyclopedia.com/doc/1G1-21157150.html.

42. Josh Gibson, *Baseball Library*, http://www.baseballlibrary.com/ballplayers /player.php?name=Josh_Gibson_1911.

43. John Drebinger, "Cox Retracts Admissions on Betting . . . OWNERS HEAR ROBESON – Organized Baseball Urged to Admit Negro Players – Up to Each Club, Lardis Replies," *NYT*, Dec. 4, 1943, 17. Landis, of course, did not add gender to the list. In 1931, a Tennessee farm team had signed a teen-aged pitcher named Jackie Mitchell. She faced the Yankees in an exhibition game and made news when she struck out both Babe Ruth and Lou Gehrig. The following day Landis nullified Mitchell's contract, asserting baseball was "too strenuous" for females. See http://www .baseball -almanac.com/articles /kenesaw_landis_biography.shtml.

44. Paul Robeson and Philip Sheldon Foner, *Paul Robeson Speaks: Writings, Speeches, Interviews 1918–1974* (New York: Citadel Press Books, 1978), 152.

45. Drebinger, *NYT*, Dec. 4, 1943, 17.

46. Peter Golenbock, "Breaking Baseball's Color Barrier," excerpt from *Bums: An Oral History of the Brooklyn Dodgers* (New York: Putnam Adult Books, 1984), http://thatsbaseball1.tripod.com/id147.htm.

47. *Ibid.*

48. Ward and Burns, *Baseball: An Illustrated History*, 44.

49. James D. Robenalt, *The Harding Affair, Love and Espionage During the Great War* (New York: Palgrave Macmillan, 2009).

50. Rich Cohen, *Tough Jews: Fathers, Sons, and Gangster Dreams* (London: Vintage Books, 1999), 53; see also Linda Grant, "Defenders of the faith," *The Guardian*, July 6, 2002, http://www.guardian.ca.uk/books/2002 /jul/06/.featuresreviews.guardianreview10.

Chapter 7
LEGAL LYNCHING OF SACCO AND VANZETTI
Biased Judicial System Gives American Justice an International Black Eye

1. George and Willene Hendrick (eds.), *Carl Sandburg, Selected Poems*, "Legal Midnight Hour," *Poems of Protest*, (New York: Harvest Books, 1996), 63, https://books.google.com/books?id=NmUWLxwhsWMC&pg=PA63& lpg=PA63&dq=Legal+Midnight+HOur&source=bl&ots=jdNNhBN71d &sig=lQvIQTdcF-rkWNxkArGjowqa1Aw&hl=en&sa=X&ved=0ahUKEwj 7m9XJ-vfSAhUDx2MKHciPCTUQ6AEIGjAA#v=onepage&q=Legal%20 Midnight%20HOur&f=false. Accessed March 25, 2017.

2. Clyde Haberman, "New Yorkers Speaking Softly," http://cityroom.blog .nytimes. com/2011/07/12/new–yorkers–speaking–softly/. In July of 2011, Republican Congressional candidate Bob Turner invoked Roosevelt's 100 percent American speech in his successful campaign for Democrat Anthony Weiner's former seat in New York's Ninth District.

3. F. Russell, *Sacco and Vanzetti: The Case Resolved* (New York: Harper & Row, 1986), 80.

4. Boston Police Strike, http://www.u-s-history.com/pages/h1348.html. Accessed August 2, 2017.

5. "First Lady Biography Edith Wilson," http://www.firstladies.org/biographies

/firstladies.aspx?biography=29. Accessed August 2, 2017.

6. Robert Grant and Joseph Katz, *The Great Trials of the Twenties: The Watershed Decade in America's Courtrooms* (New York: Sarpedon, 1998), 50.

7. Elizabeth Gage, *The Day Wall Street Exploded: A Story of America in its First Age of Terror* (Oxford: Oxford Univ. Press, 2009), caption and photograph of flyer following page 150.

8. "Vanzetti Files Plea in Fight to Cheat Death," *The Lima News*, Lima, Ohio, May 5, 1927, 7.

9. "Radicals' Cause May be Assisted," *The North Adams Transcript*, July 11, 1927, 1; Moshik Temkin, *The Sacco-Vanzetti Affair: America on Trial* (New Haven: Yale Univ. Press, 2009), Kindle location 203–205.

10. Will, "The Trial That Scarred A Nation," cited in Temkin, *The Sacco-Vanzetti Affair*, n. 88, Kindle location 4410.

11. Russell, *Sacco and Vanzetti: The Case Resolved*, 116.

12. See, e.g., Isa Engleberg, *Working in Groups: Communication Principles and Strategies* (My Communication Kit Series, 2006), 133.

13. Grant and Katz, *The Great Trials of the Twenties*, 42.

14. Felix Frankfurter, "The Case of Sacco and Vanzetti," *The Atlantic Monthly*, March 1927. In Francis Russell's otherwise highly credible account, *Sacco and Vanzetti: The Case Resolved*, pages 110–116, Russell dubiously defends Thayer's fairness, based primarily on two biased sources: interviews of the jurors, with their own verdict to defend, and court personnel who might likewise be presumed to support their presiding judge from attacks on his performance. Russell states that both groups believed Thayer ran a very fair trial and dismisses, without discussion, Thayer's prejudicial out-of-court statements sworn to by reputable disinterested parties, who later submitted similar affidavits to the Lowell Commission. Most troubling of all, Russell rejects veteran attorney Thompson's testimony before the Lowell Commission that Thayer used a sarcastic and abrupt tone of voice and dismissive body language to convey his intense dislike for the defendants and their lead counsel. Russell fails to address the substantial impact of nonverbal cues from tone of voice and body language. Words used by a speaker – all that is left in a written record – generally account for 30 to 40 percent of communication. (See note 12, above.)

15. "Sacco Vanzetti Ordeal Haunts Longtime Advocate," *Boston Globe*, June 18, 1998, http://www.highbeam.com/doc/1p2-8487281.htm.

16. Gage, *The Day Wall Street Exploded*, 312–313, citing Louis Post, "The Deportations Delirium of Nineteen-Twenty: A Personal Narrative of an Historic Official Experience" (Chicago: C.H. Kerr & Company, 1923), 307.

17. *Ibid.*

18. *Ibid.*, 322–323.

19. *Ibid.*

20. Temkin, *The Sacco-Vanzetti Affair*, Kindle location 575–579.

21. *Ibid.*, location 590–592.

22. *Ibid.*, location 608–610.

23. Grant and Katz, *The Great Trials of the Twenties*, 48-49.

24. *Ibid.*, 49.

25. Leslie Burdick, "Sacco and Vanzetti – The Jury is Still Out," *The Sun*, Lowell,

Massachusetts, Aug. 2, 1977, 30.

26. Paul Avrich, *Sacco and Vanzetti: The Anarchist Background* (Princeton: Princeton Univ. Press, 1991), 204–207.

Chapter 8
TEENAGE SOCIOPATHS
Life or Death for Leopold and Loeb?

1. Simon Baatz, *For the Thrill of It: Leopold, Loeb and the Murder That Shocked Chicago* (New York: Harper Collins, 2008), 70 (reproduction of ransom note).
2. Clarence Darrow, *The Story of My Life* (New York: DaCapo Press, 1996), 232.
3. *Ibid.*, 233.
4. Stone, *Clarence Darrow for the Defense*, 450.
5. Hal Higdon, *Leopold and Loeb, The Crime of the Century* (Illinois: G. P. Putnam's Sons,1996), 138.
6. *Ibid.*, 140.
7. *Ibid.*, 159.
8. Douglas O. Linder, "Famous Trials: Leopold and Loeb," http://www.law.umkc.edu/faculty/projects/ftrials/leoploeb/BIO_CAVE.HTM. Accessed June 30, 2011.
9. "Weird and Haunted Chicago: A Guide to the Ghosts, Local Legends and Unsolved Mysteries of the Windy City: Leopold and Loeb, Chicago's Thrill Killers," http://www .prairieghosts.com/leopold.html. Accessed March 6, 2015.
10. Darrow, *The Story of My Life*, 242.
11. Grant and Katz, *The Great Trials of the Twenties*, 190–191.
12. *Ibid.*
13. Baatz, *For the Thrill of It*, 401.
14. *Ibid.*, 402.
15. *Ibid.*, 406.
16. Dershowitz, *America on Trial*, 261.
17. Linder, "Famous Trials: Leopold and Loeb," http://www.law.umkc.edu/faculty/projects/ftrials/leoploeb/BIO_CAVE.HTM. Accessed June 29, 2011.
18. Baatz, *For the Thrill of It*, 462.
19. "Governor Ryan declares moratorium on executions, will appoint commission to review capital punishment system," press release, Jan. 31, 2000, http://www.illinois.gov/PressReleases/ShowPressRelease.cfm?. Accessed June 30, 2011.
20. Mark Berman, "Pennsylvania's Governor Suspends the Death Penalty," *The Washington Post*, February 13, 2015, http://www.washingtonpost.com/news/post-nation/wp/2015/02/13/pennsylvania-suspends-the-death-penalty/. Accessed February 23, 2015.
21. *Roper v. Simmons* (2005) 543 U.S. 551, 575.
22. *Miller v. Alabama* 567 U.S. at (2012) [slip opn. p. 15], http://caselaw.findlaw.com/us-supreme-court/10-9646.html.

Chapter 9
THE DARK SIDE OF THE SCOPES TRIAL
White Supremacists on Both Sides Embrace Genocidal Acts

1. Quote from John Scopes, http://www.goodreads.com/quotes/922052-i
    -furnished-the-body-that-was-needed-to-sit-in. Accessed June 30, 2011.
2. Edward J. Larson, *Summer for the Gods: The Scopes Trial and America's
    Continuing Debate Over Science and Religion* (New York: Basic Books, Perseus
    Book Group, 1997), 265.
3. Larson, *Summer for the Gods*, 83.
4. *Ibid.*, 12–13.
5. *Ibid.*, 15.
6. *Ibid.* 40–41.
7. The Butler Act as reprinted in *NYT,* July 18, 1925, 1.
8. Larson, *Summer for the Gods*, 71 and fn. 28, citing Darrow biographer Kevin
    Tierney *Darrow: A Biography* (New York: Booksales, 1981).
9. Harry Laughlin's "Model Eugenical Sterilization Law," reproduced by Asst.
    Prof. Alex Wellerstein of the Stevenson Institute of Technology in "Harry
    Laughlin's Model Law," http://alexwellerstein.com/laughlin/. Accessed
    March 6, 2015.
10. George W. Hunter, *A Civic Biology Presented in Problems* (New York: American
    Book Co., 1914), 195 –196, reproduced at Google Books, http://books
    .google.com/books?id=-yl
11. *Ibid.*, 261.
12. *Ibid.* 263. See also David Klinghoffer, "The Dark Side of Darwinism,"
    The Huffington Post, July 1, 2010, www.huffingtonpost.com/david
    -klinghoffer/the-dark-side. Accessed March 6, 2015.
13. Jack Shafer, "Fourth Estate: 1924: The Wildest Convention in U.S.
    History," *Politico, March 7, 2916,* http://www.politico.com/magazine/
    story/2016/03/1924-the-craziest-convention-in-us-history-213708.   See
    also Patricia Bernstein, "We used to talk about immigrants this way –
    nearly a century ago,"*TribTalk,* February 24, 2017, https://www.tribtalk.
    org/2017/02/24/we-used-to-talk-about-immigrants-this-way-nearly-a-
    century-ago/IMMIGRATION.
14. Larson, *Summer for the Gods*, 140.
15. Stone, *Clarence Darrow for the Defense*, 486.
16. Larson, *Summer for the Gods*, 142 and fn. 100.
17. Stone, *Clarence Darrow for the Defense*, 493.
18. Larson, *Summer for the Gods*, 150.
19. *Ibid.*, 154 and fn. 18.
20. Douglas O. Linder, "What is THE trial of the century?" Jan. 28, 1999,
    http://www.law.umkc.edu/faculty/projects/ftrials/century.html.
    Accessed June 30, 2011.
21. *Ibid.*
22. Edward McGlynn Gaffney, Jr., "How the Scopes Trial Framed the Modern
    Debate Over Science and Religion," *LAT,* July 12, 1998, http://articles
    .latimes.com/1998/jul/12/ books/bk-2824. Accessed June 30, 2011.

23. Although the ACLU attacked the statute under which Scopes was convicted on several constitutional grounds, the only argument that persuaded the Tennessee Supreme Court was that the state constitution then prohibited judges from setting fines over $50, i.e., the Scopes jury should have decided to award the $100 minimum fine, not the trial judge. The high court then went further and recommended that the prosecutor decline to retry the case since Scopes was no longer teaching in Tennessee. (*Scopes v. State*, 154 Tenn. 105 (1927).) The prosecutor followed that recommendation and dropped the case.

24. George William Hunter, *New Civic Biology: Presented in Problems* (New York: American Book Co., 1926), 250–51, 411–12.

25. *Buck v. Bell*, 274 U.S. 200 (1927). Justice Oliver Wendell Holmes, Jr., authored the 8 to 1 opinion authorizing involuntary tubal ligation of teenager Carrie Buck. The high court assumed this procedure was for the public benefit, based solely on a state-employed doctor labeling both Carrie (who had given birth to a baby after being raped) and her mother "feebleminded and promiscuous." In the opinion, Justice Holmes famously stated, "Three generations of imbeciles are enough" (274 U.S. 200 at 207). This characterization of the family later proved unfounded. See Margarita Tartakovsky, "Eugenics & The Story of Carrie Buck," PsychCentral, http://psychcentral.com/blog/archives/2011/01/24/eugenics-the-story-of-carrie-buck/. Accessed April 8, 2015. Fifteen years after *Buck v. Bell*, in *Skinner v. Oklahoma* 16 U.S. 535 (1942), the U.S. Supreme Court curtailed the broad sweep of its prior decision. It used a strict scrutiny test to declare unconstitutional an Oklahoma law that authorized sterilization of a chicken thief as a man within a class of targeted felons while excluding those who committed similar white-collar crimes.

26. Timothy Ryback, "Hitler's Bedtime Reading," October 17, 2008, http://www.thedailybeast.com/articles/2008/10/17/hitlers-bedtime-reading.htm. Accessed March 6, 2015.

27. Klinghoffer, "The Dark Side of Darwinism," *The Huffington Post*, July 1, 2010, www.huffingtonpost.com/david-klinghoffer/the-dark-side. Accessed March 6, 2015.

28. *Epperson v. Arkansas*, 393 U.S. 97 (1968).

Chapter 10
A BLACK MAN'S CASTLE
The Sweet Murder Trials Launch the NAACP Legal Defense Fund as the KKK Collapses

1. Stone, *Clarence Darrow for the Defense*, 538.

2. Boyle, *Arc of Justice*, 118.

3. *Ibid.*, 155.

4. Douglas O. Linder, "Famous Trials: The Sweet Trials," http://www.law.umkc.edu/faculty/projects/ftrials/sweet/sweetaccount.HTM. Accessed June 29, 2011); Marcet Haldeman-Julius, *Clarence Darrow's Two Great Trials* (Girard, Kansas: Haldeman-Julius Company, 1927), 45.

5. Linder, *op. cit.* Accessed June 30, 2011.

6. Boyle, *Arc of Justice*, 32, 37.
7. *Ibid.*, 196.
8. *Ibid.*, 225.
9. *Ibid.*, 139.
10. *Ibid.*, 245–246.
11. Linder, "Famous Trials: The Sweet Trials." Opening Statement of Arthur Garfield Hays, http://law2.umkc.edu/faculty/projects/ftrials/sweet/transcriptexcerpts.HTM# Opening Statement. Accessed June 30, 2011.
12. "Stephenson Sentenced," *Indianapolis News*, Nov. 16, 1925, 1.
13. Boyle, *Arc of Justice*, 289.
14. Linder, "Famous Trials: The Sweet Trials, Transcript Excerpts," http://www.law.umkc.edu/faculty/projects/ftrials/sweet/transcriptexcerpts.HTM. Accessed June 30, 2011.
15. Haldeman-Julius, *Clarence Darrow's Two Great Trials*, 54.
16. "Sweet Trial Is Race Issue, Darrow Insists," *Detroit Free Press*, April 21, 1926.
17. Haldeman-Julius, *Clarence Darrow's Two Great Trials*, 55.
18. Boyle, *Arc of Justice*, 329. Additional excerpts from the closing argument of Thomas Chawke are set forth in Linder, "Famous Trials: The Sweet Trials," http://law2.umkc.edu/faculty/projects/ftrials/sweet/chawkespeech.html. Accessed June 30, 2011.
19. Linder, "Famous Trials: The Sweet Trials, Darrow Summation," http://www.law.umkc.edu/faculty/projects/ftrials/sweet/darrowsummation.html. Accessed June 30, 2011.
20. "Charge to the jury in the case of MICHIGAN v. HENRY SWEET Detroit, Michigan by Judge Frank Murphy," May 13, 1926, http://law2.umkc.edu/faculty/projects/ftrials/sweet/chargetojury.html. Accessed June 30, 2011.
21. "The Law of Love," *This Case Is Close to My Heart*, American History Feature, HistoryNet.Com, August 2000, http://www.historynet.com/this-case-is-close-to-my-heart-page-1-august-2000-american-history-feature.htm/6. Accessed June 30, 2011.
22. Linder, "Famous Trials: The Sweet Trials, Darrow Summation," *op. cit.* Accessed June 30, 2011.
23. Boyle, *Arc of Justice*, 344 and fn. 14.
24. Darrow, *The Story of My Life*, 311.
25. David Cunningham, "The Ku Klux Klan in History and Today," OUP Blog: Oxford University Press's Academic Insights for the Thinking World, January 14, 2015, http://blog.oup.com/2015/01/klansville-usa-david-cunningham-ku-klux-klan/ Accessed April 11, 2015.
26. *Korematsu v. United States*, 323 U.S.214, 65 S. Ct. 193, 240, Justice Murphy dissenting (1944).
27. The phrase "White Supremacy" appears twice in the Chief Justice's opinion in *Loving v. Virginia* 388 U.S. 1, (1967). According to Prof. Sheryll Cashin, author of *Loving: Interracial Intimacy in America and the Threat to White Supremacy* (Boston: Beacon Press, 2017), Warren was the first justice to use the term in any Supreme Court opinion. Sheryll Cashin, "Interracial Love Is Saving America," Opinion, *NYT Sunday Review,* June 4, 2017, 3.
28. G. Edward White, "The Unacknowledged Lesson: Earl Warren and the

Japanese Relocation Controversy," *VQR,* Autumn 1979, quoting Earl Warren, *The Memoirs of Chief Justice Earl Warren* (Lanham, Maryland: Madison Books, Roman and Littlefield, 1977), http://www.vqronline .org/essay/unacknowledged-lesson-earl-warren-and-japanese-relocation -controversy. Accessed June 5, 2017.

29. Chris Hayes, *A Colony in a Nation* (New York: W.W. Norton & Company, 2017), 116.

30. Caroline Light, "'Stand Your Ground' Expansion That Expands Inequality," *NYT,* March 23, 2017, https://www.nytimes.com/2017/03/23/opinion/a -stand-your-ground-expansion-that-expands-inequality.html.

31. *Ibid.*

Chapter 11
ALABAMA STAND-OFF
The Railroading of the Scottsboro Boys Prompts Two
Landmark Supreme Court Decisions

1. Elizabeth Blair, "The Strange Story the Man Who Wrote *Strange Fruit*" NPR, Sept. 5, 2012, http://www.npr.org/2012/09/05/158933012/the -strange-story-of-the-man-behind-strange-fruit.

2. Maria Weston Chapman (ed.), *The Liberty Bell: Testimony Against Slavery* (Whitefish, Montana: Kessinger Publishing, 2007), 29–30; quoting a letter from Alexis de Tocqueville.

3. Campbell Parker, "History of Lynchings in the South Documents. Nearly 4000 Names," *NYT,* February 10, 2015, http://www.nytimes .com/2015/02/10/us/history-of-lynchings-in-the-south-documents -nearly-4000-names.html. The new list of documented lynchings from 1877 to 1950 includes about 700 names not on any prior lists. Accessed February 25, 2015.

4. A diagram showing where on the train each defendant and the two alleged victims were found is provided in Douglas Linder, "The Trials of the Scottsboro Boys," http://law2.umkc.edu/faculty/projects/ftrials /scottsboro/SB_train.html. Accessed September 10, 2012.

5. "The Scottsboro Boys: Jim Crow on Trial," *Crime Magazine, An Encyclopedia of Crime,* July 13, 2009, http://www.crimemagazine.com/scottsboro_boys .htm. Accessed June 30, 2011.

6. James Goodman, *Stories of Scottsboro* (New York: Pantheon Books, 1994), 16.

7. Douglas O. Linder, "The Trials of the Scottsboro Boys," http://law2.umkc .edu/faculty/projects/ftrials/scottsboro/SB_acct.html. Accessed June 30, 2011.

8. James R. Acker, *Scottsboro and Its Legacy* (Westport, Connecticut.: Praeger Publishing, 2008), 26; see also David Aretha, *The Trial of the Scottsboro Boys* (Greensboro, North Carolina: Morgan Reynolds Publishing, 2008).

9. Stone, *Clarence Darrow for the Defense,* 559.

10. *Weems et al. v. State* (1932) 224 Ala. 524, 141 So. 215.

11. *Powell v. State of Alabama* 287 U.S. 45, 71 (1932).

12. Goodman, *Stories of Scottsboro,* 211.

13. Garry Morgan, "Sheriff Matt Wann, a brave man and the untold story,

secrets and questions, the story of a murder," Scottsboro Stories, October 27, 2010, http://scottsborostories.blogspot.com/2010/10/sheriff-matt-wann-brave-man-and-untold.html. Accessed March 10, 2013.

14. Douglas O. Linder, "Famous Trials: The Scottsboro Boys; Excerpts from the summation of Wade Wright," http://www.law.umkc.edu/faculty/projects/FTrials /scottsboro/wr-summations.html. Accessed June 30, 2011.

15. Douglas O. Linder, "Famous Trials: Judge Horton Orders a New Trial in the Case of Haywood Patterson," June 22, 1933, http://law2.umkc.edu/faculty /projects/FTrials/scottsboro/Exhorton.htm. Accessed June 30, 2011.

16. F. Raymond Daniell, "Roosevelt Is Asked to Intervene to Protect Scottsboro Negroes," NYT, Nov. 20, 1933, 1.

17. Huddie William Ledbetter (known professionally as "Leadbelly"), "Scottsboro Boys" song, https://genius.com/Leadbelly-scottsboro-boys-lyrics.

18. Langston Hughes, "Scottsboro," https://www.poetrynook.com/poem /scottsboro-0.

19. Morgan, "Sheriff Matt Wann, a brave man and the untold story, secrets and questions, the story of a murder," http://scottsborostories.blogspot .com/2010/10/sheriff-matt-wann-brave-man-and-untold.html.

20. "The Best of the Century," Time, Dec. 31, 1999, http://www.time.com /time/magazine/article/0, 9171, 993039, 00.html. Accessed June 30, 2011.

21. See Mary L. Dudziak, Cold War Civil Rights (Princeton, New Jersey: Princeton Univ. Press, 2000).

22. See Jack Epstein, "Baseball's conscience finally gets his due," SFC, July 10, 2005, A1,13, citing Irwin Silber, Press Box Red: The Story of Lester Rodney, the Communist Who Helped Break the Color Line in American Sports (Philadelphia: Temple Univ. Press, 2003).

23. "Desegregation of the Armed Forces: Chronology," Truman Library, http://www.trumanlibrary.org/whistlestop/studycollections/desegregation /large/indexphp?action=chronology. Accessed June 29, 2011.

24. Thomas B. Edsall, "Lott Decried for Part of Salute to Thurmond: GOP Senate Leader Hails Colleague's Run as Segregationist," Common Dreams .org, Dec. 7, 2003, http:// www.commondreams.org/headlines02/1207-01 .htm. Accessed June 30, 2011.

25. "Alabama Anything But Gentlemanly," Time, May 10,1948, http://www .time.com/time/magazine/article/0,9171,804636,00.html. Accessed June 30, 2011.

26. Jessica Mitford, A Fine Old Conflict (New York: Vintage Books 1956, 1977), 193.

27. Leslie Brody, Irrepressible: The Life and Times of Jessica Mitford (Berkeley, California: Counterpoint, 2010), 174.

28. David E. Stannard, Honor Killing: How the Infamous "Massie Affair" Transformed Hawai'i (New York: Viking Penguin Books, 2005), 305.

Chapter 12
THE MASSIE AFFAIR
False Charges of Gang Rape Set the Stage for Hawaiian Statehood

1. The "Fake Summons Used in the Kidnapping of Joseph Kahahawai in January 1932" is reproduced in Prof. Douglas O. Linder's Famous Trials, "The Massie (Honor Killing) Trials *1931–2*", http://law2.umkc.edu /faculty/projects/ftrials/massie/summons.html. Accessed April 8, 2015.

2. John F. Galliher, Larry W. Koch, David Patrick Keys, Teresa J. Guess, *America Without the Death Penalty: States Lead the Way* (Boston: Northeastern Univ. Press, 2005), 159. Campbell Parker, "History of Lynchings in the South Documents Nearly 4000 Names," *NYT*, February 10, 2015, http:// www.ytimes.com/2015/02/10/us/history-of-lynchings-in-the-south -documents-nearly-4000-names.html. Accessed February 11, 2015.

3. Stannard, *Honor Killing: How the Infamous "Massie Affair" Transformed Hawai'i* (New York: Viking Penguin Books, 2005), 55.

4. Uelmen, *Lessons From the Trial: The People v. O. J. Simpson*, 114.

5. Stannard, *Honor Killing*, 103.

6. *American Experience: The Massie Affair*, PBS, http://www.pbs.org/wgbh /amexmassie/peopleevents/p_suspects.html. Accessed June 30, 2011.

7. Douglas O. Linder, "Famous Trials: The Massie Trials: A Commentary," 2007, http://law2.umkc.edu/faculty/projects/ftrials/massie / massietrialsaccount.html. Accessed June 28, 2011.

8. *Ibid.*

9. Uelmen, *Lessons From the Trial*, 129.

10. Stannard, *Honor Killing*, 212.

11. Cobey Black, *Hawaii Scandal* (Waipahu, Hawaii: Island Heritage, 2002), 94.

12. *Ibid.* 94–97.

13. Stannard, *Honor Killing*, 212–215.

14. *Ibid.*, 222.

15. Galliher *et al.*, *America Without the Death Penalty*, 161 and fn. 54.

16. *Personal Justice Denied, Report of the Commission on Wartime Relocation and Internment of Civilians* (Seattle, Washington: Univ. of Washington Press, 1982), Chapter 11, Military Rule, fn. 31, http://www.hps.gov/history /history/online-books/personal-justice-denied/chapll.htm.

17. Linder, "Famous Trials: The Massie Affair," http://www.law.umkc.edu /faculty/projects/FTRIALS/massie/massietrialsaccount.htm. Accessed June 28, 2011.

18. Peter Van Slingerland, *Something Terrible Has Happened: The Account of the Sensational Thalia Massie Affair Which Burst From Prewar Hawaii to Incense a Nation* (New York: Harper & Row, 1966), "Confession of the Killer of Joe Kahahawai, Deacon Jones," 316–322, quote at 319.

19. Stannard, *Honor Killing*, 267.

20. Linder, "Famous Trials: The Massie Affair," http://www.law.umkc.edu /faculty/projects/FTRIALS/massie/massietrialsaccount.htm. Accessed June 28, 2011.

21. "Races: Lust in Paradise," *Time*, Dec. 28, 1931, http://www.time.com /time/magazine/article/0,9171,753207,00.html. In. 161, fn. 53. Accessed

June 30, 2011.

22. Stone, *Clarence Darrow for the Defense*, 565.

23. Stannard, *Honor Killing*, 400.

24. Darrow, *The Story of My Life*, 458.

25. Stannard, *Honor Killing*, 301.

26. *Ibid.*, 322.

27. *Ibid.*, 321.

28. Van Slingerland, *Something Terrible Has Happened*, 318.

29. Darrow, *The Story of My Life*, 467.

30. Van Slingerland, *Something Terrible Has Happened*, 316–322.

31. Linder, "Famous Trials: The Massie Affair," http://www.law.umkc.edu/faculty/projects/FTRIALS/massie/massietrialsaccount.html. Accessed June 28, 2011.

32. Richard A. Hawkins, "Princess Abigail Kawananakoa: The Forgotten Territorial Native Hawaiian Leader," *Hawai'i Journal of History*, Vol. 37 (2003) 163, http://www.evols.li brary.manoa.hawaii.edu/bitstream/10524/354/2/JL37167.pdf. Accessed June 30, 2011.

33. Linder, "Famous Trials: The Massie Affair," *op. cit.* Accessed June 28, 2011.

34. "Remarks by the President at the Funeral Service for Senator Daniel Ken Inouye," December 12, 2012, https://obamawhitehouse.archives.gov/the-press-office/2012/12/21/remarks-president-funeral-service-senator-daniel-ken-inouye. Accessed June 6, 2017.

Chapter 13
THE LINDBERGH BABY KILLING
Law Enforcement Helps Cover Up Key Evidence in "The Crime of the Century"

1. Douglas O. Linder, "Famous Trials: Richard Hauptmann Lindbergh Kidnapping Trial," http://law2.umkc.edu/faculty/projects/ftrials/Hauptmann/hauptmannletter.html.

2. Knappman et al., ed., *Great American Trials: From the Salem Witch Trials to Rodney King* (Detroit: Visible Ink Press, 1994), 320.

3. Jim Fisher, *FBI Summary Report: The Lindbergh Case* (New Brunswick, New Jersey: Rutgers Univ. Press, 1987, 1994), 129.

4. *Ibid.*, 129 and fn. 7, citing Al Dunlap, "Why No Lie Detector for the Lindbergh Case?" *The Detective*, Sept. 1932.

5. *Ibid.*, 437, fn. 13.

6. Lloyd Gardner, *The Case That Never Dies: The Lindbergh Kidnapping* (New Brunswick, New Jersey: Rutgers Univ. Press, 2004), 107–108.

7. *Ibid.*, 220, fn. 60.

8. Ludovic Kennedy, *The Airman and the Carpenter: The Lindbergh Kidnapping and the Framing of Richard Hauptmann* (New York: Viking Penguin, 1985), 240, fn. 2.

9. Gregory Ahlgren and Stephen Monier, *The Crime of the Century: The Lindbergh Kidnapping Hoax* (Boston: Brandon Books, 1993), 140.

10. *Brady v. Maryland*, 373 U.S. 83 (1963).

11. Fisher, in *The Lindbergh Case*, 249–250, relies on a police diary notation, but acknowledges that the FBI was quite skeptical at the time of the voice

identification by Lindbergh of such few words spoken two-and-a-half years earlier. Lloyd Gardner, in *The Case That Never Dies*, 188–191 and 202, questions the reliability of Fisher's source, noting that the contemporaneous reports were that Lindbergh could not identify Hauptmann when asked to do so before trial. Ahlgren and Monier in *The Crime of the Century: The Lindbergh Kidnapping Hoax*, 165–166, criticize the inherent unreliability of the method by which Lindbergh was asked to identify Hauptmann's voice both before and at trial.

12. Gardner, *The Case That Never Dies*, 162–163 and fn. 48.

13. Kennedy, *The Airman and the Carpenter*, 179.

14. Gardner, *The Case That Never Dies*, 161.

15. *Ibid.*, 344 and fn. 45.

16. Dershowitz, *America on Trial*, 274, citing Sidney P. Whipple, *The Trial of Bruno Richard Hauptmann* (Birmingham, Alabama: The Notable Trials Library, 1989), 561–563.

17. Kennedy, *The Airman and the Carpenter*, 342.

18. "Darrow Urges Delay," *NYT*, April 2, 1936, 2.

19. Ahlgren and Monier, *The Lindbergh Kidnapping Hoax*, 272–275.

20. Fisher, *The Lindbergh Case*, 5.

21. Hugo Adam Bedau and Michael L. Radelet, "Miscarriages of Justice in Potentially Capital Cases," 40 *Stanford Law Review* 21 (1987) 124–25 and fn. 582. The two professors noted that the Hauptmann trial featured an "atmosphere of near-hysteria" and a "grossly incompetent defense attorney." In addition, review of a number of independent analyses of the proceedings led them to conclude: "There is no doubt that the conviction rested in part on corrupt prosecutorial practices, suppression of evidence, intimidation of witnesses, perjured testimony, and Hauptmann's prior record." See also Mary E. Williams (ed.), *Is the Death Penalty Fair?* (Farmington Hills, Minnesota: Greenhaven Press, 2003), 48 ["Doubt about the guilt of the condemned man is a common thread in some of the most celebrated murder trials in this nation's history. Bruno Richard Hauptmann's chances for a fair trial in the Lindbergh kidnapping – and the ability truly to ascertain his guilt or innocence – were compromised by perjured testimony, tampering with exhibits, and the suppression by the New Jersey state police of exculpatory evidence."]

22. Kim Chandler, "Man Freed From Death Row: Prosecutors Will 'Answer to God,'" Associated Press, April 4, 2015. http://abcnews.go.com/US/wireStory /ala-man-death-row-prosecutors-answer-god-300960941. Accessed April 4, 2015.

23. C. Ronald Huff, "Wrongful Conviction: Causes and Public Policy Issues," 18 *Criminal Justice*. 15 (Spring 2003), 18.

24. Kennedy, *The Airman and the Carpenter*, 6.

25. "The Lindbergh Kidnapping Hoax," http://www.lindberghkidnapping hoax.com/. Accessed June 30, 2011.

26. See discussion in Geis and Bienen, *Crimes of the Century: From Leopold and Loeb to O. J. Simpson*, 116–120, "Bruno Richard Hauptmann (1932), Public Outrage, and Criminal Justice."

27. Michael Newton, *The Encyclopedia of Unsolved Crimes* (New York: Checkmark Books, 2004), 257.
28. Gardner, *The Case That Never Dies*, 344.
29. Robert R. Bryan, "The Execution of the Innocent: The Tragedy of the Hauptmann-Lindbergh and Bigelow Cases," 18 *NYU Review of Law and Social Change* (1990–91), 831, 833; see also authorities cited in fn. 20.
30. Geis and Bienen, *Crimes of the Century*, 116.
31. Fisher, *The Lindbergh Case*, 5.

CONCLUSION

1. Michael D. Shear and Matt Apuzzo, "Trump Fires Comey Amid Russia Inquiry," *NYT*, May 10, 2017; reproduction of termination letter to Director Comey signed by President Trump, 1.
2. David R. Davies (ed.), *The Press and Race* (Jackson, Mississippi: Univ. Press of Mississippi, 2001), 41, quoting the *Jackson Daily News* and *The Meridian Star*.
3. Ward Churchill and Jim Vander Wall, *The COINTELPRO Papers* (Cambridge, Massahusetts: South End Press, 1990, 2002), 95–99, quoting from internal FBI memos. In 1975, the Select Committee to Study Governmental Operations with respect to Intelligence Activities United States Senate, chaired by Senator Frank Church, undertook extensive hearings and issued reports ("the Church Committee Report"). The Church Committee found, to its astonishment, that Hoover had instructed all the FBI's branch offices to treat the nonviolent Southern Christian Leadership Conference, led by Dr. King, as a "Black Nationalist 'Hate Group.'"(See the Church Committee's Final Report, Book III, "COINTELPRO: The FBI's Covert Action Programs Against American Citizens" (Washington, D.C.: U.S. Gov't Printing Office, April 23, 1976), 4 (citing a memo from headquarters to all SACs, dated 8/25/67, p. 2.) The Committee further found that "From December 1963 until his death in 1968, Martin Luther King, Jr. was the target of an intensive campaign by the Federal Bureau of Investigation to 'neutralize' him as an effective civil rights leader. In the words of the man in charge of the FBI's 'war' against Dr. King: 'No holds were barred. We have used [similar] techniques against Soviet agents.'" See Church Committee, Final Report, "Dr. Martin Luther King, Jr.: A Case Study," Intro., 1.
4. *Ibid.*, 2. At J. Edgar Hoover's request, Attorney Gen. Robert Kennedy approved wiretaps on Dr. King's home. The SCLC headquarters and Dr. King's associates were also bugged, as were motel rooms where Dr. King stayed. Hoover was outraged when the Nobel committee announced that King would be the recipient of its 1964 Peace Prize. In response, the FBI tried blackmail. Within days of the announcement, the FBI sent King a package featuring a string of "highlights" from illegal audiotapes of his sex life, and an anonymous threat to go public and reveal him as an "evil, abnormal beast." The letter warned "you are done" and gave him 34 days to do the "one thing left for you to do. You know what it is. . . . There is but one way out for you. You better take it before your filthy, abnormal fraudulent self is bared to the nation." (Churchill and

Vander Wall, *The COINTELPRO Papers*, 99.) The Senate Committee heard conflicting testimony on this episode. Its report notes, "According to the Chief of the FBI's Domestic Intelligence Division, the tape was intended to precipitate a separation between Dr. King and his wife in the belief that the separation would reduce Dr. King's stature . . . . Dr. King and his advisers interpreted [the note] as a threat to release the tape recording unless Dr. King committed suicide." *Ibid.*, 2.

5. Campbell Robertson, "Last Chapter for a Court With a Place in History," *NYT*, September 17, 2012, http://topics.nytimes.com/top/reference/timestopics/people/r/campbell_robertson/index.html. Accessed April 13, 2015.

6. Warren Hinckle, *If You Have a Lemon, Make Lemonade* (New York: W.W. Norton, 1973), 30.

7. Bob Herbert, "What Color Is That Baby?" *NYT* editorial page, May 11, 2009.

8. "Baldus Study (Capital Punishment)," U.S. Civil Liberties Org., http://uscivilliberties.org/themes/3159-baldus-study.html. Accessed April 17, 2015.

9. *McCleskey v. Kemp*, 481 U.S. 279 at 313 (1987).

10. Adam Liptak, "David C. Baldus, 75, Dies; Studied Race and the Law,"*NYT*, June 15, 2011, A23; referencing John C. Jeffries, Jr.'s *Justice Lewis F. Powell, Jr.: A Biography* (New York: Fordham University Press, 2001), 451.

11. See, e.g., Anthony Amsterdam, "Race and the Death Penalty Before and After *McCleskey*," *Columbia Human Rights Law Review* 39: 34 (2007); Steven Graines and Justin Wyatt, "The Rehnquist Court, Legal Process Theory, and *McCleskey v. Kemp*," *American Journal of Criminal Law* 28: 1 (2000).

12. Leigh Raiford, *Imprisoned in a Luminous Glare* (Chapel Hill, North Carolina: Univ. of North Carolina Press, 2011), 210.

13. Gwen Ifill, *The Breakthrough: Politics and Race in the Age of Obama* (New York: Random House, Anchor Books, 2009), 148.

14. The term first became popular in the 1990s and has made a recent resurgence. See, e.g., Kai Ryssdal,"Angry white men love Trump, and here's why," August 22, 2016, https://www.marketplace.org/2016/08/12/elections/angry-white-men-love-trump-and-heres-why. Michael Kimmel, *Angry White Men: American Masculinity at the End of an Era* (New York: Nation Books, 2013).

15. John Wocjik, COMMENTARY Holocaust Museum Dr. Tiller: "Janet Napolitano Saw It Coming," June 12, 2009, www.peoplesworld.org /commentary-holocaust-museum-drtiller-janet-napolitano-saw-it-coming/. Accessed June 25, 2011.

16. Kate Taylor, "The Thorny Path to a National Black Museum," *NYT*, Jan. 23, 2011, 1, 22.

17. Emily Yahr, "Read George W. Bush's speech at the African American Museum, 13 years after signing the bill to build it," *The Washington Post*, Sept. 24, 2016, p/2016/09/24/read-george-w-bushs-speech-at-the-african-american-museum-13-years-after-signing-the-bill-to-build-it/?utm_term=.b1c344ea2b55. Accessed June 10, 2017.

18. President Obama's Second Inaugural Address (transcript), *The Washington*

Post, January 21, 2013, http://www.washingtonpost.com/politics /president-obamas-second-inaugural-address-transcript/2013/01/21 /f148d234-63d6-11e2-85f5-a8a9228e55e7_story.html Accessed March 6, 2015. Accessed June 10, 2017.

19. *Ibid.*

20. Michelle Alexander, *The New Jim Crow: Mass Incarceration in the Age of Color Blindness* (New Press, 2010), Kindle location 2355–2361; http://www .disinfo.com/2011/04/more-black-men-now-in-prison-system-than-were -enslaved-before-the-civil-war-began/; "Obama's America and the New Jim Crow: The Recurring Racial Nightmare, The Cyclical Rebirth of Caste," quoted at http://nathanielturner.com/obamasamericaandnewjimcrow .htm. Accessed June 25, 2011.

21. Earl Ofari Hutchinson, "Why Obama Won't Pardon Jack Johnson – Friendly Fire," Los Angeles Newspaper Group, http://www.insidesocal .com/friendlyfire/2010/02/why-obama-wont-pardon-jack-joh.html. Accessed June 30, 2011.

22. "U.S. Has Highest Levels of Illegal Drug Use," *About Health*, June 19, 2014. http://alcoholism.about.com/od/sa/a/drug_use.htm, also stating that usage correlates with higher incomes, see Michelle Alexander's *The New Jim Crow*, chapter three, "The Color of Justice." Alexander summarizes a number of studies that evidence extraordinary percentages of African-Americans imprisoned for drug crimes in recent decades. Human Rights Watch reported that, in 2000, blacks comprised 80 to 90 percent of imprisoned drug offenders in several states and were incarcerated at rates far exceeding their percentage of the offending population in many more. That same year, the National Institute on Drug Abuse reported that white students used both cocaine and heroin at seven times the rate of black students; another study showed that white teenagers were significantly more likely to sell drugs than black students.

23. Hayes, *A Colony in a Nation*, 109.

24. *Ibid.*, 136, 218.

25. Newt Gingrich and Pat Nolan, "Prison reform: A smart way for states to save money and lives," *The Washington Post*, Jan. 7, 2011, http:// www.washingtonpost.com/wp-dyn/content/article/2011/01/06 /AR2011010604386.html. Accessed June 30, 2011.

26. Naomi Shavin, "Criminal Justice: A Republican Governor Is Leading the Country's Most Successful Prison Reform," *The New Republic*, March 31, 2015, http://www.newrepublic.com/article/121425/gop-governor -nathan-deal-leading-us-prison-reform?utmsource=Sailthru&utm _medium=email&utm_term=TNR%20Daily%20Newsletter&utm _campaign=Daily%20Newsletter%20-%204%2F1%2F15. Accessed April 1, 2015.

27. Geneva Sands, "AG Sessions orders tougher prison sentences as the 'right and moral thing to do,'" *ABC News*, May 12, 2017, http://abcnews. go.com/Politics/ag-sessions-orders-tougher-prison-sentences-moral-thing/story?id=47371598. Accessed May 31, 2017.

28. James Forman, Jr., "Justice Springs Eternal," *NYT Sunday Review*, March

25, 2017, 1, https://www.nytimes.com/2017/03/25/opinion/sunday /justice -springs-eternal.html.

29. Matt Welch, "Rand Paul: Sessions Misled Me on Drug Sentencing Senator slams the Attorney General's new directive, and offers new explanation for his confirmation vote," Reason.com, May 16, 2017, http://reason.com/blog/2017/05/16/rand-paul-sessions-misled-me-on -drug-sen. Accessed May 31, 2017.

30. Eli Watkins, "Trump calls Portland stabbings 'unacceptable,'" *CNN*, May 30, 2017, http://www.cnn.com/2017/05/29/politics/donald-trump -portland-attack/. Accessed June 1, 2017. His short tweet appeared to some commentators as insincere; see, e.g., Chauncey DeVega, "Donald Trump's weak condemnation of the Portland attack speaks volumes: He should have stayed silent," *Salon*, May 31, 2017, http://www.salon .com/2017/05/31 /donald-trumps-weak-condemnation-of-the-portland -attack-speaks -volumes-he-should-have-stayed-silent/; Renée Graham, "Too little, too late," *The Boston Globe*, May 30, 2017, https://www.bostonglobe .com/opinion/2017/05/30/too-little-too-late-from-trump-portland -killings /aYdyX06toF0IK55OIRMcIP/story.html. Philip Bump, "Trump's quick to tweet about terror and TV, slower on things like the attack in Portland," *The Washington Post*, May 30, 2017, https://www.washingtonpost .com/news/politics/wp/2017/05/30/trumps-quick-to-tweet-about -terror-and-tv-slower-on-things-like-the-attack-in-portland/?utm_term =.b9b9adac8cad. Accessed June 1, 2017.

31. "MAX stabbing suspect unrepentant at arraignment," KOIN6, May 30, 2017, http://koin.com/2017/05/30/jeremy-christian-expected-in-court -tuesday/. Accessed June 1, 2017.

32. Gillian Flaccus, AP, "Portland Stabbing Victim Micah Fletcher Says City Has 'White Savior Complex,'" May 31, 2017, http://time.com/4800489 /portland-oregon-stabbing-micah-fletcher/. Accessed June 2, 2017.

33. Jaweed Kaleem, "Clashes break out as supporters and opponents of Trump descend on Portland," *LAT*, June 4, 2017, http://www.latimes.com/nation /la-na-portland-protests-20170604-story.html. Accessed June 5, 2017.

34. Hayes, *A Colony in a Nation*, 159.

35. Keith Payne, *The Broken Ladder: How Inequality Affects the Way We Think, Live, and Die* (New York: Viking Books, 2017, Kindle Edition, 2017) loc. 82 of 4116, p. 3 of 246.

36. Nicholas Kristof, "What Monkeys Can Teach Us About Fairness," *NYT Sunday Review*, June 4, 2017, 9.

37. "Transcript: Read Full Text of President Barack Obama's Speech in Selma," *Time Magazine*, March 7, 2015, time.com/3736357/barack-obama-selma -speech-transcript.

38. Jeremy Borden, Sari Horowitz and Jerry Markon, "Officials: Suspect in church slayings unrepentant amid outcry over racial hatred," June 19, 2015, *The Washington Post*. http://www.msn.com/en-us/news/crime /officials-suspect-in-church-slayings-unrepentant-amid-outcry-over-racial- hatred/ar-AAbQ4A6. Accessed March 26, 2017.

39. Full text of President Obama's eulogy for Clementa Pinckney, http://www.

onenewspage.com/n/World/755393nbl/Full-text-of-President-Obama
-eulogy-for.htm. Accessed June 27, 2015.

40. Kira Lerner, "South Carolina Trump Supporters Say They'll Never Forgive
    Nikki Haley For Removing Confederate Flag," Feb. 17, 2016, https://
    thinkprogress.org/south-carolina-trump-supporters-say-theyll-never-forgive
    -nikki-haley-for-removing-confederate-flag-8a6cd2c0a83e. Accessed April
    20, 2017.

41. "Mitch Landrieu's Speech on the Removal of Confederate Monuments
    in New Orleans," *NYT,* Opinion, May 23, 2017, https://www.nytimes
    .com/2017/05/23/opinion/mitch-landrieus-speech-transcript.html?_r=0.
    Accessed May 24, 2017. Equal Justice Initiative Executive Director Bryan
    Stevenson has launched a nonprofit project to plant markers throughout the
    South and elsewhere where provable lynchings took place to commemorate
    the victims and vie with the widespread homage to heroes of the Confederacy.
    "EJI's Lynching Marker Project Grows," September 12, 2016, http://eji.org
    /news/eji-lynching-marker-project-grows. Accessed May 10, 20117.

42. "Mitch Landrieu's Speech on the Removal of Confederate Monuments in
    New Orleans," *op. cit.,* note 41.

43. On the whole, across the country, African Americans are victims of
    homicide at a rate of nearly 20 per 100,000. For whites the rate is 2.5."
    Hayes, *A Colony in a Nation,* 23.

44. Kate Zavadski, "AMERICAN EVIL: Dylann Roof's Racist Manifesto Is
    Chilling, Shooter was obsessed with 'black on white' crime and called
    slavery a 'myth.'" *The Daily Beast,* June 20, 2015, http://www.thedailybeast
    .com/articles/2015/06/20/dylann-roof-s-racist-manifesto-is-ignorant-and
    -chilling.html. Accessed May 10, 2017.

45. "Dylann Roof facing competency hearing," CNN, Jan. 4, 2017, http://www
    .cnn.com/2017/01/04/us/dylann-roof-statement-sentencing/. Accessed
    May 10, 2017.

46. Troutfishing, "Trump Links To White Supremacist Group That Helped
    Inspire Dylann Roof Massacre," *Daily Kos,* November 2, 2016, http://
    www.dailykos.com/stories/2016/11/2/1589993/-Trump-Links-To-White
    -Supremacist-Group-That-Helped-Inspire-Dylann-Roof-Massacre. Accessed
    May 10, 2017.

47. John Greenberg, "Trump's Pants on Fire Tweet That Blacks killed 81%
    of White Homicide Victims," *Politifact,* November 22, 2015, http://www
    .politifact.com/truth-o-meter/statements/2015/nov/23/donald-trump
    /trump-tweet-blacks-white-homicide-victims/. Accessed May 9, 2017.

48. *Ibid.* 27–28, 133, 175.

49. The 2016 Pew Poll is cited in Chris Cillizza, *CNN Politics,* "Nancy Pelosi just
    went off on Republicans attacking Democrats over the Scalise shooting,"
    June 15, 2017; the 2014 Pew Poll is cited by Prof. Payne in *The Broken
    Ladder,* at 112.

50. "Nancy Pelosi: 'On days like today, there are no Democrats or Republicans,
    only Americans'" *LAT,* June 14, 2017, http://www.latimes.com/politics
    /essential/la-pol-ca-essential-politics-updates-nancy-pelosi-on-days-like
    -today-1497450832-htmlstory.html.

51. Chris Cillizza, "Paul Ryan gave a spot-on speech on the baseball shooting," CNN, June 14, 2017, http://www.cnn.com/2017/06/14/politics/paul-ryan-steve-scalise/index.html.

52. "The Donald," comments, *Reddit*, June 17, 2017, https://www.reddit.com/r/The_Donald/comments/6h8yn2/president_donald_trump_we_can_all_agree_we_are/.

53. *Liveleak*, June 16, 2017, https://www.liveleak.com/view?i=15b_149764093 2& comments=1. Accessed June 17, 2017.

54. "The Hawaii Judge Who Stopped Trump's Travel Ban Has Been Receiving Death Threats," March 23, 2017, https://www.buzzfeed.com/mbvd/hawaii-judge-who-stopped-trump-travel-ban-is-targeted?utm_term= .xuG934m92#.fi7j8oMj; Q13 FOX, "Threats against judges in travel ban cases leads to increased security," February 9, 2017, http://q13fox.com/2017/02/09/threats-against-judges-in-travel-ban-cases-leads-to-increased-security/." Trump Lashes Out After His Second Travel Ban Order Was Blocked By A Judge," *Buzz Feed News,* March 15, 2017, https://www.buzzfeed.com/buzzfeednews/the-new-travel-ban-goes-into-effect-tonight?utm_term= .blyDeWkDJ#.jivrzKArQ. Also see *CNBC Politics,* "After judge blocks Trump's revised travel ban, president vows to 'fight this terrible ruling,'" March 15, 2017, http://www.cnbc.com/2017/03/15/us-judge-in-hawaii-grants-motion -for-nationwide-temporary-restraining-owner-of-trumps-travel-ban.html. Accessed May 10, 2017.

55. Daniel Lombroso and Loni Applebaum, "White Nationalists Salute 'Hail Trump!': White Nationalists Salute the President-Elect" (video), https://www.theatlantic.com/politics/archive/2016/11/richard-spencer-speech-npi/508379/. Accessed March 26, 2017.

56. "Remember Timothy Caughman," *NYT*, p. A22, March 24, 2017, citing interview of President Obama on January 6, 2017, on Channel4News /videos/10154420518126939/.

57. "Resolution on Racial Reconciliation on the 150th Anniversary of the Southern Baptist Convention," http://www.sbc.net/resolutions/899. Accessed June 15, 2017.

58. Rachel Zoll and Angie Wang, "Southern Baptists reach consensus, denouncing 'alt-right' movement,'" *The Christian Science Monitor,* June 15, 2017, http://www.csmonitor.com/USA/2017/0615/Southern-Baptists-reach-consensus-denouncing-alt-right-movement. Accessed June 15, 2017.

59. Alexandra Pelosi, "The Words That Built America," HBO documentary July 4, 2017, http://www.hbo.com/documentaries/the-words-that-built-america. "The Words That Built America" can be downloaded from HBO. The documentary will be donated to the National Constitution Center. The Preamble to the Constitution, the Bill of Rights and the Reconstruction Amendments are included in this book in the Appendix for the convenience of readers.

60. Claire Shipman, Cindy Smith and Lee Ferran, "Man Asks Entire Town for Forgiveness for Racism," Feb. 6, 2009, http://abcnews.go.com/GMA/story?id=6813984&page=1. Accessed March 30, 2015.

61. Sheila Byrd, *The Sun Herald,* "Barbour apologizes to activists arrested in

1961," May 24, 2011, 1.

62. Chris Hayes describes "The central component of the white fear that sustains the Colony [in a Nation is] . . . the simple inability to recognize, deeply, fully, totally, the humanity of those on the other side." Hayes, *A Colony in a Nation*, 127.

63. "Charge to the jury in the case of MICHIGAN v. HENRY SWEET, Detroit, Michigan, by Judge Frank Murphy," May 13, 1926, http://law2.umkc.edu /faculty/projects/ftrials/sweet/chargetojury.html. Accessed June 30, 2011.

APPENDIX

PREAMBLE TO THE CONSTITUTION (1789)

WE THE PEOPLE of the United States, in order to form a more perfect Union, establish Justice, insure domestic Tranquility, provide for the common defence, promote the general Welfare, and secure the Blessings of Liberty to ourselves and our posterity, do ordain and establish this Constitution for the United States of America.

THE BILL OF RIGHTS (1791)

AMENDMENT I
Congress shall make no law respecting an establishment of religion, or prohibiting the free exercise thereof; or abridging the freedom of speech, or of the press; or the right of the people peaceably to assemble, and to petition the government for a redress of grievances.

AMENDMENT II
A well regulated militia, being necessary to the security of a free state, the right of the people to keep and bear arms, shall not be infringed.

AMENDMENT III
No soldier shall, in time of peace be quartered in any house, without the consent of the owner, nor in time of war, but in a manner to be prescribed by law.

AMENDMENT IV
The right of the people to be secure in their persons, houses, papers, and effects, against unreasonable searches and seizures, shall not be violated, and no warrants shall issue, but upon probable cause, supported by oath or affirmation, and particularly describing the place to be searched, and the persons or things to be seized.

AMENDMENT V
No person shall be held to answer for a capital, or otherwise infamous crime, unless on a presentment or indictment of a grand jury, except in cases arising in the land or naval forces, or in the militia, when in actual service in time of war or public danger; nor shall any person be subject for the same offense to be twice put in jeopardy of life or limb; nor shall be compelled in any criminal case to be a witness against himself, nor be deprived of life, liberty, or property, without due process of law; nor shall private property be taken for public use, without just compensation.

AMENDMENT VI

In all criminal prosecutions, the accused shall enjoy the right to a speedy and public trial, by an impartial jury of the state and district wherein the crime shall have been committed, which district shall have been previously ascertained by law, and to be informed of the nature and cause of the accusation; to be confronted with the witnesses against him; to have compulsory process for obtaining witnesses in his favor, and to have the assistance of counsel for his defense.

AMENDMENT VII

In suits at common law, where the value in controversy shall exceed twenty dollars, the right of trial by jury shall be preserved, and no fact tried by a jury, shall be otherwise reexamined in any court of the United States, than according to the rules of the common law.

AMENDMENT VIII

Excessive bail shall not be required, nor excessive fines imposed, nor cruel and unusual punishments inflicted.

AMENDMENT IX

The enumeration in the Constitution, of certain rights, shall not be construed to deny or disparage others retained by the people.

AMENDMENT X

The powers not delegated to the United States by the Constitution, nor prohibited by it to the states, are reserved to the states respectively, or to the people.

RECONSTRUCTION AMENDMENTS (1865–1870)

THIRTEENTH AMENDMENT (1865)

SECTION 1

Neither slavery nor involuntary servitude, except as a punishment for crime whereof the party shall have been duly convicted, shall exist within the United States, or any place subject to their jurisdiction.

SECTION 2

Congress shall have power to enforce this article by appropriate legislation.

FOURTEENTH AMENDMENT (1868)

SECTION 1

All persons born or naturalized in the United States and subject to the jurisdiction thereof, are citizens of the United States and of the State wherein they reside. No State shall make or enforce any law which shall abridge the privileges or immunities of citizens of the United States; nor shall any State deprive any person of life, liberty, or property, without due process of law; nor deny to any person within its jurisdiction the equal protection of the laws.

SECTION 2

Representatives shall be apportioned among the several States according to their respective numbers, counting the whole number of persons in each State, excluding Indians not taxed. But when the right to vote at any election for the choice of electors for President and Vice President of the United States, Representatives in Congress, the Executive and Judicial officers of a State, or the members of the Legislature thereof, is denied to any of the male inhabitants of such State, being twenty-one years of age, and citizens of the United States, or in any way abridged, except for participation in rebellion, or other crime, the basis of representation therein shall be reduced in the proportion which the number of such male citizens shall bear to the whole number of male citizens twenty-one years of age in such State.

SECTION 3

No person shall be a Senator or Representative in Congress, or elector of President and Vice President, or hold any office, civil or military, under the United States, or under any State, who, having previously taken an oath, as a member of Congress, or as an officer of the United States, or as a member of any State legislature, or as an executive or judicial officer of any State, to support the Constitution of the United States, shall have engaged in insurrection or rebellion against the same, or given aid or comfort to the enemies thereof. But Congress may by a vote of two-thirds of each House, remove such disability.

SECTION 4

The validity of the public debt of the United States, authorized by law, including debts incurred for payment of pensions and bounties for services in suppressing insurrection or rebellion, shall not be questioned. But neither the United States nor any State shall assume or pay any debt or obligation incurred in aid of insurrection or rebellion against the United States, or any claim for the loss or emancipation of any slave; but all such debts, obligations and claims shall be held illegal and void.

FIFTEENTH AMENDMENT (1870)

SECTION 1

The right of citizens of the United States to vote shall not be denied or abridged by the United States or by any State on account of race, color, or previous condition of servitude.

SECTION 2

The Congress shall have power to enforce this article by appropriate legislation.

BIBLIOGRAPHY

For web sources, see Endnotes.

Principal Newspaper Sources:
Atlanta Constitution, New York Times, San Francisco Examiner, Washington Post

Books:
Acker, James R., *Scottsboro and Its Legacy* (Westport, Connecticut: Praeger Publishing, 2008).

Addams, Jane, *Twenty Years at Hull House* (New York: The MacMillan Co., 1910).

Ahlgren, G., and Monier, S., *The Crime of the Century: The Lindbergh Kidnapping Hoax* (Boston: Brandon Books, 1993).

Alef, D., *William Randolph Hearst: Media Myth and Mystique [Titans of Fortune]*, Kindle Edition (Titans of Fortune Publishing, 2010).

Alexander, Michelle, *The New Jim Crow: Mass Incarceration in the Age of Color Blindness* (New York: New Press, 2010).

Auerbach, Jerold S., *Unequal Justice: Lawyers and Social Change in Modern America* (New York: Oxford Univ. Press, 1976).

Avrich, Paul, *Sacco and Vanzetti: The Anarchist Background* (Princeton, New Jersey: Princeton Univ. Press, 1991).

Baatz, S., *For the Thrill of It: Leopold, Loeb and the Murder That Shocked Chicago* (New York: Harper Collins, 2008).

Bartoletti, Susan Campbell, *Kids on Strike* (New York: Houghton Mifflin Company, 1999).

Black, Gregory D., *Hollywood Censored: Morality Codes, Catholics, and the Movies* (Cambridge, United Kingdom: Cambridge University Press, 1996).

Blackmon, Douglas A., *Slavery by Another Name: The Re-Enslavement of Black Americans From the Civil War to World War II* (New York: Anchor Books, 2009).

Blum, H., *American Lightning: Terror, Mystery, the Birth of Hollywood and the Crime of the Century* (New York: Crown Publishers, 2008).

Boyle, K., *Arc of Justice: A Saga of Race, Civil Rights and Murder in the Jazz Age* (New York: Henry Holt & Co., 2004).

Brody, Leslie, *Irrepressible: The Life and Times of Jessica Mitford* (Berkeley, California: Counterpoint, 2010).

Broussard, A. S., *Black San Francisco: The Struggle for Racial Equality in the West, 1900–1954* (Lawrence, Kansas: University Press of Kansas, 1993).

Browning, Reed, *Cy Young: A Baseball Life* (Amherst, Massachusetts: University of Massachusetts Press, 2003).

Cahn, William, *A Pictorial History of American Labor* (New York: Crown Publishers, 1972).

Carlson, P., *Roughneck: The Life and Times of Big Bill Haywood* (New York: W.W. Norton & Co., 1983).

Carroll, P. N., and Noble, D. W., *The Free and the Unfree: A Progressive History of the United States* (New York: Penguin Books, 2001, 3d rev. ed.).

Chapman, Maria, *The Liberty Bell: Testimony Against Slavery* (Whitefish, Montana: Kessinger Publishing, 2007).

Craig, William, J., *A History of the Boston Braves, A Time Gone By* (Charleston, South Carolina: The History Press, 2012).

Cobb, James C., *Georgia Odyssey: A Short History of the State* (Atlanta, Georgia: Univ. of Georgia Press, 2008).

Cohen, R., *Tough Jews: Fathers, Sons, and Gangster Dreams* (London: Vintage Books, 1999).

Curriden, M., and Phillips, J. L., *Contempt of Court: The Turn-of-the-Century Lynching That Launched a Hundred Years of Federalism* (New York: Anchor Books, 2001).

Dallek, Robert, *Flawed Giant* (New York: Oxford Univ. Press, 1998).

Darrow, Clarence, *The Story of My Life* (New York: Da Capo, 1996; orginally published: New York: Charles Scribner's Sons, 1932).

Davies, David R. (ed.), *The Press and Race* (Jackson, Mississippi: Univ. Press of Mississippi, 2001).

Davis, Deborah, *Guest of Honor: Booker T. Washington, Theodore Roosevelt and the White House Dinner That Shocked a Nation* (New York: Atria Books, 2012).

Dershowitz, A. M., *America on Trial: Inside The Legal Battles That Transformed Our Nation* (New York: Warner Books, 2004).

Dinnerstein, Leonard, *The Leo Frank Case* (rev. ed.) (Atlanta, Georgia: The Univ. of Georgia Press, 2008).

Fisher, Jim, *The Lindbergh Case* (New Brunswick, New Jersey: Rutgers Univ. Press, 1988).

Foner, Eric, *Reconstruction: America's Unfinished Revolution* (New York: Harper & Row, 1988).

Frommer, Harvey, *Shoeless Joe and Ragtime Baseball* (Omaha, Nebraska: Univ. of Nebraska, 2008).

Gage, Elizabeth, *The Day Wall Street Exploded: A Story of America in its First Age of Terror* (Oxford: Oxford Univ. Press, 2009).

Gardner, Lloyd, *The Case That Never Dies: The Lindbergh Kidnapping* (New Brunswick, New Jersey: Rutgers Univ. Press, 2004).

Gay, T. M., *Tris Speaker, The Rough-and-Tumble Life of a Baseball Legend* (Kearney, Nebraska: Morris Book Publishing, 2007).

Geis, Gilbert, and Beinen, Leigh, *Crimes of the Century* (Boston: Northeastern Univ. Press, 1998).

Gilmore, Glenda Elizabeth, *Gender and Jim Crow: Women and the Politics of White Supremacy in North Carolina, 1896–1920* (Durham, North Carolina: Univ. of North Carolina Press, 1996).

Gitlin, Martin, *Powerful Sports Moments: The Most Significant Sports Events in American History* (New York: Rowman and Littlefield, 2017).

Goodman, James, *Stories of Scottsboro* (New York: Pantheon Books, 1994).

Grant, Robert, and Katz, Joseph, *The Great Trials of the Twenties: The Watershed Decade in America's Courtrooms* (New York: Sarpedon, 1998).

Grossman, M., *Political Corruption in America: An Encyclopedia of Scandals, Power, and Greed* (Santa Barbara, California: ABC-Clio, 2003).

Haldeman-Julius, M., *Clarence Darrow's Two Great Trials* (Girard, Kansas: Haldeman-Julius Company, 1927).

Hayes, Chris, *A Colony in a Nation* (New York: W.W. Norton & Company, 2017).

Higdon, H., *Leopold and Loeb, The Crime of the Century* (New York: G.P. Putnam's Sons, 1975).

Hinckle, W., *If You Have a Lemon, Make Lemonade* (New York: W.W. Norton & Co, 1973).

Horan, James D., and Swiggett, Howard, *The Pinkerton Story* (New York: G.P. Putnam's Sons, 1972).

Hunter, George W., *A Civic Biology Presented in Problems* (New York: American Book Co., 1914).

_____, *New Civic Biology: Presented in Problems* (New York: American Book Co., 1926).

Kennedy, Ludovic, *The Airman and the Carpenter: The Lindbergh Kidnapping and the Framing of Richard Hauptmann* (New York: Viking Press, 1985).

Kimmel, Michael, *Angry White Men: American Masculinity at the End of an Era* (New York: Nation Books, 2013).

Knappman, E. W., *Great American Trials* (Detroit: Visible Ink Press, 1994).

Lanahan, D. J., *Justice for All: Legendary Trials of the 20th century* (Bloomington, Indiana: Author House, 2006).

Larson, E. J., *Summer for the Gods: The Scopes Trial and America's Continuing Debate Over Science and Religion* (New York: Perseus Books, 1997).

Levin, Murray B., *Political Hysteria in America: The Democratic Capacity for Repression* (New York: Basic Books, 1971).

Lukas, J. Anthony, *Big Trouble* (New York: Touchstone Books, 1997).

Morris, E., *Theodore Rex* (New York: Random House, 2001).

Nash, J. R., *The Great Pictorial History of World Crime* (Lanham, Maryland: Rowman & Littlefield, 2004).

Newton, Michael, *The Encyclopedia of Unsolved Crimes* (New York: Checkmark Books, 2004).

Ogletree, Charles J., Jr., and Sarat, Austin (eds.), *From Lynch Mobs to the Killing State: Race and the Death Penalty in America* (New York: New York University Press, 2006).

Ogletree, Charles J., Jr. (ed.), *When Law Fails: Making Sense of Miscarriages of Justice* (New York: New York University Press, 2009).

Oney, S., *And the Dead Shall Rise: The Murder of Mary Phagan and the Lynching of Leo Frank* (New York: Pantheon, 2003).

Payne, Keith, *The Broken Ladder: How Inequality Affects the Way We Think, Live, and Die* (New York: Viking, 2017).

Perman, Michael, *Struggle for Mastery: Disfranchisement in the South, 1888–1908* (Chapel Hill, North Carolina: Univ. of North Carolina Press, 2001).

Pietrusza, David, *Judge and Jury: The Life and Times of Judge Kenesaw Mountain Landis* (Lanham, Maryland: Taylor Trade Publishing, 2001, Kindle Edition 2011).

————, *Rothstein: The Life, Times, and Murder of the Criminal Genius Who Fixed the 1919 World Series* (New York: Basic Books, 2003: Kindle Edition, 2011).

Raiford, Leigh, *Imprisoned in a Luminous Glare: Photography and the African-American Freedom Struggle* (Chapel Hill, North Carolina: Univ. of North Carolina Press, 2011).

Rauchway, E., *Murdering McKinley: The Making of Theodore Roosevelt's America* (New York: Hill and Wang, 2003).

Rayback, J. G., *A History of American Labor* (New York: The Free Press, 1966).

Rhodes, D., *Ty Cobb: Safe at Home* (Guilford, Connecticut: Lyons Press, 2008).

Robenalt, James D., *The Harding Affair, Love and Espionage During the Great War* (New York: Palgrave Macmillan, 2009).

Robeson, Paul, and Foner, Philip S., *Paul Robeson Speaks: Writings, Speeches, Interviews 1918–1974* (New York: Citadel Press Books, 1978).

Russell, F., *Sacco and Vanzetti: The Case Resolved.* (New York: Harper & Row, 1986).

Stannard, D. E., *Honor Killing: How the Infamous "Massie Affair" Transformed Hawai'i* (New York: Viking Penguin Books, 2005).

Stiglitz, Joseph, *The Price of Inequality: How Today's Divided Society Endangers Our Future* (New York: W.W. Norton & Company, 2012; Kindle Edition, 2013).

Stone, Irving, *Clarence Darrow for the Defense* (New York: Signet Books, 1941, 1969).

Temkin, Moshik, *The Sacco-Vanzetti Affair* (New Haven, Connecticut: Yale University Press, 2011; Kindle Edition., 2009).

Uelman, Gerald, *Lessons From the Trial: The People v. O. J. Simpson* (Kansas City, Missouri: Andrews and McMeel, 1996).

Uruburu, P., *American Eve: Evelyn Nesbit, Stanford White, the Birth of the "It" Girl and the Crime of the Century* (New York: Riverhead Books, 2008).

Van Slingerland, P., *Something Terrible Has Happened: The Account of the*

Sensational Thalia Massie Affair Which Burst From Prewar Hawaii to Incense a Nation (New York: Harper & Row, 1966).

Ward, G. C., and Burns, K., *Baseball: An Illustrated History* (New York: Alfred A. Knopf, 1994).

Washington, Booker T., (eds.) Louis R. Harlan and W. Smock, with Barbara S. Kraft, *The Booker T. Washington Papers*, 14 vols (Urbana, Illinois: University of Illinois Press, 1972–1989).

Williams, Edward Bennett, *One Man's Freedom* (New York: Atheneum Press, 1962).

Journal Articles and Pamphlets:

Bedau, Hugo Adam, and Michael L. Radelet, "Miscarriages of Justice in Potentially Capital Cases." *Stanford Law Review* 40, no. 21 (1987): 124, 125.

Bryan, Robert R., "The Execution of the Innocent: The Tragedy of the Hauptmann-Lindbergh and Bigelow Cases." *NYU Review of Law and Social Change*, Vol. 18 (1990).

Dixon, Thomas, Jr., "Booker T. Washington and the Negro." *Saturday Evening Post*, August 19, 1905.

Frankfurter, Felix, "The Case of Sacco and Vanzetti." *The Atlantic Monthly*, March 1927.

Goldman, Emma, "The Tragedy at Buffalo." *Free Society*, October 6, 1901.

Hoffmann, Joseph, L. and King, Nancy, J., "Rethinking the Federal Role in State Criminal Justice," *NYU Law Review.*, Vol. 84 (2009), 791, 797.

Levinson, Justin, D., "Forgotten Racial Equality: Implicit Bias, Decision making, and Misremembering," *Duke Law Journal*, Vol. 57 (2007), 345, 350.

"Radical-Right Terror Plagues Nation: Hatemongers Migrating Online to Spread Ideology," *Southern Poverty Law Center Report*, Spring 2015, Vol 45, No. 1.

Reinhardt, Steven, "The Demise of Habeas Corpus and the Rise of Qualified Immunity: The Court's Ever Increasing Limitations on the Development and Enforcement of Constitutional Rights and

Some Particularly Unfortunate Consequences," *Michigan Law Review,* May 2015, Vol 113: 1219, 1240.

"SPLC Fights Back Against Bigotry in White House," *Southern Poverty Law Center Report,* Spring 2017, Vol. 47, No. 1.

Walsh, Michael, "Great Expectations," *Smithsonian,* June 2010, 54.

INDEX

ACKNOWLEDGEMENTS

Once again, I want to offer profuse thanks to my good friend David Alexander, who first suggested I would reach a wider audience if I revised my 2012 book *The Sky's the Limit* into shorter books. I published a shorter one on the continued impact of the 1968 Newton trial in October 2016 (*American Justice on Trial: People v. Newton*), with quotes from interviewed participants and commentators, to serve as a companion to the identically named documentary project I am producing for Arc of Justice Productions, Inc. You can follow that project at www.americanjusticeontrial.com. I have now finished this book focused on early 20th century trials that helped shape today's America, most of which I first included in Part One of *The Sky's the Limit*. Here, those riveting trials are reexamined with emphasis on the insights they readily provide into today's political climate.

Among the extraordinary resources now available on the web, I am especially beholden to Prof. Douglas Linder of the School of Law of the University of Missouri at Kansas City for the impressive collection of original source material accessible at his web site, Famous Trials. I am very grateful as well to experts who read and gave me feedback on earlier drafts of many of the chapters in this book: Giants pregame host and baseball historian Marty Lurie for reviewing what I wrote about the 1919 Black Sox scandal and early professional baseball; since-retired AFL-CIO Chief of Staff Jon Hiatt and AFL-CIO Director of Policy and Special Counsel Damon Silvers for reviewing the chapter on labor history; Rutgers history professor Lloyd Gardner and New Jersey State Police museum archivist Mark Falzini for input on the Lindbergh chapter. None of these fine people are responsible for any mistakes I may have incorporated into the final version of the chapters they looked at or for any opinions expressed in this book.

For his help in polishing this book, I would like to specially thank my extraordinary editor Dan White (*The Cactus Eaters* and *Under the Stars:*

How America Fell in Love with Camping). I again wish to express my deep appreciation to Mark Weiman of Regent Press and Suzanne Waligore for their excellent work and belief in this project, to Emily Burch for her graphic art talents on the book's cover and to Christopher Bernard, again, for his meticulous proofreading talents.

Thanks most of all to my family: my sister Leslie Pearlman for her editing suggestions and proofreading skills; daughters Jamie Benvenutti and Amalia Benvenutti-Glasgow for their web research and other technical assistance; my daughter Anna Benvenutti-Hoffmann for her insightful feedback on early drafts of most chapters of this book; and to my husband Peter Benvenutti – my amazing other half – for being a sounding board, editor and constant source of support in bringing this entire project to fruition.

ABOUT THE AUTHOR

Retired judge Lise Pearlman is an acclaimed author and nationally recognized speaker on famous trials of the 20th century. Her first history book, *The Sky's the Limit: People v. Newton, The REAL Trial of the 20th Century?* (Regent Press, 2012), from which this new shorter book is derived, won awards in the categories of law, history, and multi-culturalism. Her second book, *American Justice on Trial: People v. Newton* (Regent Press, 2016), is a companion to a documentary project of the same name. Judge Pearlman is president of the board of the non-profit company Arc of Justice Production, Inc., which is making that film (the following website, www.americanjusticeontrial.com, provides information on the film).

As the country's leading expert on the 1968 Newton "Trial of the Century," Pearlman also appeared as a commentator in the 2015 Stanley Nelson Film "The Black Panthers: Vanguard of the Revolution." Judge Pearlman's second book *American Justice on Trial* was a finalist in the 2017 U.S. Book Awards for American History. Pearlman was an undergraduate in the first class that included women at Yale University. After graduating from U.C. Berkeley Law School, she clerked for California Chief Justice Donald White.

Ms. Pearlman is avalable for national speaking engagements.

www.lisepearlman.com

CPSIA information can be obtained
at www.ICGtesting.com
Printed in the USA
FFOW03n1810161017
41183FF